THE

NEPA

REFERENCE GUIDE

D1519135

Compiled and edited by

Danny C. Reinke, Ph.D.

and

Lucinda Low Swartz, Esq.

Battelle Press
Columbus · Richland

Library of Congress Cataloging-in-Publication Data

The NEPA reference guide / compiled & edited by Danny C. Reinke & Lucinda Low Swartz.
   p. cm.
   Includes bibliographical references and index.
   ISBN 1-57477-068-3 (pb. : alk. paper)
   1. Environmental law–United States. I. Reinke, Danny C.
 II. Swartz, Lucinda Low, 1955–
 KF3775.N474   1999
 344.73'046–dc21   99–21501
                                                   CIP

Printed in the United States of America

Battelle Press
505 King Avenue
Columbus, Ohio 43201-2693
614-424-6393; 1-800-451-3543
Fax: 614-424-3819
Homepage: http://www.battelle.org/bookstore
E-mail: press@battelle.org

In 1995, we marked the twenty-fifth anniversary of The National Environmental Policy Act (NEPA). Some used this anniversary to measure the great successes and promise of NEPA and others used it to measure the great disappointment and lack of substantive successes. Regardless of your respective point of view, there can be little argument that NEPA was one of the first significant environmental laws passed in the United States; and, after more than twenty-five years, it continues to be one of the most far-reaching and most litigated statutes. While the law is only a few pages long, the courts have interpreted its broad language to allow NEPA what some would call a "pervasive" reach into Federal agencies' activities.

This technical guide was developed as a one-stop reference for all the officially issued Council on Environmental Quality (CEQ) guidance. It is hoped that this reference will serve as a tool to better use the existing official guidance. The reference is not a "how- to" manual, and a conscious attempt was made to present the factual requirements without interruption. It contains the NEPA Public Law, the Clean Air Act Section 309, the Environmental Quality Improvement Act, the CEQ regulations, the CEQ 40 Questions, a CEQ memorandum guidance to all Federal agencies, the CEQ scoping guidance, the CEQ pollution prevention guidance, a CEQ memorandum on transboundary actions, the CEQ environmental justice guidance, the Environmental Protection Agency (EPA) guidance on NEPA review, a summary of precedent-setting and selected recent legal cases, and selected Executive Orders, all cross-indexed. The documents are presented here without editing of format or content, including some grammatical errors as found in the originals. This allows one to follow an issue(s) through the laws, regulations, guidance, and court cases to better understand what is required for NEPA analysis and documentation.

DCR & LLS, 1999

TABLE OF CONTENTS

THE NATIONAL ENVIRONMENTAL POLICY ACT PROCESS

The NEPA process refers to the procedures a Federal agency follows to analyze the environmental impacts of a proposal and alternatives, and to document that analysis and its results. This process is generally outlined in NEPA's Section 102(2)(C) [42 U.S.C. §4332(2)(C)] and is fully described in the Council on Environmental Quality regulations [40 CFR Parts 1500-1508]. The NEPA process includes efforts to inform and seek comments from the public, State and local agencies, Native American tribes, and other Federal agencies.

NEPA requires an evaluation of the environmental impacts of a proposed action—that is when the agency has a goal and is actively preparing to make a decision on one or more alternative means of accomplishing that goal and the effects may be meaningfully evaluated. Further, NEPA applies to "major Federal actions significantly affecting the quality of the human environment." This means that the proposal has to be a Federal action (including Federal approval of a permit or involving Federal funding for all or a significant portion of a proposal) and has to have significant environmental impacts. Determining whether a proposal "significantly" affects the environment requires the agency to look at both the context (the significance of the action as a whole, the affected region, and the affected interests) and intensity (severity of the impacts).

Thus, at the beginning of the NEPA process, a Federal agency must ask itself whether a particular proposal is a "major Federal action significantly affecting the quality of the human environment." The possible answers are:

- Clearly no: the agency categorically excludes the proposed action from further NEPA documentation (a categorical exclusion is a category of actions that, by regulation, have no significant environmental impact) and publishes in the *Federal Register* for public review and comment.

- Clearly yes: the agency proceeds to prepare an Environmental Impact Statement (EIS).

- Maybe: the agency begins to prepare an environmental assessment (EA) to determine whether the impacts could be significant.

Preparing an Environmental Impact Statement

The agency prepares and publishes a notice of intent to prepare an EIS and invites public comment on the scope of the issues and alternatives to be addressed in the document. Where more than one Federal agency, or a Federal and State or local agency, have jurisdiction over the proposed action, the Federal agencies determine which should have primary jurisdiction and therefore lead responsibility for preparing the EIS (the lead agency). Other agencies with interest or special expertise can be invited to participate as cooperating agencies.

An EIS generally contains the following:

- Purpose and Need Section: identifying the purpose and need to which the agency is responding in proposing the action and alternatives

- Alternatives Section: exploring and evaluating all reasonable alternatives, including alternatives that are not within the jurisdiction of the lead agency and the no action alternative

- Affected Environment Section: describing the existing environment of the area that would be affected by the proposed action and alternatives

- Environmental Consequences Section: describing the environmental impacts of the proposed action and alternatives and possible mitigation measures that could be taken to avoid or reduce potential impacts

The EIS is prepared in two stages, draft and final. The draft EIS is filed with the Environmental Protection Agency and is publicly circulated for a minimum of 45 days. The lead agency obtains the comments of Federal agencies with jurisdiction by law or special expertise, State and local agencies, affected Native American tribes, and the public. After receiving and considering the comments received on the draft EIS, the agency prepares a final EIS. The final EIS is also filed with the Environmental Protection Agency.

At least 30 days following publication of the final EIS, the agency may issue a record of decision (ROD). The ROD is a concise public record that states what the decision is, identifies the alternatives considered by the agency, specifies which alternative is the most environmentally preferable, and states whether all practical means to avoid or minimize environmental harm were adopted.

Preparing an Environmental Assessment

An EA is a concise (preferably 10-15 pages) public document that provides sufficient evidence and analysis for determining whether to prepare an EIS; that is, whether the impacts of the proposal are expected to be significant. An agency must involve environmental agencies, applicants, and the public to the extent practicable in preparing an EA. If, after completion of the EA, the agency concludes that the impacts will not be significant, it issues a finding of no significant impact and, in most cases, can proceed to implement its proposal. If, after completion of the EA, the agency concludes that there may be significant impacts, then the agency proceeds to issue a notice of intent to prepare an EIS.

This section contains the text of the NEPA, the Environmental Quality Improvement Act, and the Clean Air Act. Below is a brief description of each.

National Environmental Policy Act of 1969

NEPA was enacted in December 1969 and signed into law on January 1, 1970. NEPA declares a national policy "to use all practicable means and measures... to create and maintain conditions under which man and nature can exist in productive harmony, and fulfill the social, economic, and other requirements of present and future generations of Americans" [NEPA, Section 101(a); 42 U.S.C. § 4331(a)]. Federal agencies are to promote this policy and consider environmental values in decision making by preparing a "detailed statement" on "every recommendation or report on proposals for legislation and other major Federal actions significantly affecting the quality of the human environment" [NEPA, Section 102(2)(C); 42 U.S.C. § 4332(2)(C)]. Among other things, the detailed statement—which is referred to as an environmental impact statement (EIS)—describes the environmental impacts of the proposed action and alternatives to the proposed action. NEPA also created the Council on Environmental Quality (CEQ) to serve as an environmental advisor to the President [NEPA, Sections 201-209; 42 U.S.C. §§ 4341-47].

Environmental Quality Improvement Act

The Environmental Quality Improvement Act was passed in April 1970 and creates the Office of Environmental Quality [42 U.S.C. § 4372]. This office provides staff support for CEQ. The head of CEQ serves as the director of the office.

Clean Air Act, Section 309

This section authorizes the EPA to review and comment on EISs prepared by Federal agencies and filed with EPA. 42 U.S.C. § 7609. Pursuant to this authority, EPA has established a rating system by which it judges both the technical adequacy of the document as well as the severity of the environmental impacts associated with the proposed action. EPA applies this rating system to all draft EISs.

In addition, Section 309 authorizes EPA to refer to CEQ any proposed action that it believes is unsatisfactory from the standpoint of public health or welfare or environmental quality. CEQ has established procedures for considering such referrals (see 40 CFR Part 1504).

NATIONAL ENVIRONMENTAL POLICY ACT OF 1969

As amended (Pub. L. 91-190, 42 U.S.C. 4321-4347, January 1, 1970, as amended by Pub. L. 94-52, July 3, 1975, Pub. L. 94-83, August 9, 1975, and Pub. L. 97-258, § 4(b), Sept. 13, 1982)

An Act to establish a national policy for the environment, to provide for establishment of a Council on Environmental Quality, and for other purposes.

Be it enacted by the Senate and House of Representatives of the United States of America in Congress assembled, that this Act may be cited as the "National Environmental Policy Act of 1969."

Purpose

Sec. 2 [42 USC § 4321]. The purposes of this Act are: To declare a national policy which will encourage productive and enjoyable harmony between man and his environment; to promote efforts which will prevent or eliminate damage to the environment and biosphere and stimulate the health and welfare of man; to enrich the understanding of the ecological systems and natural resources important to the Nation; and to establish a Council on Environmental Quality.

TITLE I

Congressional Declaration of National Environmental Policy

Sec. 101 [42 USC § 4331].
(a) The Congress, recognizing the profound impact of man's activity on the interrelations of all components of the natural environment, particularly the profound influences of population growth, high-density urbanization, industrial expansion, resource exploitation, and new and expanding technological advances and recognizing further the critical importance of restoring and maintaining environmental quality to the overall welfare and development of man, declares that it is the continuing policy of the Federal Government, in cooperation with State and local governments, and other concerned public and private organizations, to use all practicable means and measures, including financial and technical assistance, in a manner calculated to foster and promote the general welfare, to create and maintain conditions under which man and nature can exist in productive harmony, and fulfill the social, economic, and other requirements of present and future generations of Americans.

(b) In order to carry out the policy set forth in this Act, it is the continuing responsibility of the Federal Government to use all practicable means, consistent with other essential considerations of national policy, to improve and coordinate Federal plans, functions, programs, and resources to the end that the Nation may -
　　(1) fulfill the responsibilities of each generation as trustee of the environment for succeeding generations;
　　(2) assure for all Americans safe, healthful, productive, and esthetically and culturally pleasing surroundings;
　　(3) attain the widest range of beneficial uses of the environment without degradation, risk to health or safety, or other undesirable and unintended consequences;
　　(4) preserve important historic, cultural and natural aspects of our national heritage, and maintain, wherever possible, an environment which supports diversity, and variety of individual choice;
　　(5) achieve a balance between population and resource use which will permit high standards of living and a wide sharing of life's amenities; and
　　(6) enhance the quality of renewable resources and approach the maximum attainable recycling of depletable resources.

(c) The Congress recognizes that each person should enjoy a healthful environment and that each person has a responsibility to contribute to the preservation and enhancement of the environment.

Sec. 102 [42 USC § 4332]. The Congress authorizes and directs that, to the fullest extent possible: (1) the policies, regulations, and public laws of the United States shall be interpreted and administered in accordance with the policies set forth in this Act, and (2) all agencies of the Federal Government shall—

(A) utilize a systematic, interdisciplinary approach which will insure the integrated use of the natural and social sciences and the environmental design arts in planning and in decision making which may have an impact on man's environment;

(B) identify and develop methods and procedures, in consultation with the Council on Environmental Quality established by Title II of this Act, which will insure that presently unquantified environmental amenities and values may be given appropriate consideration in decision making along with economic and technical considerations;

(C) include in every recommendation or report on proposals for legislation and other major Federal actions significantly affecting the quality of the human environment, a detailed statement by the responsible official on –

(i) the environmental impact of the proposed action,

(ii) any adverse environmental effect which cannot be avoided should the proposal be implemented,

(iii) alternatives to the proposed action,

(iv) the relationship between local short-term uses of man's environment and the maintenance and enhancement of long-term productivity, and

(v) any irreversible and irretrievable commitments of resources which would be involved in the proposed action should it be implemented.

Prior to making any detailed statement, the responsible Federal official shall consult with and obtain the comments of any Federal agency which has jurisdiction by law or special expertise with respect to any environmental impact involved. Copies of such statement and the comments and views of the appropriate Federal, State, and local agencies, which are authorized to develop and enforce environmental standards, shall be made available to the President, the Council on Environmental Quality and to the public as provided by section 552 of title 5, United States Code, and shall accompany the proposal through the existing agency review processes;

(D) Any detailed statement required under subparagraph (C) after January 1, 1970, for any major Federal action funded under a program of grants to States shall not be deemed to be legally insufficient solely by reason of having been prepared by a State agency or official, if:

(i) the State agency or official has statewide jurisdiction and has the responsibility for such action,

(ii) the responsible Federal official furnishes guidance and participates in such preparation,

(iii) the responsible Federal official independently evaluates such statement prior to its approval and adoption, and

(iv) after January 1, 1976, the responsible Federal official provides early notification to, and solicits the views of, any other State or any Federal land management entity of any action or any alternative thereto which may have significant impacts upon such State or affected Federal land management entity and, if there is any disagreement on such impacts, prepares a written assessment of such impacts and views for incorporation into such detailed statement.

The procedures in this subparagraph shall not relieve the Federal official of his responsibilities for the scope, objectivity, and content of the entire statement or of any other responsibility under this Act; and further, this subparagraph does not affect the legal sufficiency of statements prepared by State agencies with less than statewide jurisdiction.

(E) study, develop, and describe appropriate alternatives to recommended courses of action in any proposal which involves unresolved conflicts concerning alternative uses of available resources;

(F) recognize the worldwide and long-range character of environmental problems and, where consistent with the foreign policy of the United States, lend appropriate support to initiatives, resolutions, and programs designed to maximize international cooperation in anticipating and preventing a decline in the quality of mankind's world environment;

(G) make available to States, counties, municipalities, institutions, and individuals, advice and information useful in restoring, maintaining, and enhancing the quality of the environment;

(H) initiate and utilize ecological information in the planning and development of resource-oriented projects; and

(I) assist the Council on Environmental Quality established by Title II of this Act.

Sec. 103 [42 USC § 4333]. All agencies of the Federal Government shall review their present statutory authority, administrative regulations, and current policies and procedures for the purpose of determining whether there are any deficiencies or inconsistencies therein which prohibit full compliance with the purposes and provisions of this Act and shall propose to the President not later than July 1, 1971, such measures as may be necessary to bring their authority and policies into conformity with the intent, purposes, and procedures set forth in this Act.

Sec. 104 [42 USC § 4334]. Nothing in Section 102 [42 USC § 4332] or 103 [42 USC § 4333] shall in any way affect the specific statutory obligations of any Federal agency (1) to comply with criteria or standards of environmental quality, (2) to coordinate or consult with any other Federal or State agency, or (3) to act, or refrain from acting contingent upon the recommendations or certification of any other Federal or State agency.

Sec. 105 [42 USC § 4335]. The policies and goals set forth in this Act are supplementary to those set forth in existing authorizations of Federal agencies.

TITLE II

Council on Environmental Quality

Sec. 201 [42 USC § 4341]. The President shall transmit to the Congress annually beginning July 1, 1970, an Environmental Quality Report (hereinafter referred to as the "report") which shall set forth (1) the status and condition of the major natural, manmade, or altered environmental classes of the Nation, including, but not limited to, the air, the aquatic, including marine, estuarine, and fresh water, and the terrestrial environment, including, but not limited to, the forest, dryland, wetland, range, urban, suburban, and rural environment; (2) current and foreseeable trends in the quality, management and utilization of such environments and the effects of those trends on the social, economic, and other requirements of the Nation; (3) the adequacy of available natural resources for fulfilling human and economic requirements of the Nation in the light of expected population pressures; (4) a review of the programs and activities (including regulatory activities) of the Federal Government, the State and local governments, and nongovernmental entities or individuals with particular reference to their effect on the environment and on the conservation, development and utilization of natural resources; and (5) a program for remedying the deficiencies of existing programs and activities, together with recommendations for legislation.

Sec. 202 [42 USC § 4342]. There is created in the Executive Office of the President a Council on Environmental Quality (hereinafter referred to as the "Council"). The Council shall be composed of three members who shall be appointed by the President to serve at his pleasure, by and with the advice and consent of the Senate. The President shall designate one of the members of the Council to serve as Chairman. Each member shall be a person who, as a result of his training, experience, and attainment, is exceptionally well qualified to analyze and interpret environmental trends and information of all kinds; to appraise programs and activities of the Federal Government in the light of the policy set forth in Title I of this Act; to be conscious of and responsive to the scientific, economic, social, aesthetic, and cultural needs and interests of the Nation; and to formulate and recommend national policies to promote the improvement of the quality of the environment.

Sec. 203 [42 USC § 4343].

(a) The Council may employ such officers and employees as may be necessary to carry out its functions under this Act. In addition, the Council may employ and fix the compensation of such experts and consultants as may be necessary for the carrying out of its functions under this Act, in accordance with section 3109 of title 5, United States Code (but without regard to the last sentence thereof).

(b) Notwithstanding section 1342 of Title 31, the Council may accept and employ voluntary and uncompensated services in furtherance of the purposes of the Council.

Sec. 204 [42 USC § 4344]. It shall be the duty and function of the Council.

(1) to assist and advise the President in the preparation of the Environmental Quality Report required by section 201 [42 USC § 4341] of this title;

(2) to gather timely and authoritative information concerning the conditions and trends in the quality of the environment both current and prospective, to analyze and interpret such information for the purpose of determining whether such conditions and trends are interfering, or are likely to interfere, with the achievement of the policy set forth in Title I of this Act, and to compile and submit to the President studies relating to such conditions and trends;

(3) to review and appraise the various programs and activities of the Federal government in the light of the policy set forth in Title I of this Act for the purpose of determining the extent to which such programs and activities are contributing to the achievement of such policy, and to make recommendations to the President with respect thereto;

(4) to develop and recommend to the President national policies to foster and promote the improvement of environmental quality to meet the conservation, social, economic, health, and other requirements and goals of the Nation;

(5) to conduct investigations, studies, surveys, research, and analyses relating to ecological systems and environmental quality;

(6) to document and define changes in the natural environment, including the plant and animal systems, and to accumulate necessary data and other information for a continuing analysis of these changes or trends and an interpretation of their underlying causes;

(7) to report at least once each year to the President on the State and condition of the environment; and

(8) to make and furnish such studies, reports thereon, and recommendations with respect to matters of policy and legislation as the President may request.

Sec. 205 [42 USC § 4345]. In exercising its powers, functions, and duties under this Act, the Council shall –

(1) consult with the Citizens' Advisory Committee on Environmental Quality established by Executive Order No. 11472, dated May 29, 1969, and with such representatives of science, industry, agriculture, labor, conservation organizations, State and local governments and other groups, as it deems advisable; and

(2) utilize, to the fullest extent possible, the services, facilities, and information (including statistical information) of public and private agencies and organizations, and individuals, in order that duplication of effort and expense may be avoided, thus assuring that the Council's activities will not unnecessarily overlap or conflict with similar activities authorized by law and performed by established agencies.

Sec. 206 [42 USC § 4346]. Members of the Council shall serve full time and the Chairman of the Council shall be compensated at the rate provided for Level II of the Executive Schedule Pay Rates [5 USC § 5313]. The other members of the Council shall be compensated at the rate provided for Level IV of the Executive Schedule Pay Rates (5 USC § 5315).

Sec. 207 [42 USC § 4346a]. The Council may accept reimbursements from any private nonprofit organization or from any department, agency, or instrumentality of the Federal Government, any State, or local government, for the reasonable travel expenses incurred by an officer or employee of the

Council in connection with his attendance at any conference, seminar, or similar meeting conducted for the benefit of the Council.

Sec. 208 [42 USC § 4346b]. The Council may make expenditures in support of its international activities, including expenditures for: (1) international travel; (2) activities in implementation of international agreements; and (3) the support of international exchange programs in the United States and in foreign countries.

Sec. 209 [42 USC § 4347]. There are authorized to be appropriated to carry out the provisions of this chapter not to exceed $300,000 for fiscal year 1970, $700,000 for fiscal year 1971, and $1,000,000 for each fiscal year thereafter.

ENVIRONMENTAL QUALITY IMPROVEMENT ACT OF 1970

HISTORY: Public Law 91-224, April 3, 1970; 84 Stat. 114, 42 U.S.C. 4371; Amended by PL 94-52, July 3, 1975; PL 94-298, May 29, 1976; PL 95-300, June 26, 1978; PL 97-350, Oct. 18, 1982; PL 98-581, Oct. 30, 1984

Sec. 201 Short Title

This title may be cited as the "Environmental Quality Improvement Act of 1970."

Sec. 202 Findings, Declarations, and Purposes [42 U.S.C. 4371]

(a) The Congress finds—

(1) that man has caused changes in the environment;

(2) that many of these changes may affect the relationship between man and his environment; and

(3) that population increases and urban concentration contribute directly to pollution and the degradation of our environment.

(b) (1) The Congress declares that there is a national policy for the environment which provides for the enhancement of environmental quality. This policy is evidenced by statutes heretofore enacted relating to the prevention, abatement, and control of environmental pollution, water and land resources, transportation, and economic and regional development.

(2) The primary responsibility for implementing this policy rests with State and local governments.

(3) The Federal Government encourages and supports implementation of this policy through appropriate regional organizations established under existing law.

(c) The purposes of this title are—

(1) To assure that each Federal department and agency conducting or supporting public works activities which affect the environment shall implement the policies established under existing law; and

(2) to authorize an Office of Environmental Quality, which, notwithstanding any other provision of law, shall provide the professional and administrative staff for the Council on Environmental Quality established by Public Law 91-190.

Sec. 203 Office of Environmental Quality [42 U.S.C. 4372]

(a) There is established in the Executive Office of the President an office to be known as the Office of Environmental Quality (hereafter in this title referred to as the "Office"). The Chairman of the Council on Environmental Quality established by Public Law 91-190 shall be the Director of the Office. There shall be in the Office a Deputy Director who shall be appointed by the President, by and with the advice and consent of the Senate.

(b) The compensation of the Deputy Director shall be fixed by the President at a rate not in excess of the annual rate of compensation payable to the Deputy Director of the Bureau of the Budget.

(c) The Director is authorized to employ such officers and employees (including experts and consultants) as may be necessary to enable the Office to carry out its functions under this title and Public Law 91-190, except that he may employ no more than ten specialists and other experts without regard to the provisions of title 5, United States Code, governing appointments in the competitive service, and pay such specialists and experts without regard to the provisions of chapter 51 and subchapter III of chapter 53 of such title relating to classification and General Schedule pay rates, but no such specialist or expert shall be paid at a rate in excess of the maximum rate for GS-18 of the General Schedule under section 5332 of title 5.

(d) In carrying out his functions the Director shall assist and advise the President on policies and programs of the Federal Government affecting environmental quality by–

(1) providing the professional and administrative staff and support for the Council on Environmental Quality established by Public Law 91-190;

(2) assisting the Federal agencies and departments in appraising the effectiveness of existing and proposed facilities, programs, policies, and activities of the Federal Government, and those specific major projects designated by the President which do not require individual project authorization by Congress, which affect environmental quality;

(3) reviewing the adequacy of existing systems for monitoring and predicting environmental changes in order to achieve effective coverage and efficient use of research facilities and other resources;

(4) promoting the advancement of scientific knowledge of the effects of actions and technology on the environment and encourage the development of the means to prevent or reduce adverse effects that endanger the health and well-being of man;

(5) assisting in coordinating among the Federal departments and agencies those programs and activities which affect, protect, and improve environmental quality;

(6) assisting the Federal departments and agencies in the development and interrelationship of environmental quality criteria and standards established through the Federal Government;

(7) collecting, analyzing, and interpreting data and information on environmental quality, ecological research, and evaluation.

(e) The Director is authorized to contract with public or private agencies, institutions, and organizations and with individuals without regard to sections 3648 and 3709 of the Revised Statutes (31 U.S.C. 529; 41 U.S.C. 5) in carrying out his functions.

Sec. 204 Report [42 U.S.C. 4373]

Each Environmental Quality Report required by Public Law 91-190 shall, upon transmittal to Congress, be referred to each standing committee having jurisdiction over any part of the subject matter of the Report.

Sec. 205 Authorization [42 U.S.C. 4374]

There are hereby authorized to be appropriated for the operations of the Office of Environmental Quality and the Council on Environmental Quality not to exceed the following sums for the following fiscal years which sums are in addition to those contained in Public Law 91-190:

(a) $2,126,000 for the fiscal year ending September 30, 1979 [§205(a) amended by PL 97-350]

(b) $3,000,000 for each of the fiscal years ending September 30, 1980, and September 30, 1981.

(c) $440,000 for the fiscal years ending September 30, 1982, 1983, and 1984. [§205(c) added by PL 97-350]

(d) $480,000 for each of the fiscal years ending September 30, 1985 and September 30, 1986. [§205(d) added by PL 98-581]

Sec. 206 Office Management Fund [42 U.S.C. 4375]

(a) There is established an Office of Environmental Quality Management Fund (hereinafter referred to as the "Fund") to receive advance payments from other agencies or accounts that may be used solely to finance–

(1) study contracts that are jointly sponsored by the Office and one or more other Federal agencies; and

(2) Federal interagency environmental projects (including task forces) in which the Office participates.

(b) Any study contract or project that is to be financed under subsection (a) may be initiated only with the approval of the Director.

(c) The Director shall promulgate regulations setting forth policies and procedures for operation of the Fund [§206 added by PL 98-581].

CLEAN AIR ACT SEC. 309*

(a) The Administrator shall review and comment in writing on the environmental impact of any matter relating to duties and responsibilities granted pursuant to this chapter or other provisions of the authority of the Administrator, contained in any (1) legislation proposed by any Federal department or agency, (2) newly authorized Federal projects for construction and any major Federal agency action (other than a project for construction) to which section 4332(2)(C) of this title applies, and (3) proposed regulations published by any department or agency of the Federal Government. Such written comment shall be made public at the conclusion of any such review.

(b) In the event the Administrator determines that any such legislation, action, or regulation is unsatisfactory from the standpoint of public health or welfare or environmental quality, he shall publish his determination and the matter shall be referred to the Council on Environmental Quality.

*July 14, 1955, c. 360, § 309, as added Dec. 31, 1970, Pub. L. 91-604 § 12(a), 42 U.S.C. § 7609 (1970).

PART II CEQ REGULATIONS AND POLICY GUIDANCE

Executive Order No. 11514 (March 5,1970) issued after the enactment of NEPA gave CEQ authority to oversee Federal agency compliance with NEPA and to issue guidelines implementing the procedural provisions of the statute. CEQ issued Interim Guidelines in April 1970 (35 Fed. Reg. 7391 (1970)). The Interim Guidelines were replaced by Guidelines in April 1971 (36 Fed. Reg. 7724 (1971)). Then, in 1973, CEQ substantially expanded the guidelines to reflect the experience Federal agencies had in preparing and utilizing EISs. CEQ first published these guidelines in draft form and sought public comment on them (38 Fed. Reg. 10856 (1973)). In response to comments, the final Guidelines, issued in final form in August 1973 (38 Fed. Reg. 20550 (1973)), increased opportunities for public comment in the EIS process and tried to provide more detailed guidance to Federal agencies on their responsibilities in light of court cases interpreting NEPA.

The Guidelines, however, were not directives. Some courts cited the CEQ Guidelines as persuasive, while others ignored them. Inconsistent agency practices resulted, making it difficult for those outside of government to understand and to participate in the environmental review process. Thus, in 1977, President Carter issued Executive Order No. 11991 (May 24, 1977) giving CEQ authority to issue regulations that would be binding on all Federal agencies. CEQ issued such regulations in 1978 and they became effective in 1979 (43 Fed. Reg. 55990 (1978)); the regulations were amended once in 1986 (51 Fed. Reg. 15625 (1986)). It is these regulations, which have as their basis the earlier guidelines, that specify the procedural requirements outlined in NEPA Section 102(2)(C).

REGULATIONS FOR IMPLEMENTING THE PROCEDURAL PROVISIONS OF THE NATIONAL ENVIRONMENTAL POLICY ACT

PART 1500–PURPOSE, POLICY, AND MANDATE

AUTHORITY: NEPA, the Environmental Quality Improvement Act of 1970, as amended (42 U.S.C. 4371 *et seq.*), sec. 309 of the Clean Air Act, as amended (42 U.S.C. 7609) and Executive Order 11514, Mar. 5, 1970, as amended by Executive Order 11991, May 24, 1977).

SOURCE: 43 FR 55990, Nov. 28, 1978, unless otherwise noted.

§ 1500.1 Purpose.

(a) The National Environmental Policy Act (NEPA) is our basic national charter for protection of the environment. It establishes policy, sets goals (section 101), and provides means (section 102) for carrying out the policy. Section 102(2) contains "action-forcing" provisions to make sure that Federal agencies act according to the letter and spirit of the Act. The regulations that follow implement section 102(2). Their purpose is to tell Federal agencies what they must do to comply with the procedures and achieve the goals of the Act. The President, the Federal agencies, and the courts share responsibility for enforcing the Act so as to achieve the substantive requirements of section 101.

(b) NEPA procedures must insure that environmental information is available to public officials and citizens before decisions are made and before actions are taken. The information must be of high quality. Accurate scientific analysis, expert agency comments, and public scrutiny are essential to implementing NEPA. Most important, NEPA documents must concentrate on the issues that are truly significant to the action in question, rather than amassing needless detail.

(c) Ultimately, of course, it is not better documents but better decisions that count. NEPA's purpose is not to generate paperwork—even excellent paperwork—but to foster excellent action. The NEPA process is intended to help public officials make decisions that are based on understanding of environmental consequences, and take actions that protect, restore, and enhance the environment. These regulations provide the direction to achieve this purpose.

§ 1500.2 Policy.

Federal agencies shall to the fullest extent possible:

(a) Interpret and administer the policies, regulations, and public laws of the United States in accordance with the policies set forth in the Act and in these regulations.

(b) Implement procedures to make the NEPA process more useful to decision makers and the public; to reduce paperwork and the accumulation of extraneous background data; and to emphasize real environmental issues and alternatives. Environmental impact statements shall be concise, clear, and to the point, and shall be supported by evidence that agencies have made the necessary environmental analyses.

(c) Integrate the requirements of NEPA with other planning and environmental review procedures required by law or by agency practice so that all such procedures run concurrently rather than consecutively.

(d) Encourage and facilitate public involvement in decisions which affect the quality of the human environment.

(e) Use the NEPA process to identify and assess the reasonable alternatives to proposed actions that will avoid or minimize adverse effects of these actions upon the quality of the human environment.

(f) Use all practicable means, consistent with the requirements of the Act and other essential considerations of national policy, to restore and enhance the quality of the human environment and avoid or minimize any possible adverse effects of their actions upon the quality of the human environment.

§ 1500.3 Mandate.

Parts 1500 through 1508 of this title provide regulations applicable to and binding on all Federal agencies for implementing the procedural provisions of the National Environmental Policy Act of 1969, as amended (Pub. L. 91-190, 42 U.S.C. 4321 *et seq.*) (NEPA or the Act) except where compliance would be inconsistent with other statutory requirements. These regulations are issued pursuant to NEPA, the Environmental Quality Improvement Act of 1970, as amended (42 U.S.C. 4371 *et seq.*) section 309 of the Clean Air Act, as amended (42 U.S.C. 7609) and Executive Order 11514, Protection and Enhancement of Environmental Quality (March 5, 1970, as amended by Executive Order 11991, May 24, 1977). These regulations, unlike the predecessor guidelines, are not confined to sec. 102(2)(C) (environmental impact statements). The regulations apply to the whole of section 102(2). The provisions of the Act and of these regulations must be read together as a whole in order to comply with the spirit and letter of the law. It is the Council's intention that judicial review of agency compliance with these regulations not occur before an agency has filed the final environmental impact statement, or has made a final finding of no significant impact (when such a finding will result in action affecting the environment), or takes action that will result in irreparable injury. Furthermore, it is the Council's intention that any trivial violation of these regulations not give rise to any independent cause of action.

§ 1500.4 Reducing paperwork.

Agencies shall reduce excessive paperwork by:
(a) Reducing the length of environmental impact statements (§ 1502.2(c)), by means such as setting appropriate page limits (§§ 1501.7(b)(1) and 1502.7).
(b) Preparing analytic rather than encyclopedic environmental impact statements (§ 1502.2(a)).
(c) Discussing only briefly issues other than significant ones (§ 1502.2(b)).
(d) Writing environmental impact statements in plain language (§ 1502.8).
(e) Following a clear format for environmental impact statements (§ 502.10).
(f) Emphasizing the portions of the environmental impact statement that are useful to decisionmakers and the public (§§ 1502.14 and 1502.15) and reducing emphasis on background material (§ 1502.16).
(g) Using the scoping process, not only to identify significant environmental issues deserving of study, but also to deemphasize insignificant issues, narrowing the scope of the environmental impact statement process accordingly (§ 1501.7).
(h) Summarizing the environmental impact statement (§ 1502.12) and circulating the summary instead of the entire environmental impact statement if the latter is unusually long (§ 1502.19).
(i) Using program, policy, or plan environmental impact statements and tiering from statements of broad scope to those of narrower scope, to eliminate repetitive discussions of the same issues (§§ 1502.4 and 1502.20).
(j) Incorporating by reference (§ 1502.21).
(k) Integrating NEPA requirements with other environmental review and consultation requirements (§ 1502.25).
(l) Requiring comments to be as specific as possible (§ 1503.3).
(m) Attaching and circulating only changes to the draft environmental impact statement, rather than rewriting and circulating the entire statement when changes are minor (§ 1503.4(c)).
(n) Eliminating duplication with State and local procedures, by providing for joint preparation (§ 1506.2), and with other Federal procedures, by providing that an agency may adopt appropriate environmental documents prepared by another agency (§ 1506.3).
(o) Combining environmental documents with other documents (§ 1506.4).
(p) Using categorical exclusions to define categories of actions which do not individually or cumulatively have a significant effect on the human environment and which are therefore exempt from requirements to prepare an environmental impact statement (§ 1508.4).

(q) Using a finding of no significant impact when an action not otherwise excluded will not have a significant effect on the human environment and is therefore exempt from requirements to prepare an environmental impact statement (§ 1508.13).

[43 FR 55990, Nov. 29, 1978; 44 FR 873, Jan. 3, 1979]

§ 1500.5 Reducing delay.

Agencies shall reduce delay by:
(a) Integrating the NEPA process into early planning (§ 1501.2).
(b) Emphasizing interagency cooperation before the environmental impact statement is prepared, rather than submission of adversary comments on a completed document (§ 1501.6).
(c) Insuring the swift and fair resolution of lead agency disputes (§ 1501.5).
(d) Using the scoping process for an early identification of what are and what are not the real issues (§ 1501.7).
(e) Establishing appropriate time limits for the environmental impact statement process (§§ 1501.7(b)(2) and 1501.8).
(f) Preparing environmental impact statements early in the process (§ 1502.5).
(g) Integrating NEPA requirements with other environmental review and consultation requirements (§ 1502.25).
(h) Eliminating duplication with State and local procedures by providing for joint preparation (§ 1506.2) and with other Federal procedures by providing that an agency may adopt appropriate environmental documents prepared by another agency (§ 1506.3).
(i) Combining environmental documents with other documents (§ 1506.4).
(j) Using accelerated procedures for proposals for legislation (§ 1506.8).
(k) Using categorical exclusions to define categories of actions which do not individually or cumulatively have a significant effect on the human environment (§ 1508.4) and which are therefore exempt from requirements to prepare an environmental impact statement.
(1) Using a finding of no significant impact when an action not otherwise excluded will not have a significant effect on the human environment (§ 1508.13) and is therefore exempt from requirements to prepare an environmental impact statement.

§ 1500.6 Agency authority.

Each agency shall interpret the provisions of the Act as a supplement to its existing authority and as a mandate to view traditional policies and missions in the light of the Act's national environmental objectives. Agencies shall review their policies, procedures, and regulations accordingly and revise them as necessary to insure full compliance with the purposes and provisions of the Act. The phrase "to the fullest extent possible" in section 102 means that each agency of the Federal Government shall comply with that section unless existing law applicable to the agency's operations expressly prohibits or makes compliance impossible.

PART 1501–NEPA AND AGENCY PLANNING

AUTHORITY: NEPA, the Environmental Quality Improvement Act of 1970, as amended (42 U.S.C. 4371 *et seq.*), sec. 309 of the Clean Air Act, as amended (42 U.S.C. 7609) and Executive Order 11514, Mar. 5, 1970, as amended by Executive Order 11991, May 24, 1977.

SOURCE: 43 FR 55992, Nov. 29, 1978, unless otherwise noted.

§ 1501.1 Purpose.

The purposes of this part include:
(a) Integrating the NEPA process into early planning to insure appropriate consideration of NEPA's policies and to eliminate delay.
(b) Emphasizing cooperative consultation among agencies before the environmental impact statement is prepared rather than submission of adversary comments on a completed document.
(c) Providing for the swift and fair resolution of lead agency disputes.
(d) Identifying at an early stage the significant environmental issues deserving of study and deemphasizing insignificant issues, narrowing the scope of the environmental impact statement accordingly.
(e) Providing a mechanism for putting appropriate time limits on the environmental impact statement process.

§ 1501.2 Apply NEPA early in the process.

Agencies shall integrate the NEPA process with other planning at the earliest possible time to insure that planning and decisions reflect environmental values, to avoid delays later in the process, and to head off potential conflicts. Each agency shall:
(a) Comply with the mandate of section 102(2)(A) to "utilize a systematic, interdisciplinary approach which will insure the integrated use of the natural and social sciences and the environmental design arts in planning and in decision making which may have an impact on man's environment," as specified by § 1507.2.
(b) Identify environmental effects and values in adequate detail so they can be compared to economic and technical analyses. Environmental documents and appropriate analyses shall be circulated and reviewed at the same time as other planning documents.
(c) Study, develop, and describe appropriate alternatives to recommended courses of action in any proposal which involves unresolved conflicts concerning alternative uses of available resources as provided by section 102(2)(E) of the Act.
(d) Provide for cases where actions are planned by private applicants or other non-Federal entities before Federal involvement so that:
(1) Policies or designated staff are available to advise potential applicants of studies or other information foreseeably required for later Federal action.
(2) The Federal agency consults early with appropriate State and local agencies and Indian tribes and with interested private persons and organizations when its own involvement is reasonably foreseeable.
(3) The Federal agency commences its NEPA process at the earliest possible time.

§ 1501.3 When to prepare an environmental assessment.

(a) Agencies shall prepare an environmental assessment (§ 1508.9) when necessary under the procedures adopted by individual agencies to supplement these regulations as described in § 1507.3. An assessment is not necessary if the agency has decided to prepare an environmental impact statement.
(b) Agencies may prepare an environmental assessment on any action at any time in order to assist agency planning and decision making.

§ 1501.4 Whether to prepare an environmental impact statement.

In determining whether to prepare an environmental impact statement the Federal agency shall:
(a) Determine under its procedures supplementing these regulations (described in § 1507.3) whether the proposal is one which:
(1) Normally requires an environmental impact statement, or
(2) Normally does not require either an environmental impact statement or an environmental assessment (categorical exclusion).

(b) If the proposed action is not covered by paragraph (a) of this section, prepare an environmental assessment (§ 1508.9). The agency shall involve environmental agencies, applicants, and the public, to the extent practicable, in preparing assessments required by § 1508.9(a)(1).

(c) Based on the environmental assessment make its determination whether to prepare an environmental impact statement.

(d) Commence the scoping process (§ 1501.7), if the agency will prepare an environmental impact statement.

(e) Prepare a finding of no significant impact (§ 1508.13), if the agency determines on the basis of the environmental assessment not to prepare a statement.

(1) The agency shall make the finding of no significant impact available to the affected public as specified in § 1506.6.

(2) In certain limited circumstances, which the agency may cover in its procedures under § 1507.3, the agency shall make the finding of no significant impact available for public review (including State and areawide clearinghouses) for 30 days before the agency makes its final determination whether to prepare an environmental impact statement and before the action may begin. The circumstances are:

(i) The proposed action is, or is closely similar to, one which normally requires the preparation of an environmental impact statement under the procedures adopted by the agency pursuant to § 1507.3, or

(ii) The nature of the proposed action is one without precedent.

§ 1501.5 Lead agencies.

(a) A lead agency shall supervise the preparation of an environmental impact statement if more than one Federal agency either:

(1) Proposes or is involved in the same action; or

(2) Is involved in a group of actions directly related to each other because of their functional interdependence or geographical proximity.

(b) Federal, State, or local agencies, including at least one Federal agency, may act as joint lead agencies to prepare an environmental impact statement (§ 1506.2).

(c) If an action falls within the provisions of paragraph (a) of this section the potential lead agencies shall determine by letter or memorandum which agency shall be the lead agency and which shall be cooperating agencies. The agencies shall resolve the lead agency question so as not to cause delay. If there is disagreement among the agencies, the following factors (which are listed in order of descending importance) shall determine lead agency designation:

(1) Magnitude of agency's involvement.

(2) Project approval/disapproval authority.

(3) Expertise concerning the action's environmental effects.

(4) Duration of agency's involvement.

(5) Sequence of agency's involvement.

(d) Any Federal agency, or any State or local agency or private person substantially affected by the absence of lead agency designation, may make a written request to the potential lead agencies that a lead agency be designated.

(e) If Federal agencies are unable to agree on which agency will be the lead agency or if the procedure described in paragraph (c) of this section has not resulted within 45 days in a lead agency designation, any of the agencies or persons concerned may file a request with the Council asking it to determine which Federal agency shall be the lead agency.

A copy of the request shall be transmitted to each potential lead agency. The request shall consist of:

(1) A precise description of the nature and extent of the proposed action.

(2) A detailed statement of why each potential lead agency should or should not be the lead agency under the criteria specified in paragraph (c) of this section.

(f) A response may be filed by any potential lead agency concerned within 20 days after a request is filed with the Council. The Council shall determine as soon as possible but not later than 20 days after receiving the request and all responses to it which Federal agency shall be the lead agency and which other Federal agencies shall be cooperating agencies.

§ 1501.6 Cooperating agencies.

The purpose of this section is to emphasize agency cooperation early in the NEPA process. Upon request of the lead agency, any other Federal agency which has jurisdiction by law shall be a cooperating agency. In addition any other Federal agency which has special expertise with respect to any environmental issue, which should be addressed in the statement may be a cooperating agency upon request of the lead agency. An agency may request the lead agency to designate it a cooperating agency.

(a) The lead agency shall:

(1) Request the participation of each cooperating agency in the NEPA process at the earliest possible time.

(2) Use the environmental analysis and proposals of cooperating agencies with jurisdiction by law or special expertise, to the maximum extent possible consistent with its responsibility as lead agency.

(3) Meet with a cooperating agency at the latter's request.

(b) Each cooperating agency shall:

(1) Participate in the NEPA process at the earliest possible time.

(2) Participate in the scoping process (described below in § 1501.7).

(3) Assume on request of the lead agency responsibility for developing information and preparing environmental analyses including portions of the environmental impact statement concerning which the cooperating agency has special expertise.

(4) Make available staff support at the lead agency's request to enhance the latter's interdisciplinary capability.

(5) Normally use its own funds. The lead agency shall, to the extent available funds permit, fund those major activities or analyses it requests from cooperating agencies. Potential lead agencies shall include such funding requirements in their budget requests.

(c) A cooperating agency may in response to a lead agency's request for assistance in preparing the environmental impact statement (described in paragraph (b) (3), (4), or (5) of this section) reply that other program commitments preclude any involvement or the degree of involvement requested in the action that is the subject of the environmental impact statement. A copy of this reply shall be submitted to the Council.

§ 1501.7 Scoping.

There shall be an early and open process for determining the scope of issues to be addressed and for identifying the significant issues related to a proposed action. This process shall be termed scoping. As soon as practicable after its decision to prepare an environmental impact statement and before the scoping process the lead agency shall publish a notice of intent (§ 1508.22) in the *Federal Register* except as provided in § 1507.3(e).

(a) As part of the scoping process the lead agency shall:

(1) Invite the participation of affected Federal, State, and local agencies, any affected Indian tribe, the proponent of the action, and other interested persons (including those who might not be in accord with the action on environmental grounds), unless there is a limited exception under § 1507.3(c). An agency may give notice in accordance with § 1506.6.

(2) Determine the scope (§ 1508.25) and the significant issues to be analyzed in depth in the environmental impact statement.

(3) Identify and eliminate from detailed study the issues which are not significant or which have been covered by prior environmental review (§ 1506.3), narrowing the discussion of these issues in the statement to a brief presentation of why they will not have a significant effect on the human environment or providing a reference to their coverage elsewhere.

(4) Allocate assignments for preparation of the environmental impact statement among the lead and cooperating agencies, with the lead agency retaining responsibility for the statement.

(5) Indicate any public environmental assessments and other environmental impact statements which are being or will be prepared that are related to but are not part of the scope of the impact statement under consideration.

(6) Identify other environmental review and consultation requirements so the lead and cooperating agencies may prepare other required analyses and studies concurrently with, and integrated with, the environmental impact statement as provided in § 1502.25.

(7) Indicate the relationship between the timing of the preparation of environmental analyses and the agency's tentative planning and decision making schedule.

(b) As part of the scoping process the lead agency may:

(1) Set page limits on environmental documents (§ 1502.7).

(2) Set time limits (§ 1501.8).

(3) Adopt procedures under § 1507.3 to combine its environmental assessment process with its scoping process.

(4) Hold an early scoping meeting or meetings which may be integrated with any other early planning meeting the agency has. Such a scoping meeting will often be appropriate when the impacts of a particular action are confined to specific sites.

(c) An agency shall revise the determinations made under paragraphs (a) and (b) of this section if substantial changes are made later in the proposed action, or if significant new circumstances or information arise which bear on the proposal or its impacts.

§ 1501.8 Time limits.

Although the Council has decided that prescribed universal time limits for the entire NEPA process are too inflexible, Federal agencies are encouraged to set time limits appropriate to individual actions (consistent with the time intervals required by § 1506.10). When multiple agencies are involved the reference to agency below means lead agency.

(a) The agency shall set time limits if an applicant for the proposed action requests them: *Provided*, that the limits are consistent with the purposes of NEPA and other essential considerations of national policy.

(b) The agency may:

(1) Consider the following factors in determining time limits:

(i) Potential for environmental harm.

(ii) Size of the proposed action.

(iii) State of the art of analytic techniques.

(iv) Degree of public need for the proposed action, including the consequences of delay.

(v) Number of persons and agencies affected.

(vi) Degree to which relevant information is known and if not known the time required for obtaining it.

(vii) Degree to which the action is controversial.

(viii) Other time limits imposed on the agency by law, regulations, or executive order.

(2) Set overall time limits or limits for each constituent part of the NEPA process, which may include:

(i) Decision on whether to prepare an environmental impact statement (if not already decided).

(ii) Determination of the scope of the environmental impact statement.

(iii) Preparation of the draft environmental impact statement.

(iv) Review of any comments on the draft environmental impact statement from the public and agencies.

(v) Preparation of the final environmental impact statement.

(vi) Review of any comments on the final environmental impact statement.

(vii) Decision on the action based in part on the environmental impact statement.

(3) Designate a person (such as the project manager or a person in the agency's office with NEPA responsibilities) to expedite the NEPA process.

(c) State or local agencies or members of the public may request a Federal Agency to set time limits.

PART 1502–ENVIRONMENTAL IMPACT STATEMENT

AUTHORITY: NEPA, the Environmental Quality Improvement Act of 1970, as amended (42 U.S.C. 4371 *et seq.*), sec. 309 of the Clean Air Act, as amended (42 U.S.C. 7609) and Executive Order 11514, Mar. 5, 1970, as amended by Executive Order 11991, May 24, 1977.

SOURCE: 43 FR 55994, Nov. 29, 1978, unless otherwise noted.

§ 1502.1 Purpose.

The primary purpose of an environmental impact statement is to serve as an action-forcing device to insure that the policies and goals defined in the Act are infused into the ongoing programs and actions of the Federal Government. It shall provide full and fair discussion of significant environmental impacts and shall inform decisionmakers and the public of the reasonable alternatives which would avoid or minimize adverse impacts or enhance the quality of the human environment. Agencies shall focus on significant environmental issues and alternatives and shall reduce paperwork and the accumulation of extraneous background data. Statements shall be concise, clear, and to the point, and shall be supported by evidence that the agency has made the necessary environmental analyses. An environmental impact statement is more than a disclosure document. It shall be used by Federal officials in conjunction with other relevant material to plan actions and make decisions.

§ 1502.2 Implementation.

To achieve the purposes set forth in § 1502.1 agencies shall prepare environmental impact statements in the following manner:

(a) Environmental impact statements shall be analytic rather than encyclopedic.

(b) Impacts shall be discussed in proportion to their significance. There shall be only brief discussion of other than significant issues. As in a finding of no significant impact, there should be only enough discussion to show why more study is not warranted.

(c) Environmental impact statements shall be kept concise and shall be no longer than absolutely necessary to comply with NEPA and with these regulations. Length should vary first with potential environmental problems and then with project size.

(d) Environmental impact statements shall State how alternatives considered in it and decisions based on it will or will not achieve the requirements of sections 101 and 102(1) of the Act and other environmental laws and policies.

(e) The range of alternatives discussed in environmental impact statements shall encompass those to be considered by the ultimate agency decision maker.

(f) Agencies shall not commit resources prejudicing selection of alternatives before making a final decision (§ 1506.1).

(g) Environmental impact statements shall serve as the means of assessing the environmental impact of proposed agency actions, rather than justifying decisions already made.

§ 1502.3 Statutory requirements for statements.

As required by sec. 102(2)(C) of NEPA environmental impact statements (§ 1508.11) are to be included in every recommendation or report.

On proposals (§ 1508.23).

For legislation and (§ 1508.17).

Other major Federal actions (§ 1508.18).

Significantly (§ 1508.27).

Affecting (§§ 1508.3, 1508.8).

The quality of the human environment (§ 1508.14).

§ 1502.4 Major Federal actions requiring the preparation of environmental impact statements.

(a) Agencies shall make sure the proposal which is the subject of an environmental impact statement is properly defined. Agencies shall use the criteria for scope (§ 1508.25) to determine which proposal(s) shall be the subject of a particular statement. Proposals or parts of proposals which are related to each other closely enough to be, in effect, a single course of action shall be evaluated in a single impact statement.

(b) Environmental impact statements may be, and are sometimes required, for broad Federal actions such as the adoption of new agency programs or regulations (§ 1508.18). Agencies shall prepare statements on broad actions so that they are relevant to policy and are timed to coincide with meaningful points in agency planning and decision making.

(c) When preparing statements on broad actions (including proposals by more than one agency), agencies may find it useful to evaluate the proposal(s) in one of the following ways:

(1) Geographically, including actions occurring in the same general location, such as body of water, region, or metropolitan area.

(2) Generically, including actions which have relevant similarities, such as common timing, impacts, alternatives, methods of implementation, media, or subject matter.

(3) By stage of technological development including Federal or federally assisted research, development or demonstration programs for new technologies which, if applied, could significantly affect the quality of the human environment. Statements shall be prepared on such programs and shall be available before the program has reached a stage of investment or commitment to implementation likely to determine subsequent development or restrict later alternatives.

(d) Agencies shall as appropriate employ scoping (§ 1501.7), tiering (§ 1502.20), and other methods listed in §§ 1500.4 and 1500.5 to relate broad and narrow actions and to avoid duplication and delay.

§ 1502.5 Timing.

An agency shall commence preparation of an environmental impact statement as close as possible to the time the agency is developing or is presented with a proposal (§ 1508.23) so that preparation can be completed in time for the final statement to be included in any recommendation or report on the proposal. The statement shall be prepared early enough so that it can serve practically as an important contribution to the decision making process and will not be used to rationalize or justify decisions already made (§§ 1500.2(c), 1501.2, and 1502.2). For instance:

(a) For projects directly undertaken by Federal agencies the environmental impact statement shall be prepared at the feasibility analysis (go no-go) stage and may be supplemented at a later stage if necessary.

(b) For applications to the agency appropriate environmental assessments or statements shall be commenced no later than immediately after the application is received. Federal agencies are encouraged to begin preparation of such assessments or statements earlier, preferably jointly with applicable State or local agencies.

(c) For adjudication, the final environmental impact statement shall normally precede the final staff recommendation and that portion of the public hearing related to the impact study. In appropriate circumstances the statement may follow preliminary hearings designed to gather information for use in the statements.

(d) For informal rulemaking the draft environmental impact statement shall normally accompany the proposed rule.

§ 1502.6 Interdisciplinary preparation.

Environmental impact statements shall be prepared using an interdisciplinary approach which will insure the integrated use of the natural and social sciences and the environmental design arts (section 102(2)(A) of the Act). The disciplines of the preparers shall be appropriate to the scope and issues identified in the scoping process (§ 1501.7).

§ 1502.7 Page limits.

The text of final environmental impact statements (e.g., paragraphs (d) through (g) of § 1502.10) shall normally be less than 150 pages and for proposals of unusual scope or complexity shall normally be less than 300 pages.

§ 1502.8 Writing.

Environmental impact statements shall be written in plain language and may use appropriate graphics so that decisionmakers and the public can readily understand them. Agencies should employ writers of clear prose or editors to write, review, or edit statements, which will be based upon the analysis and supporting data from the natural and social sciences and the environmental design arts.

§ 1502.9 Draft, final, and supplemental statements.

Except for proposals for legislation as provided in § 1506.8 environmental impact statements shall be prepared in two stages and may be supplemented.

(a) Draft environmental impact statements shall be prepared in accordance with the scope decided upon in the scoping process. The lead agency shall work with the cooperating agencies and shall obtain comments as required in Part 1503 of this chapter. The draft statement must fulfill and satisfy to the fullest extent possible the requirements established for final statements in section 102(2)(C) of the Act. If a draft statement is so inadequate as to preclude meaningful analysis, the agency shall prepare and circulate a revised draft of the appropriate portion. The agency shall make every effort to disclose and discuss at appropriate points in the draft statement all major points of view on the environmental impacts of the alternatives including the proposed action.

(b) Final environmental impact statements shall respond to comments as required in Part 1503 of this chapter. The agency shall discuss at appropriate points in the final statement any responsible opposing view which was not adequately discussed in the draft statement and shall indicate the agency's response to the issues raised.

(c) Agencies:

(1) Shall prepare supplements to either draft or final environmental impact statements if:

(i) The agency makes substantial changes in the proposed action that are relevant to environmental concerns; or

(ii) There are significant new circumstances or information relevant to environmental concerns and bearing on the proposed action or its impacts.

(2) May also prepare supplements when the agency determines that the purposes of the Act will be furthered by doing so.

(3) Shall adopt procedures for introducing a supplement into its formal administrative record, if such a record exists.

(4) Shall prepare, circulate, and file a supplement to a statement in the same fashion (exclusive of scoping) as a draft and final statement unless alternative procedures are approved by the Council.

§ 1502.10 Recommended format.

Agencies shall use a format for environmental impact statements which will encourage good analysis and clear presentation of the alternatives including the proposed action. The following standard format for environmental impact statements should be followed unless the agency determines that there is a compelling reason to do otherwise:

(a) Cover sheet.

(b) Summary.

(c) Table of contents.

(d) Purpose of and need for action.

(e) Alternatives including proposed action (sections 102(2)(C)(iii) and 102(2)(E) of the Act).

(f) Affected environment.

(g) Environmental consequences (especially sections 102(2)(C)(i), (ii), (iv), and (v) of the Act).

(h) List of preparers.

(i) List of Agencies, Organizations, and persons to whom copies of the statement are sent.

(j) Index.

(k) Appendices (if any).

If a different format is used, it shall include paragraphs (a), (b), (c), (h), (i), and (j), of this section and shall include the substance of paragraphs (d), (e), (f), (g), and (k) of this section, as further described in §§ 1502.11 through 1502.18, in any appropriate format.

§ 1502.11 Cover sheet.

The cover sheet shall not exceed one page. It shall include:

(a) A list of the responsible agencies including the lead agency and any cooperating agencies.

(b) The title of the proposed action that is the subject of the statement (and if appropriate the titles of related cooperating agency actions), together with the State(s) and county(ies) (or other jurisdiction if applicable) where the action is located.

(c) The name, address, and telephone number of the person at the agency who can supply further information.

(d) A designation of the statement as a draft, final, or draft or final supplement.

(e) A one paragraph abstract of the statement.

(f) The date by which comments must be received (computed in cooperation with EPA under § 1506.10).

The information required by this section may be entered on Standard Form 424 (in items 4, 6, 7, 10, and 18).

§ 1502.12 Summary.

Each environmental impact statement shall contain a summary which adequately and accurately summarizes the statement. The summary shall stress the major conclusions, areas of controversy (including issues raised by agencies and the public), and the issues to be resolved (including the choice among alternatives). The summary will normally not exceed 15 pages.

§ 1502.13 Purpose and need.

The statement shall briefly specify the underlying purpose and need to which the agency is responding in proposing the alternatives including the proposed action.

§ 1502.14 Alternatives including the proposed action.

This section is the heart of the environmental impact statement. Based on the information and analysis presented in the sections on the Affected Environment (§ 1502.15) and the Environmental Consequences (§ 1502.16), it should present the environmental impacts of the proposal and the alternatives in comparative form, thus sharply defining the issues and providing a clear basis for choice among options by the decision maker and the public. In this section agencies shall:

(a) Rigorously explore and objectively evaluate all reasonable alternatives, and for alternatives which were eliminated from detailed study, briefly discuss the reasons for their having been eliminated.

(b) Devote substantial treatment to each alternative considered in detail including the proposed action so that reviewers may evaluate their comparative merits.

(c) Include reasonable alternatives not within the jurisdiction of the lead agency.

(d) Include the alternative of no action.

(e) Identify the agency's preferred alternative or alternatives, if one or more exists, in the draft statement and identify such alternative in the final statement unless another law prohibits the expression of such a preference.

(f) Include appropriate mitigation measures not already included in the proposed action or alternatives.

§ 1502.15 Affected environment.

The environmental impact statement shall succinctly describe the environment of the area(s) to be affected or created by the alternatives under consideration. The descriptions shall be no longer than is necessary to understand the effects of the alternatives. Data and analyses in a statement shall be commensurate with the importance of the impact, with less important material summarized, consolidated, or simply referenced. Agencies shall avoid useless bulk in statements and shall concentrate effort and attention on important issues. Verbose descriptions of the affected environment are themselves no measure of the adequacy of an environmental impact statement.

§ 1502.16 Environmental consequences.

This section forms the scientific and analytic basis for the comparisons under § 1502.14. It shall consolidate the discussions of those elements required by sections 102(2)(C) (i), (ii), (iv), and (v) of NEPA which are within the scope of the statement and as much of section 102(2)(C)(iii) as is necessary to support the comparisons. The discussion will include the environmental impacts of the alternatives including the proposed action, any adverse environmental effects which cannot be avoided should the proposal be implemented, the relationship between short-term uses of man's environment and the maintenance and enhancement of long-term productivity, and any irreversible or irretrievable commitments of resources which would be involved in the proposal should it be implemented. This section should not duplicate discussions in § 1502.14. It shall include discussions of:

(a) Direct effects and their significance (§ 1508.8).

(b) Indirect effects and their significance (§ 1508.8).

(c) Possible conflicts between the proposed action and the objectives of Federal, regional, State, and local (and in the case of a reservation, Indian tribe) land use plans, policies and controls for the area concerned. (See § 1506.2(d).)

(d) The environmental effects of alternatives including the proposed action. The comparisons under § 1502.14 will be based on this discussion.

(e) Energy requirements and conservation potential of various alternatives and mitigation measures.

(f) Natural or depletable resource requirements and conservation potential of various alternatives and mitigation measures.

(g) Urban quality, historic and cultural resources, and the design of the built environment, including the reuse and conservation potential of various alternatives and mitigation measures.

(h) Means to mitigate adverse environmental impacts (if not fully covered under § 1502.14(f)).

§ 1502.17 List of preparers.

The environmental impact statement shall list the names, together with their qualifications (expertise, experience, professional disciplines), of the persons who were primarily responsible for preparing the environmental impact statement or significant background papers, including basic components of the statement (§§ 1502.6 and 1502.8). Where possible the persons who are responsible for a particular analysis, including analyses in background papers, shall be identified. Normally the list will not exceed two pages.

§ 1502.18 Appendix.

If an agency prepares an appendix to an environmental impact statement the appendix shall:

(a) Consist of material prepared in connection with an environmental impact statement (as distinct from material which is not so prepared and which is incorporated by reference (§ 1502.21)).

(b) Normally consist of material which substantiates any analysis fundamental to the impact statement.

(c) Normally be analytic and relevant to the decision to be made.

(d) Be circulated with the environmental impact statement or be readily available on request.

§ 1502.19 Circulation of the environmental impact statement.

Agencies shall circulate the entire draft and final environmental impact statements except for certain appendices as provided in § 1502.18(d) and unchanged statements as provided in § 1503.4(c). However, if the statement is unusually long, the agency may circulate the summary instead, except that the entire statement shall be furnished to:

(a) Any Federal agency which has jurisdiction by law or special expertise with respect to any environmental impact involved and any appropriate Federal, State or local agency authorized to develop and enforce environmental standards.

(b) The applicant, if any.

(c) Any person, organization, or agency requesting the entire environmental impact statement.

(d) In the case of a final environmental impact statement any person, organization, or agency which submitted substantive comments on the draft. If the agency circulates the summary and thereafter receives a timely request for the entire statement and for additional time to comment, the time for that requestor only shall be extended by at least 15 days beyond the minimum period.

§ 1502.20 Tiering.

Agencies are encouraged to tier their environmental impact statements to eliminate repetitive discussions of the same issues and to focus on the actual issues ripe for decision at each level of environmental review (§ 1508.28). Whenever a broad environmental impact statement has been prepared (such as a program or policy statement) and a subsequent statement or environmental assessment is then prepared on an action included within the entire program or policy (such as a site specific action) the subsequent statement or environmental assessment need only summarize the issues discussed in the broader statement and incorporate discussions from the broader statement by reference and shall concentrate on the issues specific to the subsequent action. The subsequent document shall State where the earlier document is available. Tiering may also be appropriate for different stages of actions. (§ 1508.28).

§ 1502.21 Incorporation by reference.

Agencies shall incorporate material into an environmental impact statement by reference when the effect will be to cut down on bulk without impeding agency and public review of the action. The incorporated material shall be cited in the statement and its content briefly described. No material may be incorporated by reference unless it is reasonably available for inspection by potentially interested persons within the time allowed for comment. Material based on proprietary data which is itself not available for review and comment shall not be incorporated by reference.

§ 1502.22 Incomplete or unavailable information.

When an agency is evaluating reasonably foreseeable significant adverse effects on the human environment in an environmental impact statement and there is incomplete or unavailable information, the agency shall always make clear that such information is lacking.

(a) If the incomplete information relevant to reasonably foreseeable significant adverse impacts is essential to a reasoned choice among alternatives and the overall costs of obtaining it are not exorbitant, the agency shall include the information in the environmental impact statement.

(b) If the information relevant to reasonably foreseeable significant adverse impacts cannot be obtained because the overall costs of obtaining it are exorbitant or the means to obtain it are not known, the agency shall include within the environmental impact statement: (1) A statement that such information is incomplete or unavailable; (2) a statement of the relevance of the incomplete or unavailable information to evaluating reasonably foreseeable significant adverse impacts on the human environment; (3) a summary of existing credible scientific evidence which is relevant to evaluating the reasonably foreseeable significant adverse impacts on the human environment, and (4) the agency's evaluation of such impacts based upon theoretical approaches or research methods generally accepted in the scientific community. For the purposes of this section, "reasonably foreseeable" includes impacts which have catastrophic consequences, even if their probability of occurrence is low, provided that the analysis of the impacts is supported by credible scientific evidence, is not based on pure conjecture, and is within the rule of reason.

(c) The amended regulation will be applicable to all environmental impact statements for which a Notice of Intent (40 CFR 1508.22) is published in the *Federal Register* on or after May 27, 1986. For environmental impact statements in progress, agencies may choose to comply with the requirements of either the original or amended regulation.

[51 FR 15625, Apr. 25, 1986]

§ 1502.23 Cost-benefit analysis.

If a cost-benefit analysis relevant to the choice among environmentally different alternatives is being considered for the proposed action, it shall be incorporated by reference or appended to the statement as an aid in evaluating the environmental consequences. To assess the adequacy of compliance with section 102(2)(B) of the Act the statement shall, when a cost-benefit analysis is prepared, discuss the relationship between that analysis and any analyses of unquantified environmental impacts, values, and amenities. For purposes of complying with the Act, the weighing of the merits and drawbacks of the various alternatives need not be displayed in a monetary cost-benefit analysis and should not be when there are important qualitative considerations. In any event, an environmental impact statement should at least indicate those considerations, including factors not related to environmental quality, which are likely to be relevant and important to a decision.

§ 1502.24 Methodology and scientific accuracy.

Agencies shall insure the professional integrity, including scientific integrity, of the discussions and analyses in environmental impact statements. They shall identify any methodologies used and shall make explicit reference by footnote to the scientific and other sources relied upon for conclusions in the statement. An agency may place discussion of methodology in an appendix.

§ 1502.25 Environmental review and consultation requirements.

(a) To the fullest extent possible, agencies shall prepare draft environmental impact statements concurrently with and integrated with environmental impact analyses and related surveys and studies required by the Fish and Wildlife Coordination Act (16 U.S.C. 661 *et seq.*), the National Historic Preservation Act of 1966 (16 U.S.C. 470 *et seq.*), the Endangered Species Act of 1973 (16 U.S.C. 1531 *et seq.*), and other environmental review laws and executive orders.

(b) The draft environmental impact statement shall list all Federal permits, licenses, and other entitlements which must be obtained in implementing the proposal. If it is uncertain whether a Federal permit, license, or other entitlement is necessary, the draft environmental impact statement shall so indicate.

PART 1503–COMMENTING

AUTHORITY: NEPA, the Environmental Quality Improvement Act of 1970, as amended (42 U.S.C. 4371 *et seq.*), sec. 309 of the Clean Air Act, as amended (42 U.S.C. 7609) and Executive Order 11514, Mar. 5, 1970, as amended by Executive Order 11991, May 24, 1977.

SOURCE: 43 FR 55997, Nov. 28, 1978, unless otherwise noted.

§ 1503.1 Inviting comments.

(a) After preparing a draft environmental impact statement and before preparing a final environmental impact statement the agency shall:

(1) Obtain the comments of any Federal agency which has jurisdiction by law or special expertise with respect to any environmental impact involved or which is authorized to develop and enforce environmental standards.

(2) Request the comments of:

(i) Appropriate State and local agencies which are authorized to develop and enforce environmental standards;

(ii) Indian tribes, when the effects may be on a reservation; and

(iii) Any agency which has requested that it receive statements on actions of the kind proposed. Under Executive Order No. 12372, the Office of Management and Budget, through its system of clearinghouse, provides a means of securing the views of State and local environmental agencies. The clearinghouses may be used, by mutual agreement of the lead agency and the clearinghouse, for securing State and local reviews of the draft environmental impact statements.

(3) Request comments from the applicant, if any.

(4) Request comments from the public, affirmatively soliciting comments from those persons or organizations who may be interested or affected.

(b) An agency may request comments on a final environmental impact statement before the decision is finally made. In any case other agencies or persons may make comments before the final decision unless a different time is provided under § 1506.10.

§ 1503.2 Duty to comment.

Federal agencies with jurisdiction by law or special expertise with respect to any environmental impact involved and agencies which are authorized to develop and enforce environmental standards shall comment on statements within their jurisdiction, expertise, or authority. Agencies shall comment within the time period specified for comment in § 1506.10. A Federal agency may reply that it has no comment. If a cooperating agency is satisfied that its views are adequately reflected in the environmental impact statement, it should reply that it has no comment.

§ 1503.3 Specificity of comments.

(a) Comments on an environmental impact statement or on a proposed action shall be as specific as possible and may address either the adequacy of the statement or the merits of the alternatives discussed or both.

(b) When a commenting agency criticizes a lead agency's predictive methodology, the commenting agency should describe the alternative methodology which it prefers and why.

(c) A cooperating agency shall specify in its comments whether it needs additional information to fulfill other applicable environmental reviews or consultation requirements and what information it needs. In particular, it shall specify any additional information it needs to comment adequately on the draft statement's analysis of significant site-specific effects associated with the granting or approving by that cooperating agency of necessary Federal permits, licenses, or entitlement.

(d) When a cooperating agency with jurisdiction by law objects to or expresses reservations about the proposal on grounds of environmental impacts, the agency expressing the objection or reservation shall specify the mitigation measures it considers necessary to allow the agency to grant or approve applicable permit, license, or related requirements or concurrences.

§ 1503.4 Response to comments.

(a) An agency preparing a final environmental impact statement shall assess and consider comments both individually and collectively, and shall respond by one or more of the means listed below, stating its response in the final statement. Possible responses are to:
(1) Modify alternatives including the proposed action.
(2) Develop and evaluate alternatives not previously given serious consideration by the agency.
(3) Supplement, improve, or modify its analyses.
(4) Make factual corrections.
(5) Explain why the comments do not warrant further agency response, citing the sources, authorities, or reasons which support the agency's position and, if appropriate, indicate those circumstances which would trigger agency reappraisal or further response.
(b) All substantive comments received on the draft statement (or summaries thereof where the response has been exceptionally voluminous), should be attached to the final statement whether or not the comment is thought to merit individual discussion by the agency in the text of the statement.
(c) If changes in response to comments are minor and are confined to the responses described in paragraphs (a)(4) and (5) of this section, agencies may write them on errata sheets and attach them to the statement instead of rewriting the draft statement. In such cases only the comments, the responses, and the changes and not the final statement need be circulated (§ 1502.19). The entire document with a new cover sheet shall be filed as the final statement (§ 1506.9).

PART 1504—PREDECISION REFERRALS TO THE COUNCIL OF PROPOSED FEDERAL ACTIONS DETERMINED TO BE ENVIRONMENTALLY UNSATISFACTORY

AUTHORITY: NEPA, the Environmental Quality Improvement Act of 1970, as amended (42 U.S.C. 4371 *et seq.*), sec. 309 of the Clean Air Act, as amended (42 U.S.C. 7609) and Executive Order 11514, Mar. 5, 1970, as amended by Executive Order 11991, May 24, 1977.

SOURCE: 43 FR 55998, Nov. 29, 1978, unless otherwise noted.

§ 1504.1 Purpose.

(a) This part establishes procedures for referring to the Council Federal interagency disagreements concerning proposed major Federal actions that might cause unsatisfactory environmental effects. It provides means for early resolution of such disagreements.
(b) Under section 309 of the Clean Air Act (42 U.S.C. 7609), the Administrator of the Environmental Protection Agency is directed to review and comment publicly on the environmental impacts of Federal activities, including actions for which environmental impact statements are prepared. If after this review the Administrator determines that the matter is "unsatisfactory from the standpoint of public health or welfare or environmental quality," section 309 directs that the matter be referred to the Council (hereafter "environmental referrals").
(c) Under section 102(2)(C) of the Act other Federal agencies may make similar reviews of environmental impact statements, including judgments on the acceptability of anticipated environmental impacts. These reviews must be made available to the President, the Council and the public.

§ 1504.2 Criteria for referral.

Environmental referrals should be made to the Council only after concerted, timely (as early as possible in the process), but unsuccessful attempts to resolve differences with the lead agency. In determining what environmental objections to the matter are appropriate to refer to the Council, an agency should weigh potential adverse environmental impacts, considering:

(a) Possible violation of national environmental standards or policies.

(b) Severity.

(c) Geographical scope.

(d) Duration.

(e) Importance as precedents.

(f) Availability of environmentally preferable alternatives.

§ 1504.3 Procedure for referrals and response.

(a) A Federal agency making the referral to the Council shall:

(1) Advise the lead agency at the earliest possible time that it intends to refer a matter to the Council unless a satisfactory agreement is reached.

(2) Include such advice in the referring agency's comments on the draft environmental impact statement, except when the statement does not contain adequate information to permit an assessment of the matter's environmental acceptability.

(3) Identify any essential information that is lacking and request that it be made available at the earliest possible time.

(4) Send copies of such advice to the Council.

(b) The referring agency shall deliver its referral to the Council not later than twenty-five (25) days after the final environmental impact statement has been made available to the Environmental Protection Agency, commenting agencies, and the public. Except when an extension of this period has been granted by the lead agency, the Council will not accept a referral after that date.

(c) The referral shall consist of:

(1) A copy of the letter signed by the head of the referring agency and delivered to the lead agency informing the lead agency of the referral and the reasons for it, and requesting that no action be taken to implement the matter until the Council acts upon the referral. The letter shall include a copy of the statement referred to in (c)(2) of this section.

(2) A statement supported by factual evidence leading to the conclusion that the matter is unsatisfactory from the standpoint of public health or welfare or environmental quality. The statement shall:

(i) Identify any material facts in controversy and incorporate (by reference if appropriate) agreed upon facts,

(ii) Identify any existing environmental requirements or policies which would be violated by the matter,

(iii) Present the reasons why the referring agency believes the matter is environmentally unsatisfactory,

(iv) Contain a finding by the agency whether the issue raised is of national importance because of the threat to national environmental resources or policies or for some other reason,

(v) Review the steps taken by the referring agency to bring its concerns to the attention of the lead agency at the earliest possible time, and

(vi) Give the referring agency's recommendations as to what mitigation alternative, further study, or other course of action (including abandonment of the matter) are necessary to remedy the situation.

(d) Not later than twenty-five (25) days after the referral to the Council the lead agency may deliver a response to the Council, and the referring agency. If the lead agency requests more time and gives assurance that the matter will not go forward in the interim, the Council may grant an extension. The response shall:

(1) Address fully the issues raised in the referral.

(2) Be supported by evidence.

(3) Give the lead agency's response to the referring agency's recommendations.

(e) Interested persons (including the applicant) may deliver their views in writing to the Council. Views in support of the referral should be delivered not later than the referral. Views in support of the response shall be delivered not later than the response.

(f) Not later than twenty-five (25) days after receipt of both the referral and any response or upon being informed that there will be no response (unless the lead agency agrees to a longer time), the Council may take one or more of the following actions:

(1) Conclude that the process of referral and response has successfully resolved the problem.

(2) Initiate discussions with the agencies with the objective of mediation with referring and lead agencies.

(3) Hold public meetings or hearings to obtain additional views and information.

(4) Determine that the issue is not one of national importance and request the referring and lead agencies to pursue their decision process.

(5) Determine that the issue should be further negotiated by the referring and lead agencies and is not appropriate for Council consideration until one or more heads of agencies report to the Council that the agencies' disagreements are irreconcilable.

(6) Publish its findings and recommendations (including where appropriate a finding that the submitted evidence does not support the position of an agency).

(7) When appropriate, submit the referral and the response together with the Council's recommendation to the President for action.

(g) The Council shall take no longer than 60 days to complete the actions specified in paragraph (f) (2), (3), or (5) of this section.

(h) When the referral involves an action required by statute to be determined on the record after opportunity for agency hearing, the referral shall be conducted in a manner consistent with 5 U.S.C. 557(d) (Administrative Procedure Act).

PART 1505–NEPA AND AGENCY DECISION MAKING

AUTHORITY: NEPA, the Environmental Quality Improvement Act of 1970, as amended (42 U.S.C. 4371 *et seq.*), sec. 309 of the Clean Air Act, as amended (42 U.S.C. 7609) and Executive Order 11514, Mar. 5, 1970, as amended by Executive Order 11991, May 24, 1977.

SOURCE: 43 FR 55999, Nov. 29, 1978, unless otherwise noted.

§ 1505.1 Agency decision making procedures.

Agencies shall adopt procedures (§ 1507.3) to ensure that decisions are made in accordance with the policies and purposes of the Act. Such procedures shall include but not be limited to:

(a) Implementing procedures under section 102(2) to achieve the requirements of sections 101 and 102(1).

(b) Designating the major decision points for the agency's principal programs likely to have a significant effect on the human environment and assuring that the NEPA process corresponds with them.

(c) Requiring that relevant environmental documents, comments, and responses be part of the record in formal rulemaking or adjudicatory proceedings.

(d) Requiring that relevant environmental documents, comments, and responses accompany the proposal through existing agency review processes so that agency officials use the statement in making decisions.

(e) Requiring that the alternatives considered by the decision maker are encompassed by the range of alternatives discussed in the relevant environmental documents and that the decision maker consider the alternatives described in the environmental impact statement. If another decision document accompanies the relevant environmental documents to the decision maker, agencies are encouraged to make available to the public before the decision is made any part of that document that relates to the comparison of alternatives.

§ 1505.2 Record of decision in cases requiring environmental impact statements.

At the time of its decision (§ 1506.10) or, if appropriate, its recommendation to Congress, each agency shall prepare a concise public record of decision. The record, which may be integrated into any other record prepared by the agency, shall:

(a) State what the decision was.

(b) Identify all alternatives considered by the agency in reaching its decision, specifying the alternative or alternatives which were considered to be environmentally preferable. An agency may discuss preferences among alternatives based on relevant factors including economic and technical considerations and agency statutory missions. An agency shall identify and discuss all such factors including any essential considerations of national policy which were balanced by the agency in making its decision and State how those considerations entered into its decision.

(c) State whether all practicable means to avoid or minimize environmental harm from the alternative selected have been adopted, and if not, why they were not. A monitoring and enforcement program shall be adopted and summarized where applicable for any mitigation.

§ 1505.3 Implementing the decision.

Agencies may provide for monitoring to assure that their decisions are carried out and should do so in important cases. Mitigation (§ 1505.2(c)) and other conditions established in the environmental impact statement or during its review and committed as part of the decision shall be implemented by the lead agency or other appropriate consenting agency. The lead agency shall:

(a) Include appropriate conditions in grants, permits or other approvals.

(b) Condition funding of actions on mitigation.

(c) Upon request, inform cooperating or commenting agencies on progress in carrying out mitigation measures which they have proposed and which were adopted by the agency making the decision.

(d) Upon request, make available to the public the results of relevant monitoring.

PART 1506–OTHER REQUIREMENTS OF NEPA

AUTHORITY: NEPA, the Environmental Quality Improvement Act of 1970, as amended (42 U.S.C. 4371 *et seq.*), sec. 309 of the Clean Air Act, as amended (42 U.S.C. 7609) and Executive Order 11514, Mar. 5, 1970, as amended by Executive Order 11991, May 24, 1977.

SOURCE: 43 FR 56000, Nov. 29, 1978, unless otherwise noted.

§ 1506.1 Limitations on actions during NEPA process.

(a) Until an agency issues a record of decision as provided in § 1505.2 (except as provided in paragraph (c) of this section), no action concerning the proposal shall be taken which would:

(1) Have an adverse environmental impact; or

(2) Limit the choice of reasonable alternatives.

(b) If any agency is considering an application from a non-Federal entity, and is aware that the applicant is about to take an action within the agency's jurisdiction that would meet either of the criteria in paragraph (a) of this section, then the agency shall promptly notify the applicant that the agency will take appropriate action to insure that the objectives and procedures of NEPA are achieved.

(c) While work on a required program environmental impact statement is in progress and the action is not covered by an existing program statement, agencies shall not undertake in the interim any major Federal action covered by the program which may significantly affect the quality of the human environment unless such action:

(1) Is justified independently of the program;

(2) Is itself accompanied by an adequate environmental impact statement; and

(3) Will not prejudice the ultimate decision on the program. Interim action prejudices the ultimate decision on the program when it tends to determine subsequent development or limit alternatives.

(d) This section does not preclude development by applicants of plans or designs or performance of other work necessary to support an application for Federal, State or local permits or assistance. Nothing in this section shall preclude Rural Electrification Administration approval of minimal expenditures not affecting the environment (*e.g.* long leadtime equipment and purchase options) made by non-governmental entities seeking loan guarantees from the Administration.

§ 1506.2 Elimination of duplication with State and local procedures.

(a) Agencies authorized by law to cooperate with State agencies of statewide jurisdiction pursuant to section 102(2)(D) of the Act may do so.

(b) Agencies shall cooperate with State and local agencies to the fullest extent possible to reduce duplication between NEPA and State and local requirements, unless the agencies are specifically barred from doing so by some other law. Except for cases covered by paragraph (a) of this section, such cooperation shall to the fullest extent possible include:

(1) Joint planning processes.

(2) Joint environmental research and studies.

(3) Joint public hearings (except where otherwise provided by statute).

(4) Joint environmental assessments.

(c) Agencies shall cooperate with State and local agencies to the fullest extent possible to reduce duplication between NEPA and comparable State and local requirements, unless the agencies are specifically barred from doing so by some other law. Except for cases covered by paragraph (a) of this section, such cooperation shall to the fullest extent possible include joint environmental impact statements. In such cases one or more Federal agencies and one or more State or local agencies shall be joint lead agencies. Where State laws or local ordinances have environmental impact statement requirements in addition to but not in conflict with those in NEPA, Federal agencies shall cooperate in fulfilling these requirements as well as those of Federal laws so that one document will comply with all applicable laws.

(d) To better integrate environmental impact statements into State or local planning processes, statements shall discuss any inconsistency of a proposed action with any approved State or local plan and laws (whether or not federally sanctioned). Where an inconsistency exists, the statement should describe the extent to which the agency would reconcile its proposed action with the plan or law.

§ 1506.3 Adoption.

(a) An agency may adopt a Federal draft or final environmental impact statement or portion thereof provided that the statement or portion thereof meets the standards for an adequate statement under these regulations.

(b) If the actions covered by the original environmental impact statement and the proposed action are substantially the same, the agency adopting another agency's statement is not required to recirculate it except as a final statement. Otherwise the adopting agency shall treat the statement as a draft and recirculate it (except as provided in paragraph (c) of this section).

(c) A cooperating agency may adopt without recirculating the environmental impact statement of a lead agency when, after an independent review of the statement, the cooperating agency concludes that its comments and suggestions have been satisfied.

(d) When an agency adopts a statement which is not final within the agency that prepared it, or when the action it assesses is the subject of a referral under Part 1504, or when the statement's adequacy is the subject of a judicial action which is not final, the agency shall so specify.

§ 1506.4 Combining documents.

Any environmental document in compliance with NEPA may be combined with any other agency document to reduce duplication and paperwork.

§ 1506.5 Agency responsibility.

(a) *Information.* If an agency requires an applicant to submit environmental information for possible use by the agency in preparing an environmental impact statement, then the agency should assist the applicant by outlining the types of information required. The agency shall independently evaluate the information submitted and shall be responsible for its accuracy. If the agency chooses to use the information submitted by the applicant in the environmental impact statement, either directly or by reference, then the names of the persons responsible for the independent evaluation shall be included in the list of preparers (§ 1502.17). It is the intent of this paragraph that acceptable work not be redone, but that it be verified by the agency.

(b) *Environmental assessments.* If an agency permits an applicant to prepare an environmental assessment, the agency, besides fulfilling the requirements of paragraph (a) of this section, shall make its own evaluation of the environmental issues and take responsibility for the scope and content of the environmental assessment.

(c) *Environmental impact statements.* Except as provided in §§ 1506.2 and 1506.3 any environmental impact statement prepared pursuant to the requirements of NEPA shall be prepared directly by or by a contractor selected by the lead agency or where appropriate under § 1501.6(b), a cooperating agency. It is the intent of these regulations that the contractor be chosen solely by the lead agency, or by the lead agency in cooperation with cooperating agencies, or where appropriate by a cooperating agency to avoid any conflict of interest. Contractors shall execute a disclosure statement prepared by the lead agency, or where appropriate the cooperating agency, specifying that they have no financial or other interest in the outcome of the project. If the document is prepared by contract, the responsible Federal official shall furnish guidance and participate in the preparation and shall independently evaluate the statement prior to its approval and take responsibility for its scope and contents. Nothing in this section is intended to prohibit any agency from requesting any person to submit information to it or to prohibit any person from submitting information to any agency.

§ 1506.6 Public involvement.

Agencies shall:

(a) Make diligent efforts to involve the public in preparing and implementing their NEPA procedures.

(b) Provide public notice of NEPA-related hearings, public meetings, and the availability of environmental documents so as to inform those persons and agencies who may be interested or affected.

(1) In all cases the agency shall mail notice to those who have requested it on an individual action.

(2) In the case of an action with effects of national concern notice shall include publication in the *Federal Register* and notice by mail to national organizations reasonably expected to be interested in the matter and may include listing in the *102 Monitor.* An agency engaged in rulemaking may provide notice by mail to national organizations who have requested that notice regularly be provided. Agencies shall maintain a list of such organizations.

(3) In the case of an action with effects primarily of local concern the notice may include:

(i) Notice to State and areawide clearinghouses pursuant to Executive Order 12372 the Intergovernmental Review Process.

(ii) Notice to Indian tribes when effects may occur on reservations.

(iii) Following the affected State's public notice procedures for comparable actions.

(iv) Publication in local newspapers (in papers of general circulation rather than legal papers).

(v) Notice through other local media.

(vi) Notice to potentially interested community organizations including small business associations.

(vii) Publication in newsletters that may be expected to reach potentially interested persons.

(viii) Direct mailing to owners and occupants of nearby or affected property.

(ix) Posting of notice on and off site in the area where the action is to be located.

(c) Hold or sponsor public hearings or public meetings whenever appropriate or in accordance with statutory requirements applicable to the agency. Criteria shall include whether there is:

(1) Substantial environmental controversy concerning the proposed action or substantial interest in holding the hearing.

(2) A request for a hearing by another agency with jurisdiction over the action supported by reasons why a hearing will be helpful. If a draft environmental impact statement is to be considered at a public hearing, the agency should make the statement available to the public at least 15 days in advance (unless the purpose of the hearing is to provide information for the draft environmental impact statement).

(d) Solicit appropriate information from the public.

(e) Explain in its procedures where interested persons can get information or status reports on environmental impact statements and other elements of the NEPA process.

(f) Make environmental impact statements, the comments received, and any underlying documents available to the public pursuant to the provisions of the Freedom of Information Act (5 U.S.C. 552), without regard to the exclusion for interagency memoranda where such memoranda transmit comments of Federal agencies on the environmental impact of the proposed action. Materials to be made available to the public shall be provided to the public without charge to the extent practicable, or at a fee which is not more than the actual costs of reproducing copies required to be sent to other Federal agencies, including the Council.

§ 1506.7 Further guidance.

The Council may provide further guidance concerning NEPA and its procedures including:

(a) A handbook which the Council may supplement from time to time, which shall in plain language provide guidance and instructions concerning the application of NEPA and these regulations.

(b) Publication of the Council's Memoranda to Heads of Agencies.

(c) In conjunction with the Environmental Protection Agency and the publication of the 102 Monitor, notice of:

(1) Research activities;

(2) Meetings and conferences related to NEPA; and

(3) Successful and innovative procedures used by agencies to implement NEPA.

§ 1506.8 Proposals for legislation.

(a) The NEPA process for proposals for legislation (§ 1508.17) significantly affecting the quality of the human environment shall be integrated with the legislative process of the Congress. A legislative environmental impact statement is the detailed statement required by law to be included in a recommendation or report on a legislative proposal to Congress. A legislative environmental impact statement shall be considered part of the formal transmittal of a legislative proposal to Congress; however, it may be transmitted to Congress up to 30 days later in order to allow time for completion of an accurate statement which can serve as the basis for public and Congressional debate. The statement must be available in time for Congressional hearings and deliberations.

(b) Preparation of a legislative environmental impact statement shall conform to the requirements of these regulations except as follows:

(1) There need not be a scoping process.

(2) The legislative statement shall be prepared in the same manner as a draft statement, but shall be considered the "detailed statement" required by statute; *Provided*, That when any of the following conditions exist both the draft and final environmental impact statement on the legislative proposal shall be prepared and circulated as provided by §§ 1503.1 and 1506.10.

(i) A Congressional Committee with jurisdiction over the proposal has a rule requiring both draft and final environmental impact statements.

(ii) The proposal results from a study process required by statute (such as those required by the Wild and Scenic Rivers Act (16 U.S.C. 1271 *et seq.*) and the Wilderness Act (16 U.S.C. 1131 *et seq.*)).

(iii) Legislative approval is sought for Federal or federally assisted construction or other projects which the agency recommends be located at specific geographic locations. For proposals requiring an environmental impact statement for the acquisition of space by the General Services Administration, a draft statement shall accompany the Prospectus or the 11(b) Report of Building Project Surveys to the Congress, and a final statement shall be completed before site acquisition.

(iv) The agency decides to prepare draft and final statements.

(c) Comments on the legislative statement shall be given to the lead agency which shall forward them along with its own responses to the Congressional committees with jurisdiction.

§ 1506.9 Filing requirements.

Environmental impact statements together with comments and responses shall be filed with the Environmental Protection Agency, attention Office of Federal Activities (A-104), 401 M Street SW., Washington, D.C. 20460. Statements shall be filed with EPA no earlier than they are also transmitted to commenting agencies and made available to the public. EPA shall deliver one copy of each statement to the Council, which shall satisfy the requirement of availability to the President. EPA may issue guidelines to agencies to implement its responsibilities under this section and § 1506.10 below.

§ 1506.10 Timing of agency action.

(a) The Environmental Protection Agency shall publish a notice in the *Federal Register* each week of the environmental impact statements filed during the preceding week. The minimum time periods set forth in this section shall be calculated from the date of publication of this notice.

(b) No decision on the proposed action shall be made or recorded under § 1505.2 by a Federal agency until the later of the following dates:

(1) Ninety (90) days after publication of the notice described above in paragraph (a) of this section for a draft environmental impact statement.

(2) Thirty (30) days after publication of the notice described above in paragraph (a) of this section for a final environmental impact statement.

An exception to the rules on timing may be made in the case of an agency decision which is subject to a formal internal appeal. Some agencies have a formally established appeal process which allows other agencies or the public to take appeals on a decision and make their views known, after publication of the final environmental impact statement. In such cases, where a real opportunity exists to alter the decision, the decision may be made and recorded at the same time the environmental impact statement is published. This means that the period for appeal of the decision and the 30-day period prescribed in paragraph (b)(2) of this section may run concurrently. In such cases the environmental impact statement shall explain the timing and the public's right of appeal. An agency engaged in rulemaking under the Administrative Procedure Act or other statute for the purpose of protecting the public health or safety, may waive the time period in paragraph (b)(2) of this section and publish a decision on the final rule simultaneously with publication of the notice of the availability of the final environmental impact statement as described in paragraph (a) of this section.

(c) If the final environmental impact statement is filed within ninety (90) days after a draft environmental impact statement is filed with the Environmental Protection Agency, the minimum thirty (30) day period and the minimum ninety (90) day period may run concurrently. However, subject to paragraph (d) of this section agencies shall allow not less than 45 days for comments on draft statements.

(d) The lead agency may extend prescribed periods. The Environmental Protection Agency may upon a showing by the lead agency of compelling reasons of national policy reduce the prescribed periods and may upon a showing by any other Federal agency of compelling reasons of national policy also extend prescribed periods, but only after consultation with the lead agency. (Also see § 1507.3(d).) Failure to file timely comments shall not be a sufficient reason for extending a period. If the lead agency does not concur with the extension of time, EPA may not extend it for more than 30 days. When the Environmental Protection Agency reduces or extends any period of time it shall notify the Council.

§ 1506.11 Emergencies.

Where emergency circumstances make it necessary to take an action with significant environmental impact without observing the provisions of these regulations, the Federal agency taking the action should consult with the Council about alternative arrangements. Agencies and the Council will limit such arrangements to actions necessary to control the immediate impacts of the emergency. Other actions remain subject to NEPA review.

§ 1506.12 Effective date.

The effective date of these regulations is July 30, 1979, except that for agencies that administer programs that qualify under section 102(2)(D) of the Act or under section 104(h) of the Housing and Community Development Act of 1974 an additional four months shall be allowed for the State or local agencies to adopt their implementing procedures.

(a) These regulations shall apply to the fullest extent practicable to ongoing activities and environmental documents begun before the effective date. These regulations do not apply to an environmental impact statement or supplement if the draft statement was filed before the effective date of these regulations. No completed environmental documents need be redone by reasons of these regulations. Until these regulations are applicable, the Council's guidelines published in the *Federal Register* of August 1, 1973, shall continue to be applicable. In cases where these regulations are applicable the guidelines are superseded. However, nothing shall prevent an agency from proceeding under these regulations at an earlier time.

(b) NEPA shall continue to be applicable to actions begun before January 1, 1970, to the fullest extent possible.

PART 1507–AGENCY COMPLIANCE

AUTHORITY: NEPA, the Environmental Quality Improvement Act of 1970, as amended (42 U.S.C. 4371 *et seq.*), sec. 309 of the Clean Air Act, as amended (42 U.S.C. 7609), and Executive Order 11514 (Mar. 5 1970, as amended by Executive Order 11991, May 24, 1977.

SOURCE: 43 FR 56002, Nov. 29, 1978, unless otherwise noted.

§ 1507.1 Compliance.

All agencies of the Federal Government shall comply with these regulations. It is the intent of these regulations to allow each agency flexibility in adapting its implementing procedures authorized by § 1507.3 to the requirements of other applicable laws.

§ 1507.2 Agency capability to comply.

Each agency shall be capable (in terms of personnel and other resources) of complying with the requirements enumerated below. Such compliance may include use of other's resources, but the using agency shall itself have sufficient capability to evaluate what others do for it. Agencies shall:

(a) Fulfill the requirements of section 102(2)(A) of the Act to utilize a systematic interdisciplinary approach which will insure the integrated use of the natural and social sciences and the environmental design arts in planning and in decision making which may have an impact on the human environment. Agencies shall designate a person to be responsible for overall review of agency NEPA compliance.

(b) Identify methods and procedures required by section 102(2)(B) to insure that presently unquantified environmental amenities and values may be given appropriate consideration.

(c) Prepare adequate environmental impact statements pursuant to section 102(2)(C) and comment on statements in the areas where the agency has jurisdiction by law or special expertise or is authorized to develop and enforce environmental standards.

(d) Study, develop, and describe alternatives to recommended courses of action in any proposal which involves unresolved conflicts concerning alternative uses of available resources. This requirement of section 102(2)(E) extends to all such proposals, not just the more limited scope of section 102(2)(C)(iii) where the discussion of alternatives is confined to impact statements.

(e) Comply with the requirements of section 102(2)(H) that the agency initiate and utilize ecological information in the planning and development of resource-oriented projects.

(f) Fulfill the requirements of sections 102(2)(F), 102(2)(G), and 102(2)(I), of the Act and of Executive Order 11514, Protection and Enhancement of Environmental Quality, Sec. 2.

§ 1507.3 Agency procedures.

(a) Not later than eight months after publication of these regulations as finally adopted in the *Federal Register*, or five months after the establishment of an agency, whichever shall come later, each agency shall as necessary adopt procedures to supplement these regulations. When the agency is a department major subunits are encouraged (with the consent of the department) to adopt their own procedures. Such procedures shall not paraphrase these regulations. They shall confine themselves to implementing procedures. Each agency shall consult with the Council while developing its procedures and before publishing them in the *Federal Register* for comment. Agencies with similar programs should consult with each other and the Council to coordinate their procedures, especially for programs requesting similar information from applicants. The procedures shall be adopted only after an opportunity for public review and after review by the Council for conformity with the Act and these regulations. The Council shall complete its review within 30 days. Once in effect they shall be filed with the Council and made readily available to the public. Agencies are encouraged to publish explanatory guidance for these regulations and their own procedures. Agencies shall continue to review their policies and procedures and in consultation with the Council to revise them as necessary to ensure full compliance with the purposes and provisions of the Act.

(b) Agency procedures shall comply with these regulations except where compliance would be inconsistent with statutory requirements and shall include:

(1) Those procedures required by §§ 1501.2(d), 1502.9(c)(3), 1505.1, 1506.6(e), and 1508.4.

(2) Specific criteria for and identification of those typical classes of action:

(i) Which normally do require environmental impact statements.

(ii) Which normally do not require either an environmental impact statement or an environmental assessment (categorical exclusions (§ 1508.4)).

(iii) Which normally require environmental assessments but not necessarily environmental impact statements.

(c) Agency procedures may include specific criteria for providing limited exceptions to the provisions of these regulations for classified proposals. They are proposed actions which are specifically authorized under criteria established by an Executive Order or statute to be kept secret in the interest of national defense or foreign policy and are in fact properly classified pursuant to such Executive Order or statute. Environmental assessments and environmental impact statements which address classified proposals may be safeguarded and restricted from public dissemination in accordance with agencies' own regulations applicable to classified information. These documents may be organized so that classified portions can be included as annexes, in order that the unclassified portions can be made available to the public.

(d) Agency procedures may provide for periods of time other than those presented in § 1506.10 when necessary to comply with other specific statutory requirements.

(e) Agency procedures may provide that where there is a lengthy period between the agency's decision to prepare an environmental impact statement and the time of actual preparation, the notice of intent required by § 1501.7 may be published at a reasonable time in advance of preparation of the draft statement.

PART 1508–TERMINOLOGY AND INDEX

AUTHORITY: NEPA, the Environmental Quality Improvement Act of 1970, as amended (42 U.S.C. 4371 *et seq.*), sec. 309 of the Clean Air Act, as amended (42 U.S.C. 7609), and Executive Order 11514 (Mar. 5, 1970, as amended by Executive Order 11991, May 24, 1977.

SOURCE: 43 FR 56003, Nov. 29, 1978, unless otherwise noted.

§ 1508.1 Terminology.

The terminology of this part shall be uniform throughout the Federal Government.

§ 1508.2 Act.

"Act" means the National Environmental Policy Act, as amended (42 U.S.C. 4321, *et seq.*) which is also referred to as "NEPA."

§ 1508.3 Affecting.

"Affecting" means will or may have an effect on.

§ 1508.4 Categorical exclusion.

"Categorical exclusion" means a category of actions which do not individually or cumulatively have a significant effect on the human environment and which have been found to have no such effect in procedures adopted by a Federal agency in implementation of these regulations (§ 1507.3) and for which, therefore, neither an environmental assessment nor an environmental impact statement is required. An agency may decide in its procedures or otherwise, to prepare environmental assessments for the reasons stated in § 1508.9 even though it is not required to do so. Any procedures under this section shall provide for extraordinary circumstances in which a normally excluded action may have a significant environmental effect.

§ 1508.5 Cooperating agency.

"Cooperating agency" means any Federal agency other than a lead agency which has jurisdiction by law or special expertise with respect to any environmental impact involved in a proposal (or a reasonable alternative) for legislation or other major Federal action significantly affecting the quality of the human environment. The selection and responsibilities of a cooperating agency are described in § 1501.6. A State or local agency of similar qualifications or, when the effects are on a reservation, an Indian Tribe, may by agreement with the lead agency become a cooperating agency.

§ 1508.6 Council.

"Council" means the Council on Environmental Quality established by Title II of the Act.

§ 1508.7 Cumulative impact.

"Cumulative impact" is the impact on the environment which results from the incremental impact of the action when added to other past, present, and reasonably foreseeable future actions regardless of what agency (Federal or non-Federal) or person undertakes such other actions. Cumulative impacts can result from individually minor but collectively significant actions taking place over a period of time.

§ 1508.8 Effects.

"Effects" include:
(a) Direct effects, which are caused by the action and occur at the same time and place.
(b) Indirect effects, which are caused by the action and are later in time or farther removed in distance, but are still reasonably foreseeable. Indirect effects may include growth inducing effects and other effects related to induced changes in the pattern of land use, population density or growth rate, and related effects on air and water and other natural systems, including ecosystems.

Effects and impacts as used in these regulations are synonymous. Effects includes ecological (such as the effects on natural resources and on the components, structures, and functioning of affected ecosystems), aesthetic, historic, cultural, economic, social, or health, whether direct, indirect, or cumulative. Effects may also include those resulting from actions which may have both beneficial and detrimental effects, even if on balance the agency believes that the effect will be beneficial.

§ 1508.9 Environmental assessment.

"Environmental assessment":
(a) Means a concise public document for which a Federal agency is responsible that serves to:
(1) Briefly provide sufficient evidence and analysis for determining whether to prepare an environmental impact statement or a finding of no significant impact.
(2) Aid an agency's compliance with the Act when no environmental impact statement is necessary.
(3) Facilitate preparation of a statement when one is necessary.
(b) Shall include brief discussions of the need for the proposal, of alternatives as required by section 102(2)(E), of the environmental impacts of the proposed action and alternatives, and a listing of agencies and persons consulted.

§ 1508.10 Environmental document.

"Environmental document" includes the documents specified in § 1508.9 (environmental assessment), § 1508.11 (environmental impact statement), § 1508.13 (finding of no significant impact), and § 1508.22 (notice of intent).

§ 1508.11 Environmental impact statement.

"Environmental impact statement" means a detailed written statement as required by section 102(2)(C) of the Act.

§ 1508.12 Federal agency.

"Federal agency" means all agencies of the Federal Government. It does not mean the Congress, the Judiciary, or the President, including the performance of staff functions for the President in his Executive Office. It also includes for purposes of these regulations States and units of general local government and Indian tribes assuming NEPA responsibilities under section 104(h) of the Housing and Community Development Act of 1974.

§ 1508.13 Finding of no significant impact (FONSI).

"Finding of no significant impact" means a document by a Federal agency briefly presenting the reasons why an action, not otherwise excluded (§ 1508.4), will not have a significant effect on the human environment and for which an environmental impact statement therefore will not be prepared. It shall include the environmental assessment or a summary of it and shall note any other environmental documents related to it (§ 1501.7(a)(5)). If the assessment is included, the finding need not repeat any of the discussion in the assessment but may incorporate it by reference.

§ 1508.14 Human environment.

"Human environment" shall be interpreted comprehensively to include the natural and physical environment and the relationship of people with that environment. (See the definition of "effects" (§ 1508.8).) This means that economic or social effects are not intended by themselves to require preparation of an environmental impact statement. When an environmental impact statement is prepared and economic or social and natural or physical environmental effects are interrelated, then the environmental impact statement will discuss all of these effects on the human environment.

§ 1508.15 Jurisdiction by law.

"Jurisdiction by law" means agency authority to approve, veto, or finance all or part of the proposal.

§ 1508.16 Lead agency.

"Lead agency" means the agency or agencies preparing or having taken primary responsibility for preparing the environmental impact statement.

§ 1508.17 Legislation.

"Legislation" includes a bill or legislative proposal to Congress developed by or with the significant cooperation and support of a Federal agency, but does not include requests for appropriations. The test for significant cooperation is whether the proposal is in fact predominantly that of the agency rather than another source. Drafting does not by itself constitute significant cooperation. Proposals for legislation include requests for ratification of treaties. Only the agency which has primary responsibility for the subject matter involved will prepare a legislative environmental impact statement.

§ 1508.18 Major Federal action.

"Major Federal action" includes actions with effects that may be major and which are potentially subject to Federal control and responsibility. Major reinforces but does not have a meaning independent of significantly (§ 1508.27). Actions include the circumstance where the responsible officials fail to act and that failure to act is reviewable by courts or administrative tribunals under the Administrative Procedure Act or other applicable law as agency action.

(a) Actions include new and continuing activities, including projects and programs entirely or partly financed, assisted, conducted, regulated, or approved by Federal agencies; new or revised agency rules, regulations, plans, policies, or procedures; and legislative proposals (§§ 1506.8, 1508.17). Actions do not include funding assistance solely in the form of general revenue sharing funds, distributed under the State and Local Fiscal Assistance Act of 1972, 31 U.S.C. 1221 *et seq.*, with no Federal agency control over the subsequent use of such funds. Actions do not include bringing judicial or administrative civil or criminal enforcement actions.

(b) Federal actions tend to fall within one of the following categories:

(1) Adoption of official policy, such as rules, regulations, and interpretations adopted pursuant to the Administrative Procedure Act, 5 U.S.C. 551 *et seq.*; treaties and international conventions or agreements; formal documents establishing an agency's policies which will result in or substantially alter agency programs.

(2) Adoption of formal plans, such as official documents prepared or approved by Federal agencies which guide or prescribe alternative uses of Federal resources, upon which future agency actions will be based.

(3) Adoption of programs, such as a group of concerted actions to implement a specific policy or plan; systematic and connected agency decisions allocating agency resources to implement a specific statutory program or executive directive.

(4) Approval of specific projects, such as construction or management activities located in a defined geographic area. Projects include actions approved by permit or other regulatory decision as well as Federal and federally assisted activities.

§ 1508.19 Matter.

"Matter" includes for purposes of Part 1504:

(a) With respect to the Environmental Protection Agency, any proposed legislation, project, action or regulation as those terms are used in section 309(a) of the Clean Air Act (42 U.S.C. 7609).

(b) With respect to all other agencies, any proposed major Federal action to which section 102(2)(C) of NEPA applies.

§ 1508.20 Mitigation.

"Mitigation" includes:

(a) Avoiding the impact altogether by not taking a certain action or parts of an action.

(b) Minimizing impacts by limiting the degree or magnitude of the action and its implementation.

(c) Rectifying the impact by repairing, rehabilitating, or restoring the affected environment.

(d) Reducing or eliminating the impact over time by preservation and maintenance operations during the life of the action.

(e) Compensating for the impact by replacing or providing substitute resources or environments.

§ 1508.21 NEPA process.

"NEPA process" means all measures necessary for compliance with the requirements of section 2 and Title I of NEPA.

§ 1508.22 Notice of intent (NOI).

"Notice of intent" means a notice that an environmental impact statement will be prepared and considered. The notice shall briefly:

(a) Describe the proposed action and possible alternatives.

(b) Describe the agency's proposed scoping process including whether, when, and where any scoping meeting will be held.

(c) State the name and address of a person within the agency who can answer questions about the proposed action and the environmental impact statement.

§ 1508.23 Proposal.

"Proposal" exists at that stage in the development of an action when an agency subject to the Act has a goal and is actively preparing to make a decision on one or more alternative means of accomplishing that goal and the effects can be meaningfully evaluated. Preparation of an environmental impact statement on a proposal should be timed (§ 1502.5) so that the final statement may be completed in time for the statement to be included in any recommendation or report on the proposal. A proposal may exist in fact as well as by agency declaration that one exists.

§ 1508.24 Referring agency.

"Referring agency" means the Federal agency which has referred any matter to the Council after a determination that the matter is unsatisfactory from the standpoint of public health or welfare or environmental quality.

§ 1508.25 Scope.

Scope consists of the range of actions, alternatives, and impacts to be considered in an environmental impact statement. The scope of an individual statement may depend on its relationships to other statements (§§ 1502.20 and 1508.28). To determine the scope of environmental impact statements, agencies shall consider 3 types of actions, 3 types of alternatives, and 3 types of impacts. They include:

(a) Actions (other than unconnected single actions) which may be:

(1) Connected actions, which means that they are closely related and therefore should be discussed in the same impact statement. Actions are connected if they:

(i) Automatically trigger other actions which may require environmental impact statements.

(ii) Cannot or will not proceed unless other actions are taken previously or simultaneously.

(iii) Are interdependent parts of a larger action and depend on the larger action for their justification.

(2) Cumulative actions, which when viewed with other proposed actions have cumulatively significant impacts and should therefore be discussed in the same impact statement.

(3) Similar actions, which when viewed with other reasonably foreseeable or proposed agency actions, have similarities that provide a basis for evaluating their environmental consequences together, such as common timing or geography. An agency may wish to analyze these actions in the same impact statement. It should do so when the best way to assess adequately the combined impacts of similar actions or reasonable alternatives to such actions is to treat them in a single impact statement.

(b) Alternatives, which include:

(1) No action alternative.

(2) Other reasonable courses of actions.

(3) Mitigation measures (not in the proposed action).

(c) Impacts, which may be: (1) Direct; (2) indirect; (3) cumulative.

§ 1508.26 Special expertise.

"Special expertise" means statutory responsibility, agency mission, or related program experience.

§ 1508.27 Significantly.

"Significantly" as used in NEPA requires considerations of both context and intensity:

(a) *Context*. This means that the significance of an action must be analyzed in several contexts such as society as a whole (human, national), the affected region, the affected interests, and the locality. Significance varies with the setting of the proposed action. For instance, in the case of a site-specific action, significance would usually depend upon the effects in the locale rather than in the world as a whole. Both short- and long-term effects are relevant.

(b) *Intensity*. This refers to the severity of impact. Responsible officials must bear in mind that more than one agency may make decisions about partial aspects of a major action. The following should be considered in evaluating intensity:

(1) Impacts that may be both beneficial and adverse. A significant effect may exist even if the Federal agency believes that on balance the effect will be beneficial.

(2) The degree to which the proposed action affects public health or safety.

(3) Unique characteristics of the geographic area such as proximity to historic or cultural resources, park lands, prime farmlands, wetlands, wild and scenic rivers, or ecologically critical areas.

(4) The degree to which the effects on the quality of the human environment are likely to be highly controversial.

(5) The degree to which the possible effects on the human environment are highly uncertain or involve unique or unknown risks.

(6) The degree to which the action may establish a precedent for future actions with significant effects or represents a decision in principle about a future consideration.

(7) Whether the action is related to other actions with individually insignificant but cumulatively significant impacts. Significance exists if it is reasonable to anticipate a cumulatively significant impact on the environment. Significance cannot be avoided by terming an action temporary or by breaking it down into small component parts.

(8) The degree to which the action may adversely affect districts, sites, highways, structures, or objects listed in or eligible for listing in the National Register of Historic Places or may cause loss or destruction of significant scientific, cultural, or historical resources.

(9) The degree to which the action may adversely affect an endangered or threatened species or its habitat that has been determined to be critical under the Endangered Species Act of 1973.

(10) Whether the action threatens a violation of Federal, State, or local law or requirements imposed for the protection of the environment.

[43 FR 56003, Nov. 29, 1978; 44 FR 874, Jan. 3, 1979]

§ 1508.28 Tiering.

"Tiering" refers to the coverage of general matters in broader environmental impact statements (such as national program or policy statements) with subsequent narrower statements or environmental analyses (such as regional or basinwide program statements or ultimately site-specific statements) incorporating by reference the general discussions and concentrating solely on the issues specific to the statement subsequently prepared. Tiering is appropriate when the sequence of statements or analyses is:

(a) From a program, plan, or policy environmental impact statement to a program, plan, or policy statement or analysis of lesser scope or to a site-specific statement or analysis.

(b) From an environmental impact statement on a specific action at an early stage (such as need and site selection) to a supplement (which is preferred) or a subsequent statement or analysis at a later stage (such as environmental mitigation). Tiering in such cases is appropriate when it helps the lead agency to focus on the issues which are ripe for decision and exclude from consideration issues already decided or not yet ripe.

FORTY MOST ASKED QUESTIONS CONCERNING CEQ'S NATIONAL ENVIRONMENTAL POLICY ACT REGULATIONS

Summary: The Council on Environmental Quality, as part of its oversight of implementation of the National Environmental Policy Act, held meetings in the ten Federal regions with Federal, State, and local officials to discuss administration of the implementing regulations. The forty most asked questions were compiled in a memorandum to agencies for the information of relevant officials. In order efficiently to respond to public inquiries this memorandum is reprinted in this issue of the *Federal Register* (Vol. 46, No. 55, March 17, 1981).

Subject: Questions and Answers About the NEPA Regulations

1a. Range of Alternatives. What is meant by "range of alternatives" as referred to in Sec. 1505.1(e)?[1]

A. The phrase "range of alternatives" refers to the alternatives discussed in environmental documents. It includes all reasonable alternatives, which must be rigorously explored and objectively evaluated, as well as those other alternatives, which are eliminated from detailed study with a brief discussion of the reasons for eliminating them. Section 1502.14. A decision maker must not consider alternatives beyond the range of alternatives discussed in the relevant environmental documents. Moreover, a decision maker must, in fact, consider all the alternatives discussed in an EIS. Section 1505.1(e).

1b. How many alternatives have to be discussed when there is an infinite number of possible alternatives?

A. For some proposals there may exist a very large or even an infinite number of possible reasonable alternatives. For example, a proposal to designate wilderness areas within a National Forest could be said to involve an infinite number of alternatives from 0 to 100 percent of the forest. When there are potentially a very large number of alternatives, only a reasonable number of examples, covering the full spectrum of alternatives, must be analyzed and compared in the EIS. An appropriate series of alternatives might include dedicating 0, 10, 30, 50, 70, 90, or 100 percent of the Forest to wilderness. What constitutes a reasonable range of alternatives depends on the nature of the proposal and the facts in each case.

2a. Alternatives Outside the Capability of Applicant or Jurisdiction of Agency. If an EIS is prepared in connection with an application for a permit or other Federal approval, must the EIS rigorously analyze and discuss alternatives that are outside the capability of the applicant or can it be limited to reasonable alternatives that can be carried out by the applicant?

A. Section 1502.14 requires the EIS to examine all reasonable alternatives to the proposal. In determining the scope of alternatives to be considered, the emphasis is on what is "reasonable" rather than on whether the proponent or applicant likes or is itself capable of carrying out a particular alternative. Reasonable alternatives include those that are practical or feasible from the technical and economic standpoint and using common sense, rather than simply desirable from the standpoint of the applicant.

2b. Must the EIS analyze alternatives outside the jurisdiction or capability of the agency or beyond what Congress has authorized?

A. An alternative that is outside the legal jurisdiction of the lead agency must still be analyzed in the EIS if it is reasonable. A potential conflict with local or Federal law does not necessarily render an alternative unreasonable, although such conflicts must be considered. Section 1506.2(d).

Alternatives that are outside the scope of what Congress has approved or funded must still be evaluated in the EIS if they are reasonable, because the EIS may serve as the basis for modifying the Congressional approval or funding in light of NEPA's goals and policies. Section 1500.1(a).

3. No-Action Alternative. What does the "no action" alternative include? If an agency is under a court order or legislative command to act, must the EIS address the "no action" alternative?

A. Section 1502.14(d) requires the alternatives analysis in the EIS to "include the alternative of no action." There are two distinct interpretations of "no action" that must be considered, depending on the nature of the proposal being evaluated. The first situation might involve an action such as updating a land management plan where ongoing programs initiated under existing legislation and regulations will continue, even as new plans are developed. In these cases "no action" is "no change" from current management direction or level of management intensity. To construct an alternative that is based on no management at all would be a useless academic exercise. Therefore, the "no action" alternative may be thought of in terms of continuing with the present course of action until that action is changed. Consequently, projected impacts of alternative management schemes would be compared in the EIS to those impacts projected for the existing plan. In this case, alternatives would include management plans of both greater and lesser intensity, especially greater and lesser levels of resource development.

The second interpretation of "no action" is illustrated in instances involving Federal decisions on proposals for projects. "No action" in such cases would mean the proposed activity would not take place, and the resulting environmental effects from taking no action would be compared with the effects of permitting the proposed activity or an alternative activity to go forward.

Where a choice of "no action" by the agency would result in predictable actions by others, this consequence of the "no action" alternative should be included in the analysis. For example, if denial of permission to build a railroad to a facility would lead to construction of a road and increased truck traffic, the EIS should analyze this consequence of the "no action" alternative.

In light of the above, it is difficult to think of a situation where it would not be appropriate to address a "no action" alternative. Accordingly, the regulations require the analysis of the no action alternative even if the agency is under a court order or legislative command to act. This analysis provides a benchmark, enabling decisionmakers to compare the magnitude of environmental effects of the action alternatives. It is also an example of a reasonable alternative outside the jurisdiction of the agency which must be analyzed. Section 1502.14(c). See Question 2 above. Inclusion of such an analysis in the EIS is necessary to inform the Congress, the public, and the President as intended by NEPA. Section 1500.I(a).

4a. Agency's Preferred Alternative. What is the "agency's preferred alternative"?

A. The "agency's preferred alternative" is the alternative which the agency believes would fulfill its statutory mission and responsibilities, giving consideration to economic, environmental, technical and other factors. The concept of the "agency's preferred alternative" is different from the "environmentally preferable alternative," although in some cases one alternative may be both. See Question 6 below. It is identified so that agencies and the public can understand the lead agency's orientation.

4b. Does the "preferred alternative" have to be identified in the Draft EIS and the Final EIS or just in the Final EIS?

A. Section 1502.14(e) requires the section of the EIS on alternatives to "identify the agency's preferred alternative if one or more exists, in the draft statement, and identify such alternative in the final statement..." This means that if the agency has a preferred alternative at the Draft EIS stage, that alternative must be labeled or identified as such in the Draft EIS. If the responsible Federal official in fact has no preferred alternative at the Draft EIS stage, a preferred alternative need not be identified there. By the time the Final EIS is filed, Section 1502.14(e) presumes the existence of a preferred alternative and requires its identification in the Final EIS "unless another law prohibits the expression of such a preference."

4c. Who recommends or determines the "preferred alternative?"

A. The lead agency's official with line responsibility for preparing the EIS and assuring its adequacy is responsible for identifying the agency's preferred alternative(s). The NEPA regulations do not dictate which official in an agency shall be responsible for preparation of EISs, but agencies can identify this official in their implementing procedures, pursuant to Section 1507.3.

Even though the agency's preferred alternative is identified by the EIS preparer in the EIS, the statement must be objectively prepared and not slanted to support the choice of the agency's preferred alternative over the other reasonable and feasible alternatives.

5a. Proposed Action v. Proposed Alternative. Is the "proposed action" the same thing as the "preferred alternative"?

A. The "proposed action" may be, but is not necessarily, the agency's "preferred alternative." The proposed action may be a proposal in its initial form before undergoing analysis in the EIS process. If the proposed action is internally generated, such as preparing a land management plan, the proposed action might end up as the agency's preferred alternative. On the other hand the proposed action may be granting an application to a non-federal entity for a permit. The agency may or may not have a "preferred alternative" at the Draft EIS stage (see Question 4 above). In that case the agency may decide at the Final EIS stage, on the basis of the Draft EIS and the public and agency comments, that an alternative other than the proposed action is the agency's "preferred alternative."

5b. Is the analysis of the "proposed action" in an EIS to be treated differently from the analysis of alternatives?

A. The degree of analysis devoted to each alternative in the EIS is to be substantially similar to that devoted to the "proposed action." Section 1502.14 is titled "Alternatives including the proposed action" to reflect such comparable treatment. Section 1502.14(b) specifically requires "substantial treatment" in the EIS of each alternative including the proposed action. This regulation does not dictate an amount of information to be provided, but rather, prescribes a level of treatment, which may in turn require varying amounts of information, to enable a reviewer to evaluate and compare alternatives.

6a. Environmentally Preferable Alternative. What is the meaning of the term "environmentally preferable alternative" as used in the regulations with reference to Records of Decision? How is the term "environment" used in the phrase?

A. Section 1505.2(b) requires that, in cases where an EIS has been prepared, the Record of Decision (ROD) must identify all alternatives that were considered, "...specifying the alternative or alternatives which were considered to be environmentally preferable." The environmentally preferable alternative is the alternative that will promote the national environmental policy as expressed in NEPA's Section 101. Ordinarily, this means the alternative that causes the least damage to the biological and physical environment; it also means the alternative which best protects, preserves, and enhances historic, cultural, and natural resources.

The Council recognizes that the identification of the environmentally preferable alternative may involve difficult judgments, particularly when one environmental value must be balanced against another. The public and other agencies reviewing a Draft EIS can assist the lead agency to develop and determine environmentally preferable alternatives by providing their views in comments on the Draft EIS. Through the identification of the environmentally preferable alternative, the decision maker is clearly faced with a choice between that alternative and others, and must consider whether the decision accords with the Congressionally declared policies of the Act.

6b. Who recommends or determines what is environmentally preferable?

A. The agency EIS staff is encouraged to make recommendations of the environmentally preferable alternative(s) during EIS preparation. In any event the lead agency official responsible for the EIS is encouraged to identify the environmentally preferable alternative(s) in the EIS. In all cases, commentors from other agencies and the public are also encouraged to address this question. The agency must identify the environmentally preferable alternative in the ROD.

7. Difference Between Section of EIS on Alternatives and Environmental Consequences. What is the difference between the sections in the EIS on "alternatives" and "environmental consequences"? How do you avoid duplicating the discussion of alternatives in preparing these two sections?

A. The "alternatives" section is the heart of the EIS. This section rigorously explores and objectively evaluates all reasonable alternatives including the proposed action. Section 1502.14. It should include relevant comparisons on environmental and other grounds. The "environmental consequences" section of the EIS discusses the specific environmental impacts or effects of each of the alternatives including the proposed action. Section 1502.16. In order to avoid duplication between these two sections, most of the "alternatives" section should be devoted to describing and comparing the alternatives. Discussion of the environmental impacts of these alternatives should be limited to a concise descriptive summary of such impacts in a comparative form, including charts or tables, thus sharply defining the issues and providing a clear basis for choice among options. Section 1502.14. The "environmental consequences" section should be devoted largely to a scientific analysis of the direct and indirect environmental effects of the proposed action and of each of the alternatives. It forms the analytic basis for the concise comparison in the "alternatives" section.

8. Early Application of NEPA. Section 1501.2(d) of the NEPA regulations requires agencies to provide for the early application of NEPA to cases where actions are planned by private applicants or non-Federal entities and are, at some stage, subject to Federal approval of permits, loans, loan guarantees, insurance or other actions. What must and can agencies do to apply NEPA early in these cases?

A. Section 1501.2(d) requires Federal agencies to take steps toward ensuring that private parties and State and local entities initiate environmental studies as soon as Federal involvement in their proposals can be foreseen. This section is intended to ensure that environmental factors are considered at an early stage in the planning process and to avoid the situation where the applicant for a Federal permit or approval has completed planning and eliminated all alternatives to the proposed action by the time the EIS process commences or before the EIS process has been completed.

Through early consultation, business applicants and approving agencies may gain better appreciation of each other's needs and foster a decision making process which avoids later unexpected confrontations.

Federal agencies are required by Section 1507.3(b) to develop procedures to carry out Section 1501.2(d). The procedures should include an "outreach program", such as a means for prospective applicants to conduct pre-application consultations with the lead and cooperating agencies. Applicants need to find out, in advance of project planning, what environmental studies or other information will be required, and what mitigation requirements are likely, in connection with the later Federal NEPA process. Agencies should designate staff to advise potential applicants of the agency's NEPA information requirements and should publicize their pre-application procedures and information requirements in newsletters or other media used by potential applicants.

Complementing Section 1501.2(d), Section 1506.5(a) requires agencies to assist applicants by outlining the types of information required in those cases where the agency requires the applicant to submit environmental data for possible use by the agency in preparing an EIS.

Section 1506.5(b) allows agencies to authorize preparation of environmental assessments by applicants. Thus, the procedures should also include a means for anticipating and utilizing applicants' environmental studies or "early corporate environmental assessments" to fulfill some of the Federal agency's NEPA obligations. However, in such cases the agency must still evaluate independently the environmental issues and take responsibility for the environmental assessment.

These provisions are intended to encourage and enable private and other non-Federal entities to build environmental considerations into their own planning processes in a way that facilitates the application of NEPA and avoids delay.

9. **Applicant Who Needs Other Permits.** To what extent must an agency inquire into whether an applicant for a Federal permit, funding or other approval of a proposal will also need approval from another agency for the same proposal or some other related aspect of it?

A. Agencies must integrate the NEPA process into other planning at the earliest possible time to insure that planning and decisions reflect environmental values, to avoid delays later in the process, and to head off potential conflicts. Specifically, the agency must "provide for cases where actions are planned by . . . applicants," so that designated staff are available to advise potential applicants of studies or other information that will foreseeably be required for the later Federal action; the agency shall consult with the applicant if the agency foresees its own involvement in the proposal; and it shall insure that the NEPA process commences at the earliest possible time. Section 1501.2(d). (See Question 8.)

The regulations emphasize agency cooperation early in the NEPA process. Section 1501.6. Section 1501.7 on "scoping" also provides that all affected Federal agencies are to be invited to participate in scoping the environmental issues and to identify the various environmental review and consultation requirements that may apply to the proposed action. Further, Section 1502.25(b) requires that the draft EIS list all the Federal permits, licenses and other entitlements that are needed to implement the proposal.

These provisions create an affirmative obligation on Federal agencies to inquire early, and to the maximum degree possible, to ascertain whether an applicant is or will be seeking other Federal assistance or approval, or whether the applicant is waiting until a proposal has been substantially developed before requesting Federal aid or approval.

Thus, a Federal agency receiving a request for approval or assistance should determine whether the applicant has filed separate requests for Federal approval or assistance with other Federal agencies. Other Federal agencies that are likely to become involved should then be contacted, and the NEPA process coordinated, to insure an early and comprehensive analysis of the direct and indirect effects of the proposal and any related actions. The agency should inform the applicant that action on its application may be delayed unless it submits all other Federal applications (where feasible to do so), so that all the relevant agencies can work together on the scoping process and preparation of the EIS.

10a. Limitations on Action During 30-Day Review Period for Final EIS. What actions by agencies and/or applicants are allowed during EIS preparation and during the 30-day review period after publication of a final EIS?

A. No Federal decision on the proposed action shall be made or recorded until at least 30 days after the publication by EPA of notice that the particular EIS has been filed with EPA. Sections 1505.2 and 1506.10. Section 1505.2 requires this decision to be stated in a public Record of Decision.

Until the agency issues its Record of Decision, no action by an agency or an applicant concerning the proposal shall be taken which would have an adverse environmental impact or limit the choice of reasonable alternatives. Section 1506.1(a). But this does not preclude preliminary planning or design work which is needed to support an application for permits or assistance. Section 1506.1(d).

When the impact statement in question is a program EIS, no major action concerning the program may be taken which may significantly affect the quality of the human environment, unless the particular action is justified independently of the program, is accompanied by its own adequate environmental impact statement and will not prejudice the ultimate decision on the program. Section 1506.1(c).

10b. Do these limitations on action (described in Question 10a) apply to State or local agencies that have statutorily delegated responsibility for preparation of environmental documents required by NEPA, for example, under the HUD Block Grant program?

A. Yes, these limitations do apply, without any variation from their application to Federal agencies.

11. Limitations on Actions by an Applicant EIS Process. What actions must a lead agency take during the NEPA process when it becomes aware that a non-federal applicant is about to take an action within the agency's jurisdiction that would either have an adverse environmental impact or limit the choice of reasonable alternatives (e.g., prematurely commit money or other resources towards the completion of the proposal)?

A. The Federal agency must notify the applicant that the agency will take strong affirmative steps to insure that the objectives and procedures of NEPA are fulfilled. Section 1506.1(b). These steps could include seeking injunctive measures under NEPA, or the use of sanctions available under either the agency's permitting authority or statutes setting forth the agency's statutory mission. For example, the agency might advise an applicant that if it takes such action the agency will not process its application.

12a. Effective Date and Enforceability of the Regulations. What actions are subject to the Council's new regulations, and what actions are grandfathered under the old guidelines?

A. The effective date of the Council's regulations was July 30, 1979 (except for certain HUD programs under the Housing and Community Development Act, 42 U.S.C. 5304(h), and certain State highway programs that qualify under Section 102(2)(D) of NEPA for which the regulations became effective on November 30, 1979). All the provisions of the regulations are binding as of that date, including those covering decision making, public participation, referrals, limitations on actions, EIS supplements, etc. For example, a Record of Decision would be prepared even for decisions where the draft EIS was filed before July 30, 1979.

But in determining whether or not the new regulations apply to the preparation of a particular environmental document, the relevant factor is the date of filing of the draft of that document. Thus, the new regulations do not require the redrafting of an EIS or supplement if the draft EIS or supplement was filed before July 30, 1979. However. a supplement prepared after the effective date of the regulations for an EIS issued in final before the effective date of the regulations would be controlled by the regulations.

Even though agencies are not required to apply the regulations to an EIS or other document for which the draft was filed prior to July 30, 1979, the regulations encourage agencies to follow the regulations "to the fullest extent practicable," i.e., if it is feasible to do so, in preparing the final document. Section 1506.12(a).

12b. Are projects authorized by Congress before the effective date of the Council's regulations grandfathered?

A. No. The date of Congressional authorization for a project is not determinative of whether the Council's regulations or former Guidelines apply to the particular proposal. No incomplete projects or proposals of any kind are grandfathered in whole or in part. Only certain environmental documents, for which the draft was issued before the effective date of the regulations, are grandfathered and subject to the Council's former Guidelines.

12c. Can a violation of the regulations give rise to a cause of action?

A. While a trivial violation of the regulations would not give rise to an independent cause of action, such a cause of action would arise from a substantial violation of the regulations. Section 1500.3.

13. Use of Scoping Before Notice of Intent to Prepare EIS. Can the scoping process be used in connection with preparation of an environmental assessment, i.e., before both the decision to proceed with an EIS and publication of a notice of intent?

A. Yes. Scoping can be a useful tool for discovering alternatives to a proposal, or significant impacts that may have been overlooked. In cases where an environmental assessment is being prepared to help an agency decide whether to prepare an EIS, useful information might result from early participation by other agencies and the public in a scoping process.

The regulations State that the scoping process is to be preceded by a Notice of Intent (NOI) to prepare an EIS. But that is only the minimum requirement. Scoping may be initiated earlier, as long as there is appropriate public notice and enough information available on the proposal so that the public and relevant agencies can participate effectively.

However, scoping that is done before the assessment, and in aid of its preparation, cannot substitute for the normal scoping process after publication of the NOI, unless the earlier public notice stated clearly that this possibility was under consideration, and the NOI expressly provides that written comments on the scope of alternatives and impacts will still be considered.

14a. Rights and Responsibilities of Lead Agency and Cooperating Agencies. What are the respective rights and responsibilities of lead and cooperating agencies? What letters and memoranda must be prepared?

A. After a lead agency has been designated (Sec. 1501.5), that agency has the responsibility to solicit cooperation from other Federal agencies that have jurisdiction by law or special expertise on any environmental issue that should be addressed in the EIS being prepared. Where appropriate, the lead agency should seek the cooperation of State or local agencies of similar qualifications. When the proposal may affect an Indian reservation, the agency should consult with the Indian tribe. Section 1508.5. The request for cooperation should come at the earliest possible time in the NEPA process.

After discussions with the candidate cooperating agencies, the lead agency and the cooperating agencies are to determine by letter or by memorandum which agencies will undertake cooperating responsibilities. To the extent possible at this stage, responsibilities for specific issues should be assigned. The allocation of responsibilities will be completed during scoping. Section 1501.7(a)(4).

Cooperating agencies must assume responsibility for the development of information and the preparation of environmental analyses at the request of the lead agency. Section 1501.6(b)(3). Cooperating agencies are now required by Section 1501.6 to devote staff resources that were normally primarily used to critique or comment on the Draft EIS after its preparation, much earlier in the NEPA process–primarily at the scoping and Draft EIS preparation stages. If a cooperating agency determines that its resource limitations preclude any involvement, or the degree of involvement (amount of work) requested by the lead agency, it must so inform the lead agency in writing and submit a copy of this correspondence to the Council. Section 1501.6(c).

In other words, the potential cooperating agency must decide early if it is able to devote any of its resources to a particular proposal. For this reason the regulation states that an agency may reply to a request for cooperation that "other program commitments preclude any involvement or the degree of involvement requested in the action that is the subject of the environmental impact statement." (Emphasis added). The regulation refers to the "action," rather than to the EIS, to clarify that the agency is taking itself out of all phases of the Federal action, not just draft EIS preparation. This means that the agency has determined that it cannot be involved in the later stages of EIS review and comment, as well as decision making on the proposed action. For this reason, cooperating agencies with jurisdiction by law (those which have permitting or other approval authority) cannot opt out entirely of the duty to cooperate on the EIS. See also Question 15, relating specifically to the responsibility of EPA.

14b. How are disputes resolved between lead and cooperating agencies concerning the scope and level of detail of analysis and the quality of data in impact statements?

A. Such disputes are resolved by the agencies themselves. A lead agency, of course, has the ultimate responsibility for the content of an EIS. But it is supposed to use the environmental analysis and recommendations of cooperating agencies with jurisdiction by law or special expertise to the maximum extent possible, consistent with its own responsibilities as lead agency. Section 1501.6(a)(2).

If the lead agency leaves out a significant issue or ignores the advice and expertise of the cooperating agency, the EIS may be found later to be inadequate. Similarly, where cooperating agencies have their own decisions to make and they intend to adopt the environmental impact statement and base their decisions on it, one document should include all of the information necessary for the decisions by the cooperating agencies. Otherwise they may be forced to duplicate the EIS process by issuing a new, more complete EIS or Supplemental EIS, even though the original EIS could have sufficed if it had been properly done at the outset. Thus, both lead and cooperating agencies have a stake in producing a document of good quality. Cooperating agencies also have a duty to participate fully in the scoping process to ensure that the appropriate range of issues is determined early in the EIS process.

Because the EIS is not the Record of Decision, but instead constitutes the information and analysis on which to base a decision, disagreements about conclusions to be drawn from the EIS need not inhibit agencies from issuing a joint document, or adopting another agency's EIS, if the analysis is adequate. Thus, if each agency has its own "preferred alternative," both can be identified in the EIS. Similarly, a cooperating agency with jurisdiction by law may determine in its own ROD that alternative A is the environmentally preferable action, even though the lead agency has decided in its separate ROD that Alternative B is environmentally preferable.

14c. What are the specific responsibilities of Federal and State cooperating agencies to review draft EISs?

A. Cooperating agencies (i.e., agencies with jurisdiction by law or special expertise) and agencies that are authorized to develop or enforce environmental standards, must comment on environmental impact statements within their jurisdiction, expertise or authority. Sections 1503.2, 1508.5. If a cooperating agency is satisfied that its views are adequately reflected in the environmental impact statement, it should simply comment accordingly. Conversely, if the cooperating agency determines that a draft EIS is incomplete, inadequate or inaccurate, or it has other comments, it should promptly make such comments, conforming to the requirements of specificity in Section 1503.3.

14d. How is the lead agency to treat the comments of another agency with jurisdiction by law or special expertise which has failed or refused to cooperate or participate in scoping or EIS preparation?

A. A lead agency has the responsibility to respond to all substantive comments raising significant issues regarding a draft EIS. Section 1503.4. However, cooperating agencies are generally under an obligation to raise issues or otherwise participate in the EIS process during scoping and EIS preparation if they reasonably can do so. In practical terms, if a cooperating agency fails to cooperate at the outset, such as during scoping, it will find that its comments at a later stage will not be as persuasive to the lead agency.

15. Commenting Responsibilities of EPA. Are EPA's responsibilities to review and comment on the environmental effects of agency proposals under Section 309 of the Clean Air Act independent of its responsibility as a cooperating agency?

A. Yes. EPA has an obligation under Section 309 of the Clean Air Act to review and comment in writing on the environmental impact of any matter relating to the authority of the Administrator contained in proposed legislation, Federal construction projects, other Federal actions requiring EISs, and new regulations. 42 U.S.C. Sec. 7609. This obligation is independent of its role as a cooperating agency under the NEPA regulations.

16. Third Party Contracts. What is meant by the term "third party contracts" in connection with the preparation of an EIS? See Section 1506.5(c). When can "third party contracts" be used?

A. As used by EPA and other agencies, the term "third party contract" refers to the preparation of EISs by contractors paid by the applicant. In the case of an EIS for a National Pollution Discharge Elimination System (NPDES) permit, the applicant, aware in the early planning stages of the proposed project of the need for an EIS, contracts directly with a consulting firm for its preparation. See 40 C.F.R. 6.604(g). The "third party" is EPA which, under Section 1506.5(c), must select the consulting firm, even though the applicant pays for the cost of preparing the EIS. The consulting firm is responsible to EPA for preparing an EIS that meets the requirements of the NEPA regulations and EPA's NEPA procedures. It is in the applicant's interest that the EIS comply with the law so that EPA can take prompt action on the NPDES permit application. The "third party contract" method under EPA's NEPA procedures is purely voluntary, though most applicants have found it helpful in expediting compliance with NEPA.

If a Federal agency uses "third party contracting," the applicant may undertake the necessary paperwork for the solicitation of a field of candidates under the agency's direction, so long as the agency complies with Section 1506.5(c). Federal procurement requirements do not apply to the agency because it incurs no obligations or costs under the contract, nor does the agency procure anything under the contract.

17a. Disclosure Statement to Avoid Conflict of Interest. If an EIS is prepared with the assistance of a consulting firm, the firm must execute a disclosure statement. What criteria must the firm follow in determining whether it has any "financial or other interest in the outcome of the project" which would cause a conflict of interest?

A. Section 1506.5(c), which specifies that a consulting firm preparing an EIS must execute a disclosure statement, does not define "financial or other interest in the outcome of the project." The Council interprets this term broadly to cover any known benefits other than general enhancement of professional reputation. This includes any financial benefit such as a promise of future construction or design work on the project, as well as indirect benefits the consultant is aware of (e.g., if the project would aid proposals sponsored by the firm's other clients). For example, completion of a highway project may encourage construction of a shopping center or industrial park from which the consultant stands to benefit. If a consulting firm is aware that it has such an interest in the decision on the proposal, it should be disqualified from preparing the EIS, to preserve the objectivity and integrity of the NEPA process.

When a consulting firm has been involved in developing initial data and plans for the project, but does not have any financial or other interest in the outcome of the decision, it need not be disqualified from preparing the EIS. However, a disclosure statement in the draft EIS should clearly State the scope and extent of the firm's prior involvement to expose any potential conflicts of interest that may exist.

17b. If the firm in fact has no promise of future work or other interest in the outcome of the proposal, may the firm later bid in competition with others for future work on the project if the proposed action is approved?

A. Yes.

18. Uncertainties About Indirect Effects of a Proposal. How should uncertainties about indirect effects of a proposal be addressed, for example, in cases of disposal of Federal lands, when the identity or plans of future landowners is unknown?

A. The EIS must identify all the indirect effects that are known, and make a good faith effort to explain the effects that are not known but are "reasonably foreseeable." Section 1508.8(b). In the example, if there is total uncertainty about the identity of future land owners or the nature of future land uses, then of course, the agency is not required to engage in speculation or contemplation about their future plans. But, in the ordinary course of business, people do make judgments based upon reasonably foreseeable occurrences. It will often be possible to consider the likely purchasers and the development trends in that area or similar areas in recent years; or the likelihood that the land will be used for an energy project, shopping center, subdivision, farm or factory. The agency has the responsibility to make an informed judgment, and to estimate future impacts on that basis, especially if trends are ascertainable or potential purchasers have made themselves known. The agency cannot ignore these uncertain, but probable, effects of its decisions.

19a. Mitigation Measures. What is the scope of mitigation measures that must be discussed?

A. The mitigation measures discussed in an EIS must cover the range of impacts of the proposal. The measures must include such things as design alternatives that would decrease pollution emissions, construction impacts, esthetic intrusion, as well as relocation assistance, possible land use controls that could be enacted, and other possible efforts. Mitigation measures must be considered even for impacts that by themselves would not be considered "significant." Once the proposal itself is considered as a whole to have significant effects, all of its specific effects on the environment (whether or not "significant") must be considered, and mitigation measures must be developed where it is feasible to do so. Sections 1502.14(f), 1502.16(h), 1508.14.

19b. How should an EIS treat the subject of available mitigation measures that are (1) outside the jurisdiction of the lead or cooperating agencies, or (2) unlikely to be adopted or enforced by the responsible agency?

A. All relevant, reasonable mitigation measures that could improve the project are to be identified, even if they are outside the jurisdiction of the lead agency or the cooperating agencies, and thus would not be committed as part of the RODs of these agencies. Sections 1502.16(h), 1505.2(c). This will serve to alert agencies or officials who can implement these extra measures, and will encourage them to do so. Because the EIS is the most comprehensive environmental document, it is an ideal vehicle in which to lay out not only the full range of environmental impacts but also the full spectrum of appropriate mitigation.

However, to ensure that environmental effects of a proposed action are fairly assessed, the probability of the mitigation measures being implemented must also be discussed. Thus the EIS and the Record of Decision should indicate the likelihood that such measures will be adopted or enforced by the responsible agencies. Sections 1502.16(h), 1505.2. If there is a history of nonenforcement or opposition to such measures, the EIS and Record of Decision should acknowledge such opposition or nonenforcement. If the necessary mitigation measures will not be ready for a long period of time, this fact, of course, should also be recognized.

20. Worst Case Analysis [Withdrawn.][2]

21. Combining Environmental and Planning Documents. Where an EIS or an EA is combined with another project planning document (sometimes called "piggybacking"), to what degree may the EIS or EA refer to and rely upon information in the project document to satisfy NEPA's requirements?

A. Section 1502.25 of the regulations requires that draft EISs be prepared concurrently and integrated with environmental analyses and related surveys and studies required by other Federal statutes. In addition, Section 1506.4 allows any environmental document prepared in compliance with NEPA to be combined with any other agency document to reduce duplication and paperwork. However, these provisions were not intended to authorize the preparation of a short summary or outline EIS, attached to a detailed project report or land use plan containing the required environmental impact data. In such circumstances, the reader would have to refer constantly to the detailed report to understand the environmental impacts and alternatives which should have been found in the EIS itself.

The EIS must stand on its own as an analytical document which fully informs decisionmakers and the public of the environmental effects of the proposal and those of the reasonable alternatives. Section 1502.1. But, as long as the EIS is clearly identified and is self-supporting, it can be physically included in or attached to the project report or land use plan, and may use attached report material as technical backup.

Forest Service environmental impact statements for forest management plans are handled in this manner. The EIS identifies the agency's preferred alternative, which is developed in detail as the proposed management plan. The detailed proposed plan accompanies the EIS through the review process, and the documents are appropriately cross-referenced. The proposed plan is useful for EIS readers as an example, to show how one choice of management options translates into effects on natural resources. This procedure permits initiation of the 90-day public review of proposed forest plans, which is required by the National Forest Management Act.

All the alternatives are discussed in the EIS, which can be read as an independent document. The details of the management plan are not repeated in the EIS, and vice versa. This is a reasonable functional separation of the documents: the EIS contains information relevant to the choice among alternatives; the plan is a detailed description of proposed management activities suitable for use by the land managers. This procedure provides for concurrent compliance with the public review requirements of both NEPA and the National Forest Management Act.

Under some circumstances, a project report or management plan may be totally merged with the EIS, and the one document labeled as both "EIS" and "management plan" or "project report." This may be reasonable where the documents are short, or where the EIS format and the regulations for clear, analytical EISs also satisfy the requirements for a project report.

22. State and Federal Agencies as Joint Lead Agencies. May State and Federal agencies serve as joint lead agencies? If so, how do they resolve law, policy and resource conflicts under NEPA and the relevant State environmental policy act? How do they resolve differences in perspective where, for example, national and local needs may differ?

A. Under Section 1501.5(b), Federal, State or local agencies, as long as they include at least one Federal agency, may act as joint lead agencies to prepare an EIS. Section 1506.2 also strongly urges State and local agencies and the relevant Federal agencies to cooperate fully with each other. This should cover joint research and studies, planning activities, public hearings, environmental assessments and the preparation of joint EISs under NEPA and the relevant "little NEPA" State laws, so that one document will satisfy both laws.

The regulations also recognize that certain inconsistencies may exist between the proposed Federal action and any approved State or local plan or law. The joint document should discuss the extent to which the Federal agency would reconcile its proposed action with such plan or law. Section 1506.2(d). (See Question 23).

Because there may be differences in perspective as well as conflicts among Federal, State and local goals for resources management, the Council has advised participating agencies to adopt a flexible, cooperative approach. The joint EIS should reflect all of their interests and missions, clearly identified as such. The final document would then indicate how State and local interests have been accommodated, or would identify conflicts in goals (e.g., how a hydroelectric project, which might induce second home development, would require new land use controls). The EIS must contain a complete discussion of scope and purpose of the proposal, alternatives, and impacts so that the discussion is adequate to meet the needs of local, State and Federal decisionmakers.

23a. Conflicts of Federal Proposal With Land Use Plans, Policies or Controls. How should an agency handle potential conflicts between a proposal and the objectives of Federal, State or local land use plans, policies and controls for the area concerned? See Sec. 1502.16(c).

A. The agency should first inquire of other agencies whether there are any potential conflicts. If there would be immediate conflicts, or if conflicts could arise in the future when the plans are finished (see Question 23(b) below), the EIS must acknowledge and describe the extent of those conflicts. If there are any possibilities of resolving the conflicts, these should be explained as well. The EIS should also evaluate the seriousness of the impact of the proposal on the land use plans and policies, and whether, or how much, the proposal will impair the effectiveness of land use control mechanisms for the area. Comments from officials of the affected area should be solicited early and should be carefully acknowledged and answered in the EIS.

23b. What constitutes a "land use plan or policy" for purposes of this discussion?

A. The term "land use plans," includes all types of formally adopted documents for land use planning, zoning and related regulatory requirements. Local general plans are included, even though they are subject to future change. Proposed plans should also be addressed if they have been formally proposed by the appropriate government body in a written form, and are being actively pursued by officials of the jurisdiction. Staged plans, which must go through phases of development such as the Water Resources Council's Level A, B and C planning process should also be included even though they are incomplete.

The term "policies" includes formally adopted statements of land use policy as embodied in laws or regulations. It also includes proposals for action such as the initiation of a planning process, or a formally adopted policy statement of the local, regional or State executive branch, even if it has not yet been formally adopted by the local, regional or State legislative body.

23c. What options are available for the decision maker when conflicts with such plans or policies are identified?

A. After identifying any potential land use conflicts, the decision maker must weigh the significance of the conflicts, among all the other environmental and non-environmental factors that must be considered in reaching a rational and balanced decision. Unless precluded by other law from causing or contributing to any inconsistency with the land use plans, policies or controls, the decision maker retains the authority to go forward with the proposal, despite the potential conflict. In the Record of Decision, the decision maker must explain what the decision was, how it was made, and what mitigation measures are being imposed to lessen adverse environmental impacts of the proposal, among the other requirements of Section 1505.2. This provision would require the decision maker to explain any decision to override land use plans, policies or controls for the area.

24a. Environmental Impact Statements on Policies, Plans or Programs. When are EISs required on policies, plans or programs?

A. An EIS must be prepared if an agency proposes to implement a specific policy, to adopt a plan for a group of related actions, or to implement a specific statutory program or executive directive. Section 1509.18. In addition, the adoption of official policy in the form of rules, regulations and interpretations pursuant to the Administrative Procedure Act (APA), treaties, conventions, or other formal documents establishing governmental or agency policy which will substantially alter agency programs, could require an EIS. Section 1508.18. In all cases, the policy, plan, or program must have the potential for significantly affecting the quality of the human environment in order to require an EIS. It should be noted that a proposal "may exist in fact as well as by agency declaration that one exists." Section 1508.23.

24b. When is an area-wide or overview EIS appropriate?

A. The preparation of an area-wide or overview EIS may be particularly useful when similar actions, viewed with other reasonably foreseeable or proposed agency actions, share common timing or geography. For example, when a variety of energy projects may be located in a single watershed, or when a series of new energy technologies may be developed through Federal funding, the overview or area-wide EIS would serve as a valuable and necessary analysis of the affected environment and the potential cumulative impacts of the reasonably foreseeable actions under that program or within that geographical area.

24c. What is the function of tiering in such cases?

A. Tiering is a procedure which allows an agency to avoid duplication of paperwork through the incorporation by reference of the general discussions and relevant specific discussions from an environmental impact statement of broader scope into one of lesser scope or vice versa. In the example given in Question 24b, this would mean that an overview EIS would be prepared for all of the energy activities reasonably foreseeable in a particular geographic area or resulting from a particular development program. This impact statement would be followed by site-specific or project-specific EISs. The tiering process would make each EIS of greater use and meaning to the public as the plan or program develops, without duplication of the analysis prepared for the previous impact statement.

25a. Appendices and Incorporation by Reference. When is it appropriate to use appendices instead of including information in the body of an EIS?

A. The body of the EIS should be a succinct statement of all the information on environmental impacts and alternatives that the decision maker and the public need, in order to make the decision and to ascertain that every significant factor has been examined. The EIS must explain or summarize methodologies of research and modeling, and the results of research that may have been conducted to analyze impacts and alternatives.

Lengthy technical discussions of modeling methodology, baseline studies, or other work are best reserved for the appendix. In other words, if only technically trained individuals are likely to understand a particular discussion then it should go in the appendix, and a plain language summary of the analysis and conclusions of that technical discussion should go in the text of the EIS.

The final statement must also contain the agency's responses to comments on the draft EIS. These responses will be primarily in the form of changes in the document itself, but specific answers to each significant comment should also be included. These specific responses may be placed in an appendix. If the comments are especially voluminous, summaries of the comments and responses will suffice. (See Question 29 regarding the level of detail required for responses to comments.)

25b. How does an appendix differ from incorporation by reference?

A. First, if at all possible, the appendix accompanies the EIS, whereas the material which is incorporated by reference does not accompany the EIS. Thus the appendix should contain information that reviewers will be likely to want to examine. The appendix should include material that pertains to preparation of a particular EIS. Research papers directly relevant to the proposal, lists of affected species, discussion of the methodology of models used in the analysis of impacts, extremely detailed responses to comments, or other information, would be placed in the appendix.

The appendix must be complete and available at the time the EIS is filed. Five copies of the appendix must be sent to EPA with five copies of the EIS for filing. If the appendix is too bulky to be circulated, it instead must be placed in conveniently accessible locations or furnished directly to commentors upon request. If it is not circulated with the EIS, the Notice of Availability published by EPA must so State, giving a telephone number to enable potential commentors to locate or request copies of the appendix promptly.

Material that is not directly related to preparation of the EIS should be incorporated by reference. This would include other EISs, research papers in the general literature, technical background papers or other material that someone with technical training could use to evaluate the analysis of the proposal. These must be made available, either by citing the literature, furnishing copies to central locations, or sending copies directly to commentors upon request.

Care must be taken in all cases to ensure that material incorporated by reference, and the occasional appendix that does not accompany the EIS, are in fact available for the full minimum public comment period.

26a. Index and Keyword Index in EISs. How detailed must an EIS index be?

A. The EIS index should have a level of detail sufficient to focus on areas of the EIS of reasonable interest to any reader. It cannot be restricted to the most important topics. On the other hand, it need not identify every conceivable term or phrase in the EIS. If an agency believes that the reader is reasonably likely to be interested in a topic, it should be included.

26b. Is a keyword index required?

A. No. A keyword index is a relatively short list of descriptive terms that identifies the key concepts or subject areas in a document. For example it could consist of 20 terms which describe the most significant aspects of an EIS that a future researcher would need: type of proposal, type of impacts, type of environment, geographical area, sampling or modelling methodologies used. This technique permits the compilation of EIS data banks, by facilitating quick and inexpensive access to stored materials. While a keyword index is not required by the regulations, it could be a useful addition for several reasons. First, it can be useful as a quick index for reviewers of the EIS, helping to focus on areas of interest. Second, if an agency keeps a listing of the keyword indexes of the EISs it produces, the EIS preparers themselves will have quick access to similar research data and methodologies to aid their future EIS work. Third, a keyword index will be needed to make an EIS available to future researchers using EIS data banks that are being developed. Preparation of such an index now when the document is produced will save a later effort when the data banks become operational.

27a. List of Preparers. If a consultant is used in preparing an EIS, must the list of preparers identify members of the consulting firm as well as the agency NEPA staff who were primarily responsible?

A. Section 1502.17 requires identification of the names and qualifications of persons who were primarily responsible for preparing the EIS or significant background papers, including basic components of the statement. This means that members of a consulting firm preparing material that is to become part of the EIS must be identified. The EIS should identify these individuals even though the consultant's contribution may have been modified by the agency.

27b. Should agency staff involved in reviewing and editing the EIS also be included in the list of preparers?

A. Agency personnel who wrote basic components of the EIS or significant background papers must, of course, be identified. The EIS should also list the technical editors who reviewed or edited the statements.

27c. How much information should be included on each person listed?

A. The list of preparers should normally not exceed two pages. Therefore, agencies must determine which individuals had primary responsibility and need not identify individuals with minor involvement. The list of preparers should include a very brief identification of the individuals involved, their qualifications (expertise, professional disciplines) and the specific portion of the EIS for which they are responsible. This may be done in tabular form to cut down on length. A line or two for each person's qualifications should be sufficient.

28. Advance or Xerox Copies of EIS. May an agency file xerox copies of an EIS with EPA pending the completion of printing the document?

A. Xerox copies of an EIS may be filed with EPA prior to printing only if the xerox copies are simultaneously made available to other agencies and the public. Section 1506.9 of the regulations, which governs EIS filing, specifically requires Federal agencies to file EISs with EPA no earlier than the EIS is distributed to the public. However, this section does not prohibit xeroxing as a form of reproduction and distribution. When an agency chooses xeroxing as the reproduction method, the EIS must be clear and legible to permit ease of reading and ultimate microfiching of the EIS. Where color graphs are important to the EIS, they should be reproduced and circulated with the xeroxed copy.

29a. Responses to Comments. What response must an agency provide to a comment on a draft EIS which states that the EISs methodology is inadequate or inadequately explained? For example, what level of detail must an agency include in its response to a simple postcard comment making such an allegation?

A. Appropriate responses to comments are described in Section 1503.4. Normally the responses should result in changes in the text of the EIS, not simply a separate answer at the back of the document. But, in addition, the agency must State what its response was, and if the agency decides that no substantive response to a comment is necessary, it must explain briefly why.

An agency is not under an obligation to issue a lengthy reiteration of its methodology or any portion of an EIS if the only comment addressing the methodology is a simple complaint that the EIS methodology is inadequate. But agencies must respond to comments, however brief, which are specific in their criticism of agency methodology. For example, if a commentor on an EIS said that an agency's air quality dispersion analysis or methodology was inadequate, and the agency had included a discussion of that analysis in the EIS, little if anything need be added in response to such a comment. However, if the commentor said that the dispersion analysis was inadequate because of its use of a certain computational technique, or that a dispersion analysis was inadequately explained because computational techniques were not included or referenced, then the agency would have to respond in a substantive and meaningful way to such a comment.

If a number of comments are identical or very similar, agencies may group the comments and prepare a single answer for each group. Comments may be summarized if they are especially voluminous. The comments or summaries must be attached to the EIS regardless of whether the agency believes they merit individual discussion in the body of the final EIS.

29b. How must an agency respond to a comment on a draft EIS that raises a new alternative not previously considered in the draft EIS?

A. This question might arise in several possible situations. First, a commentor on a draft EIS may indicate that there is a possible alternative which, in the agency's view, is not a reasonable alternative. Section 1502.14(a). If that is the case, the agency must explain why the comment does not warrant further agency response, citing authorities or reasons that support the agency's position and, if appropriate, indicate those circumstances which would trigger agency reappraisal or further response. Section 1503.4(a). For example, a commentor on a draft EIS on a coal-fired power plant may suggest the alternative of using synthetic fuel. The agency may reject the alternative with a brief discussion (with authorities) of the unavailability of synthetic fuel within the time frame necessary to meet the need and purpose of the proposed facility.

A second possibility is that an agency may receive a comment indicating that a particular alternative, while reasonable, should be modified somewhat, for example, to achieve certain mitigation benefits, or for other reasons. If the modification is reasonable, the agency should include a discussion of it in the final EIS. For example, a commentor on a draft EIS on a proposal for a pumped storage power facility might suggest that the applicant's proposed alternative should be enhanced by the addition of certain reasonable mitigation measures, including the purchase and set aside of a wildlife preserve to substitute for the tract to be destroyed by the project. The modified alternative including the additional mitigation measures should be discussed by the agency in the final EIS.

A third slightly different possibility is that a comment on a draft EIS will raise an alternative which is a minor variation of one of the alternatives discussed in the draft EIS, but this variation was not given any consideration by the agency. In such a case, the agency should develop and evaluate the new alternative, if it is reasonable, in the final EIS. If it is qualitatively within the spectrum of alternatives that were discussed in the draft, a supplemental draft will not be needed. For example, a commentor on a draft EIS to designate a wilderness area within a National Forest might reasonably identify a specific tract of the forest, and urge that it be considered for designation. If the draft EIS considered designation of a range of alternative tracts which encompassed forest area of similar quality and quantity, no supplemental EIS would have to be prepared. The agency could fulfill its obligation by addressing that specific alternative in the final EIS.

As another example, an EIS on an urban housing project may analyze the alternatives of constructing 2,000, 4,000, or 6,000 units. A commentor on the draft EIS might urge the consideration of constructing 5,000 units utilizing a different configuration of buildings. This alternative is within the spectrum of alternatives already considered, and, therefore, could be addressed in the final EIS.

A fourth possibility is that a commentor points out an alternative which is not a variation of the proposal or of any alternative discussed in the draft impact statement, and is a reasonable alternative that warrants serious agency response. In such a case, the agency must issue a supplement to the draft EIS that discusses this new alternative. For example, a commentor on a draft EIS on a nuclear power plant might suggest that a reasonable alternative for meeting the projected need for power would be through peak load management and energy conservation programs. If the permitting agency has failed to consider that approach in the Draft EIS, and the approach cannot be dismissed by the agency as unreasonable, a supplement to the Draft EIS, which discusses that alternative, must be prepared. (If necessary, the same supplement should also discuss substantial changes in the proposed action or significant new circumstances or information, as required by Section 1502.9(c)(1) of the Council's regulations.)

If the new alternative was not raised by the commentor during scoping, but could have been, commentors may find that they are unpersuasive in their efforts to have their suggested alternative analyzed in detail by the agency. However, if the new alternative is discovered or developed later, and it could not reasonably have been raised during the scoping process, then the agency must address it in a supplemental draft EIS. The agency is, in any case, ultimately responsible for preparing an adequate EIS that considers all reasonable alternatives.

30. Adoption of EIS. When a cooperating agency with jurisdiction by law intends to adopt a lead agency's EIS and it is not satisfied with the adequacy of the document, may the cooperating agency adopt only the part of the EIS with which it is satisfied? If so, would a cooperating agency with jurisdiction by law have to prepare a separate EIS or EIS supplement covering the areas of disagreement with the lead agency?

A. Generally, a cooperating agency may adopt a lead agency's EIS without recirculating it if it concludes that its NEPA requirements and its comments and suggestions have been satisfied. Section 1506.3(a), (c). If necessary, a cooperating agency may adopt only a portion of the lead agency's EIS and may reject that part of the EIS with which it disagrees, stating publicly why it did so. Section 1506.3(a).

A cooperating agency with jurisdiction by law (e.g., an agency with independent legal responsibilities with respect to the proposal) has an independent legal obligation to comply with NEPA. Therefore, if the cooperating agency determines that the EIS is wrong or inadequate, it must prepare a supplement to the EIS, replacing or adding any needed information, and must circulate the supplement as a draft for public and agency review and comment. A final supplemental EIS would be required before the agency could take action. The adopted portions of the lead agency EIS should be circulated with the supplement. Section 1506.3(b). A cooperating agency with jurisdiction by law will have to prepare its own Record of Decision for its action, in which it must explain how it reached its conclusions. Each agency should explain how and why its conclusions differ, if that is the case, from those of other agencies which issued their Records of Decision earlier.

An agency that did not cooperate in preparation of an EIS may also adopt an EIS or portion thereof. But this would arise only in rare instances, because an agency adopting an EIS for use in its own decision normally would have been a cooperating agency. If the proposed action for which the EIS was prepared is substantially the same as the proposed action of the adopting agency, the EIS may be adopted as long as it is recirculated as a final EIS and the agency announces what it is doing. This would be followed by the 30-day review period and issuance of a Record of Decision by the adopting agency. If the proposed action by the adopting agency is not substantially the same as that in the EIS (i.e., if an EIS on one action is being adapted for use in a decision on another action), the EIS would be treated as a draft and circulated for the normal public comment period and other procedures. Section 1506.3(b).

31a. Application of Regulations to Independent Regulatory Agencies. Do the Council's NEPA regulations apply to independent regulatory agencies like the Federal Energy Regulatory Commission (FERC) and the Nuclear Regulatory Commission?

A. The statutory requirements of NEPA's Section 102 apply to "all agencies of the Federal government." The NEPA regulations implement the procedural provisions of NEPA as set forth in NEPA's Section 102(2) for all agencies of the Federal government. The NEPA regulations apply to independent regulatory agencies; however, they do not direct independent regulatory agencies or other agencies to make decisions in any particular way or in a way inconsistent with an agency's statutory charter. Sections 1500.3, 1500.6, 1507.1, and 1507.3.

31b. Can an Executive Branch agency like the Department of the Interior adopt an EIS prepared by an independent regulatory agency such as FERC?

A. If an independent regulatory agency such as FERC has prepared an EIS in connection with its approval of a proposed project, an Executive Branch agency (e.g., the Bureau of Land Management in the Department of the Interior) may, in accordance with Section 1506.3, adopt the EIS or a portion thereof for its use in considering the same proposal. In such a case the EIS must, to the satisfaction of the adopting agency, meet the standards for an adequate statement under the NEPA regulations (including scope and quality of analysis of alternatives) and must satisfy the adopting agency's comments and suggestions. If the independent regulatory agency fails to comply with the NEPA regulations, the cooperating or adopting agency may find that it is unable to adopt the EIS, thus forcing the preparation of a new EIS or EIS Supplement for the same action. The NEPA regulations were made applicable to all Federal agencies in order to avoid this result, and to achieve uniform application and efficiency of the NEPA process.

32. Supplements to Old EISs. Under what circumstances do old EISs have to be supplemented before taking action on a proposal?

A. As a rule of thumb, if the proposal has not yet been implemented, or if the EIS concerns an ongoing program, EISs that are more than 5 years old should be carefully reexamined to determine if the criteria in Section 1502.9 compel preparation of an EIS supplement.

If an agency has made a substantial change in a proposed action that is relevant to environmental concerns, or if there are significant new circumstances or information relevant to environmental concerns and bearing on the proposed action or its impacts, a supplemental EIS must be prepared for an old EIS so that the agency has the best possible information to make any necessary substantive changes in its decisions regarding the proposal. Section 1502.9(c).

33a. Referrals. When must a referral of an interagency disagreement be made to the Council?

A. The Council's referral procedure is a pre-decision referral process for interagency disagreements. Hence, Section 1504.3 requires that a referring agency must deliver its referral to the Council not later than 25 days after publication by EPA of notice that the final EIS is available (unless the lead agency grants an extension of time under Section 1504.3(b)).

33b. May a referral be made after this issuance of a Record of Decision?

A. No, except for cases where agencies provide an internal appeal procedure which permits simultaneous filing of the final EIS and the record of decision (ROD). Section 1506.10(b)(2). Otherwise, as stated above, the process is a pre-decision referral process. Referrals must be made within 25 days after the notice of availability of the final EIS, whereas the final decision (ROD) may not be made or filed until after 30 days from the notice of availability of the EIS. Sections 1504.3(b), 1506.10(b). If a lead agency has granted an extension of time for another agency to take action on a referral, the ROD may not be issued until the extension has expired.

34a. Records of Decision. Must Records of Decision (RODs) be made public? How should they be made available?

A. Under the regulations, agencies must prepare a "concise public record of decision," which contains the elements specified in Section 1505.2. This public record may be integrated into any other decision record prepared by the agency, or it may be separate if decision documents are not normally made public. The Record of Decision is intended by the Council to be an environmental document (even though it is not explicitly mentioned in the definition of "environmental document" in Section 1508.10). Therefore, it must be made available to the public through appropriate public notice as required by Section 1506.6(b). However, there is no specific requirement for publication of the ROD itself, either in the *Federal Register* or elsewhere.

34b. May the summary section in the final Environmental Impact Statement substitute for or constitute an agency's Record of Decision?

A. No. An environmental impact statement is supposed to inform the decision maker before the decision is made. Sections 1502.1, 1505.2. The Council's regulations provide for a 30-day period after notice is published that the final EIS has been filed with EPA before the agency may take final action. During that period, in addition to the agency's own internal final review, the public and other agencies can comment on the final EIS prior to the agency's final action on the proposal. In addition, the Council's regulations make clear that the requirements for the summary in an EIS are not the same as the requirements for a ROD. Sections 1502.12 and 1505.2.

34c. What provisions should Records of Decision contain pertaining to mitigation and monitoring?

A. Lead agencies "shall include appropriate conditions [including mitigation measures and monitoring and enforcement programs] in grants, permits or other approvals" and shall "condition funding of actions on mitigation." Section 1505.3. Any such measures that are adopted must be explained and committed in the ROD.

The reasonable alternative mitigation measures and monitoring programs should have been addressed in the draft and final EIS. The discussion of mitigation and monitoring in a Record of Decision must be more detailed than a general statement that mitigation is being required, but not so detailed as to duplicate discussion of mitigation in the EIS. The Record of Decision should contain a concise summary identification of the mitigation measures which the agency has committed itself to adopt.

The Record of Decision must also State whether all practicable mitigation measures have been adopted, and if not, why not. Section 1505.2(c). The Record of Decision must identify the mitigation measures and monitoring and enforcement programs that have been selected and plainly indicate that they are adopted as part of the agency's decision. If the proposed action is the issuance of a permit or other approval, the specific details of the mitigation measures shall then be included as appropriate conditions in whatever grants, permits, funding or other approvals are being made by the Federal agency. Section 1505.3(a), (b). If the Proposal is to be carried out by the Federal agency itself, the Record of Decision should delineate the mitigation and monitoring measures in sufficient detail to constitute an enforceable commitment, or incorporate by reference the portions of the EIS that do so.

34d. What is the enforceability of a Record of Decision?

A. Pursuant to generally recognized principles of Federal administrative law, agencies will be held accountable for preparing Records of Decision that conform to the decisions actually made and for carrying out the actions set forth in the Records of Decision. This is based on the principle that an agency must comply with its own decisions and regulations once they are adopted. Thus, the terms of a Record of Decision are enforceable by agencies and private parties. A Record of Decision can be used to compel compliance with or execution of the mitigation measures identified therein.

35. Time Required for the NEPA Process. How long should the NEPA process take to complete?

A. When an EIS is required, the process obviously will take longer than when an EA is the only document prepared. But the Council's NEPA regulations encourage streamlined review, adoption of deadlines, elimination of duplicative work, eliciting suggested alternatives and other comments early through scoping, cooperation among agencies, and consultation with applicants during project planning. The Council has advised agencies that under the new NEPA regulations even large complex energy projects would require only about 12 months for the completion of the entire EIS process. For most major actions, this period is well within the planning time that is needed in any event, apart from NEPA.

The time required for the preparation of program EISs may be greater. The Council also recognizes that some projects will entail difficult long-term planning and/or the acquisition of certain data which of necessity will require more time for the preparation of the EIS. Indeed, some proposals should be given more time for the thoughtful preparation of an EIS and development of a decision which fulfill NEPA's substantive goals.

For cases in which only an environmental assessment will be prepared, the NEPA process should take no more than 3 months, and in many cases substantially less, as part of the normal analysis and approval process for the action.

36a. Environmental Assessments (EA). How long and detailed must an environmental assessment (EA) be?

A. The environmental assessment is a concise public document which has three defined functions. (1) It briefly provides sufficient evidence and analysis for determining whether to prepare an EIS; (2) it aids an agency's compliance with NEPA when no EIS is necessary, i.e., it helps to identify better alternatives and mitigation measures; and (3) it facilitates preparation of an EIS when one is necessary. Section 1508.9(a).

Since the EA is a concise document, it should not contain long descriptions or detailed data which the agency may have gathered. Rather, it should contain a brief discussion of the need for the proposal, alternatives to the proposal, the environmental impacts of the proposed action and alternatives, and a list of agencies and persons consulted. Section 1508.9(b).

While the regulations do not contain page limits for EAs, the Council has generally advised agencies to keep the length of EAs to not more than approximately 10-15 pages. Some agencies expressly provide page guidelines (e.g., 10-15 pages in the case of the Army Corps). To avoid undue length, the EA may incorporate by reference background data to support its concise discussion of the proposal and relevant issues.

36b. Under what circumstances is a lengthy EA appropriate?

A. Agencies should avoid preparing lengthy EAs except in unusual cases, where a proposal is so complex that a concise document cannot meet the goals of Section 1508.9, and where it is extremely difficult to determine whether the proposal could have significant environmental effects. In most cases, however, a lengthy EA indicates that an EIS is needed.

37a. Findings of No Significant Impact (FONSI). What is the level of detail of information that must be included in a finding of no significant impact (FONSI)?

A. The FONSI is a document in which the agency briefly explains the reasons why an action will not have a significant effect on the human environment and, therefore, why an EIS will not be prepared. Section 1508.13. The finding itself need not be detailed, but must succinctly State the reasons for deciding that the action will have no significant environmental effects, and, if relevant, must show which factors were weighted most heavily in the determination. In addition to this statement, the FONSI must include, summarize, or attach and incorporate by reference, the environmental assessment.

37b. What are the criteria for deciding whether a FONSI should be made available for public review for 30 days before the agency's final determination whether to prepare an EIS?

A. Public review is necessary, for example, (a) if the proposal is a borderline case, i.e., when there is a reasonable argument for preparation of an EIS; (b) if it is an unusual case, a new kind of action, or a precedent-setting case such as a first intrusion of even a minor development into a pristine area; (c) when there is either scientific or public controversy over the proposal; or (d) when it involves a proposal which is or is closely similar to one which normally requires preparation of an EIS. Sections 1501.4(e)(2), 1508.27. Agencies also must allow a period of public review of the FONSI if the proposed action would be located in a floodplain or wetland. E.0. 11988, Sec. 2(a)(4); E.0. 11990, Sec. 2(b).

38. Public Availability of EAs v. FONSIs. Must EAs and FONSIs be made public? If so, how should this be done?

A. Yes, they must be available to the public. Section 1506.6 requires agencies to involve the public in implementing their NEPA procedures, and this includes public involvement in the preparation of EAs and FONSIs. These are public "environmental documents" under Section 1506.6(b), and, therefore, agencies must give public notice of their availability. A combination of methods may be used to give notice, and the methods should be tailored to the needs of particular cases. Thus, a *Federal Register* notice of availability of the documents, coupled with notices in national publications and mailed to interested national groups might be appropriate for proposals that are national in scope. Local newspaper notices may be more appropriate for regional or site-specific proposals.

The objective, however, is to notify all interested or affected parties. If this is not being achieved, then the methods should be reevaluated and changed. Repeated failure to reach the interested or affected public would be interpreted as a violation of the regulations.

39. Mitigation Measures Imposed in EAs and FONSIs. Can an EA and FONSI be used to impose enforceable mitigation measures, monitoring programs, or other requirements, even though there is no requirement in the regulations in such cases for a formal Record of Decision?

A. Yes. In cases where an environmental assessment is the appropriate environmental document, there still may be mitigation measures or alternatives that would be desirable to consider and adopt even though the impacts of the proposal will not be "significant." In such cases, the EA should include a discussion of these measures or alternatives to "assist agency planning and decision making" and to "aid an agency's compliance with [NEPA] when no environmental impact statement is necessary." Section 1501.3(b), 1508.9(a)(2). The appropriate mitigation measures can be imposed as enforceable permit conditions, or adopted as part of the agency final decision in the same manner mitigation measures are adopted in the formal Record of Decision that is required in EIS cases.

40. Propriety of Issuing EA When Mitigation Reduces Impacts. If an environmental assessment indicates that the environmental effects of a proposal are significant but that, with mitigation, those effects may be reduced to less than significant levels, may the agency make a finding of no significant impact rather than prepare an EIS? Is that a legitimate function of an EA and scoping?

[The 1987-88 CEQ Annual Report stated that CEQ intended to issue additional guidance on this topic. Editor's note.]

A. Mitigation measures may be relied upon to make a finding of no significant impact only if they are imposed by statute or regulation, or submitted by an applicant or agency as part of the original proposal. As a general rule, the regulations contemplate that agencies should use a broad approach in defining significance and should not rely on the possibility of mitigation as an excuse to avoid the EIS requirement. Sections 1508.8, 1508.27.

If a proposal appears to have adverse effects which would be significant, and certain mitigation measures are then developed during the scoping or EA stages, the existence of such possible mitigation does not obviate the need for an EIS. Therefore, if scoping or the EA identifies certain mitigation possibilities without altering the nature of the overall proposal itself, the agency should continue the EIS process and submit the proposal, and the potential mitigation, for public and agency review and comment. This is essential to ensure that the final decision is based on all the relevant factors and that the full NEPA process will result in enforceable mitigation measures through the Record of Decision.

In some instances, where the proposal itself so integrates mitigation from the beginning that it is impossible to define the proposal without including the mitigation, the agency may then rely on the mitigation measures in determining that the overall effects would not be significant (e.g., where an application for a permit for a small hydro dam is based on a binding commitment to build fish ladders, to permit adequate down stream flow, and to replace any lost wetlands, wildlife habitat and recreational potential). In those instances, agencies should make the FONSI and EA available for 30 days of public comment before taking action. Section 1501.4(e)(2).

Similarly, scoping may result in a redefinition of the entire project, as a result of mitigation proposals. In that case, the agency may alter its previous decision to do an EIS, as long as the agency or applicant resubmits the entire proposal and the EA and FONSI are available for 30 days of review and comment. One example of this would be where the size and location of a proposed industrial park are changed to avoid affecting a nearby wetland area.

[This memorandum was filed in the *Federal Register* and appears at 46 Fed. Reg. 18026 (Mar. 23, 1981).]

<u>Endnotes</u>

The first endnote appeared in the original *Federal Register*. The other endnote, which refers to subsequent CEQ actions, is for information only.

1. References throughout the document are to the Council on Environmental Quality's Regulations for Implementing the Procedural Provisions of the National Environmental Policy Act. 40 CFR Parts 1500-1508.

2. Q20 Worst Case Analysis was withdrawn by final rule issued at 51 Fed. Reg. 15618 (Apr. 25, 1986); textual errors corrected 51 F.R. p. 16,846 (May 7, 1986). The preamble to this rule is published at ELR Admin. Mat. 35055.

MEMORANDUM: GUIDANCE REGARDING NEPA REGULATIONS

40 CFR Part 1500

[This memorandum was published in the *Federal Register* and appears at 48 Fed. Reg. 34263 (1983). Editor's note]

MEMORANDUM

For: Heads of Federal Agencies

From: A. Alan Hill, Chairman, Council on Environmental Quality

Re: Guidance Regarding NEPA Regulations

The Council on Environmental Quality (CEQ) regulations implementing the National Environmental Policy Act (NEPA) were issued on November 29, 1978. These regulations became effective for, and binding upon, most Federal agencies on July 30, 1979, and for all remaining Federal agencies on November 30, 1979.

As part of the Council's NEPA oversight responsibilities it solicited through an August 14,1981, notice in the *Federal Register* public and agency comments regarding a series of questions that were developed to provide information on the manner in which Federal agencies were implementing the CEQ regulations. On July 12, 1982, the Council announced the availability of a document summarizing the comments received from the public and other agencies and also identifying issue areas which the Council intended to review. On August 12, 1982, the Council held a public meeting to address those issues and hear any other comments which the public or other interested agencies might have about the NEPA process. The issues addressed in this guidance were identified during this process.

There are many ways in which agencies can meet their responsibilities under NEPA and the 1978 regulations. The purpose of this document is to provide the Council's guidance on various ways to carry out activities under the regulations.

Scoping

The Council on Environmental Quality (CEQ) regulations direct Federal agencies which have made a decision to prepare an environmental impact statement to engage in a public scoping process. Public hearings or meetings, although often held, are not required; instead the manner in which public input will be sought is left to the discretion of the agency.

The purpose of this process is to determine the scope of the EIS so that preparation of the document can be effectively managed. Scoping is intended to ensure that problems are identified early and properly studied, that issues of little significance do not consume time and effort, that the draft EIS is thorough and balanced, and that delays occasioned by an inadequate draft EIS are avoided. The scoping process should identify the public and agency concerns; clearly define the environmental issues and alternatives to be examined in the EIS including the elimination of non-significant issues; identify related issues which originate from separate legislation, regulation, or Executive Order (e.g., historic preservation or endangered species concerns); and identify State and local agency requirements which must be addressed. An effective scoping process can help reduce unnecessary paperwork and time delays in preparing and processing the EIS by clearly identifying all relevant procedural requirements.

In April 1981, the Council issued a "Memorandum for General Counsels, NEPA Liaisons and Participants in Scoping" on the subject of Scoping Guidance. The purpose of this guidance was to give agencies suggestions as to how to more effectively carry out the CEQ scoping requirement. The availability of this document was announced in the *Federal Register* at 46 FR 25461. It is still available upon request from the CEQ General Council's office.

The concept of lead agency (§1508.16) and cooperating agency (§ 508.5) can be used effectively to help manage the scoping process and prepare the environmental impact statement. The lead agency should identify the potential cooperating agencies. It is incumbent upon the lead agency to identify any agency which may ultimately be involved in the proposed action, including any subsequent permitting actions. Once cooperating agencies have been identified, they have specific responsibility under the NEPA regulations (40 CFR 1501.6). Among other things, cooperating agencies have responsibilities to participate in the scoping process and to help identify issues which are germane to any subsequent action it must take on the proposed action. The ultimate goal of this combined agency effort is to produce an EIS which, in addition to fulfilling the basic intent of NEPA, also encompasses to the maximum extent possible all the environmental and public involvement requirements of State and Federal laws, Executive Orders, and administrative policies of the involved agencies. Examples of these requirements include the Fish and Wildlife Coordination Act, the Clean Air Act, the Endangered Species Act, the National Historic Preservation Act, the Wild and Scenic Rivers Act, the Farmland Protection Policy Act, Executive Order 11990 (Protection of Wetlands), and Executive Order 11998 (Floodplain Management).

It is emphasized that cooperating agencies have the responsibility and obligation under the CEQ regulations to participate in the scoping process. Early involvement leads to early identification of significant issues, better decision making, and avoidance of possible legal challenges. Agencies with "jurisdiction by law" must accept designation as a cooperating agency if requested (40 CFR 1501.6).

One of the functions of scoping is to identify the public involvement / public hearing procedures of all appropriate State and Federal agencies that will ultimately aid upon the proposed action. To the maximum extent possible, such procedures should be integrated into the EIS process so that joint public meetings and hearings can be conducted. Conducting joint meetings and hearings eliminates duplication and should significantly reduce the time and cost of processing an EIS and any subsequent approvals. The end result will be a more informed public cognizant of all facets of the proposed action.

It is important that the lead agency establish a process to properly manage scoping. In appropriate situations the lead agency should consider designating a project coordinator and forming an interagency project review team. The project coordinator would be the key person in monitoring time schedules and responding to any problems which may arise in both scoping and preparing the EIS. The project review team would be established early in scoping and maintained throughout the process of preparing the EIS. This review team would include State and local agency representatives. The review team would meet periodically to ensure that the EIS is complete, concise, and prepared in a timely manner.

A project review team has been used effectively on many projects. Some of the more important functions this review team can serve include: (1) a source of information, (2) a coordination mechanism, and (3) a professional review group. As an information source, the review team can identify all Federal, State, and local environmental requirements, agency public meeting and hearing procedures, concerned citizen groups, data needs and sources of existing information, and the significant issues and reasonable alternatives for detailed analysis, excluding the nonsignificant issues. As a coordination mechanism, the team can ensure the rapid distribution of appropriate information or environmental studies, and can reduce the time required for formal consultation on a number of issues (e.g., endangered species or historic preservation). As a professional review group the team can assist in establishing and monitoring a tight time schedule for preparing the EIS by identifying critical points in the process, discussing and recommending solutions to the lead agency as problems arise, advising whether a requested analysis or information item is relevant to the issues under consideration, and providing timely and substantive review comments on any preliminary reports or analyses that may be prepared during the process. The presence of professionals from all scientific disciplines which have a significant role in the proposed action could greatly enhance the value of the team.

The Council recognizes that there may be some problems with the review team concept, such as limited agency travel funds and the amount of work necessary to coordinate and prepare for the periodic team meetings. However, the potential benefits of the team concept are significant and the Council encourages agencies to consider utilizing interdisciplinary project review teams to aid in EIS preparation. A regularly scheduled meeting time and location should reduce coordination problems. In some instances, meetings can be arranged so that many projects are discussed at each session. The benefits of the concept are obvious: timely and effective preparation of the EIS, early identification and resolution of any problems which may arise, and elimination, or at least reduction of, the need for additional environmental studies subsequent to the approval of the EIS.

Since the key purpose of scoping is to identify the issues and alternatives for consideration, the scoping process should end once the issues and alternatives to be addressed in the EIS have been clearly identified. Normally this would occur during the final stages of preparing the draft EIS and before it is officially circulated for public and agency review.

The Council encourages the lead agency to notify the public of the results of the scoping process to ensure that all issues have been identified. The lead agency should document the results of the scoping process in its administrative record.

The NEPA regulations place a new and significant responsibility on agencies and the public alike during the scoping process to identify all significant issues and reasonable alternatives to be addressed in the EIS. Most significantly, the Council has found that scoping is an extremely valuable aid to better decision making. Thorough scoping may also have the effect of reducing the frequency with which proposed actions are challenged in court on the basis of an inadequate EIS. Through the techniques identified in this guidance, the lead agency will be able to document that an open public involvement process was conducted, that all reasonable alternatives were identified, that significant issues were identified and non-significant issues eliminated, and that the environmental public involvement requirements of all agencies were met, to the extent possible, in a single "one-stop" process.

Categorical Exclusions

Section 1507 of the CEQ regulations directs Federal agencies when establishing implementing procedures to identify those actions which experience has indicated will not have a significant environmental effect and to categorically exclude them from NEPA review. In our August 1981 request for public comments, we asked the question "Have categorical exclusions been adequately identified and defined?"

The responses the Council received indicated that there was considerable belief that categorical exclusions were not adequately identified and defined. A number of commentators indicated that agencies had not identified all categories of actions that meet the categorical exclusion definition (§1508.4) or that agencies were overly restrictive in their interpretations of categorical exclusions. Concerns were expressed that agencies were requiring too much documentation for projects that were not major Federal actions with significant effects and also that agency procedures to add categories of actions to their existing lists of categorical exclusions were too cumbersome.

The National Environmental Policy Act and the CEQ regulations are concerned primarily with those "major Federal actions significantly affecting the quality of the human environment" (42 U.S.C. 4332). Accordingly, agency procedures, resources, and efforts should focus on determining whether the proposed Federal action is a major Federal action significantly affecting the quality of the human environment. If the answer to this question is yes, an environmental impact statement must be prepared. If there is insufficient information to answer the question, an environmental assessment is needed to assist the agency in determining if the environmental impacts are significant and require an

EIS. If the assessment shows that the impacts are not significant, the agency must prepare a finding of no significant impact. Further stages of this Federal action may be excluded from requirements to prepare NEPA documents.

The CEQ regulations were issued in 1978 and most agency implementing regulations and procedures were issued shortly thereafter. In recognition of the experience with the NEPA process that agencies have had since the CEQ regulations were issued, the Council believes that it is appropriate for agencies to examine their procedures to insure that the NEPA process utilizes this additional knowledge and experience. Accordingly, the Council strongly encourages agencies to reexamine their environmental procedures and specifically those portions of the procedures where "categorical exclusions" are discussed to determine if revisions are appropriate. The specific issues which the Council is concerned about are (1) the use of detailed lists of specific activities for categorical exclusions, (2) the excessive use of environmental assessments/findings of no significant impact and (3) excessive documentation.

The Council has noted some agencies have developed lists of specific activities which qualify as categorical exclusions. The Council believes that if this approach is applied narrowly it will not provide the agency with sufficient flexibility to make decisions on a project-by-project basis with full consideration to the issues and impacts that are unique to a specific project. The Council encourages the agencies to consider broadly defined criteria which characterize types of actions that, based on the agency's experience, do not cause significant environmental effects. If this technique is adopted, it would be helpful for the agency to offer several examples of activities frequently performed by that agency's personnel which would normally fall in these categories. Agencies also need to consider whether the cumulative effects of several small actions would cause sufficient environmental impact to take the actions out of the categorically excluded class.

The Council also encourages agencies to examine the manner in which they use the environmental assessment process in relation to their process for identifying projects that meet the categorical exclusion definition. A report[1] to the Council indicated that some agencies have a very high ratio of findings of no significant impact to environmental assessments each year while producing only a handful of EISs. Agencies should examine their decision making process to ascertain if some of these actions do not, in fact, fall within the categorical exclusion definition, or, conversely, if they deserve full EIS treatment.

As previously noted, the Council received a number of comments that agencies require an excessive amount of environmental documentation for projects that meet the categorical exclusion definition. The Council believes that sufficient information will usually be available during the course of normal project development to determine the need for an EIS and, further, that the agency's administrative record will clearly document the basis for its decision. Accordingly, the Council strongly discourages procedures that would require the preparation of additional paperwork to document that an activity has been categorically excluded.

Categorical exclusions promulgated by an agency should be reviewed by the Council at the draft stage. After reviewing comments received during the review period and prior to publication in final form, the Council will determine whether the categorical exclusions are consistent with the NEPA regulations.

Adoption Procedures

During the recent effort undertaken by the Council to review the current NEPA regulations, several participants indicated Federal agencies were not utilizing the adoption procedures as authorized by the CEQ regulations. The concept of adoption was incorporated into the Council's NEPA Regulations (40 CFR 1506.3) to reduce duplicative EISs prepared by Federal agencies. The experiences gained during the 1970s revealed situations in which two or more agencies had an action relating to the same project;

---

[1] Environmental Law Institute, NEPA In Action Environmental Offices in Nineteen Federal Agencies, A Report To the Council on Environmental Quality, October 1981.

however, the timing of the actions was different. In the early years of NEPA implementation, agencies independently approached their activities and decisions. This procedure lent itself to two or even three EISs on the same project. In response to this situation the CEQ regulations authorized agencies, in certain instances, to adopt environmental impact statements prepared by other agencies.

In general terms, the regulations recognize three possible situations in which adoption is appropriate. One is where the Federal agency participated in the process as a cooperating agency (40 CFR 1506.3(c)). In this case, the cooperating agency may adopt a final EIS and simply issue its record of decision.[2] However, the cooperating agency must independently review the EIS and determine that its own NEPA procedures have been satisfied.

A second case concerns the Federal agency which was not a cooperating agency, but is, nevertheless, undertaking an activity which was the subject of an EIS. (40 CFR 1506.3(b)). This situation would arise because an agency did not anticipate that it would be involved in a project which was the subject of another agency's EIS. In this instance, where the proposed action is substantially the same as that action described in the EIS, the agency may adopt the EIS and recirculate (file with EPA and distribute to agencies and the public) it as a final EIS. However, the agency must independently review the EIS to determine that it is current and that its own NEPA procedures have been satisfied. When recirculating the final EIS the agency should provide information which identifies what Federal action is involved.

The third situation is one in which the proposed action is not substantially the same as that covered by the EIS. In this case, any agency may adopt an EIS or a portion thereof by circulating the EIS as a draft or as a portion of the agency's draft and preparing a final EIS (40 CFR 1506.3(a)). Repetitious analysis and time consuming data collection can be easily eliminated utilizing this procedure.

The CEQ regulations specifically address the question of adoption only in terms of preparing EISs. However, the objectives that underlie this portion of the regulations—i.e., reducing delays and eliminating duplication—apply with equal force to the issue of adopting other environmental documents. Consequently, the Council encourages agencies to put in place a mechanism for adopting environmental assessments prepared by other agencies. Under such procedures the agency could adopt the environmental assessment and prepare a Finding of No Significant Impact based on that assessment. In doing so, the agency should be guided by several principles:
  - First, when an agency adopts such an analysis it must independently evaluate the information contained therein and take full responsibility for its scope and content.
  - Second, if the proposed action meets the criteria set out in 40 CFR 1501.4(e)(2), a Finding of No Significant Impact would be published for 30 days of public review before a final determination is made by the agency on whether to prepare an environmental impact statement.

Contracting Provisions

Section 1506.5(c) of the NEPA regulations contains the basic rules for agencies which choose to have an environmental impact statement prepared by a contractor. That section requires the lead or cooperating agency to select the contractor, to furnish guidance and to participate in the preparation of the environmental impact statement. The regulation requires contractors who are employed to prepare an environmental impact statement to sign a disclosure statement stating that they have no financial or other interest in the outcome of the project. The responsible Federal official must independently evaluate the statement prior to its approval and take responsibility for its scope and contents.

During the recent evaluation of comments regarding agency implementation of the NEPA process, the Council became aware of confusion and criticism about the provisions of Section 1506.5(c). It appears that a great deal of misunderstanding exists regarding the interpretation of the conflict of interest

---

[2] Records of decision must be prepared by each agency responsible for making a decision, and cannot be adopted by another agency.

provision. There is also some feeling that the conflict of interest provision should be completely eliminated.[3]

Applicability of §1506.5(c)

This provision is only applicable when a Federal lead agency determines that it needs contractor assistance in preparing an EIS. Under such circumstances, the lead agency or a cooperating agency should select the contractor to prepare the EIS.[4]

This provision does not apply when the lead agency is preparing the EIS based on information provided by a private applicant. In this situation, the private applicant can obtain its information from any source. Such sources could include a contractor hired by the private applicant to do environmental, engineering, or other studies necessary to provide sufficient information to the lead agency to prepare an EIS. The agency must independently evaluate the information and is responsible for its accuracy.

Conflict of Interest Provisions

The purpose of the disclosure statement requirement is to avoid situations in which the contractor preparing the environmental impact statement has an interest in the outcome of the proposal. Avoidance of this situation should, in the Council's opinion, ensure a better and more defensible statement for the Federal agencies. This requirement also serves to assure the public that the analysis in the environmental impact statement has been prepared free of subjective, self-serving research and analysis.

Some persons believe these restrictions are motivated by undue and unwarranted suspicion about the bias of contractors. The Council is aware that many contractors would conduct their studies in a professional and unbiased manner. However, the Council has the responsibility of overseeing the administration of the National Environmental Policy Act in a manner most consistent with the statute's directives and the public's expectations of sound government. The legal responsibilities for carrying out NEPA's objectives rest solely with Federal agencies. Thus, if any delegation of work is to occur, it should be arranged to be performed in as objective a manner as possible.

Preparation of environmental impact statements by parties who would suffer financial losses if, for example, a "no action" alternative were selected, could easily lead to a public perception of bias. It is important to maintain the public's faith in the integrity of the EIS process, and avoidance of conflicts in the preparation of environmental impact statements is an important means of achieving this goal. The Council has discovered that some agencies have been interpreting the conflicts provision in an overly burdensome manner. In some instances, multidisciplinary firms are being excluded from environmental impact statements preparation contracts because of links to a parent company which has design and/or construction capabilities. Some qualified contractors are not bidding on environmental impact statement contracts because of fears that their firm may be excluded from future design or construction contracts. Agencies have also applied the selection and disclosure provisions to project proponents who wish to have their own contractor for providing environmental information. The result of these misunderstandings has been reduced competition in bidding for EIS preparation contracts, unnecessary delays in selecting a contractor and preparing the EIS, and confusion and resentment about the requirement. The Council believes that a better understanding of the scope of §1506.5(c) by agencies, contractors and project proponents will eliminate these problems.

---

[3] The Council also received requests for guidance on effective management of the third-party environmental impact statement approach. However, the Council determined that further study regarding the policies behind this technique is warranted, and plans to undertake that task in the future.

[4] There is no bar against the agency considering candidates suggested by the applicant, although the Federal agency must retain its independence. If the applicant is seen as having a major role in the selection of the contractor, contractors may feel the need to please both the agency and the applicant. An applicant's suggestion, if any, to the agency regarding the choice of contractors should be one of many factors involved in the selection process.

Section 1506.5(c) prohibits a person or entity entering into a contract with a Federal agency to prepare an EIS when that party has at that time and during the life of the contract pecuniary or other interests in the outcomes of the proposal. Thus, a firm which has an agreement to prepare an EIS for a construction project cannot, at the same time, have an agreement to perform the construction, nor could it be the owner of the construction site. However, if there are no such separate interests or arrangements, and if the contract for EIS preparation does not contain any incentive clauses or guarantees of any future work on the project, it is doubtful that an inherent conflict of interest will exist. Further, §1506.5(c) does not prevent an applicant from submitting information to an agency. The lead Federal agency should evaluate potential conflicts of interest prior to entering into any contract for the preparation of environmental documents.

Selection of Alternatives in Licensing and Permitting Situations

Numerous comments have been received questioning an agency's obligation, under the National Environmental Policy Act, to evaluate alternatives to a proposed action developed by an applicant for a Federal permit or license. This concern arises from a belief that projects conceived and developed by private parties should not be questioned or second-guessed by the government. There has been discussion of developing two standards to determining the range of alternatives to be evaluated: The "traditional" standard for projects which are initiated and developed by a Federal agency, and a second standard of evaluating only those alternatives presented by an applicant for a permit or license.

Neither NEPA nor the CEQ regulations make a distinction between actions initiated by a Federal agency and by applicants. Early NEPA case law, while emphasizing the need for a rigorous examination of alternatives, did not specifically address this issue. In 1981, the Council addressed the question in its document, "Forty Most Asked Questions Concerning CEQ's National Environmental Policy Act Regulations."[5] The answer indicated that the emphasis in determining the scope of alternatives should be on what is "reasonable". The Council said that, "reasonable alternatives include those that are practical or feasible from the technical and economic standpoint and using common sense rather than simply desirable from the standpoint of the applicant."

Since issuance of that guidance, the Council has continued to receive requests for further clarification of this question. Additional interest has been generated by a recent appellate court decision. *Roosevelt Campobello International Park Commission v. E.P.A.*[6] dealt with EPA's decision of whether to grant a permit under the National Pollutant Discharge Elimination System to a company proposing a refinery and deep-water terminal in Maine. The court discussed both the criteria used by EPA in its selecting of alternative sites to evaluate, and the substantive standard used to evaluate the sites. The court determined that EPA's choice of alternative sites was "focused by the primary objectives of the permit applicant ..." and that EPA had limited its consideration of sites to only those sites which were considered feasible, given the applicant's stated goals. The court found that EPA's criteria for selection of alternative sites was sufficient to meet its NEPA responsibilities.

This decision is in keeping with the concept that an agency's responsibilities to examine alternative sites has always been "bounded by some notion of feasibility" to avoid NEPA from becoming "an exercise in frivolous boilerplate."[7] NEPA has never been interpreted to require examination of purely conjectural possibilities whose implementation is deemed remote and speculative. Rather, the agency's duty is to consider "alternatives as they exist and are likely to exist."[8] In the Roosevelt Campobello case, for example, EPA examined three alternative sites and two alternative modifications of the project at the

---

[5] 46 FR 18026 (1981).

[6] 684 F.2d 1041 (lst Cir. 1982).

[7] *Vermont Yankee Nuclear Power Corp. v. NRDC*, 435 U.S. 519,551 (1978).

[8] *Monarch Chemical Works, Inc. v. Exon*, 466 F.Supp. 639,650 (1979), quoting *Carolina Environmental Study Group v. U.S.*, 510 F.2d 796,801(1975).

preferred alternative site. Other factors to be developed during the scoping process—comments received from the public, other government agencies and institutions, and development of the agency's own environmental data—should certainly be incorporated into the decision of which alternatives to seriously evaluate in the EIS. There is, however, no need to disregard the applicant's purposes and needs and the common sense realities of a given situation in the development of alternatives.

Tiering

Tiering of environmental impact statements refers to the process of addressing a broad, general program, policy or proposal in an initial environmental impact statement (EIS), and analyzing a narrower site-specific proposal, related to the initial program, plan or policy in a subsequent EIS. The concept of tiering was promulgated in the 1978 CEQ regulations: the preceding CEQ guidelines had not addressed the concept. The Council's intent in formalizing the tiering concept was to encourage agencies, "to eliminate repetitive discussions and to focus on the actual issues ripe for decisions at each level of environmental review."[9]

Despite these intentions, the Council perceives that the concept of tiering has caused a certain amount of confusion and uncertainty among individuals involved in the NEPA process. This confusion is by no means universal; indeed, approximately half of those commenting in response to our question about tiering[10] indicated that tiering is effective and should be used more frequently. Approximately one-third of the commentators responded that they had no experience with tiering upon which to base their comments. The remaining commentators were critical of tiering. Some commentators believed that tiering added an additional layer of paperwork to the process and encouraged, rather than discouraged, duplication. Some commentators thought that the inclusion of tiering in the CEQ regulations added an extra legal requirement to the NEPA process. Other commentators said that an initial EIS could be prepared when issues were too broad to analyze properly for any meaningful consideration. Some commentators believed that the concept was simply not applicable to the types of projects with which they worked; others were concerned about the need to supplement a tiered EIS. Finally, some who responded to our inquiry questioned the courts' acceptance of tiered EIS(s).

The Council believes that misunderstanding of tiering and its place in the NEPA process is the cause of much of this criticism. Tiering, of course, is by no means the best way to handle all proposals which are subject to NEPA analysis and documentation. The regulations do not require tiering; rather, they authorize its use when an agency determines it is appropriate. It is an option for an agency to use when the nature of the proposal lends itself to tiered EIS(s).

Tiering does not add an additional legal requirement to the NEPA process. An environmental impact statement is required for proposals for legislation and other major Federal actions significantly affecting the quality of the human environment. In the context of NEPA, "major Federal actions" include adoption of official policy, formal plans, and programs as well as approval of specific projects, such as construction activities in a particular location or approval of permits to an outside applicant. Thus, where a Federal agency adopts a formal plan which will be executed throughout a particular region, and later proposes a specific activity to implement that plan in the same region, both actions need to be analyzed under NEPA to determine whether they are major actions which will significantly affect the environment. If the answer is yes in both cases, both actions will be subject to the EIS requirement, whether tiering is used or not. The agency then has one of two alternatives: either preparation of two environmental impact statements, with the second repeating much of the analysis and information found in the first environmental impact statement, or tiering the two documents. If tiering is utilized, the site-specific EIS contains a summary of the issues discussed in the first statement and the agency will incorporate by reference discussions from the first statement. Thus, the second, or site-specific statement, would focus

---

[9] Preamble, FR, Vol. 43, No. 230, p.55984, 11/29/78.

[10] "Is tiering being used to minimize repetition in an environmental assessment and in environmental impact statements?", 46 FR 41131, August 14, 1981.

primarily on the issues relevant to the specific proposal, and would not duplicate material found in the first EIS. It is difficult to understand, given this scenario, how tiering can be criticized for adding an unnecessary layer to the NEPA process; rather, it is intended to streamline the existing process.

The Council agrees with commentators who stated that there are stages in the development of a proposal for a program, plan or policy when the issues are too broad to lend themselves to meaningful analysis in the framework of an EIS. The CEQ regulations specifically define a "proposal" as existing at, "that stage in the development of an action when an agency subject to [NEPA] has a goal and is actively preparing to make a decision on one or more alterative means of accomplishing the goal and the effects can be meaningfully evaluated."[11] Tiering is not intended to force an agency to prepare an EIS before this stage is reached; rather, it is a technique to be used once meaningful analysis can be performed. An EIS is not required before that stage in the development of a proposal whether tiering is used or not.

The Council also realizes that tiering is not well suited to all agency programs. Again, this is why tiering has been established as an option for the agency to use, as opposed to a requirement.

A supplemental EIS is required when an agency makes substantial changes in the proposed action relevant to environmental concerns, or when there are significant new circumstances or information relevant to environmental concerns bearing on the proposed action, and is optional when an agency otherwise determines to supplement an EIS.[12] The standard for supplementing an EIS is not changed by the use of tiering; there will no doubt be occasions when a supplement is needed, but the use of tiering should reduce the number of those occasions.

Finally, some commentators raised the question of courts' acceptability of tiering. This concern is understandable, given several cases which have reversed agency decisions in regard to particular programmatic EIS. However, these decisions have never invalidated the concept of tiering, as stated in the CEQ regulations and discussed above. Indeed, the courts recognized the usefulness of the tiering approach in case law before the promulgation of the tiering regulation. Rather, the problems appear when an agency determines not to prepare a site-specific EIS based on the fact that a programmatic EIS was prepared. In this situation, the courts carefully examine the analysis contained in the programmatic EIS. A court may or may not find that the programmatic EIS contains appropriate analysis of impacts and alternatives to meet the adequacy test for the site-specific proposal. A recent decision by the Ninth Circuit Court of Appeals[13] invalidated an attempt by the Forest Service to make a determination regarding wilderness and non-wilderness designations on the basis of a programmatic EIS for this reason. However, it should be stressed that this and other decisions are not a repudiation of the tiering concept. In these instances, in fact, tiering has not been used; rather, the agencies have attempted to rely exclusively on programmatic or "first level" EIS(s) which did not have site-specific information. No court has found that the tiering process as provided for in the CEQ regulations is an improper manner of implementing the NEPA process.

In summary, the Council believes that tiering can be a useful method of reducing paperwork and duplication when used carefully for appropriate types of plans, programs and policies which will later be translated into site-specific projects. Tiering should not be viewed as an additional substantive requirement, but rather a means of accomplishing the NEPA requirements in as efficient a manner as possible.

---

[11] 40 CFR 1508.23 (emphasis added).

[12] 40 CFR 1502.9(c).

[13] *California v. Block*, 18 ERC 1149 (1982). [FR Doc. 83-20522 Filed 7-27-83 8:45 am]

CEQ 1981 MEMORANDUM, SCOPING GUIDANCE

MEMORANDUM: SCOPING GUIDANCE

(Council on Environmental Quality Apr. 30,1981)

I. Introduction

A. Background of this document

In 1978, with the publication of the proposed NEPA regulations (since adopted as formal rules, 40 C.F.R. Parts 1500-1508), the Council on Environmental Quality gave formal recognition to an increasingly used term—scoping. Scoping is an idea that has long been familiar to those involved in NEPA compliance: in order to manage effectively the preparation of an environmental impact statement (EIS), one must determine the scope of the document—that is, what will be covered, and in what detail. Planning of this kind was a normal component of EIS preparation. But the consideration of issues and choice of alternatives to be examined was, in too many cases, completed outside of public view. The innovative approach to scoping in the regulations is that the process is open to the public and State and local governments, as well as to affected Federal agencies. This open process gives rise to important new opportunities for better and more efficient NEPA analyses, and simultaneously places new responsibilities on public and agency participants alike to surface their concerns early. Scoping helps insure that real problems are identified early and properly studied; that issues that are of no concern do not consume time and effort; that the draft statement when first made public is balanced and thorough; and that the delays occasioned by re-doing an inadequate draft are avoided. Scoping does not create problems that did not already exist; it ensures that problems that would have been raised anyway are identified early in the process.

Many members of the public as well as agency staffs engaged in the NEPA process have told the Council that the open scoping requirement is one of the most far-reaching changes engendered by the NEPA regulations. They have predicted that scoping could have a profound positive effect on environmental analyses, on the impact statement process itself, and ultimately on decision making.

Because the concept of open scoping was new, the Council decided to encourage agencies' innovation without unduly restrictive guidance. Thus, the regulations relating to scoping are very simple. They state that "there shall be an early and open process for determining the scope of issues to be addressed" which "shall be termed scoping," but they lay down few specific requirements (section 1501.7[14]). They require an open process with public notice; identification of significant and insignificant issues; allocation of EIS preparation assignments; identification of related analysis requirements in order to avoid duplication of work and the planning of a schedule for EIS preparation that meshes with the agency's decision making schedule. (section 1501.7(a)). The regulations encourage, but do not require, setting time limits and page limits for the EIS, and holding scoping meetings (section 1501.7(b)). Aside from these general outlines, the regulations left the agencies on their own. The Council did not believe, and still does not, that it is necessary or appropriate to dictate the specific manner in which over 100 Federal agencies should deal with the public. However, the Council has received several requests for more guidance. In 1980 we decided to investigate the agency and public response to the scoping requirement, to find out what was working and what was not, and to share this with all agencies and the public.

The Council first conducted its own survey, asking Federal agencies to report some of their scoping experiences. The Council then contracted with the American Arbitration Association and Clark McGlennon Associates to survey the scoping techniques of major agencies and to study several

---

[14] All citations are to be the NEPA regulations, 40 C.F.R. Parts 1500-1508 unless otherwise specified.

innovative methods in detail.[15] Council staff conducted a two-day workshop in Atlanta in June 1980, to discuss with Federal agency NEPA staff and several EIS contractors what seems to work best in scoping of different types of proposals, and discussed scoping with Federal, State and local officials in meetings in all 10 Federal regions.

This document is a distillation of all the work that has been done so far by many people to identify valuable scoping techniques. It is offered as a guide to encourage success and to help avoid pitfalls. Since scoping methods are still evolving, the Council welcomes any comments on this guide, and may add to it or revise it in coming years.

B. What scoping is and what it can do

Scoping is often the first contact between proponents of a proposal and the public. This fact is the source of the power of scoping and of the trepidation that it sometimes evokes. If a scoping meeting is held, people on both sides of an issue will be in the same room and, if all goes well, will speak to each other. The possibilities that flow from this situation are vast. Therefore, a large portion of this document is devoted to the productive management of meetings and the de-fusing of possible heated disagreements.

Even if a meeting is not held, the scoping process leads EIS preparers to think about the proposal early on, in order to explain it to the public and affected agencies. The participants respond with their own concerns about significant issues and suggestions of alternatives. Thus, as the draft EIS is prepared, it will include, from the beginning, a reflection or at least an acknowledgment of the cooperating agencies' and the public's concerns. This reduces the need for changes after the draft is finished, because it reduces the chances of overlooking a significant issue or reasonable alternative. It also in many cases increases public confidence in NEPA and the decision making process, thereby reducing delays, such as from litigation, later on when implementing the decisions. As we will discuss further in this document, the public generally responds positively when its views are taken seriously, even if they cannot be wholly accommodated.

But scoping is not simply another "public relations" meeting requirement. It has specific and fairly limited objectives: (a) to identify the affected public and agency concerns; (b) to facilitate an efficient EIS preparation process, through assembling the cooperating agencies, assigning EIS writing tasks, ascertaining all the related permits and reviews that must be scheduled concurrently, and setting time or page limits; (c) to define the issues and alternatives that will be examined in detail in the EIS, while simultaneously devoting less attention and time to issues which cause no concern; and (d) to save time in the overall process by helping to ensure that draft statements adequately address relevant issues, reducing the possibility that new comments will cause a statement to be rewritten or supplemented.

Sometimes the scoping process enables early identification of a few serious problems with a proposal, which can be changed or solved because the proposal is still being developed. In these cases, scoping the EIS can actually lead to the solution of a conflict over the proposed action itself. We have found that this extra benefit of scoping occurs fairly frequently. But it cannot be expected in most cases, and scoping can still be considered successful when conflicts are clarified but not solved. This guide does not presume that resolution of conflicts over proposals is a principal goal of scoping, because it is only possible in limited circumstances. Instead, the Council views the principal goal of scoping to be an adequate and efficiently prepared EIS. Our suggestions and recommendations are aimed at reducing the conflicts among affected interests that impede this limited objective. But we are aware of the possibilities of more general conflict resolution that are inherent in any productive discussions among interested parties. We urge all participants in scoping processes to be alert to this larger context, in which scoping could prove to be the first step in environmental problem solving.

---

[15] The results of this examination are reported in "Scoping the Content of EISs: An Evaluation of Agencies' Experiences," which is available from the Council or the Resource Planning Analysis Offices of the U.S. Geological Survey, 750 National Center, Reston, Va. 22092.

Scoping can lay a firm foundation for the rest of the decision making process. If the EIS can be relied upon to include all the necessary information for formulating policies and making rational choices, the agency will be better able to make a sound and prompt decision. In addition, if it is clear that all reasonable alternatives are being seriously considered, the public will usually be more satisfied with the choice among them.

II. Advice for Government Agencies Conducting Scoping

A. General context

Scoping is a process, not an event or a meeting. It continues throughout the planning for an EIS, and may involve a series of meetings, telephone conversations, or written comments from different interested groups. Because it is a process, participants must remain flexible. The scope of an EIS occasionally may need to be modified later if a new issue surfaces, no matter how thorough the scoping was. But it makes sense to try to set the scope of the statement as early as possible.

Scoping may identify people who already have knowledge about a site or an alternative proposal or a relevant study, and induce them to make it available. This can save a lot of research time and money. But people will not come forward unless they believe their views and materials will receive serious consideration. Thus, scoping is a crucial first step toward building public confidence in a fair environmental analysis and ultimately a fair decision making process.

One further point to remember: the lead agency cannot shed its responsibility to assess each significant impact or alternative even if one is found after scoping. But anyone who hangs back and fails to raise something that reasonably could have been raised earlier on will have a hard time prevailing during later stages of the NEPA process or if litigation ensues. Thus, a thorough scoping process does provide some protection against subsequent lawsuits.

B. Step-by-step through the process

1. Start scoping after you have enough information

Scoping cannot be useful until the agency knows enough about the proposed action to identify most of the affected parties, and to present a coherent proposal and a suggested initial list of environmental issues and alternatives. Until that time, there is no way to explain to the public or other agencies what you want them to get involved in. So, the first stage is to gather preliminary information from the applicant, or to compose a clear picture of your proposal, if it is being developed by the agency.

2. Prepare an information packet

In many cases, scoping of the EIS has been preceded by preparation of an environmental assessment (EA) as the basis for the decision to proceed with an EIS. In such cases, the EA will, of course, include the preliminary information that is needed.

If you have not prepared an EA, you should put together a brief information packet consisting of a description of the proposal, an initial list of impacts and alternatives, maps, drawings, and any other material or references that can help the interested public to understand what is being proposed. The proposed work plan of the EIS is not usually sufficient for this purpose. Such documents rarely contain a description of the goals of the proposal to enable readers to develop alternatives.

At this stage, the purpose of the information is to enable participants to make an intelligent contribution to scoping the EIS. Because they will be helping to plan what will be examined during the environmental review, they need to know where you are now in that planning process.

Include in the packet a brief explanation of what scoping is and what procedure will be used, to give potential participants a context for their involvement. Be sure to point out that you want comments from participants on very specific matters. Also reiterate that no decision has yet been made on the contents of the EIS, much less on the proposal itself. Thus, explain that you do not yet have a preferred alternative, but that you may identify the preferred alternative in the draft EIS. See Section 1502.14(e)). This should reduce the tendency of participants to perceive the proposal as already a definite plan. Encourage them to focus on recommendations for improvements to the various alternatives.

Some of the complaints alleging that scoping can be a waste of time stem from the fact that the participants may not know what the proposal is until they arrive at a meeting. Even the most intelligent among us can rarely make useful, substantive comments on the spur of the moment. Don't expect helpful suggestions to result if participants are put in such a position.

3. Design the scoping process for each project

There is no established or required procedure for scoping. The process can be carved out by meetings, telephone conversations, written comments, or a combination of all three. It is important to tailor the type, the timing and the location of public and agency comments to the proposal at hand.

For example, a proposal to adopt a land management plan for a National Forest in a sparsely populated region may not lend itself to calling a single meeting in a central location. While people living in the area and elsewhere may be interested, any meeting place will be inconvenient for most of the potential participants. One solution is to distribute the information packet, solicit written comments, list a telephone number with the name of the scoping coordinator, and invite comments to be phoned in. Otherwise, small meetings in several locations may be necessary when face-to-face communications is important.

In another case, a site-specific construction project may be proposed. This would be a better candidate for a central scoping meeting. But you must first find out if anyone would be interested in attending such a meeting. If you simply assume that a meeting is necessary, you may hire a hall and a stenographer, assemble your staff for a meeting, and find that nobody shows up.

There are many proposals that just do not generate sufficient public interest to cause people to attend another public meeting. So a wise early step is to contact known local citizens groups and civic leaders.

In addition, you may suggest in your initial scoping notice and information packet that all those who desire a meeting should call to request one. That way you will only hear from those who are seriously interested in attending.

The question of where to hold a meeting is a difficult one in many cases. Except for site-specific construction projects, it may be unclear where the interested parties can be found. For example, an EIS on a major energy development program may involve policy issues and alternatives to the program that are of interest to public groups all over the nation, and to agencies headquartered in Washington, D.C., while the physical impacts might be expected to be felt most strongly in a particular region of the country. In such a case, if personal contact is desired, several meetings would be necessary, especially in the affected region and in Washington, to enable all interests to be heard.

As a general guide, unless a proposal has no site specific impacts, scoping meetings should not be confined to Washington. Agencies should try to elicit the views of people who are closer to the affected regions.

The key is to be flexible. It may not be possible to plan the whole scoping process at the outset unless you know who all the potential players are. You can start with written comments, move on to an informal meeting, and hold further meetings if desired.

There are several reasons to hold a scoping meeting. First, some of the best effects of scoping stem from the fact that all parties have the opportunity to meet one another and to listen to the concerns of the others. There is no satisfactory substitute for personal contact to achieve this result. If there is any possibility that resolution of underlying conflicts over a proposal may be achieved, this is always enhanced by the development of personal and working relationships among the parties.

Second, even in a conflict situation people usually respond positively when they are treated as partners in the project review process. If they feel confident that their views were actually heard and taken seriously, they will be more likely to be satisfied that the decision making process was fair even if they disagree with the outcome. It is much easier to show people that you are listening to them if you hold a face-to-face meeting where they can see you writing down their points, than if their only contact is through written comments.

If you suspect that a particular proposal could benefit from a meeting with the affected public at any time during its review, the best time to have the meeting is during this early scoping stage. The fact that you are willing to discuss openly a proposal before you have committed substantial resources to it will often enhance the chances for reaching an accord.

If you decide that a public meeting is appropriate, you still must decide what type of meeting, or how many meetings, to hold. We will discuss meetings in detail below in "Conducting a Public Meeting". But as part of designing the scoping process, you must decide between a single meeting and multiple ones for different interest groups, and whether to hold a separate meeting for government agency participants.

The single large public meeting brings together all the interested parties, which has both advantages and disadvantages. If the meeting is efficiently run, a lot of interests and issues can be covered in a short time. And a single meeting does reduce agency travel time and expense. In some cases, it may be an advantage to have all interested groups hear each others' concerns, possibly promoting compromise. It is definitely important to have the staffs of the cooperating agencies, as we have the lead agency, hear the public views of what the significant issues are, and it will be difficult and expensive for the cooperating agencies to attend several meetings. But if there are opposing groups of citizens who feel strongly on both sides of an issue, the setting of the large meeting may needlessly create tension and an emotional confrontation between the groups. Moreover, some people may feel intimidated in such a setting, and won't express themselves at all.

The principal drawback of the large meeting is that it is generally unwieldy. To keep order, discussion is limited, dialogue is difficult, and often all participants are frustrated—agency and public alike. Large meetings can serve to identify the interest groups for future discussion, but often little else is accomplished. Large meetings often become "events" where grandstanding substitutes for substantive comments. Many agencies resort to a formal hearing-type format to maintain control, and this can cause resentments among participants who come to the meeting expecting a responsive discussion.

For these reasons, we recommend that meetings be kept small and informal, and that you hold several, if necessary, to accommodate the different interest groups. The other solution is to break a large gathering into small discussion groups, which is discussed below. Using either method increases the likelihood that participants will level with you and communicate their underlying concerns, rather than make an emotional statement just for effect.

Moreover, in our experience, a separate meeting for cooperating agencies is quite productive. Working relationships can be forged for the effective participation of all involved in the preparation of the EIS. Work assignments are made by the lead agency, a schedule may be set for production of parts of the draft EIS, and information gaps can be identified early. But a productive meeting such as this is not possible at the very beginning of the process. It can only result from the same sort of planning and preparation that goes into the public meetings. We discuss below the special problems of cooperating agencies, and their information needs for effective participation in scoping.

4. Issuing the public notice

The preliminary look at the proposal, in which you develop the information packet discussed above, will enable you to tell what kind of public notice will be most appropriate and effective.

Section 1501.7 of the NEPA regulations requires that a notice of intent to prepare an EIS must be published in the *Federal Register* prior to initiating scoping.[16] This means that one of the appropriate means of giving public notice of the upcoming scoping process could be the same *Federal Register* notice. And because the notice of intent must be published anyway, the scoping notice would be essential if free. But use of the *Federal Register* is not an absolute requirement, and other means of public notice often are more effective, including local newspapers, radio and TV, posting notices in public places, etc. (See Section 1506.6 of the regulations.)

What is important is that the notice actually reach the affected public. If the proposal is an important new national policy in which national environmental groups can be expected to be interested, these groups can be contacted by form letter with ease. (See the Conservation Directory for a list of national groups.[17]) Similarly, for proposals that may have major implications for the business community, trade associations can be helpful means of alerting affected groups. The *Federal Register* notice can be relied upon to notify others that you did not know about. But the *Federal Register* is of little use for reaching individuals or local groups interested in a site-specific proposal. Therefore, notices in local papers, letters to local government officials and personal contact with a few known interested individuals would be more appropriate. Land owners abutting any proposed project site should be notified individually.

Remember that issuing press releases to newspapers, and radio and TV stations is not enough, because they may not be used by the media unless the proposal is considered "newsworthy." If the proposal is controversial, you can try alerting reporters or editors to an upcoming scoping meeting for coverage in special weekend sections used by many papers. But placing a notice in the legal notices section of the paper is the only guarantee that it will be published.

5. Conducting a public meeting

In our study of agency practice in conducting scoping, the most interesting information on what works and doesn't work involves the conduct of meetings. Innovative techniques have been developed, and experience shows that these can be successful.

One of the most important factors turns out to be the training and experience of the moderator. The U.S. Office of Personnel Management and others give training courses on how to run a meeting effectively. Specific techniques are taught to keep the meeting on course and to deal with confrontations. These techniques are sometimes called "meeting facilitation skills."

When holding a meeting, the principle thing to remember about scoping is that it is a process to initiate preparation of an EIS. It is not concerned with the ultimate decision on the proposal. A fruitful scoping process leads to an adequate environmental analysis, including all reasonable alternatives and

---

[16] Several agencies have found it useful to conduct scoping for environmental assessments. EAs are prepared where answering the question of whether an EIS is necessary requires identification of significant environmental issues; and consideration of alternatives in an EA can often be useful even where an EIS is not necessary. In both situations scoping can be valuable. Thus, the Council has stated that scoping may be used in connection with preparation of an EA; that is, before publishing any notice of intent to prepare an EIS, as in normal scoping, appropriate public notice is required, as well as adequate information on the proposal to make scoping worthwhile. But scoping at this early stage cannot substitute for the normal scoping process unless the earlier public notice stated clearly that this would be the case, and the notice of intent expressly provides that written comments suggesting impacts and alternatives for study will still be considered.

[17] The Conservation Directory is a publication of the National Wildlife Federation, 1421 16th St., N.W., Washington, D.C. 20036, $4.00.

mitigation measures. This limited goal is in the interest of all the participants, and thus offers the possibility of agreement by the parties on this much at least. To run a successful meeting you must keep the focus on this *positive* purpose.

At the point of scoping, therefore, in one sense all the parties involved have a common goal, which is a thorough environmental review. If you emphasize this in the meeting, you can stop any grandstanding speeches without a heavy hand by simply asking the speaker if he or she has any concrete suggestions for the group on issues to be covered in the EIS. By frequently drawing the meeting back to this central purpose of scoping, the opponents of a proposal will see that you have not already made a decision, and they will be forced to deal with the real issues. In addition, when people see that you are genuinely seeking their opinion, some will volunteer useful information about a particular subject or site that they may know better than anyone on your staff.

As we stated above, we found that informal meetings in small groups are the most satisfactory for eliciting useful issues and information. Small groups can be formed in two ways: you can invite different interest groups to different meetings, or you can break a large number into small groups for discussion.

One successful model is used by the Army Corps of Engineers, among others. In cases where a public meeting is desired, it is publicized and scheduled for a location that will be convenient for as many potential participants as possible. The information packet is made available in several ways: by sending it to those known to be interested, giving a telephone number in the public notices for use in requesting one, and providing more at the door of the meeting place as well. As participants enter the door, each is given a number. Participants are asked to register their name, address and/or telephone number for use in future contact during scoping and the rest of the NEPA process.

The first part of the meeting is devoted to a discussion of the proposal in general, covering its purpose, proposed location, design, and any other aspects that can be presented in a lecture format. A question and answer period concerning this information is often held at this time. Then, if there are more than 15 or 20 attendees at the meeting, the next step is to break it into small groups for more intensive discussion. At this point, the numbers held by the participants are used to assign them to small groups by sequence, random drawing, or any other method. Each group should be no larger than 12, and 8 to 10 is better. The groups are informed that their task is to prepare a list of significant environmental issues and reasonable alternatives for analysis in the EIS. These lists will be presented to the main group and combined into a master list after the discussion groups are finished. The rules for how priorities are to be assigned to the issues identified by each group should be made clear before the large group breaks up.

Some agencies ask each group member to vote for the 5 or 10 most important issues. After tallying the votes of individual members, each group would only report out those issues that received a certain number of votes; in this way, only those items of most concern to the members would even make the list compiled by each group. Some agencies go further, and only let each group report out the top few issues identified. But you must be careful not to ignore issues that may be considered a medium priority by many people. They may still be important, even if not in the top rank. Thus, instead of simply voting, the members of the groups should rank the listed issues in order of perceived importance. Points may be assigned to each item on the basis of the rankings by each member, so that the group can compile a list of its issues in priority order. Each group should then be asked to assign cut-off numbers to separate high, medium and low priority items. Each group should then report out to the main meeting all of its issues, but with priorities clearly assigned.

One member of the lead agency or cooperating agency staff should join each group to answer questions and to listen to the participants' expressions of concern. It has been the experience of many of those who have tried this method that it is better not to have the agency person lead the group discussions. There does need to be a leader who should be chosen by the group members. In this way, the agency staff member will not be perceived as forcing his opinions on the others.

If the agency has a sufficient staff of formally trained "meeting facilitators," they may be able to achieve the same result even where agency staff people lead the discussion groups. But absent such training, the staff should not lead the discussion groups. A good technique is to have the agency person serve as the recording secretary for the group, writing down each impact and alternative that is suggested for study by the participants. This enhances the neutral status of the agency representative, and ensures that he is perceived as listening and reacting to the views of the group. Frequently, the recording of issues is done with a large pad mounted on the wall like a blackboard, which has been well received by agency and public alike, because all can see that the views expressed actually have been heard and understood.

When the issues are listed, each must be clarified or combined with others to eliminate duplication or fuzzy concepts. The agency staff person can actually lead in this effort because of his need to reflect on paper exactly what the issues are. After the group has listed all the environmental impacts and alternatives and any other issues that the members wish to have considered, they are asked to discuss the relative merits and importance of each listed item. The group should be reminded that one of its tasks is to eliminate insignificant issues. Following this, the members assign priorities or vote using one of the methods described above.

The discussion groups are then to return to the large meeting to report on the results of their ranking. At this point, further discussion may be useful to seek a consensus on which issues are really insignificant. But the moderator must not appear to be ruthlessly eliminating issues that the participants ranked of high or medium importance. The best that can usually be achieved is to de-emphasize some of them by placing them in the low priority category.

6. What to do with the comments

After you have comments from the cooperating agencies and the interested public, you must evaluate them and make judgments about which issues are in fact significant and which ones are not. The decision of what the EIS should contain is ultimately made by the lead agency. But you will now know what the interested participants consider to be the principal areas for study and analysis. You should be guided by these concerns or be prepared to briefly explain why you do not agree. Every issue that is raised as a priority matter during scoping should be addressed in some manner in the EIS, either by in-depth analysis, or at least a short explanation showing that the issue was examined, but not considered significant for one or more reasons.

Some agencies have complained that the time savings claimed for scoping have not been realized because after public groups raise numerous minor matters, they cannot focus the EIS on the significant issues. It is true that it is always easier to add issues than it is to subtract them during scoping. And you should realize that trying to eliminate a particular environmental impact or alternative from study may arouse the suspicions of some people. Cooperating agencies may be even more reluctant to eliminate issues in their areas of special expertise than the public participants. But the way to approach it is to seek consensus on which issues are less important. These issues may then be de-emphasized in the EIS by a brief discussion of why they were not examined in depth.

If no consensus can be reached, it is still your responsibility to select the significant issues. The lead agency cannot abdicate its role and simply defer to the public. Thus, a group of participants at a scoping meeting should not be able to "vote" an insignificant matter into a big issue. If a certain issue is raised and, in your professional judgment, you believe it is not significant, explain clearly and briefly in the EIS why it is not significant. There is no need to devote time and pages to it in the EIS if you can show that it is not relevant or important to the proposed action. But you should address in some manner all matters that were raised in the scoping process, either by an extended analysis or a brief explanation showing that you acknowledge the concern.

Several agencies have made a practice of sending out a post-scoping document to make public the decisions that have been made on what issues to cover in the EIS. This is not a requirement, but in certain controversial cases it can be worthwhile. Especially when scoping has been conducted by written comments, and there has been no face-to-face contact, a post-scoping document is the only assurance to the participants that they were heard and understood until the draft EIS comes out. Agencies have acknowledged to us that "letters instead of meetings seem to get disregarded easier." Thus, a reasonable *quid pro quo* for relying on comment letters would be to send out a post-scoping document as feedback to the commentors.

The post-scoping document may be as brief as a list of impacts and alternatives selected for analysis. It may consist of the "scope of work" produced by the lead and cooperating agency for their own EIS work or for the contractor, or it may be a special document that describes all the issues and explains why they were selected.

7. Allocating work assignments and setting schedules

Following the public participation in whatever form, and the selection of issues to be covered, the lead agency must allocate the EIS preparation work among the available resources. If there are no cooperating agencies, the lead agency allocates work among its own personnel or contractors. If there are cooperating agencies involved, they may be assigned specific research or writing tasks. The NEPA regulations require that they normally devote their own resources to the issues in which they have special expertise or jurisdiction by law. (Sections 1501.6(b)(3), (5), and 1501.7(a)(4)).

In all cases, the lead agency should set a schedule for completion of the work, designate a project manager and assign the reviewers, and must set a time limit for the entire NEPA analysis if requested to do so by an applicant. (Section 1501.8).

8. A few ideas to try

a. Route design workshop

As part of a scoping process, a successful innovation by one agency involved route selection for a railroad. The agency invited representatives of the interested groups (identified at a previous public meeting) to try their hand at designing alternative routes for a proposed rail segment. Agency staff explained design constraints and evaluation criteria such as the desire to minimize damage to prime agricultural land and valuable wildlife habitat. The participants were divided into small groups for a few hours of intensive work. After learning of the real constraints on alternative routes, the participants had a better understanding of the agency's and applicant's viewpoints. Two of the participants actually supported alternative routes that affected their own land because the overall impacts of these routes appeared less adverse.

The participants were asked to rank the five alternatives they had devised and the top two were included in the EIS. But the agency did not permit the groups to apply the same evaluation criteria to the routes proposed by the applicant or the agency. Thus, public confidence in the process was not as high as it could have been, and probably was reduced when the applicant's proposal was ultimately selected.

The Council recommends that when a hands-on design workshop is used, the assignment of the group be expanded to include evaluation of the reasonableness of all the suggested alternatives.

b. Hotline

Several agencies have successfully used a special telephone number, essentially a hotline, to take public comments before, after, or instead of a public meeting. It helps to designate a named staff member to receive these calls so that some continuity and personal relationships can be developed.

c. Videotape of sites

A videotape of proposed sites is an excellent tool for explaining site differences and limitations during the lecture-format part of a scoping meeting.

d. Videotape meetings

One agency has videotaped whole scoping meetings. Staff found that the participants took their roles more seriously and the taping appeared not to precipitate grandstanding tactics.

e. Review committee

Success has been reported from one agency which sets up review committees, representing all interested groups, to oversee the scoping process. The committees help to design the scoping process. In cooperation with the lead agency, the committee reviews the materials generated by the scoping meeting. Again, however, the final decision on EIS content is the responsibility of the lead agency.

f. Consultant as meeting moderator

In some hotly contested cases, several agencies have used the EIS consultant to actually run the scoping meeting. This is permitted under the NEPA regulations and can be useful to defuse a tense atmosphere if the consultant is perceived as a neutral third party. But the responsible agency officials must attend the meetings. There is no substitute for developing a relationship between the agency officials and the affected parties. Moreover, if the responsible officials are not prominently present, the public may interpret that to mean that the consultant is actually making the decisions about the EIS, and not the lead agency.

g. Money saving tips

Remember that money can be saved by using conference calls instead of meetings, tape-recording the meetings instead of hiring a stenographer, and finding out whether people want a meeting before announcing it.

C. Pitfalls

We list here some of the problems that have been experienced in certain scoping cases in order to enable others to avoid the same difficulties.

1. Closed meetings

In response to informal advice from CEQ that holding separate meetings for agencies and the public would be permitted under the regulations and could be more productive, one agency scheduled a scoping meeting for the cooperating agencies some weeks in advance of the public meeting. Apparently, the lead agency felt that the views of the cooperating agencies would be more candidly expressed if the meeting were closed. In any event, several members of the public learned of the meeting and asked to be present. The lead agency acquiesced only after newspaper reporters were able to make a story out of the closed session. At the meeting, the members of the public were informed that they would not be allowed to speak, nor to record the proceedings. The ill feeling aroused by this chain of events may not be repaired for a long time. Instead, we would suggest the following possibilities:

a. Although separate meetings for agencies and public groups may be more efficient, there is no magic to them. By all means, if someone insists on attending the agency meeting, let him. There is nothing as secret going on there as he may think there is if you refuse him admittance. Better yet, have your meeting of cooperating agencies *after* the public meeting. That may be the most logical time anyway, since only then can the scope of the EIS be decided upon and assignments made among the agencies. If it is well done, the public meeting will satisfy most people and show them that you are listening to them.

b. Always permit recording. In fact, you should suggest it for public meetings. All parties will feel better if there is a record of the proceeding. There is no need for a stenographer, and tape is inexpensive. It may even be better then a typed transcript, because staff and decision makers who did not attend the meeting can listen to the exchange and may learn a lot about public perceptions of the proposal.

c. When people are admitted to a meeting, it makes no sense to refuse their requests to speak. However, you can legitimately limit their statements to the subject at hand—scoping. You do not have to permit some participants to waste the others' time if they refuse to focus on the impacts and alternatives for inclusion in the EIS. Having a tape of the proceedings could be useful after the meeting if there is some question that speakers were improperly silenced. But it takes an experienced moderator to handle a situation like this.

d. The scoping stage is the time for building confidence and trust on all sides of a proposal, because this is the only time when there is a common enterprise. The attitudes formed at this stage can carry through the project review process. Certainly, it is difficult for things to get better. So, foster the good will as long as you can by listening to what is being said during scoping. It is possible that out of that dialogue may appear recommendations for changes and mitigation measures that can turn a controversial fight into an acceptable proposal.

2. *Contacting interested groups*

Some problems have arisen in scoping where agencies failed to contact all the affected parties, such as industries or State and local governments. In one case, a panel was assembled to represent various interests in scoping an EIS on a wildlife-related program. The agency had an excellent format for the meeting, but the panel did not represent industries that would be affected by the program or interested State and local governments. As a result, the EIS may fail to reflect the issues of concern to these parties.

Another agency reported to us that it failed to contact parties directly, because staff feared that if they missed someone they would be accused of favoritism. Thus, they relied on the issuance of press releases, which were not effective. Many people who did not learn about the meetings in time sought additional meeting opportunities, which cost extra money and delayed the process.

In our experience, the attempt to reach people is worth the effort. Even if you miss someone, it will be clear that you tried. You can enlist a few representatives of an interest group to help you identify and contact others. Trade associations, chambers of commerce, local civic groups, and local and national conservation groups can spread the word to members.

3. *Tiering*

Many people are not familiar with the way environmental impact statements can be "tiered" under the NEPA regulations so that issues are examined in detail at the stage that decisions on them are being made. See Section 1508.28 of the regulations. For example, if a proposed program is under review, it is possible that site-specific actions are not yet proposed. In such a case, these actions are not addressed in the EIS on the program, but are reserved for a later tier of analysis. If tiering is being used, this concept must be made clear at the outset of any scoping meeting so that participants do not concentrate on issues that are not going to be addressed at this time. If you can specify when these other issues will be addressed, it will be easier to convince people to focus on the matters at hand.

4. Scoping for unusual programs

One interesting scoping case involved proposed changes in the Endangered Species Program. Among the impacts to be examined were the effects of this conservation program on user activities such as mining, hunting, and timber harvest, instead of the other way around. Because of this reverse twist in the impacts to be analyzed, some participants had difficulty focusing on useful issues. Apparently, if the subject of the EIS is unusual, it will be even harder than normal for scoping participants to grasp what is expected of them.

In the case of the Endangered Species Program EIS, the agency planned an intensive 3-day scoping session, successfully involved the participants, and reached accord on several issues that would be important for the future implementation of the program. But the participants were unable to focus on impacts and program alternatives for the EIS. We suggest that if the intensive session had been broken up into 2 or 3 meetings separated by days or weeks, the participants might have been able to get used to the new way of thinking required, and thereby participate more productively. Programmatic proposals are often harder to deal with in a scoping context than site-specific projects. Thus, extra care should be taken in explaining the goals of the proposal and making the information available well in advance of any meetings.

D. Lead and Cooperating Agencies

Some problems with scoping revolve around the relationship between lead and cooperating agencies. Some agencies are still uncomfortable with these roles. The NEPA regulations, and the *40 Questions and Answers about the NEPA Regulations*, 46 Fed. Reg. 18026, (March 23, 1981) describe in detail the way agencies are now asked to cooperate on environmental analyses. (See Questions 9, 14, and 30.) We will focus here on the early phase of that cooperation.

It is important for the lead agency to be as specific as possible with the cooperating agencies. Tell them what you want them to contribute during scoping: environmental impacts and alternatives. Some agencies still do not understand the purpose of scoping.

Be sure to contact and involve representatives of the cooperating agencies who are responsible for NEPA-related functions. The lead agency will need to contact staff of the cooperating agencies who can both help to identify issues and alternatives and commit resources to a study, agree to a schedule for EIS preparation, or approve a list of issues as sufficient. In some agencies, that will be at the district or State office level (e.g., Corps of Engineers, Bureau of Land Management, and Soil Conservation Service) for all but exceptional cases; in other agencies you must go to regional offices for scoping comments and commitments (e.g., EPA, Fish and Wildlife Service, Water and Power Resources Service). In still others, the field offices do not have NEPA responsibilities or expertise and you will deal directly with headquarters (e.g., Federal Energy Regulatory Commission, Interstate Commerce Commission). In all cases, you are looking for the office that can give you the answers you need. So, keep trying until you find the organizational level of the cooperating agency that can give you useful information and that has the authority to make commitments.

As stated in *40 Questions and Answers about the NEPA Regulations*, the lead agency has the ultimate responsibility for the content of the EIS, but if it leaves out a significant issue or ignores the advice and expertise of the cooperating agency, the EIS may be found later to be inadequate (46 Fed. Reg. 18030, Questions 14b.) At the same time, the cooperating agency will be concerned that the EIS contain material sufficient to satisfy its decision making needs. Thus, both agencies have a stake in producing a document of good quality. The cooperating agencies should be encouraged not only to participate in scoping but also to review the decisions made by the lead agency about what to include in the EIS. Lead agencies should allow any information needed by a cooperating agency to be included, and any issues of concern to the cooperating agency should be covered, but it usually will have to be at the expense of the cooperating agency.

Cooperating agencies have at least as great a need as the general public for advance information on a proposal before any scoping takes place. Agencies have reported to us that information from the lead agency is often too sketchy or comes too late for informed participation. Lead agencies must clearly explain to all cooperating agencies what the proposed action is conceived to be at this time, and what present alternatives and issues the lead agency sees, before expecting other agencies to devote time and money to a scoping session. Informal contacts among the agencies before scoping gets underway are valuable to establish what the cooperating agencies will need for productive scoping to take place.

Some agencies will be called upon to be cooperators more frequently than others, and they may lack the resources to respond to the numerous requests. The NEPA regulations permit agencies without jurisdiction by law (i.e., no approval authority over the proposal) to decline the cooperating agency role. (Section 1501.6(c)). But agencies that do have jurisdiction by law cannot opt out entirely and may have to reduce their cooperating effort devoted to each EIS. (See Section 1501.6(c) and *40 Questions and Answers about the NEPA Regulations*, 46 Fed. Reg. 18030, Question 14a.) Thus, cooperators would be greatly aided by a priority list from the lead agency showing which proposals most need their help. This will lead to a more efficient allocation of resources.

Some cooperating agencies are still holding back at the scoping stage in order to retain a critical position for later in the process. They either avoid the scoping sessions or fail to contribute, and then raise objections in comments on the draft EIS. We cannot emphasize enough that the whole point of scoping is to avoid this situation. As we stated in *40 Questions and Answers about the NEPA Regulation*, "if the new alternative [or other issue] was not raised by the comments or during scoping, but could have been, commentors may find that they are unpersuasive in their efforts to have their suggested alternative analyzed in detail by the [lead] agency." (46 Fed. Reg. 18035, Question 29b.)

III. Advice for Public Participants

Scoping is a new opportunity for you to enter the earliest phase of the decision making process on proposals that affect you. Through this process you have access to public officials before decisions are made and the right to explain your objections and concern. But this opportunity carries with it a new responsibility. No longer may individuals hang back until the process is almost complete and then spring forth with a significant issue or alternative that might have been raised earlier. You are now part of the review process, and your role is to inform the responsible agencies of the potential impacts that should be studied, the problems a proposal may cause that you foresee, and the alternatives and mitigating measures that offer promise.

As noted above, and in *40 Questions and Answers*, no longer will a comment raised for the first time after the draft EIS is finished be accorded the same serious consideration it would otherwise have merited if the issue had been raised during scoping. Thus, you have a responsibility to come forward early with known issues.

In return, you get the chance to meet the responsible officials and to make the case for your alternative before they are committed to a course of action. To a surprising degree, this avenue has been found to yield satisfactory results. There's no guarantee, of course, but when the alternative you suggest is really better, it is often hard for a decision-maker to resist.

There are several problems that commonly arise that public participants should be aware of.

A. Public input is often only negative

The optimal timing of scoping within the NEPA process is difficult to judge. On the one hand, as explained above (Section 11. 8.1.), if it is attempted too early, the agency cannot explain what it has in mind and informed participation will be impossible. On the other hand, if it is delayed, the public may find that significant decisions are already made, and their comments may be discounted or will be too late to change the project. Some agencies have found themselves in a tactical cross-fire when public criticism arises before they can even define their proposal sufficiently to see whether they have a worthwhile plan. Understandably, they would be reluctant after such an experience to invite public criticism early in the planning process through open scoping. But it is in your interest to encourage agencies to come out with proposals in the early stage because that enhances the possibility of your comments being used. Thus, public participants in scoping should reduce the emotion level wherever possible and use the opportunity to make thoughtful, rational presentations on impacts and alternatives. Polarity over issues too early hurts all parties. If agencies get positive and useful public responses from the scoping process, they will more frequently come forward with proposals early enough so that they can be materially improved by your suggestions.

B. Issues are too broad

The issues that participants tend to identify during scoping are much too broad to be useful for analytical purposes. For example, "cultural impacts"—what does this mean? What precisely are the impacts that should be examined? When the EIS preparers encounter a comment as vague as this, they will have to make their own judgment about what you meant, and you may find that your issues are not covered. Thus, you should refine the broad general topics, and specify which issues need evaluation and analysis.

C. Impacts are not identified

Similarly, people (including agency staff) frequently identify "causes" as issues but fail to identify the principal "effects" that the EIS should evaluate in depth. For example, oil and gas development is a cause of many impacts. Simply listing this generic category is of little help. You must go beyond the obvious causes to the specific effects that are of concern. If you want scoping to be seen as more than just another public meeting, you will need to put in extra work.

IV. Brief Points for Applicants

Scoping can be an invaluable part of your early project planning. Your main interest is in getting a proposal through the review process. This interest is best advanced by finding out early where the problems with the proposal are, who the affected parties are, and where accommodations can be made. Scoping is an ideal meeting place for all the interest groups if you have not already contacted them. In several cases, we found that the compromises made at this stage allowed a project to move efficiently through the permitting process virtually unopposed.

The NEPA regulations place an affirmative obligation on agencies to "provide for cases where actions are planned by private applicants" so that designated staff are available to consult with the applicants, to advise applicants of information that will be required during review, and to insure that the NEPA process commences at the earliest possible time. (Section 1501.2(d)). This section of the regulations is intended to ensure that environmental factors are considered at an early stage in the applicant's planning process. (See *40 Questions and Answers about the NEPA Regulations*, 46 Fed. Reg. 18028, Questions 8 and 9.)

Applicants should take advantage of this requirement in the regulations by approaching the agencies early to consult on alternatives, mitigation requirements, and the agency's information needs. This early contact with the agency can facilitate a prompt initiation of the scoping process in cases where an EIS will be prepared. You will need to furnish sufficient information about your proposal to enable the lead agency to formulate a coherent presentation for cooperating agencies and the public. But don't wait until your choices are all made and the alternatives have been eliminated (Section 1506.1).

During scoping, be sure to attend any of the public meetings, unless the agency is dividing groups by interest affiliation. You will be able to answer any questions about the proposal, and even more important, you will be able to hear the objections raised, and find out what the real concerns of the public are. This is, of course, vital information for future negotiations with the affected parties.

COUNCIL ON ENVIRONMENTAL QUALITY GUIDANCE ON POLLUTION PREVENTION AND THE NATIONAL ENVIRONMENTAL POLICY ACT

HISTORY: 58 FR 6478, Jan. 29, 1993

MEMORANDUM

TO: Heads of Federal Departments and Agencies

FROM: Michael R. Deland

SUBJECT: Pollution Prevention and the National Environmental Policy Act

Date: January 12, 1993

Introduction

Although substantial improvements in environmental quality have been made in the last 20 years by focusing Federal energies and Federal dollars on pollution abatement and on cleaning up pollution once it has occurred, achieving similar improvements in the future will require that polluters and regulators focus more of their efforts on pollution prevention. For example, reducing non-point source pollution—such as runoff from agricultural lands and urban roadways—and addressing cross-media environmental problems—such as the solid waste disposal problem posed by the sludge created in the abatement of air and water pollution—may not be possible with "end-of-the-pipe" solutions. Pollution prevention techniques seek to reduce the amount and/or toxicity of pollutants being generated. In addition, such techniques promote increased efficiency in the use of raw materials and in conservation of natural resources, and can be a more cost-effective means of controlling pollution than does direct regulation. Many strategies have been developed and used to reduce pollution and protect resources, including using fewer toxic inputs, redesigning products, altering manufacturing and maintenance processes, and conserving energy.

This memorandum seeks to encourage all Federal departments and agencies, in furtherance of their responsibilities under the National Environmental Policy Act (NEPA), to incorporate pollution prevention principles, techniques, and mechanisms into their planning and decision making processes and to evaluate and report those efforts, as appropriate, in documents prepared pursuant to NEPA.

Background

NEPA provides a long-standing umbrella for a renewed emphasis on pollution prevention in all Federal activities. Indeed, NEPA's very purpose is "to promote efforts which will prevent or eliminate damage to the environment ....." 42 USC 4321.[18]

Section 101 of NEPA contains Congress' express recognition of "the profound impact of man's activity on the interrelations of all components of the natural environment" and declaration of the policy of the Federal government "to use all practicable means and measures...to create and maintain conditions under which man and nature can exist in productive harmony...." 42 USC 4331(a). In order to carry out

---

[18] For a discussion of such strategies and activities, see the Council on Environmental Quality's 20th Environmental Quality report, at 215-257 (1989); 21st Environmental Quality report, at 79-133 (1990); and 22nd Environmental Quality report, at 151-158 (1991).

this environmental policy, Congress required all agencies of the Federal government to act to preserve, protect, and enhance the environment. See 42 USC 4331(b).

Further, section 102 of NEPA requires the Federal agencies to document the consideration of environmental values in their decision making in "detailed statements" known as environmental impact statements (EIS). 42 USC 4332(2)(c)). As the United States Supreme Court has noted, the "sweeping policy goals announced in section 101 of NEPA are thus realized through a set of 'action-forcing' procedures that require that agencies take a 'hard look' at environmental consequences." *Robertson v. Methow Valley Citizens Council,* 490 U.S. 332 (1989).

The very premise of NEPA's policy goals, and the thrust for implementation of those goals in the Federal government through the EIS process, is to avoid, minimize, or compensate for adverse environmental impacts before an action is taken. Virtually the entire structure of NEPA compliance has been designed by CEQ with the goal of preventing, eliminating, or minimizing environmental degradation. Thus, compliance with the goals and procedural requirements of NEPA, thoughtfully and fully implemented, can contribute to the reduction of pollution from Federal projects, and from projects funded, licensed, or approved by Federal agencies.

Defining Pollution Prevention

CEQ defines and uses the term "pollution prevention" broadly. In keeping with NEPA and the CEQ regulations implementing the procedural provisions of the statute, CEQ is not seeking to limit agency discretion in choosing a particular course of action, but rather is providing direction on the incorporation of pollution prevention considerations into agency planning and decision making.

"Pollution prevention" as used in this guidance includes, but is not limited to, reducing or eliminating hazardous or other polluting inputs which can contribute to both point and non-point source pollution; modifying manufacturing, maintenance, or other industrial practices; modifying product designs; recycling (especially in-process, closed loop recycling); preventing the disposal and transfer of pollution from one media to another; and increasing energy efficiency and conservation. Pollution prevention can be implemented at any stage—input, use or generation, and treatment—and may involve any technique—process modification, waste stream segregation, inventory control, good housekeeping or best management practices, employee training, recycling, and substitution. Indeed, any reasonable mechanism which successfully avoids, prevents, or reduces pollutant discharges or emissions other than by the traditional method of treating pollution at the discharge end of a pipe or a stack should, for purposes of this guidance, be considered pollution prevention.[19]

Federal Agency Responsibilities

Pursuant to the policy goals found in NEPA section 101 and the procedural requirements found in NEPA section 102 and in the CEQ regulations, the Federal departments and agencies should take every opportunity to include pollution prevention considerations in the early planning and decision making processes for their actions, and, where appropriate, should document those considerations in any EISs

---

[19] It should be noted that EPA, in accordance with the Pollution Prevention Act of 1990 (Pub. L. 101-508, 6601 *et seq.*), uses a different definition, one which describes pollution prevention in terms of source reduction and other practices which reduce or eliminate the creation of pollutants through increased efficiency in the use of raw materials, energy, water, or other resources or the protection of natural resources by conservation. "Source reduction" is defined as any practice which reduces the amount of any hazardous substance, pollutant, or contaminant entering any waste stream or otherwise released into the environment prior to recycling, treatment, or disposal and which reduces the hazards to public health and the environment associated with the release of such substances, pollutants, or contaminants.

or environmental assessments (EAs) prepared for those actions.[20] In this context, Federal actions encompass policies and projects initiated by a Federal agency itself, as well as activities initiated by a non-Federal entity, which need Federal funding or approval. Federal agencies are encouraged to consult EPA's Pollution Prevention Information Clearinghouse, which can serve as a source of innovative ideas for reducing pollution.

1. Federal policies, projects, and procurements

The Federal government develops and implements a wide variety of policies, legislation, rules, and regulations; designs, constructs, and operates its own facilities; owns and manages millions of acres of public lands; and has a substantial role as a purchaser and consumer of commercial goods and services—all of these activities provide tremendous opportunities for pollution prevention which the Federal agencies should grasp to the fullest extent practicable. Indeed, some agencies have already begun their own creative pollution prevention initiatives.

a. Land management

The United States Forest Service has instituted best management practices in several national forests. These practices include leaving slash and downed logs in harvest units, maintaining wide buffer zones around streams, and encouraging biological diversity by mimicking historic burn patterns and other natural processes in timber sale design and layout. The beneficial effects have been a reduction in erosion, creation of fish and wildlife habitat, and the elimination of the need to burn debris after logging—in other words, a reduction of air and water pollution.

The National Park Service and the Bureau of Reclamation have implemented integrated pest management programs which minimize or eliminate the use of pesticides. In addition, in some parks storm water runoffs from parking lots have been eliminated by replacing asphalt with the use of a "geo-block" system (interlocking concrete blocks with openings for grass plantings). The lot is mowed as a lawn but has the structural strength to support vehicles.

The Tennessee Valley Authority (TVA) has developed a transmission line right-of-way maintenance program which requires buffer zones around sensitive areas for herbicide applications, and use of herbicides which have soil retention properties which allow less frequent treatment and better control. TVA is also testing whole tree chipping to clear rights-of-way in a single pass application, allowing for construction vehicle access but reducing the need for access roads with the nonpoint source pollution associated with leveling, drainage, or compaction. In addition, TVA is using more steel transmission line poles to replace traditional wooden poles which have been treated with chemicals.

For construction projects it undertakes, the Department of Veterans Affairs discusses in NEPA documents and implements pollution prevention measures such as oil separation in storm water drainage of parking structures, soil erosion and sedimentation controls, and the use of recycled asphalt.

b. Office programs

Many agencies, including the Department of Agriculture's Economic Research Service and Soil Conservation Service, Department of the Army, Department of the Interior, Consumer Product Safety Commission, and Tennessee Valley Authority, have implemented pollution prevention initiatives in their daily office activities. These initiatives embrace recycling programs covering items such as paper

---

[20] Under section 309 of the Clean Air Act (42 USC 7609), EPA is directed to review and comment on all major Federal actions, including construction projects, proposed legislation, and proposed regulations. In addition, the Pollution Prevention Act of 1990 directs EPA to encourage source reduction practices in other Federal agencies. EPA is using this authority to identify opportunities for pollution prevention in the Federal agencies and to suggest how pollution prevention concepts can be addressed by the agencies in their EISs and incorporated into the wide range of government activities.

products (e.g., white paper, newsprint, cardboard), aluminum, waste oil, batteries, tires, and scrap metal; procurement and use of "environmentally safe" products and products with recycled material content (e.g., batteries, tires, cement mixed with fly ash and recycled oil, plastic picnic tables); purchase and use of alternative-fueled vehicles in agency fleets; and encouragement of carpooling with employee education programs and locator assistance.

In planning the relocation of its headquarters, the Consumer Product Safety Commission (CPSC) is considering only buildings located within walking distance of the subway system as possible sites. By conveniently siting its headquarters facility, CPSC expects to triple the number of employees relying on public transportation for commuting and to substantially increase the number of agency visitors using public transportation for attendance at agency meetings or events.

c. Waste reduction

The Department of Energy (DOE) has instituted an aggressive waste minimization program which has produced substantial results. DOE's nuclear facilities have reduced the sizes of radiological control areas in order to reduce low-level radioactive waste. Other facilities have scrap metal segregation programs which reduce solid waste and allow useable material to be sold and recycled. DOE facilities also are replacing solvents and cleaners containing hazardous materials with less or non-toxic materials.

The Department of the Army has a similar waste reduction program and is vigorously pursuing source reduction changes to industrial processes to eliminate toxic chemical usage that ultimately generates hazardous wastes. The Army's program includes material substitution techniques as well as alternative application technologies. For example, in an EIS and subsequent record of decision for proposed actions on Kwajalein Atoll, the Army committed to segregate solvents from waste oils in the Kwajalein power plant which will prevent continual contamination of large quantities of used engine oil with solvents. Oil recycling equipment will also be installed on power plant diesel generators, allowing reuse of waste oil.

The Federal Aviation Administration (FAA) has also implemented a waste minimization program designed to eliminate or reduce the amount and toxicity of wastes generated by all National Airspace System facilities. This program includes using chemical life extenders and recycling additives to reduce the quantity and frequency of wastes generated at FAA facilities and providing chlorofluorocarbon (CFC) recycling equipment to each sector in the FAA so that CFCs used in industrial chillers, refrigeration equipment, and air conditioning units can be recaptured, recycled, and reused.

d. Inventory control

DOE is improving procurement and inventory control of chemicals and control of materials entering radiologically controlled areas. This can minimize or prevent non-radioactive waste from entering a radioactive waste stream, thus reducing the amount of low-level waste needing disposal.

In two laboratories operated by the Consumer Product Safety Commission, pollution prevention is being practiced by limiting quantities of potentially hazardous materials on hand.

The Tennessee Valley Authority's nuclear program has established a chemical traffic control program to control the use and disposal of hazardous materials. As a result of the program, hazardous materials are being replaced by less hazardous alternatives and use of hazardous chemicals and products has been reduced by 66%.

2. Federal approvals

In addition to initiating their own policies and projects, Federal agencies provide funding in the form of loans, contracts, and grants and/or issue licenses, permits, and other approvals for projects initiated by private parties and State and local government agencies. As with their own projects and consistent with their statutory authorities, Federal agencies could urge private applicants to include pollution prevention considerations into the siting, design, construction, and operation of privately owned and operated projects. These considerations could then be included in the NEPA documentation prepared for the federally-funded or federally-approved project, and any pollution prevention commitments made by the applicant would be monitored and enforced by the agency. Thus, using their existing regulatory authority, Federal agencies can effectively promote pollution prevention throughout the private sector. Below are some existing examples of incorporation of pollution prevention into Federal approvals.

The Nuclear Regulatory Commission has required licensees to perform mitigation measures during nuclear power plant construction. These measures include controlling drainage by means of ditches, berms, and sedimentation basins; prompt revegetation to control erosion; and stockpiling and reusing topsoil. Similarly, mitigation measures required during the construction of transmission facilities include the removal of vegetation by cutting and trimming rather than bulldozing, and avoiding multiple stream crossings, wet areas, and areas with steep slopes and highly erodible soils. The mitigation conditions in licenses serve to prevent pollution from soil erosion and to minimize waste from construction.

In the implementation of its programs, the Department of Agriculture encourages farmers to follow management practices designed to reduce the environmental impacts of farming. Such practices include using biological pest controls and integrated pest management to reduce the toxicity and application of pesticides, controlling nutrient loadings by installing buffer strips around streams and replacing inorganic fertilizers with animal manures, and reducing soil erosion through modified tillage and irrigation practices. Further, encouraging the construction of structures such as waste storage pits, terraces, irrigation water conveyances or pipelines, and lined or grassed waterways reduces runoff and percolation of chemicals into the groundwater.

The Department of Transportation's Maritime Administration is conducting research on a Shipboard Piloting Expert System. If installed on vessels, this system would provide a navigation and pilotage assistance capability which would instantly provide warnings to a ship master or pilot of pending hazards and recommended changes in vessel heading to circumvent the hazard. The system could prevent tanker collisions or groundings which cause catastrophic releases of pollutants.

The Department of the Interior's Minerals Management Service (MMS) prepares EISs which examine the effects of potential Outer Continental Shelf (OCS) oil exploration on the environment and the various mitigation measures that may be needed to minimize such effects. Some pollution prevention measures which are analyzed in these EISs and which have been adopted for specific lease sales include measures designed to minimize the effects of drilling fluids discharge, waste disposal, oil spills, and air emissions. For example, MMS requires OCS operations to use curbs, gutters, drip pans, and drains on drilling platforms and rig decks to collect contaminants such as oil which may be recycled.

Incorporating Pollution Prevention Into NEPA Documents

NEPA and the CEQ regulations establish a mechanism for building environmental considerations into Federal decision making. Specifically, the regulations require Federal agencies to "integrate the NEPA process with other planning at the earliest possible time to insure that planning and decisions reflect environmental values, to avoid delays later in the process, and to head off potential conflicts." 40 CFR 1501.2. This mechanism can be used to incorporate pollution prevention in the early planning stages of a proposal.

In addition, prior to preparation of an EIS, the Federal agency proposing the action is required to conduct a scoping process during which the public and other Federal agencies are able to participate in discussions concerning the scope of issues to be addressed in the EIS. See 40 CFR 1501.7. Including pollution prevention as an issue in the scoping process would encourage those outside the Federal agency to provide insights into pollution prevention technologies which might be available for use in connection with the proposal or its possible alternatives.

Pollution prevention should also be an important component of mitigation of the adverse impacts of a Federal action. To the extent practicable, pollution prevention considerations should be included in the proposed action and in the reasonable alternatives to the proposal, and should be addressed in the environmental consequences section of the EIS. See 40 CFR 1502.14(f), 1502.16(h), and 1508.20.

Finally, when an agency reaches a decision on an action for which an EIS was completed, a public record of decision must be prepared which provides information on the alternatives considered and the factors weighed in the decision making process. Specifically, the agency must State whether all practicable means to avoid or minimize environmental harm were adopted, and if not, why they were not. A monitoring and enforcement program must be adopted if appropriate for mitigation. See 40 CFR 1505.2(c). These requirements for the record of decision and for monitoring and enforcement could be an effective means to inform the public of the extent to which pollution prevention is included in a decision and to outline how pollution prevention measures will be implemented.

A discussion of pollution prevention may also be appropriate in an EA. While an EA is designed to be a brief discussion of the environmental impacts of a particular proposal, the preparer could also include suitable pollution prevention techniques as a means to lessen any adverse impacts identified. See 40 CFR 1508.9. Pollution prevention measures which contribute to an agency's finding of no significant impact must be carried out by the agency or made part of a permit or funding determination.

Conclusion

Pollution prevention can provide both environmental and economic benefits, and CEQ encourages Federal agencies to consider pollution prevention principles in their planning and decision making processes in accordance with the policy goals of NEPA Section 101 and to include such considerations in documents prepared pursuant to NEPA section 102, as appropriate.[21] In its role as a regulator, a policymaker, a manager of Federal lands, a grantor of Federal funds, a consumer, and an operator of Federal facilities which can create pollution, the Federal government is in a position to help lead the nation's efforts to prevent pollution before it is created. The Federal agencies should act now to develop and incorporate pollution prevention considerations in the full range of their activities.

David B. Struhs,

Chief of Staff

---

[21] As a guidance document, this memorandum does not impose any new legal requirements on the agencies and does not require any changes to be made to any existing agency environmental regulations.

COUNCIL ON ENVIRONMENTAL QUALITY GUIDANCE ON NEPA ANALYSES FOR TRANSBOUNDARY IMPACTS, JULY 1, 1997

The purpose of this guidance is to clarify the applicability of the National Environmental Policy Act (NEPA) to proposed Federal actions in the United States, including its territories and possessions, that may have transboundary effects extending across the border and affecting another country's environment. While the guidance arises in the context of negotiations undertaken with the governments of Mexico and Canada to develop an agreement on transboundary environmental impact assessment in North America,[22] the guidance pertains to all Federal agency actions that are normally subject to NEPA, whether covered by an international agreement or not.

It is important to State at the outset the matters to which this guidance is addressed and those to which it is not. This guidance does not expand the range of actions to which NEPA currently applies. An action that does not otherwise fall under NEPA would not now fall under NEPA by virtue of this guidance. Nor does this guidance apply NEPA to so-called "extraterritorial actions"; that is, U.S. actions that take place in another country or otherwise outside the jurisdiction of the United States.[23] The guidance pertains only to those proposed actions currently covered by NEPA that take place within the United States and its territories, and it does not change the applicability of NEPA law, regulations or case law to those actions. Finally, the guidance is consistent with long-standing principles of international law.

NEPA Law and Policy

NEPA declares a national policy that encourages productive and enjoyable harmony between human beings and their environment, promotes efforts which will prevent or eliminate damage to the environment and biosphere, stimulates the health and welfare of human beings, and enriches the understanding of ecological systems.[24] Section 102(1) of NEPA "authorizes and directs that, to the fullest extent possible .... the policies, regulations and public laws of the United States shall be interpreted and administered in accordance with the policies set forth in [the] Act."[25] NEPA's explicit statement of policies calls for the Federal government "to use all practical means and measures .... to create and maintain conditions under which man and nature can exist in productive harmony...."[26] In addition, Congress directed Federal agencies to "use all practical means .... to improve and coordinate Federal plans, functions, programs, and resources to the end that the Nation may .... attain the widest range of beneficial uses of the environment without degradation, risk to health or safety, or other undesirable and unintended consequences."[27] Section 102(2)(C) requires Federal agencies to assess the environmental impacts of and alternatives to proposed major Federal actions significantly affecting the quality of the human environment.[28] Congress also recognized the "worldwide and long-range

---

[22] The negotiations were authorized in Section 10.7 of the North American Agreement on Environmental Cooperation, which is a side agreement to the North American Free Trade Agreement. The guidance is also relevant to the ECE Convention on Environmental Impact Assessment In a Transboundary Context, signed in Espoo, Finland in February, 1991, but not yet in force.

[23] For example, NEPA does apply to actions undertaken by the National Science Foundation in Antarctica. *Environmental Defense Fund v. Massey*, 986 F.2d 528 (D.C. Cir. 1993).

[24] 42 USC 4321.

[25] 42 USC 4332(1).

[26] 42 USC 4331(a).

[27] 42 USC 4331 (b)(3).

[28] 42 USC 4332(2)(C).

character of environmental problems" in NEPA and directed agencies to assist other countries in anticipating and preventing a decline in the quality of the world environment.[29]

Neither NEPA nor the Council on Environmental Quality's (CEQ) regulations implementing the procedural provisions of NEPA define agencies' obligations to analyze effects of actions by administrative boundaries. Rather, the entire body of NEPA law directs Federal agencies to analyze the effects of proposed actions to the extent they are reasonably foreseeable consequences of the proposed action, regardless of where those impacts might occur. Agencies must analyze indirect effects which are caused by the action, are later in time or farther removed in distance, but are still reasonably foreseeable, including growth-inducing effects and related effects on the ecosystem,[30] as well as cumulative effects.[31] Case law interpreting NEPA has reinforced the need to analyze impacts regardless of geographic boundaries within the United States,[32] and has also assumed that NEPA requires analysis of major Federal actions that take place entirely outside of the United States but could have environmental effects within the United States.[33]

Courts that have addressed impacts across the United States' borders have assumed that the same rule of law applies in a transboundary context. In *Swinomish Tribal Community v. Federal Energy Regulatory Commission*,[34] Canadian intervenors were allowed to challenge the adequacy of an environmental impact statement (EIS) prepared by FERC in connection with its approval of an amendment to the City of Seattle's license that permitted raising the height of the Ross Dam on the Skagit River in Washington State. Assuming that NEPA required consideration of Canadian impacts, the court concluded that the report had taken the requisite "hard look" at Canadian impacts. Similarly, in *Wilderness Society v. Morton*,[35] the court granted intervenor status to Canadian environmental organizations that were challenging the adequacy of the trans-Alaska pipeline EIS. The court granted intervenor status because it found that there was a reasonable possibility that oil spill damage could significantly affect Canadian resources, and that Canadian interests were not adequately represented by other parties in the case.

In sum, based on legal and policy considerations, CEQ has determined that agencies must include analysis of reasonably foreseeable transboundary effects of proposed actions in their analysis of proposed actions in the United States.

Practical Considerations

CEQ notes that many proposed Federal actions will not have transboundary effects, and cautions agencies against creating boilerplate sections in NEPA analyses to address this issue. Rather, Federal agencies should use the scoping process[36] to identify those actions that may have transboundary environmental effects and determine at that point their information needs, if any, for such analyses. Agencies should be particularly alert to actions that may affect migratory species, air quality, watersheds, and other components of the natural ecosystem that cross borders, as well as to interrelated social and

---

[29] 42 USC 4332(2)(F).

[30] 40 CFR 1508.8(b).

[31] 40 CFR 1508.7.

[32] See, for example, *Sierra Club v. U.S. Forest Service*, 46 F.3d 835 (8th Cir. 1995); *Resources Ltd., Inc. v. Robertson*, 35 F.3d 1300 and 8 F.3d 1394 (9th Cir. 1993); *Natural Resources Defense Council v. Hodel*, 865 F.2d 288 (D.C. Cir. 1988); *County of Josephine v. Watt*, 539 F.Supp. 696 (N.D. Cal. 1982).

[33] See *Sierra Club v. Adams*, 578 F.2d 389 (D.C. Cir. 1978); *NORML v. Dept. of State*, 452 F.Supp. 1226 (D.D.C. 1978).

[34] 627 F.2d 499 (D.C. Cir. 1980).

[35] 463 F.2d 1261 (D.C. Cir. 1972).

[36] 40 CFR 1501.7. Scoping is a process for determining the scope of the issues to be addressed and the parties that need to be involved in that process prior to writing the environmental analyses.

---

economic effects.[37] Should such potential impacts be identified, agencies may rely on available professional sources of information and should contact agencies in the affected country with relevant expertise.

Agencies have expressed concern about the availability of information that would be adequate to comply with NEPA standards that have been developed through the CEQ regulations and through judicial decisions. Agencies do have a responsibility to undertake a reasonable search for relevant, current information associated with an identified potential effect. However, the courts have adopted a "rule of reason" to judge an agency's actions in this respect, and do not require agencies to discuss "remote and highly speculative consequences".[38] Furthermore, CEQ's regulation at 40 CFR 1502.22 dealing with incomplete or unavailable information sets forth clear steps to evaluating effects in the context of an EIS when information is unobtainable.[39] Additionally, in the context of international agreements, the parties may set forth a specific process for obtaining information from the affected country which could then be relied upon in most circumstances to satisfy agencies' responsibility to undertake a reasonable search for information.

Agencies have also pointed out that certain Federal actions that may cause transboundary effects do not, under U.S. law, require compliance with Sections 102(2)(C) and 102(2)(E) of NEPA. Such actions include actions that are statutorily exempted from NEPA, Presidential actions, and individual actions for which procedural compliance with NEPA is excused or modified by virtue of the CEQ regulations[40] and various judicial doctrines interpreting NEPA.[41] Nothing in this guidance changes the agencies' ability to rely on those rules and doctrines.

International Law

It has been customary law since the 1905 Trail Smelter Arbitration that no nation may undertake acts on its territory that will harm the territory of another state.[42] This rule of customary law has been recognized as binding in Principle 21 of the Stockholm Declaration on the Human Environment and Principle 2 of the 1992 Rio Declaration on Environment and Development. This concept, along with the duty to give notice to others to avoid or avert such harm, is incorporated into numerous treaty obligations undertaken by the United States. Analysis of transboundary impacts of Federal agency actions that occur in the United States is an appropriate step towards implementing those principles.

---

[37] It is a well accepted rule that under NEPA, social and economic impacts by themselves do not require preparation of an EIS. 40 CFR 1508.14.

[38] *Trout Unlimited v. Morton*, 509 F.2d 1276, 1283 (9th Cir. 1974). See also, *Northern Alaska Environmental Center v. Lujan*, 961 F.2d 886, 890 (9th Cir. 1992); *Idaho Conservation League v, Mumma*, 956 F.2d 1508, 1519 (9th Cir. 1992); *San Luis Obispo Mothers for Peace v. N.R.C.*, 751 F.2d 1287, 1300 (D.C. Cir. 1984); *Scientists Institute for Public Information, Inc. v. Atomic Energy Commission*, 481 F.2d 1079, 1092 (D.C. Cir. 1973).

[39] See Preamble to Amendment of 40 CFR 1502.22, deleting prior requirement for "worst case analysis" at 51 *Federal Register* 15625, April 25, 1986, for a detailed explanation of this regulation.

[40] For example, agencies may contact CEQ for approval of alternative arrangements for compliance with NEPA in the case of emergencies. 40 CFR 1506.11.

[41] For example, courts have recognized that NEPA does not require an agency to make public information that is otherwise properly classified information for national security reasons, *Weinberger v. Catholic Action of Hawaii*, 454 U.S. 139 (1981).

[42] Trail Smelter Arbitration, *U.S. v. Canada* 3 UN Rep. Int'l Arbit. Awards 1911 (1941). The case involved a smelter in British Columbia that was causing environmental harm in the State of Washington. The decision held that "under principles of International Law, as well as the law of the United States, no State has the right to use or permit the use of its territory in such a manner as to cause injury by fumes in or to the territory of another or the properties or persons therein, when the case is of serious consequence and the injury is described by clear and convincing injury." *Ibid.* at 1965). Also see the American Law Institute's *Restatement of the Foreign Relations Law of the United States 3d, Section 601,* ("State obligations with respect to environment of other States and the common environment").

Conclusion

NEPA requires agencies to include analysis of reasonably foreseeable transboundary effects of proposed actions in their analysis of proposed actions in the United States. Such effects are best identified during the scoping stage, and should be analyzed to the best of the agency's ability using reasonably available information. Such analysis should be included in the EA or EIS prepared for the proposed action.

COUNCIL ON ENVIRONMENTAL QUALITY GUIDANCE ON ENVIRONMENTAL JUSTICE UNDER THE NATIONAL ENVIRONMENTAL POLICY ACT

Introduction

Executive Order 12898, "Federal Actions to Address Environmental Justice in Minority Populations and Low-Income Populations,"[43] provides that "each Federal agency shall make achieving environmental justice part of its mission by identifying and addressing, as appropriate, disproportionately high and adverse human health or environmental effects of its programs, policies, and activities on minority populations and low-income populations." The Executive Order makes clear that its provisions apply fully to Native American programs.

In the memorandum to heads of departments and agencies that accompanied Executive Order 12898, the President specifically recognized the importance of procedures under the National Environmental Policy Act (NEPA),[44] for identifying and addressing environmental justice concerns. The memorandum states that "[e]ach Federal agency shall analyze the environmental effects, including human health, economic and social effects, of Federal actions, including effects on minority communities and low-income communities, when such analysis is required by [NEPA]." The memorandum particularly emphasizes the importance of NEPA's public participation process, directing that "each Federal agency shall provide opportunities for community input in the NEPA process." Agencies are further directed to "identify potential effects and mitigation measures in consultation with affected communities, and improve the accessibility of meetings, crucial documents, and notices."

The Council on Environmental Quality (CEQ) has oversight of the Federal government's compliance with Executive Order 12898 and NEPA.[45] CEQ, in consultation with EPA and other affected agencies, has developed this guidance to further assist Federal agencies with their NEPA procedures so that environmental justice concerns are effectively identified and addressed. To the extent practicable and permitted by law, agencies may supplement this guidance with more specific procedures tailored to particular programs or activities of an individual department, agency, or office.

Executive Order 12898 and the Presidential Memorandum

In addition to the general directive in Executive Order 12898 that each agency identify and address, as appropriate, "disproportionately high and adverse human health or environmental effects of its programs, policies, and activities on minority populations and low-income populations,"[46] there are several provisions of the Executive Order and a number of supporting documents to which agencies should refer when identifying and addressing environmental justice concerns in the NEPA process.

First, the Executive Order itself contains particular emphasis on four issues that are pertinent to the NEPA process:

---

[43] 59 Fed. Reg. 7629 (1994).

[44] 42 U.S.C. §4321 *et seq.*

[45] Certain oversight functions in the Executive Order are delegated to the Deputy Assistant to the President for Environmental Policy. Following the merger of the White House Office on Environmental Policy with CEQ, the Chair of CEQ assumed those functions. The Environmental Protection Agency (EPA) has lead responsibility for implementation of the Executive Order as Chair of the Interagency Working Group (IWG) on Environmental Justice.

[46] Executive Order No. 12898, 59 Fed. Reg. at 7630 (Section 1-101).

- The Executive Order requires the development of agency-specific environmental justice strategies.[47] Thus, agencies have developed and should periodically revise their strategies providing guidance concerning the types of programs, policies, and activities that may, or historically have, raised environmental justice concerns at the particular agency. These guidances may suggest possible approaches to addressing such concerns in the agency's NEPA analyses, as appropriate.

- The Executive Order recognizes the importance of research, data collection, and analysis, particularly with respect to multiple and cumulative exposures to environmental hazards for low-income populations, minority populations, and Indian tribes.[48] Thus, data on these exposure issues should be incorporated into NEPA analyses as appropriate.[49]

- The Executive Order provides for agencies to collect, maintain, and analyze information on patterns of subsistence consumption of fish, vegetation, or wildlife.[50] Where an agency action may affect fish, vegetation, or wildlife, that agency action may also affect subsistence patterns of consumption and indicate the potential for disproportionately high and adverse human health or environmental effects on low-income populations, minority populations, and Indian tribes.

- The Executive Order requires agencies to work to ensure effective public participation and access to information.[51] Thus, within its NEPA process and through other appropriate mechanisms, each Federal agency shall, "wherever practicable and appropriate, translate crucial public documents, notices and hearings, relating to human health or the environment for limited English speaking populations." In addition, each agency should work to "ensure that public documents, notices, and hearings relating to human health or the environment are concise, understandable, and readily accessible to the public."[52]

Second, the memorandum accompanying the Executive Order identifies four important ways to consider environmental justice under NEPA.

- Each Federal agency should analyze the environmental effects, including human health, economic, and social effects of Federal actions, including effects on minority populations, low-income populations, and Indian tribes, when such analysis is required by NEPA.[53]

- Mitigation measures identified as part of an environmental assessment (EA), a finding of no significant impact (FONSI), an environmental impact statement (EIS), or a record of decision (ROD), should, whenever feasible, address significant and adverse environmental effects of proposed Federal actions on minority populations, low-income populations, and Indian tribes.[54]

---

[47] *Ibid.* at 7630 (Section 1-103).

[48] *Ibid.* at 7631 (Section 3-3).

[49] For further information on considering cumulative effects, see Considering Cumulative Effects Under The National Environmental Policy Act (Council on Environmental Quality, Executive Office of the President, Jan. 1997).

[50] *Ibid.* at 7631 (Section 4-401).

[51] *Ibid.* at 7632 (Section 5-5).

[52] *Ibid.* at 7632 (Section 5-5).

[53] Memorandum from the President to the Heads of Departments and Agencies. Comprehensive Presidential Documents No. 279. (Feb. 11, 1994).

[54] *Ibid.*

- Each Federal agency must provide opportunities for effective community participation in the NEPA process, including identifying potential effects and mitigation measures in consultation with affected communities and improving the accessibility of public meetings, crucial documents, and notices.[55]

- Review of NEPA compliance (such as EPA's review under § 309 of the Clean Air Act) must ensure that the lead agency preparing NEPA analyses and documentation has appropriately analyzed environmental effects on minority populations, low-income populations, or Indian tribes, including human health, social, and economic effects.[56]

Third, the Interagency Working Group (IWG), established by the Executive Order to implement the order's requirements, has developed guidance on key terms in the Executive Order. The guidance, reproduced as Appendix A, reflects a general consensus based on Federal agencies' experience and understanding of the issues presented. Agencies should apply the guidance with flexibility, and may consider its terms a point of departure rather than conclusive direction in applying the terms of the Executive Order.

Executive Order 12898 and NEPA

A. NEPA Generally

NEPA's fundamental policy is to "encourage productive and enjoyable harmony between man and his environment."[57] In the statute, Congress "recognizes that each person should enjoy a healthful environment and that each person has a responsibility to contribute to the preservation and enhancement of the environment."[58] The following goals, set forth in NEPA, make clear that attainment of environmental justice is wholly consistent with the purposes and policies of NEPA[59]:

- To "assure for all Americans safe, healthful, productive, and aesthetically and culturally pleasing surroundings"[60];

- To "attain the widest range of beneficial uses of the environment without degradation, risk to health or safety, or other undesirable and unintended consequences";[61]

- To "preserve important historic, cultural, and natural aspects of our natural heritage, and maintain, wherever possible, an environment which supports diversity and variety of individual choice"[62]; and

- To "achieve a balance between population and resource use which will permit high standards of living and a wide sharing of life's amenities."[63]

These goals are promoted through the requirement that all agencies of the Federal government shall include in every recommendation or report on proposals for legislation and other major Federal actions

---

[55] *Ibid.*

[56] *Ibid.*

[57] 42 U.S.C. § 4321.

[58] 42 U.S.C. § 4331(c).

[59] 42 U.S.C. § 4331(b).

[60] 42 U.S.C. § 4331(b)(2).

[61] 42 U.S.C. § 4331(b)(3).

[62] 42 U.S.C. § 4331(b)(4).

[63] 42 U.S.C. § 4331(b)(5).

significantly affecting the quality of the human environment, a "detailed statement by the responsible official" on: the environmental impacts of the proposed action; adverse environmental effects that cannot be avoided should the proposal be implemented; alternatives to the proposed action; the relationship between local, short-term uses of man's environment and long-term productivity; and any irreversible or irretrievable commitments of resources involved in the proposed action itself.[64]

Preparation of an EA may precede preparation of an EIS, to determine whether a proposed action may "significantly affect" the quality of the human environment. The EA either will support a finding of no significant impact (FONSI), or will document the need for an EIS. Agency procedure at each step of this process should be guided by the agency's own NEPA regulations and by the CEQ regulations found at 40 C.F.R. Parts 1500-1508.

B. Principles for Considering Environmental Justice Under NEPA

Environmental justice issues may arise at any step of the NEPA process and agencies should consider these issues at each and every step of the process, as appropriate. Environmental justice issues encompass a broad range of impacts covered by NEPA, including impacts on the natural or physical environment and interrelated social, cultural and economic effects.[65] In preparing an EIS or an EA, agencies must consider both impacts on the natural or physical environment and related social, cultural, and economic impacts.[66] Environmental justice concerns may arise from impacts on the natural and physical environment, such as human health or ecological impacts on minority populations, low-income populations, and Indian tribes, or from related social or economic impacts.

1. General principles

Agencies should recognize that the question of whether agency action raises environmental justice issues is highly sensitive to the history or circumstances of a particular community or population, the particular type of environmental or human health impact, and the nature of the proposed action itself. There is not a standard formula for how environmental justice issues should be identified or addressed. However, the following six principles provide general guidance.

- Agencies should consider the composition of the affected area to determine whether minority populations, low-income populations, or Indian tribes are present in the area affected by the proposed action, and, if so, whether there may be disproportionately high and adverse human health or environmental effects on minority populations, low-income populations, or Indian tribes.

- Agencies should consider relevant public health data and industry data concerning the potential for multiple or cumulative exposure to human health or environmental hazards in the affected population and historical patterns of exposure to environmental hazards to the extent such information is reasonably available. For example, data may suggest there are disproportionately high and adverse human health or environmental effects on a minority population, low-income population, or Indian tribe from the agency action. Agencies should consider these multiple, or cumulative effects, even if certain effects are not within the control or subject to the discretion of the agency proposing the action.

- Agencies should recognize the interrelated cultural, social, occupational, historical, or economic factors that may amplify the natural and physical environmental effects of the proposed agency action. These factors should include the physical sensitivity of the community or population to

---

[64] 42 U.S.C. § 4332(c).

[65] The CEQ implementing regulations define "effects" or "impacts" to include "ecological...aesthetic, historic, cultural, economic, social or health, whether direct, indirect or cumulative." 40 C.F.R. 1508.8.

[66] 40 C.F.R. 1508.14.

particular impacts; the effect of any disruption on the community structure associated with the proposed action; and the nature and degree of impact on the physical and social structure of the community.

- Agencies should develop effective public participation strategies. Agencies should, as appropriate, acknowledge and seek to overcome linguistic, cultural, institutional, geographic, and other barriers to meaningful participation, and should incorporate active outreach to affected groups.

- Agencies should assure meaningful community representation in the process. Agencies should be aware of the diverse constituencies within any particular community when they seek community representation and should endeavor to have complete representation of the community as a whole. Agencies also should be aware that community participation must occur as early as possible if it is to be meaningful.

- Agencies should seek tribal representation in the process in a manner that is consistent with the government-to-government relationship between the United States and tribal governments, the Federal government's trust responsibility to federally-recognized tribes, and any treaty rights.

2. Additional considerations

The preceding principles must be applied in light of these further considerations that are pertinent to any analysis of environmental justice under NEPA.

- The Executive Order does not change the prevailing legal thresholds and statutory interpretations under NEPA and existing case law. For example, for an EIS to be required, there must be a sufficient impact on the physical or natural environment to be "significant" within the meaning of NEPA. Agency consideration of impacts on low-income populations, minority populations, or Indian tribes may lead to the identification of disproportionately high and adverse human health or environmental effects that are significant and that otherwise would be overlooked.[67]

- Under NEPA, the identification of a disproportionately high and adverse human health or environmental effect on a low-income population, minority population, or Indian tribe does not preclude a proposed agency action from going forward, nor does it necessarily compel a conclusion that a proposed action is environmentally unsatisfactory. Rather, the identification of such an effect should heighten agency attention to alternatives (including alternative sites), mitigation strategies, monitoring needs, and preferences expressed by the affected community or population.

- Neither the Executive Order nor this guidance prescribes any specific format for examining environmental justice, such as designating a specific chapter or section in an EIS or EA on environmental justice issues. Agencies should integrate analyses of environmental justice concerns in an appropriate manner so as to be clear, concise, and comprehensible within the general format suggested by 40 C.F.R. § 1502.10.

C. Considering Environmental Justice in Specific Phases of the NEPA Process

While appropriate consideration of environmental justice issues is highly dependent upon the particular facts and circumstances of the proposed action, the affected environment, and the affected populations, there are opportunities and strategies that are useful at particular stages of the NEPA process.

---

[67] Title VI of the Civil Rights Act of 1964, U.S.C. 2000d *et seq.*, and agency implementing regulations, prohibit recipients of Federal financial assistance from taking actions that discriminate on the basis of race, sex, color, national origin, or religion. If an agency is aware that a recipient of Federal funds may be taking action that is causing a racially discriminatory impact, the agency should consider using Title VI as a means to prevent or eliminate that discrimination.

1. Scoping

During the scoping process, an agency should preliminarily determine whether an area potentially affected by a proposed agency action may include low-income populations, minority populations, or Indian tribes, and seek input accordingly. When the scoping process is used to develop an EIS or EA, an agency should seek input from low income populations, minority populations, or Indian tribes as early in the process as information becomes available.[68] Any such determination, as well as the basis for the determination, should be more substantively addressed in the appropriate NEPA documents and communicated as appropriate during the NEPA process.

If an agency identifies any potentially affected minority populations, low-income populations, or Indian tribes, the agency should develop a strategy for effective public involvement in the agency's determination of the scope of the NEPA analysis. Customary agency practices for notifying the public of a proposed action and subsequent scoping and public events may be enhanced through better use of local resources, community and other nongovernmental organizations, and locally targeted media.

Agencies should consider enhancing their outreach through the following means:

- Religious organizations (e.g., churches, temples, ministerial associations);

- Newspapers, radio and other media, particularly media targeted to low-income populations, minority populations, or Indian tribes;

- Civic associations;

- Minority business associations;

- Environmental and environmental justice organizations;

- Legal aid providers;

- Homeowners', tenants', and neighborhood watch groups;

- Federal, State, local, and tribal governments;

- Rural cooperatives;

- Business and trade organizations;

- Community and social service organizations;

- Universities, colleges, vocational and other schools;

- Labor organizations;

- Civil rights organizations;

- Local schools and libraries;

- Senior citizens' groups;

- Public health agencies and clinics; and

- The Internet and other electronic media.

The participation of diverse groups in the scoping process is necessary for full consideration of the potential environmental impacts of a proposed agency action and any alternatives. By discussing and informing the public of the emerging issues related to the proposed action, agencies may reduce misunderstandings, build cooperative working relationships, educate the public and decision makers, and avoid potential conflicts. Agencies should recognize that the identity of the relevant "public" may

---

[68] For more information on scoping, see Memorandum from Nicolas C. Yost, *Scoping Guidance* (Council on Environmental Quality, Executive Office of the President, April 30, 1981).

evolve during the process and may include different constituencies or groups of individuals at different stages of the NEPA process. This may also be the appropriate juncture to begin government-to-government consultation with affected Indian tribes and to seek their participation as cooperating agencies. For this participation to be meaningful, the public should have access to enough information so that it is well informed and can provide constructive input.

Thorough scoping is the foundation for the analytical process and provides an early opportunity for the public to participate in the design of alternatives for achieving the goals and objectives of the proposed agency action.

2. Public participation

Early and meaningful public participation in the Federal agency decision making process is a paramount goal of NEPA. CEQ's regulations require agencies to make diligent efforts to involve the public throughout the NEPA process. Participation of low-income populations, minority populations, or tribal populations may require adaptive or innovative approaches to overcome linguistic, institutional, cultural, economic, historical, or other potential barriers to effective participation in the decision-making processes of Federal agencies under customary NEPA procedures. These barriers may range from agency failure to provide translation of documents to the scheduling of meetings at times and in places that are not convenient to working families.

3. Determining the affected environment

In order to determine whether a proposed action is likely to have disproportionately high and adverse human health or environmental effects on low-income populations, minority populations, or Indian tribes, agencies should identify a geographic scale for which they will obtain demographic information on the potential impact area. Agencies may use demographic data available from the Bureau of the Census (BOC) to identify the composition of the potentially affected population. Geographic distribution by race, ethnicity, and income, as well as a delineation of tribal lands and resources, should be examined. Census data are available in published formats, and on CD-ROM available through the BOC. This data also is available from a number of local, college, and university libraries, and the World Wide Web. Agencies may also find that Federal, tribal, State and local health, environmental, and economic agencies have useful demographic information and studies, such as the Landview II system, which is used by the BOC to assist in utilizing data from a geographic information system (GIS). Landview II has proven to be a low-cost, readily available means of graphically accessing environmental justice data. These approaches already should be incorporated into current NEPA compliance.

Agencies should recognize that the impacts within minority populations, low-income populations, or Indian tribes may be different from impacts on the general population due to a community's distinct cultural practices. For example, data on different patterns of living, such as subsistence fish, vegetation, or wildlife consumption and the use of well water in rural communities may be relevant to the analysis. Where a proposed agency action would not cause any adverse environmental impacts, and therefore would not cause any disproportionately high and adverse human health or environmental impacts, specific demographic analysis may not be warranted. Where environments of Indian tribes may be affected, agencies must consider pertinent treaty, statutory or executive order rights and consult with tribal governments in a manner consistent with the government-to-government relationship.

4. Analysis

When a disproportionately high and adverse human health or environmental effect on a low-income population, minority population, or Indian tribe has been identified, agencies should analyze how environmental and health effects are distributed within the affected community. Displaying available data spatially, through a GIS, can provide the agency and the public with an effective visualization of the

The following steps may be considered, as appropriate, in developing an innovative strategy for effective public participation:

- Coordination with individuals, institutions, or organizations in the affected community to educate the public about potential health and environmental impacts and enhance public involvement;

- Translation of major documents (or summaries thereof), provision of translators at meetings, or other efforts as appropriate to ensure that limited-English speakers potentially affected by a proposed action have an understanding of the proposed action and its potential impacts;

- Provision opportunities for limited-English speaking members of the affected public to provide comments throughout the NEPA process;

- Provision of opportunities for public participation through means other than written communication, such as personal interviews or use of audio or video recording devices to capture oral comments;

- Use of periodic newsletters or summaries to provide updates on the NEPA process to keep the public informed;

- Use of different meeting sizes or formats, or variation on the type and number of media used, so that communications are tailored to the particular community or population;

- Circulation or creation of specialized materials that reflect the concerns and sensitivities of particular populations such as information about risks specific to subsistence consumers of fish, vegetation, or wildlife;

- Use of locations and facilities that are local, convenient, and accessible to the disabled, low-income and minority communities, and Indian tribes; and

- Assistance to hearing-impaired or sight-impaired individuals.

distribution of health and environmental impacts among demographic populations. This type of data should be analyzed in light of any additional qualitative or quantitative information gathered through the public participation process.

Where a potential environmental justice issue has been identified by an agency, the agency should State clearly in the EIS or EA whether, in light of all of the facts and circumstances, a disproportionately high and adverse human health or environmental impact on minority populations, low-income populations, or Indian tribe is likely to result from the proposed action and any alternatives. This statement should be supported by sufficient information for the public to understand the rationale for the conclusion. The underlying analysis should be presented as concisely as possible, using language that is understandable to the public and that minimizes use of acronyms or jargon.

5. Alternatives

Agencies should encourage the members of the communities that may suffer a disproportionately high and adverse human health or environmental effect from a proposed agency action to help develop and comment on possible alternatives to the proposed agency action as early as possible in the process.

Where an EIS is prepared, CEQ regulations require agencies to identify an environmentally preferable alternative in the record of decision (ROD).[69] When the agency has identified a disproportionately high and adverse human health or environmental effect on low-income populations, minority populations, or Indian tribes from either the proposed action or alternatives, the distribution as well as the magnitude of the disproportionate impacts in these communities should be a factor in determining the environmentally preferable alternative. In weighing this factor, the agency should consider the views it has received from the affected communities, and the magnitude of environmental impacts associated with alternatives that have a less disproportionate and adverse effect on low-income populations, minority populations, or Indian tribes.

6. Record of decision

When an agency reaches a decision on an action for which an EIS was prepared, a public record of decision (ROD) must be prepared that provides information on the alternatives considered and the factors weighed in the decision-making process. Disproportionately high and adverse human health or environmental effects on a low-income population, minority population, or Indian tribe should be among those factors explicitly discussed in the ROD, and should also be addressed in any discussion of whether all practicable means to avoid or minimize environmental and other interrelated effects were adopted. Where relevant, the agency should discuss how these issues are addressed in any monitoring and enforcement program summarized in the ROD.[70]

Dissemination of the information in the ROD may provide an effective means to inform the public of the extent to which environmental justice concerns were considered in the decision-making process, and where appropriate, whether the agency intends to mitigate any disproportionately high and adverse human health or environmental effects within the constraints of NEPA and other existing laws. In addition to translating crucial portions of the EIS where appropriate, agencies should provide translation, where practicable and appropriate, of the ROD in non-technical, plain language for limited-English speakers. Agencies should also consider translating documents into languages other than English where appropriate and practical.

7. Mitigation

Mitigation measures include steps to avoid, mitigate, minimize, rectify, reduce, or eliminate the impact associated with a proposed agency action.[71] Throughout the process of public participation, agencies should elicit the views of the affected populations on measures to mitigate a disproportionately high and adverse human health or environmental effect on a low-income population, minority population, or Indian tribe and should carefully consider community views in developing and implementing mitigation strategies. Mitigation measures identified in an EIS or developed as part of a FONSI should reflect the needs and preferences of affected low-income populations, minority populations, or Indian tribes to the extent practicable.

---

[69] 40 C.F.R. § 1505.2(b).

[70] See 40 C.F.R. § 1505.2(c).

[71] See 40 C.F.R. § 1508.20.

D. Where No EIS or EA is Prepared

There are certain circumstances in which the policies of NEPA apply, and a disproportionately high and adverse human health or environmental impact on low-income populations, minority populations, or Indian tribes may exist, but where the specific statutory requirement to prepare an EIS or EA does not apply. These circumstances may arise because of an exemption from the requirement, a categorical exclusion of specific activities by regulation, or a claim by an agency that another environmental statute establishes the "functional equivalent" of an EIS or EA. For example, neither an EIS nor an EA is prepared for certain hazardous waste facility permits.

In circumstances in which an EIS or EA will not be prepared and a disproportionately high and adverse human health or environmental impact on low-income populations, minority populations, or Indian tribes may exist, agencies should augment their procedures as appropriate to ensure that the otherwise applicable process or procedure for a Federal action addresses environmental justice concerns. Agencies should ensure that the goals for public participation outlined in this guidance are satisfied to the fullest extent possible. Agencies also should fully develop and consider alternatives to the proposed action whenever possible, as would be required by NEPA.

Regulatory Changes

Consistent with the obligation of all agencies to promote consideration of environmental justice under NEPA and in all of their programs and activities, agencies that promulgate or revise regulations, policies, and guidances under NEPA or under any other statutory scheme should consult with CEQ and EPA to ensure that the principles and approaches presented in this guidance are fully incorporated into any new or revised regulations, policies, and guidances.

Effect of This Guidance

Agencies should apply, and comply with, this guidance prospectively. If an agency has made substantial investments in NEPA compliance, or public participation with respect to a particular agency action, prior to issuance of this guidance, the agency should ensure that application of this guidance does not result in additional delays or costs of compliance.

This guidance is intended to improve the internal management of the Executive Branch with respect to environmental justice under NEPA. The guidance interprets NEPA as implemented through the CEQ regulations in light of Executive Order 12898. It does not create any rights, benefits, or trust obligations, either substantive or procedural, enforceable by any person, or entity in any court against the United States, its agencies, its officers, or any other person.

APPENDIX A

GUIDANCE FOR FEDERAL AGENCIES ON KEY TERMS IN EXECUTIVE ORDER 12898 (see Selected Executive Orders section).

PART III CASE LAW (PRECEDENT SETTING AND/OR REPRESENTATIVE, RECENT CASE LAW)

INTRODUCTION
How to Read Legal Citations and Explanation of Abbreviations

Scott v. U.S., 411 F. Supp. 332, 345 (D.D.C. 1979), *aff'd in part, rev'd in part on other grounds*, 642 F.2d 602 (D.C. Cir. 1980). The decision in the fictitious case of Scott versus U.S. is reported at Volume 411 of the Federal Supplement reporter (reporting decisions of the U.S. District Courts); in this case, a 1979 decision of the U.S. District Court for the District of Columbia beginning at page 332; succeeding page numbers, if any, contain the specific passage or proposition for which the citation is being offered. The decision was upheld (or affirmed) in part and overturned (or reversed) in part on other grounds unrelated to the proposition for which the citation to the earlier opinion is being offered at Volume 642 of the Federal Reporter, Second Series (reporting decisions of the U.S. Courts of Appeals); in this fictitious case, a 1980 decision of the Court of Appeals for the District of Columbia Circuit) beginning at page 602. The following authorities are similarly cited by volume, page number(s) and date of issuance:

U.S. United States Reports—decisions of the U.S. Supreme Court

S.Ct. West Publishing Company's report of cases decided by the U.S. Supreme Court

L.Ed. Lawyers Co-operative Publishing Company report of cases decided by the U.S. Supreme Court

ERC Environment Reporter, Bureau of National Affairs Environmental Decisions—Cases

Statutory and Regulatory Authorities

42 U.S.C. § 4321 (1982). The statute or statutory language being cited, in this case the National Environmental Policy Act of 1969, is codified at Title 42 of the main 1982 volume of the United States Code (containing the compilation of statutes currently in force), in Section 4321; (West 1985) in a citation references the 1985 edition of West Publishing Company's annotated code.

40 C.F.R. § 1508.21 (1990). The regulation or regulatory language being cited is published in the 1990 edition of Title 40 of the Code of Federal Regulations (containing the compilation of regulations currently in force), at Section 1508.21.

Abbreviations and Acronyms Used

ACOE—U.S. Army Corps of Engineers
AEC—Atomic Energy Commission
APA—Administrative Procedures Act
Army—U.S. Department of the Army
Army Corps—U.S. Army Corps of Engineers
BLM—Bureau of Land Management
CEQ—Council on Environmental Quality
CERCLA—Comprehensive Environmental Response, Compensation, and Liability Act
DEIS—draft environmental impact statement
DOD—U.S. Department of Defense
DOE—U.S. Department of Energy
DOI—U.S. Department of the Interior
EA—environmental assessment
EIS—environmental impact statement
EPA—U.S. Environmental Protection Agency
ESA—Endangered Species Act

FAA—Federal Aviation Administration
FEIS—final environmental impact statement
FERC—Federal Energy Regulatory Commission
FHWA—Federal Highway Administration
FIFRA—Federal Insecticide, Fungicide, and Rodenticide Act
FLPMA—Federal Land Policy and Management Act
FOIA—Freedom of Information Act
FONSI—finding of no significant impact
FSEIS—final supplemental environmental impact statement
FWS—U.S. Fish and Wildlife Service
GSA—General Services Administration
HUD—U.S. Department of Housing and Urban Development
ICC—Interstate Commerce Commission
Navy—U.S. Department of the Navy
NEPA—National Environmental Policy Act
NIH—National Institutes of Health
NRC—U.S. Nuclear Regulatory Commission
NSF—National Science Foundation
RCRA—Resource Conservation and Recovery Act
ROD—record of decision
SARA—Superfund Amendments Act
USAF—U.S. Department of the Air Force
USFS—U.S. Forest Service
USGS—U.S. Geological Survey
USPS—U.S. Postal Service

Editor's note:

The cases discussed below provide a background on how the Federal courts have decided NEPA issues, and every effort was made to include the quotations as they appeared in the decisions. However, in general, citations to other cases and footnotes that were included in the decisions have not been included in the quotations. For this reason, users should refer to the court decisions themselves before using the discussion or quotations in other documents.

Aberdeen & Rockfish R. Co. v. Students Challenging Regulatory Agency Procedures, 422 U.S. 289, 95 S.Ct. 2336, 45 L.Ed.2d 191 (1975)

ISSUE(S) ADDRESSED: standing, judicial review

FACTS: In December 1971, citing sharply increasing costs and decreasing or negative profits, substantially all of the Nation's railroads collectively proposed to file tariffs increasing their freight rates. The Interstate Commerce Commission (ICC) prepared and issued a brief draft EIS regarding the environmental impact of the proposed tariff increase and concluded that there was no basis to believe that the environment would be substantially affected by the increase. Plaintiffs challenged this determination, alleging that the ICC had enacted a proposal with a significant effect on the environment without complying with NEPA.

FINDINGS: The U.S. Supreme Court stated that "NEPA does create a discrete procedural obligation on Government agencies to give written consideration of environmental issues in connection with certain major Federal actions and a right of action in adversely affected parties to enforce that obligation. When agency or departmental consideration of environmental factors in connection with that 'Federal action' is complete, notions of finality and exhaustion do not stand in the way of judicial review of the adequacy of such consideration...." 422 U.S. at 319.

The Court noted that "NEPA provides that 'such statement ... shall accompany *the proposal* through the existing agency review processes.' This sentence does not, contrary to the District Court opinion, affect the time when the 'statement' must be prepared. It simply says what must be done with the 'statement' once it is prepared - it must accompany the 'proposal.' The 'statement' referred to is the one required to be included 'in every recommendation or report on proposals for ... major Federal actions significantly affecting the quality of the human environment' and is apparently the final impact statement, for no other kind of statement is mentioned in the statute. Under *this* sentence of the statute, the time at which the agency must prepare the final 'statement' is the time at which it makes a recommendation or report on a *proposal* for Federal action." *Ibid.* at 320 (emphasis in original).

"The statute also requires that agencies consult with other environmentally expert agencies 'prior to making any detailed statement'...." *Ibid.* at 321.

***Flint Ridge Development Co. v. Scenic Rivers Association of Oklahoma*, 426 U.S. 776, 96 S.Ct. 2430, 49 L.Ed.2d 205 (1976)**

ISSUE(S) ADDRESSED: statutory conflict

FACTS: Plaintiffs challenged Department of Housing and Urban Development's (HUD) failure to prepare an EIS prior to approving the filing of a disclosure statement under the Interstate Land Sales Full Disclosure Act. Under this act, developers are required to disclose information by filing with HUD a statement of record regarding title of the land and conditions of the subdivision, among other things. The statement of record becomes effective automatically on the 30th day after filing, unless it is found to be materially incomplete or inaccurate.

FINDINGS: "NEPA's instruction that all Federal agencies comply with the impact statement requirement—and with all the other requirements of §102—'to the fullest extent possible,'... is neither accidental nor hyperbolic. Rather, the phrase is a deliberate command that the duty NEPA imposes upon the agencies to consider environmental factors not be shunted aside in the bureaucratic shuffle." 96 S.Ct. at 2438.

"Section 102 recognizes, however, that where a clear and unavoidable conflict in statutory authority exists, NEPA must give way....[T]he question we must resolve is whether, assuming an environmental impact statement would otherwise be required in this case, requiring the Secretary to prepare such a statement would create an irreconcilable and fundamental conflict with the Secretary's duties under the Disclosure Act." *Ibid.*

The Court noted that "even if the Secretary's action in this case constituted major Federal action significantly affecting the quality of the human environment so that an environmental impact statement would ordinarily be required, there would be a clear and fundamental conflict of statutory duty. The Secretary cannot comply with the statutory duty to allow statements of record to go into effect within 30 days of filing, absent inaccurate or incomplete disclosure, and simultaneously prepare impact statement on proposed developments. In these circumstances, we find that NEPA's impact statement requirement is inapplicable." *Ibid.* at 2439-40.

Kleppe v. Sierra Club, 427 U.S. 390, 96 S.Ct. 2718, 49 L.Ed.2d 576 (1976)

ISSUE(S) ADDRESSED: programmatic EIS, judicial review, cumulative impacts

FACTS: Plaintiffs claimed that Federal officials could not allow further development of coal reserves on Federal land without a comprehensive EIS on the entire region. The U.S. Supreme Court held that there was no proposal for regional development and, thus, that there was nothing on which to prepare an EIS.

FINDINGS: The mere contemplation of a certain action is not sufficient to require an EIS. "In the absence of a proposal for a regional plan of development, there is nothing that could be the subject of the analysis envisioned by the statute for an impact statement." 427 U.S. at 401.

"[U]nder the first sentence of §102(2)(C) the moment at which an agency must have a final statement ready 'is the time at which it makes a recommendation or report on a *proposal* for Federal action'...The procedural duty imposed upon agencies by this section is quite precise, and the role of the courts in enforcing that duty is similarly precise. A court has no authority to depart from the statutory language and, by a balancing of court-devised factors, determine a point during the germination process of a potential proposal at which an impact statement *should be prepared*...The contemplation of a project and the accompanying study thereof do not necessarily result in a proposal for major Federal action...." *Ibid.* at 406 (emphasis in original).

"This is not to say that §102(2)(C) imposes no duties upon an agency prior to its making a report or recommendation on a proposal for action. The section states that prior to preparing the impact statement the responsible official 'shall consult with and obtain the comments of any Federal agency which has jurisdiction by law or special expertise with respect to any environmental impact involved.' Thus, the section contemplates a consideration of environmental factors by agencies during the evolution of a report or recommendation on a proposal. But the time at which a court enters the process is when the report or recommendation on the proposal is made, and someone protests either the absence or the adequacy of the final impact statement. This is the point at which an agency's action has reached sufficient maturity to assure that judicial intervention will not hazard unnecessary disruption." *Ibid.* at 406, n.15

"NEPA does not contemplate that a court should substitute its judgment for that of the agency as to the environmental consequences of its actions. The only role for a court is to insure that the agency has taken a 'hard look' at environmental consequences." Ibid. at 410, n.21

"Thus when several proposals for actions which have cumulative or synergistic environmental impacts on a region are pending concurrently before an agency, their environmental consequences must be considered together." *Ibid.* at 410.

The "basic argument is that one comprehensive statement on the Northern Great Plains is required because all coal-related activity in that region is 'programmatically,' geographically,' and 'environmentally' related. Both the alleged 'programmatic' relationship and the alleged 'geographic' relationship resolve, ultimately, into an argument that the region is proper for a comprehensive impact statement because the petitioners themselves have approached environmental study in this area on a regional basis. Respondents point primarily to the [Northern Great Plains Regional Plan], which they claim- and petitioners deny- focused on the region described in the complaint...As for the alleged 'environmental' relationship respondents contend that the coal-related projects 'will produce a wide variety of cumulative environmental impacts.'...Cumulative environmental impacts are, indeed what require a comprehensive impact statement. But determination of the extent and effect of these factors, and particularly identification of the geographic area within which they may occur, is a task assigned to the special competency of the appropriate agencies." *Ibid.* at 412-414.

However, "[e]ven if environmental interrelationships could be shown conclusively to extend across basins and drainage areas, practical considerations of feasibility might well necessitate restricting the scope of comprehensive statements." *Ibid.* at 414.

Vermont Yankee Nuclear Power Corp. v. Natural Resources Defense Council, 435 U.S. 519, 98 S.Ct. 1197, 55 L.Ed.2d 460 (1978)

ISSUE(S) ADDRESSED: judicial review, reasonable alternatives, public involvement and disclosure

FACTS: Plaintiffs challenged the NRC's issuance of operating licenses to two nuclear power plants on the grounds that the agency failed to comply with NEPA. In one case, NRC had left to a subsequent proceeding the question of nuclear waste disposal; in another, NRC did not explore energy conservation as an alternative.

FINDINGS: "The [NRC's] prime area of concern in the licensing context...is national security, public health, and safety...NEPA, of course, has altered slightly the statutory balance, requiring 'a detailed statement by the responsible official on ... alternatives to the proposed action.' But, as should be obvious even upon a moment's reflection, the term 'alternatives' is not self-defining. To make an impact statement something more than an exercise in frivolous boilerplate the concept of alternatives must be bounded by some notion of feasibility." 98 S.Ct. at 1215.

"Common sense also teaches us that the 'detailed statement of alternatives' cannot be found wanting simply because the agency failed to include every alternative device and thought conceivable by the mind of man. Time and resources are simply too limited to hold that an impact statement fails because the agency failed to ferret out every possible alternative, regardless of how uncommon or unknown that alternative may have been at the time the project was approved." *Ibid.*

"We think these facts amply demonstrate that the concept of 'alternatives' is an evolving one, requiring the agency to explore more or fewer alternatives as they become better known and understood." *Ibid.* at 1216.

"[W]hile it is true that NEPA places upon an agency the obligation to consider every significant aspect of the environmental impact of a proposed action, it is still incumbent upon intervenors who wish to participate to structure their participation so that it is meaningful, so that it alerts the agency to the intervenors' position and contentions." *Ibid.*

"Indeed, administrative proceedings should not be a game or a forum to engage in unjustified obstructionism by making cryptic and obscure references to matters that 'ought to be' considered and then, after failing to do more than bring the matter to the agency's attention, seeking to have that agency determination vacated on the ground that the agency failed to consider matters 'forcefully presented.'" *Ibid.* at 1217.

"The fundamental policy questions appropriately resolved in Congress and in the State legislatures are not subject to reexamination in the Federal courts under the guise of judicial review of agency action. Time may prove wrong the decision to develop nuclear energy, but it is Congress or the States within their appropriate agencies which must eventually make that judgment. In the meantime courts should perform their appointed function. NEPA does set forth significant substantive goals for the Nation, but its mandate to the agencies is essentially procedural...It is to insure a fully informed and well-considered decision, not necessarily a decision the judges of the court of appeals would have reached it they had been members of the decision making unit of the agency. Administrative decisions should be set aside in this context, as in every other, only for substantial procedural or substantive reasons as mandated by statute, ... not simply because the court is unhappy with the result reached. And a single alleged oversight on a peripheral issue, urged by parties who never fully cooperated or indeed raised the issue below, must not be made the basis for overturning a decision properly made after an otherwise exhaustive proceeding." *Ibid.* at 1219.

Andrus v. Sierra Club, 442 U.S. 347, 99 S.Ct. 2335, 60 L.Ed.2d 943 (1979)

ISSUE(S) ADDRESSED: deference to CEQ regulations, definition of proposal

FACTS: Plaintiffs challenged the submission of a DOI appropriations request to Congress proposing curtailment of the National Wildlife Refuge System on the ground that the submittal was not accompanied by a "detailed statement" as required by NEPA.

FINDINGS: In this case, the U.S. Supreme Court agreed with CEQ's interpretation of NEPA with respect to whether EISs were required for appropriation requests. CEQ's regulations provide specifically that "legislation includes a bill or legislation proposal to Congress...but does not include requests for appropriations." 40 CFR 1508.17.

The Court described the CEQ regulations as a "single set of uniform, mandatory regulations applicable to all Federal agencies." 442 U.S. at 357. In addition, the Court said that "CEQ's interpretation of NEPA is entitled to substantial deference." *Ibid.* at 358.

Since appropriations "have the limited and specific purpose of providing funds for authorized programs," and since the "action-forcing" provisions of NEPA are directed precisely at the processes of "planning and...decision making,... which are associated with underling legislation, we conclude that the distinction made by CEQ's regulations is correct and that 'proposals for legislation' do not include appropriation requests." *Ibid.* at 361.

"[A]ppropriation requests do not 'propose' Federal actions at all; they instead fund action already proposed; Section 102(2)(C) is thus best interpreted as applying to those recommendation or reports that actually propose programmatic action, rather than to those which merely suggest how such actions may be funded. Any other result would create unnecessary redundancy. For example, if the mere funding of otherwise unaltered agency programs were construed to constitute major Federal actions significantly affecting the quality of the human environment, the resulting EISs would merely recapitulate the EISs that should have accompanied the initial proposals of the of the programs. And if an agency program were to be expanded or revised in a manner that constituted major Federal action significantly affecting the quality of the human environment, an EIS would have been required to accompany the underlying programmatic decision. An additional EIS at the appropriation stage would add nothing." *Ibid.* at 362-63.

Stryker's Bay Neighborhood Council, Inc. v. Karlen, 444 U.S. 223, 100 S.Ct. 497, 62 L.Ed.2d 433 (1980).

ISSUE(S) ADDRESSED: judicial review

FACTS: At issue was a plan by HUD to redesignate a site in New York City for a proposed low-income housing project. The Court of Appeals had ordered HUD to find a solution to the problem of low-income housing in a different manner.

FINDINGS: The U.S. Supreme Court held that NEPA does not require an agency to elevate environmental concerns over other, admittedly legitimate considerations. Further, "once an agency has made a decision subject to NEPA's procedural requirements, the only role for a court is to insure that the agency has considered the environmental consequences; it cannot 'interject itself within the area of discretion of the executive as to the choice of the action to be taken." 100 S.Ct. at 500.

"[T]here is no doubt that HUD considered the environmental consequences of its decision...NEPA requires no more." *Ibid.*

Weinberger v. Catholic Action of Hawaii/Peace Education Project, 454 U.S. 139, 102 S.Ct. 1917, 70 L.Ed.2d 298 (1981)

ISSUE(S) ADDRESSED: definition of proposal, national security, public involvement and disclosure

FACTS: Plaintiffs sought to require the Navy to prepare an EIS in connection with alleged plans to store nuclear weapons at a naval base in Hawaii. The Court of Appeals had issued an order requiring the Navy to prepare and release a "hypothetical" EIS. The U.S. Supreme Court reversed that holding.

FINDINGS: "Section 102(2)(C) thus serves twin aims. The first is to inject environmental considerations into the Federal agency's decision making process by requiring the agency to prepare an EIS. The second aim is to inform the public that the agency has considered environmental concerns in its decision making process. Through the disclosure of an EIS, the public is made aware that the agency has taken environmental considerations into account. Public disclosure of the EIS is expressly governed by FOIA." 102 S.Ct. at 201.

"The decision making and public disclosure goals of §102(2)(C), though certainly compatible, are not necessarily coextensive. Thus, §102(2)(C) contemplates that in a given situation a Federal agency might have to include environmental considerations in its decision making process, yet withhold public disclosure of any NEPA documents, in whole or in part, under the authority of an FOIA exemption." *Ibid.*

FOIA "exemption 1 exempts from disclosure matters that are 'A) specifically authorized under criteria established by an Executive order to be kept secret in the interest of national defense or foreign policy and B) are in fact properly classified pursuant to such Executive order.'" *Ibid.* at 202.

"Since the public disclosure requirements of NEPA are governed by FOIA, it is clear that Congress intended that the public's interest in ensuring that Federal agencies comply with NEPA must give way to the Government's need to preserve military secrets. In the instant case, an EIS concerning a proposal to store nuclear weapons at West Loch need not be disclosed....If the Navy proposes to store nuclear weapons at West Loch, the Department of Defense regulations can fairly be read to require that an EIS be prepared solely for internal purposes, even though such a document cannot be disclosed to the public. The Navy must consider environmental consequences in its decision making process, even if it is unable to meet NEPA's public disclosure goals by virtue of FOIA Exemption." *Ibid.* at 203.

"The Navy is not required to prepare an EIS regarding the hazards of storing nuclear weapons at West Lock simply because the facility is 'nuclear capable.'... [A]n EIS need not be prepared simply because a project is *contemplated*, but only when the project is *proposed*. To say that the West Loch facility is "nuclear capable' is to say little more than that the Navy has contemplated the possibility that nuclear weapons, of whatever variety, may at some time be stored here. It is the proposal to *store* nuclear weapons at West Loch that triggers the Navy's obligation to prepare an EIS." *Ibid.* at 203 (emphasis in original).

Metropolitan Edison Co. v. People Against Nuclear Energy, 460 U.S. 766, 103 S.Ct. 1556, 75 L.Ed.2d 534 (1983)

ISSUE(S) ADDRESSED: scope

FACTS: Plaintiffs challenged the adequacy of an EA, alleging that it did not address the psychological stress of living near the Three Mile Island nuclear power plant.

FINDINGS: The U.S. Supreme Court concluded that the threat to psychological health of residents near Three Mile Island nuclear plant restart was not cognizable under NEPA. NEPA is concerned with the physical environment—land, air, water, not the mere threat of impact.

The Court found that "NEPA does not require the agency to assess every impact or effect of its proposed action, but only the impact or effect on the environment." 103 S.Ct. at 1560.

"NEPA was designed to promote human welfare by alerting governmental actors to the effect of their proposed action on the physical environment." *Ibid.*

"Thus, although NEPA states its goals in sweeping terms of human health and welfare, these goals are *ends* that Congress has chosen to pursue by *means* of protecting the physical environment." (emphasis in the original). *Ibid.* at 1561.

"To determine whether [NEPA] §102 requires consideration of a particular effect, we must look at the relationship between what effect and the change in the physical environment caused by the major Federal action at issue... For example, residents of Harrisburg area have relatives in other parts of the country. Renewed operation of TMI-1 may well cause psychological health problems for these people. They may suffer 'anxiety, tension and fear, a sense of helplessness,' and accompanying physical disorder,.... because of the risk that their relatives may be harmed in a nuclear accident. However, this harm is simply too remote from the physical environment to justify requiring the NRC to evaluate the psychological health damage to these people that may be caused by renewed operation of TMI-1." *Ibid.*

"Our understanding of the congressional concerns that led to the enactment of NEPA suggest that the terms 'environmental effect' and 'environmental impact' in §102 be read to include a requirement of a reasonably close causal relationship between a change in the physical environment and the effect at issue." *Ibid.*

"[People Against Nuclear Energy] argues that the psychological health damage it alleges 'will flow directly from the risk of (a nuclear) accident.'... But a risk of an accident is not an effect on the physical environment. A risk is, by definition, unrealized in the physical world. In a causal chain from renewed operation of TMI-1 to psychological health damage, the element of risk and its perception by PANE's members are necessary middle links. We believe that the element of risk lengthens the causal chain beyond the reach of NEPA." *Ibid.* at 1562.

"Neither the language nor the history of NEPA suggests that it was intended to give citizens a general opportunity to air their policy objections to proposed Federal actions. The political process, and not NEPA, provides the appropriate forum in which to air policy disagreements. We do not mean to denigrate the fears of PANE's members, or to suggest that the psychological health damage they fear could not, in fact, occur. Nonetheless, it is difficult for us to see the differences between someone who dislikes a government decision so much that he suffers anxiety and stress, someone who fears the effects of that decision so much that he suffers similar anxiety and stress, and someone who suffers anxiety and stress that 'flow directly,'... from the risks associated with the same decision. It would be extraordinarily difficult for agencies to differentiate between 'genuine' claims that are grounded solely in disagreement with a democratically adopted policy. Until Congress provides a more explicit statutory instruction than NEPA now contains, we do not think agencies are obligated to undertake the inquiry." *Ibid.* at 1563.

"The gravity of harm does not change its character. If a harm does not have a sufficiently close connection to the physical environment, NEPA dose not apply. NEPA does not require agencies to evaluate the effects of risk *qua* risk." *Ibid.*

Baltimore Gas and Electric Co. v. Natural Resources Defense Council, Inc., 462 U.S. 87, 103 S.Ct. 2246, 76 L.Ed.2d 437 (1983)

ISSUE(S) ADDRESSED: judicial review

FACTS: In a generic rulemaking to evaluate the environmental effects of the nuclear fuel cycle for nuclear power plants, the NRC issued a rulemaking that assumed "zero release" of radiological effluents from nuclear wastes sealed in a permanent repository. Under this rule, NRC licensing boards would assume, for purposes of NEPA, that the permanent storage of certain nuclear wastes would have no significant environmental impact and thus would not affect the decision whether to license a nuclear power plant. Plaintiffs challenged the rule as arbitrary and capricious and in violation of NEPA.

FINDINGS: "As part of its generic rulemaking proceedings to evaluate the environmental effects of the nuclear fuel cycle for nuclear powerplants, the Nuclear Regulatory Commission decided that licensing boards should assume, for purposes of NEPA, that the permanent storage of certain nuclear wastes would have no significant environmental impact and thus should not affect the decision whether to license a particular nuclear powerplant." 103 S.Ct. at 1058.

"The Commission and the parties have later termed this assumption of complete repository integrity as the 'zero-release' assumption: the reasonableness of this assumption is at the core of the present controversy." *Ibid.* at 1059.

"The key requirement of NEPA, however, is that the agency consider and disclose the actual environmental effects in a manner that will ensure that the overall process, including both the generic rulemaking and the individual proceedings, brings those effects to bear on decisions to take particular actions that significantly affect the environment." *Ibid.* at 1061.

"Resolution of these fundamental policy questions lies, however, with Congress and the agencies to which Congress has delegated authority, as well as with State legislatures (not with NEPA) and, ultimately, the populace as a whole." *Ibid.*

"Congress in enacting NEPA, however, did not require agencies to elevate environmental concerns over other appropriate considerations....Rather, it required only that the agency take a 'hard look' at the environmental consequences before taking a major action." *Ibid.*

"The role of the courts is simply to ensure that the agency has adequately considered and disclosed (to the public) the environmental impact of its actions and that its decision is not arbitrary or capricious." *Ibid.*

"Congress did not enact NEPA, of course, so that an agency could contemplate the environmental impact of an action as an abstract exercise. Rather, Congress intended that the 'hard look' be incorporated as part of the agency's process of deciding whether to pursue a particular Federal action." *Ibid.* at 1062-63.

"NEPA does not require agencies to adopt any particular internal decision making structure. Here, the agency has chosen to evaluate generically the environmental impact of the fuel cycle and inform individual licensing boards, though the Table S-3 rule, of its evaluation. The generic method chosen by the agency is clearly an appropriate method of conducting the 'hard look' required by NEPA....The environmental effects of much of the fuel cycle are not plant specific, for any plant, regardless of its particular attributes, will create additional wastes that must be stored in a common long-term repository. Administrative efficiency and consistency of decision are both furthered by a generic determination of these effects without needless repetition of the litigation in individual proceedings, which are subject to review by the Commission in any event." *Ibid.* at 1063.

"[A] reviewing court must remember that the Commission is making predictions, within its area of special expertise, at the frontiers of science. When examining this kind of scientific determination, as opposed to simple findings of fact, a reviewing court must generally be at its most deferential." *Ibid.* at 1064.

"It is not our task to determine what decision, we, as Commissioners, would have reached. Our only task is to determine whether the Commission has considered the relevant factors and articulated a rational connection between the facts found and the choice made." *Ibid.* at 1065.

Robertson v. Methow Valley Citizens Council, 490 U.S. 332, 109 S.Ct. 1835, 104 L.Ed.2d 351 (1989) (This case is a companion to *Marsh v. Oregon National Resources Council*)

ISSUE(S) ADDRESSED: procedural requirements, mitigation, public involvement and disclosure, deference to CEQ

FACTS: A USFS study designated a particular national forest location as having high potential for a major ski resort. Methow Recreation applied for a special use permit to develop and operate such a resort on the site. The USFS prepared an EIS on the project, including the effects of various levels of development on wildlife and air quality and outlined steps to mitigate adverse effects. The Washington Department of Game raised special concerns about the potential losses to migratory mule deer which use the Methow Valley. Plaintiffs brought suit challenging USFS decision to issue special use permit. The U.S. Supreme Court examined (1) whether the NEPA requires Federal agencies to include in each EIS a fully developed plan to mitigate environmental harm and a 'worst case' analysis of potential environmental harm if relevant information concerning significant environmental effects is unavailable or too costly to obtain; and (2) whether the USFS may issue a special use permit for recreational use of national forest land in absence of a fully developed plan to mitigate environmental harm.

FINDINGS: "The statutory requirement that a Federal agency contemplating a major action prepare such an environmental impact statement serves NEPA's 'action-forcing' purpose in two important respects...It ensures that the agency, in reaching its decision, will have available, and will carefully consider, detailed information concerning significant environmental impacts; it also guarantees that the relevant information will be made available to the larger audience that may also play a role in both the decision making process and the implementation of that decision." 109 S.Ct. at 1845.

"Publication of an EIS, both in draft and final form, also serves a larger informational role. It gives the public the assurance that the agency 'has indeed considered environmental concerns in its decision making process,' and, perhaps more significantly, provides a springboard for public comment.'" *Ibid.*

"The sweeping policy goals announced in § 101 of NEPA are thus realized through a set of 'action-forcing' provisions that require that agencies that a 'hard look' at environmental consequences...and that provide for broad public dissemination of relevant environmental information. Although these procedures are almost certain to affect the agency's substantive decision, it is now well-settled that NEPA itself does not mandate particular results, but simply prescribes the necessary process." *Ibid.* at 1846.

"If the adverse environmental effects of the proposed action are adequately identified and evaluated, the agency is not constrained by NEPA from deciding that other values outweigh the environmental costs... In this case, for example, it would not have violated NEPA if the Forest Service, after complying with the Act's procedural requirements, had decided that the benefits to be derived from downhill skiing at Sandy Butte justified the issuance of a special use permit, not withstanding the loss of 15 percent, 50 percent, or even 100 percent of the mule deer herd. Other statutes may impose substantive environmental obligations on Federal agencies, but NEPA merely prohibits uninformed—rather than unwise—agency action." *Ibid.*

"The requirement that an EIS contain a detailed discussion of possible mitigation measures flows both from the language of the Act and, more expressly, from CEQ's implementing regulations." *Ibid.*

"[O]mission of a reasonably complete discussion of possible mitigation measures would undermine the 'action-forcing' function of NEPA. Without such a discussion, neither the agency nor other interested groups and individuals can properly evaluate the severity of the adverse effects." *Ibid.* at 1847.

"There is fundamental distinction, however, between a requirement that mitigation be discussed in sufficient detail to ensure that environmental consequences have been fairly evaluated, on the one hand, and a substantive requirement that a complete mitigation plan be actually formulated and adopted, on the other....[I]t would be inconsistent with NEPA's reliance on procedural mechanisms—as opposed to substantive, results-based standards—to demand the presence of a fully developed plan that will mitigate harm before an agency can act." *Ibid.*

The Court also held that CEQ's amendment of its regulation to delete the requirement for a "worst case analysis" was valid, and found that the worst case requirement was not a codification of prior NEPA case law. Specifically, the Court held that the regulations promulgated by CEQ were entitled to substantial deference, particularly where, as here, there appeared to have been good reason for the change (i.e., eliminating the distortion of the decision making process by overemphasizing highly speculative harms) which came after the prior regulation had been subjected to considerable criticism. See generally, *Ibid.* at 1848.

"Moreover, the amendment was designed to better serve the twin functions of an EIS—requiring agencies to take a 'hard look' at the consequences of the proposed action and providing important information to other groups and individuals. CEQ explained that by requiring that an EIS focus on reasonably foreseeable impacts, the new regulation, 'will generate information and discussion on those consequences of greatest concern to the public and of greatest relevance to the agency's decision,'...rather than distorting the decision making process by overemphasizing highly speculative harms...." *Ibid.* at 1849.

"In sum, we conclude that NEPA does not require a fully developed plan detailing what steps *will* be taken to mitigate adverse environmental impacts and does not require a 'worst case analysis.' In addition, we hold that the Forest Service has adopted a permissible interpretation of its own regulations." *Ibid.* at 1851 (emphasis in original).

Marsh v. Oregon Natural Resources Council, 490 U.S. 360, 109 S.Ct. 1851, 104 L.Ed.2d 377 (1989) (This case is a companion to *Robertson v. Methow Valley Citizens Council*)

ISSUE(S) ADDRESSED: supplementation, agency discretion

FACTS: The case arose out of a decision to construct a dam at Elk Creek in the Rogue River Basin in southwest Oregon, and presented the question of whether information developed after completion of the EIS required that a supplemental EIS be prepared before construction of the dam could continue.

FINDINGS: "The subject of post-decision supplemental environmental impact statements is not expressly addressed in NEPA. Preparation of such statements, however, is at times necessary to satisfy the Act's 'action-forcing' purpose." 109 S.Ct. at 1857-58.

"...NEPA promotes its sweeping commitment to 'prevent or eliminate damage to the environment and biosphere' by focusing government and public attention on the environmental effects of proposed agency action....By so focusing agency attention, NEPA ensures that the agency will not act on incomplete information, only to regret its decision after it is too late to correct. Similarly, the broad dissemination of information mandated by NEPA permits the public and other government agencies to react to the effects of a proposed action at a meaningful time. It would be incongruous with this approach to environmental protection, and with the Act's manifest concern with preventing uninformed action, for the blinders to adverse environmental effects, once unequivocally removed, to be restored prior to the completion of agency action simply because the relevant proposal has received initial approval. As we explained in *TVA v. Hill*, 437 U.S. 153, 188 n. 34 (1978), although 'it would make sense to hold NEPA inapplicable at some point in the life of a project, because the agency would no longer have a meaningful opportunity to *weigh* the benefits of the project versus the detrimental effects on the environment,' up to that point, 'NEPA cases have generally required agencies to file [EISs] when the remaining governmental action would be environmentally significant.'" *Ibid.* at 1858.

"[A]n agency need not supplement an EIS every time new information comes to light after the EIS is finalized. To require otherwise would render agency decision making intractable, always awaiting updated information only to find the new information outdated by the time a decision is made. On the other hand, ... NEPA does require that agencies take a 'hard look' at the environmental effects of their planned action, even after a proposal has received initial approval. Application of the 'rule of reason' thus turns on the value of the new information to the still pending decision making process. In this respect, the decision whether to prepare a supplemental EIS is similar to the decision whether to prepare an EIS in the first instance: If there remains 'major Federal action' to occur, and if the new information is sufficient to show that the remaining action will 'affect the quality of the human environment' in a significant manner or to a significant extent not already considered, a supplemental EIS must be prepared." *Ibid.* at 1859.

"[R]esolution of this dispute involves primarily issues of fact. Because analysis of the relevant documents 'requires a high level of technical expertise,' we must defer to 'the informed discretion of the responsible Federal agencies.' ....[A]s long as the Corps' decision not to supplement the FEISS was not 'arbitrary or capricious,' it should not be set aside." *Ibid.* at 1861.

"When specialists express conflicting views, an agency must have discretion to rely on the reasonable opinions of its own qualified experts even if, as an original matter, a court might find contrary views more persuasive. On the other hand, ... courts should not automatically defer to the agency's express reliance on an interest in finality without carefully reviewing the record and satisfying themselves that the agency has made a reasoned decision based on its evaluation of the significance—or lack of significance—of the new information." *Ibid.*

"Respondents' argument that significant new information required the preparation of a second [SEIS] rests on two written documents....Nor do [the documents] purport to discuss any conditions that had changed since the FEIS was completed in 1980...Before respondents commenced this litigation in October 1985, no one had suggested that either document constituted the kind of new information that made it necessary or appropriate to supplement the FEISs...." *Ibid.* at 1861-62.

"There is little doubt that if all of the information in [the documents] was both new and accurate, the Corps would have been required to prepare a second supplemental EIS....[Having taken a 'hard look' at the proffered evidence] and having determined based on careful scientific analysis that the new information was of exaggerated importance, the Corps acted within the dictates of NEPA in concluding that supplementation was unnecessary." *Ibid.* at 1865.

Lujan v. National Wildlife Federation, 497 U.S. 871. 110 S.Ct. 3177, 111 L.Ed.2d 695 (1990)

ISSUE(S) ADDRESSED: standing

FACTS: Plaintiffs challenged BLM's administration of its "land withdrawal program" as violating NEPA. As a preliminary matter, the Court considered whether plaintiffs had standing to bring the litigation. In particular, the Court considered the issue of conferring standing on plaintiffs who had alleged in affidavits the use of public lands "in the vicinity" of land that were the subject of two out of 1,250 BLM orders. These orders, plaintiffs claimed, would open public lands up to mining activities, thereby destroying their natural beauty. Plaintiffs challenged all of the 1,250 BLM orders, claiming violations of the NEPA and the Federal Land Policy and Management Act (FLPMA). Under the program, DOI undertook to review individual land classifications and withdrawals affecting some 180 million acres of public land with an eye to clearing title to lands outside Federal ownership and returning as much public land as possible to multiple use management, as directed by FLPMA. Plaintiff's suit alleged that the program violated FLPMA and NEPA. Plaintiffs abandoned its challenged to each of the 1,250 individual land actions taken by DOI, reserving only its challenge to the program as a whole.

The district court, ruling on defendants' motion for summary judgment, found that plaintiffs had no standing to seek judicial review. The Court of Appeals reversed, finding the affidavits sufficient to confer standing to challenge the two individual orders and that standing to challenge those orders conferred standing to challenge all 1,250 orders.

FINDINGS: Reversing the Court of Appeals, the U.S. Supreme Court acknowledged that neither NEPA nor FLPMA provides a private right of action for violations of it provisions. Rather an injured party must seek relief under the APA.

To demonstrate standing, a plaintiff must identify some final agency action that affects him or her and must show he or she has suffered a legal wrong or is adversely affected or aggrieved by that action within the meaning of a relevant statute. See generally, APA, Sections 702 and 704. To be "adversely affected" within the meaning of a statute, a plaintiff must be within the "zone of interests" sought to be protected by the statutory provision that forms the basis of the complaint.

Using this test of standing, the Court found that plaintiffs' interest in recreational use and aesthetic enjoyment of the Federal lands were within the "zone of interest" that NEPA and FLPMA were designed to protect, but the plaintiffs claiming use "in the vicinity" of immense tracts of land managed by BLM, had not shown they would be "adversely affected" by the BLM actions. See generally, 110 S.Ct. at 3185-86. The Court noted that the affidavits contained "averments which State only that one of respondent's members uses unspecified portions of an immense tract of territory, on some portions of which mining activity has occurred or probably will occur by virtue of the governmental action." *Ibid.* at 3189. The Court specifically rejected the D.C. Circuit's concept to "presume" the missing connection between the affiant and the affected land. *Ibid.*

The Court also held that the APA does not provide a cause of action to challenge a government program like this one at all: a program "is not an 'agency action' within the meaning of § 702, much less a 'final agency action' within the meaning of § 704." *Ibid.* at 3189. For this reason, even the supplementary affidavits submitted by plaintiffs to cure the defect in their original affidavits could not give them standing, because the APA only allows challenges to "final agency action."

"Respondent alleges that violation of law is rampant within this program—failure to revise land use plans in proper fashion, failure to submit certain recommendations to Congress, failure to consider multiple use, inordinate focus upon mineral exploitation, failure to provide required public notice, failure to provide adequate environmental impact statements. Perhaps so. But respondent cannot seek *wholesale* improvement of this program by court decree, rather than in the offices of the Department or the halls of Congress, where programmatic improvements are normally made. Under the terms of the

APA, respondent must direct its attack against some particular 'agency action' that causes it harm." *Ibid.* at 3190 (emphasis in original).

The Court also rejected plaintiff's claim to "informational standing" for the same general reason that it rejected the supplementary affidavits. Plaintiff's affidavit did not "identify any particular 'agency action' that was the source of these injuries," but instead alleged injury from the program as a whole. *Ibid.* at 3194. The plaintiffs failed to set forth specific facts necessary to survive a motion for summary judgment. The Court neither endorsed nor criticized the "informational standing" doctrine.

RELEVANT FEDERAL CIRCUIT AND DISTRICT COURT CASES

Alabama ex rel. Siegelman v. EPA, 911 F.2d 499 (11th Cir. 1990)

ISSUE(S) ADDRESSED: functional equivalence

FACTS: EPA issued a final operating permit under RCRA for the nation's largest hazardous waste management facility, located at Emelle, Alabama. The Emelle facility, owned and operated by Chemical Waste Management, Inc., received hazardous wastes from forty-eight states. The facility covered 2,730 acres of land and included twenty inactive landfill trenches, one active trench, an aqueous waste storage pond, a waste drum storage area, a liquid waste tank storage area, a liquid waste solidification unit, and a solvent and fuel recovery area. Plaintiffs challenged the issuance of the RCRA permit on the basis that EPA had not complied with NEPA.

FINDINGS: EPA is not required to comply with NEPA with respect to the issuance of permits pursuant to the RCRA. NEPA is the general statute forcing agencies to consider the environmental consequences of their actions and to allow the public a meaningful opportunity to learn about and to comment on the proposed actions.

"If there were no RCRA, NEPA would seem to apply here. But RCRA is the later and more specific statute directly governing EPA's process for issuing permits to hazardous waste management facilities. As such, RCRA is an exception to NEPA and controls here." 911 F.2d at 504.

"Still, RCRA is the functional (though not the structural or literal) equivalent and more specific counter part of NEPA. RCRA is comprehensive in its field of application." *Ibid.* at 505.

"If RCRA does not represent the best policy for protecting the public welfare when EPA issues permits for hazardous waste facilities Congress can, of course change the law." *Ibid.* at 505 n. 13.

Audubon Society of Central Arkansas v. Dailey, 977 F.2d 428 (8th Cir. 1992)

ISSUE(S) ADDRESSED: mitigation, mitigated finding of no significant impact

FACTS: In 1987, the voters of Little Rock approved a capital improvement bond issue to build streets. At the time of the bond election, the city's list of top twenty street projects included an extension of Rebsamen Park Road permitting access to Murray Lock and Dam and Murray, LaHarpe View and Rebsamen parks from the west, where previously the only entrance had been from central Little Rock. These parks run alongside the Arkansas River near downtown Little Rock. The City had plans eventually to connect these parks to others in a "chain of parks." The Army Corps determined that, though the only action affecting national waters was the placement of the fill in Jimerson Creek, NEPA required the agency to consider the environmental impact on the entire area of "the proposed road extension plus the existing Rebsamen Park Road from gateway to gateway." The Army Corps prepared an EA and FONSI which was contested in the district court. The district court held that the Army Corps had ignored the considerable effect increased traffic resulting from the bridge and its connected project would have on recreational use of Murray Park, Rebsamen Park, and other recreational areas on the south bank of the Arkansas River at Little Rock. The City argued that the Army Corps considered the effect of the traffic and that the court had no power to require the Army Corps to do anything further. Alternatively, the City requested that the court remand the matter to the Army Corps instead of affirming the order requiring an EIS.

FINDING(S): The Court of Appeals quoted favorably from the lower court opinion: "While the COE [Army Corps of Engineers] might have been taking a 'hard look,' the COE ultimately chose to ignore what it saw. All the facts and scientific projections showed the tremendous increase in traffic that will occur severely impacting the recreational uses of the area. The City's wishful thinking that the commuting public will choose Cantrell with its approximately eight more stoplights for the comparable distance and travel time over Rebsamen Park Road is without justification. The COE's misplaced reliance on the City's empty assurances that it will enforce the 35 mph speed limit flies in the face of the COE's information that the current limits are not being enforced and the public will use a speed limit 10 mph over the existing limits. The COE was not relying on reasonable opinions of any qualified experts in concluding the impacts of the project were not significant when its own consultant and personnel had made reasoned decisions to the contrary based on their evaluations of the available data." 977 F.2d at 433

"The District of Columbia Circuit has listed four factors to be considered in determining whether an agency's decision to forego an EIS is arbitrary and capricious: (1) whether the agency took a 'hard look' at the problem; (2) whether the agency identified the relevant areas of environmental concern; (3) as to the problems studied and identified, whether the agency made a convincing case that the impact was insignificant; and (4) if there was impact of true significance, whether the agency convincingly established that changes in the project sufficiently reduced it to a minimum. *Cabinet Mountains Wilderness v. Peterson*, 685 F.2d 678, 681-82 (D.C.Cir.1982); *Sierra Club v. United States Dept. of Transportation*, 753 F.2d 120, 127 (D.C.Cir.1985). While the City would limit our inquiry to the second factor in *Cabinet Mountains*, the district court's determination properly focussed on the third factor -- whether the conclusion of insignificant impact is sufficiently convincing." *Ibid.* at 434.

"The permit as issued contains as special conditions neither a speed limit, nor any requirement of speed limit enforcement, nor any provision for closing the road off at rush hours. The Environmental Assessment stated that the City agreed to establish and enforce a 35 mph speed limit, but it did not make this a condition of the permit. Other mitigation measures included the City's agreement to place gateways with stop signs at the west entrance to the parkway and the east entrance to Rebsamen Park, and inclusion of a 'mild' curve in the road design." *Ibid.* at 435.

"Thus, the Environmental Assessment itself comes very close to explicitly acknowledging that without enforcement of the 35 mph speed limit the project would have significant impact on the environment, yet the administrative record shows that the entity responsible for enforcing the speed limit has not enforced it on the existing road. An agency may certainly base its decision of 'no significant impact' on mitigating measures to be undertaken by a third party. See *Friends of Endangered Species, Inc. v. Jantzen*, 760 F.2d 976, 987 (9th Cir.1985). In such a case, the mitigating measures need not be a condition of the permit (although this helps, see *State of Louisiana v. Lee*, 758 F.2d 1081, 1083 (5th Cir.1985), *cert. denied*, 475 U.S. 1044 (1986)), nor even a contractual obligation, see *Preservation Coalition, Inc. v. Pierce*, 667 F.2d 851 (9th Cir.1982). However, the mitigating measures must be 'more than mere vague statements of good intentions.' *Ibid.* at 860-61; *Lee*, 758 F.2d at 1083. Of course, the result of the mitigating measures must be to render the net effect of the modified project on the quality of the environment less than 'significant.' See *Cabinet Mountains*, 685 F.2d at 682." *Ibid.* at 435-36.

Big Hole Ranchers Assoc. v. United States Forest Service, 686 F. Supp. 256 (D. Mont. 1988)

ISSUE(S) ADDRESSED: connected actions, cumulative actions

FACTS: Plaintiffs challenged several EAs for timber sales and road construction in Beaverhead National Forest.

FINDINGS: The court held that the question of whether the proposed actions, which were the subject of separate EAs, were connected or cumulative actions having significant impact on the environment precluded finding that the EAs were adequate and allowing summary judgment for the defendant, USFS. "An EIS serves two purposes: (1) to provide decision makers with enough information to aid in the substantive decision whether to proceed with the project in light of its environmental consequence; and (2) to provide the public with information and an opportunity to participate in gathering information." *Ibid.* at 260.

"In reviewing an agency decision not to prepare an EIS pursuant to NEPA, the court's inquiry is whether the 'responsible agency has "reasonably concluded" that the project will have no significant adverse environmental consequences.' *Save the Yaak Committee. v. Block*, 840 F.2d 714, 717 (9th Cir.1988). If substantial questions are raised regarding whether the proposed action may have a significant effect upon the human environment, a decision not to prepare an EIS is unreasonable." *Ibid.*

"[T]he issue in the present action is whether the road construction and the tree timber sales are 'connected actions' and/or 'cumulative actions' within the meaning of 40 CFR §1508.25(a)(2), requiring the Forest Service to prepare an EIS analyzing their combined environmental impacts." *Ibid.* at 261

The court cited the finding in *Yaak* as persuasive: "The road reconstruction, timber harvest, and feeder roads are all 'connected actions' that must be analyzed by the Forest Service in deciding whether to prepare an EIS or only an EA. Thus, these 'connected actions' raise material issues of fact concerning the effects that these actions may have on the human environment. Summary judgment was not appropriate." Citing *Yaak*, 840, F.2d 714, 721.
Ibid. at 262.

Blue Ocean Preservation Society v. Watkins, 754 F. Supp. 1450 (D. HI. 1991)

ISSUE(S) ADDRESSED: connected actions, definition of proposal

FACTS: The State of Hawaii developed the Hawaii Geothermal Project consisting of four phases: 1) exploration and testing of geothermal resource; 2) research regarding the feasibility of transporting the power via underwater cables; 3) a program involving the drilling of exploration wells; and 4) construction of separate geothermal power plants. DOE provided funds for the first 2 phases; in 1988, Congress appropriated an additional $5 million for use in Phase III, the first of three such appropriations anticipated from Congress over the next three years. Congress stated in a Conference Report that while Phase III was "research," not a major Federal action subject to NEPA, DOE should nevertheless earmark some of the funds for an EA/EIS for the project. In 1990, Plaintiffs sued DOE seeking to compel preparation of an EIS, and to enjoin further Federal participation in the project until the EIS was completed.

FINDINGS: "In this case, the agency, DOE, clearly 'has a goal' of implementing Phase III, and it is apparent that its ultimate goal is to see Phase IV through. There is evidence that the Department of Interior shares this goal. If DOE is, as it suggests, soliciting or drawing up contracts to perform the work, it 'is actively preparing to make a decision on one or more means of accomplishing that goal.' The fact that DOE has not set forth any written 'proposal' is immaterial because 'a proposal may exist in fact as well as by agency declaration.'" 754 F. Supp. at 1466-62.

The court rejected Congress' characterization of Phase III, and held that Phases III and IV were connected actions which must be considered in one EIS. The court further held that the "research work" contemplated by Phase III "alone easily satisfies the statutory standards for 'major Federal action' based simply on the extent of Federal funding." *See Ibid.* at 1466-68.

Cabinet Mountains Wilderness/Scotchman's Peak Grizzly Bears v. Peterson, 685 F.2d 678 (D.C. Cir. 1982)

ISSUE(S) ADDRESSED: mitigated finding of no significant impact

FACTS: The Cabinet Mountains Wilderness Area, managed by the USFS, consists of approximately 94,272 acres and is part of the Cabinet-Yaak ecosystem, one of only six ecosystems in the continental U.S. that supports populations of grizzly bears. The USFS determined that the impacts of a proposal to allow drilling in the area would not be significant because the impacts to the grizzly bear population could be mitigated. Plaintiffs argued that the USFS' failure to prepare an EIS violated NEPA.

FINDINGS: The court noted that "[t]he plan devised by the FWS was expressly adopted by the Forest Service" and that "[n]umerous specific recommendations were made to avoid this impact and mitigation measures to protect the grizzly bears were imposed upon the proposal." 685 F.2d at 680, 681.

"Under the statute the administrative agency has the 'initial and primary responsibility' to ascertain whether an EIS is required and its decision can be overturned only if it was arbitrary, capricious or an abuse of discretion." *Ibid.* at 681.

The court also stated that "changes in the project are not legally adequate to avoid an impact statement *unless they permit a determination that such impact as remains, after the change, is not significant* (emphasis in the original)." *Ibid.* at 682.

"NEPA's EIS requirement is governed by the rule of reason...and an EIS must be prepared only when significant environmental impacts will occur as a result of the proposed action. If, however, the proposal is modified prior to implementation by adding specific mitigation measures which completely compensate for any adverse environmental impacts stemming from the original proposal, the statutory threshold of significant environmental effects is not crossed and an EIS is not required. To require an EIS in such circumstances would trivialize NEPA and would 'diminish its utility in providing useful environmental analysis for major Federal actions that truly affect the environment.'" *Ibid.*

"Because the mitigation measures adopted in the present case were not part of the original proposal and were not imposed by statute or regulation, appellants contend they can not be used to justify the Forest Service's failure to prepare an EIS." *Ibid.*

"The appellants rely on a recent statement by the Council on Environmental Quality (CEQ) concerning the effect of mitigation measures on NEPA's EIS requirement. In a publication entitled 'Forty Most Asked Questions Concerning CEQ's National Environmental Policy Act Regulations'...the CEQ said:

> 'mitigation measures may be relied upon to make a finding of no significant impact only if they are imposed by statute or regulation, or submitted b an applicant or agency as part of the original proposal...'" *Ibid.*

However, the court held that the appellants' reliance on the CEQ statement was misplaced. "The CEQ is charged with administering NEPA and its interpretations are generally entitled to substantial deference... but such deference is nether required nor appropriate here. The NEPA regulations issued by the CEQ are binding on all Federal agencies. The 'Forty Questions' publication, however, is merely an informal statement, not a regulation, and we do not find it be persuasive authority....Unlike the regulations considered in the *Andrus* case, it was not the product of notice and comment procedures and does not impose a mandatory obligation on all Federal agencies." *Ibid.*

California ex rel. Van de Kamp v. Marsh, 687 F. Supp. 495, (N.D. Calif. 1988)

ISSUES ADDRESSED: reasonable alternatives, cumulative impacts, adequacy of an EA

FACTS: The Army Corps proposed to issue a permit for the filling of 180 acres of wetlands for the Oakland Airport project. The site was located immediately adjacent to existing airport facilities on diked, nontidal baylands, and was made up of seasonal wetlands which provided feeding and resting habitat for migratory shorebirds and waterfowl during the winter. Additional birds and wildlife used the wetlands year-round. The Army Corps sought public comment on the proposed permit and prepared an EA, concluding that no EIS was necessary. The Army Corps did not hold any public hearings on the project. Plaintiffs sued to set aside the permit issued to fill the wetlands based on alleged violations of NEPA and other statutes.

FINDINGS: The court found the EA inadequate for a number of reasons. In general, the court held that "[t]he Corps relied on other agencies' evaluations of the project's cumulative effect of the wetlands and wildlife impacts. The Corps did not discuss the cumulative impacts on air quality, water quality, or the noise pollution in its Decision Document." 687 F. Supp at 498.

"As a Federal agency, the Corps must provide a discussion of the environmental impacts, not only of the proposed project, but of the alternatives to the proposed project, in its EA [40 C.F.R. § 1508.9(b) (1987); 33 C.F.R. § 230.9(a) (1987)]. The Corps did not evaluate the alternative of relocating some or all of the air cargo project at nearby airports, including San Francisco International, and San Jose airport. It did not complete a detailed analysis of the environmental impacts of these alternative sites. The Corps did not consider changing the project to house only one of the air cargo companies who had requested space at the airport, and thereby shrinking the impact on the wetlands. These appear to be reasonable alternatives which had to be evaluated by the Corps. By failing to consider and evaluate them, the Corps did not strictly comply with NEPA's requirement to pursue all alternatives to the Oakland Airport site." *Ibid.* at 499.

"The Corps must provide a discussion of the environmental impacts of the project [40 C.F.R. § 1508.9(b)]. It was undisputed at trial that the 180-acre wetlands are very significant. The wildlife at the site is abundant and the site is an important part of the migration trip for the migratory birds. The Corps did not have adequate information regarding the numbers of birds, specifically the California Least Tern, which are present at the Oakland Airport, to be able to make a fully informed and well-considered decision about the birdlife at the proposed site. The trapping studies of the Salt Marsh Harvest Mouse were not accurate and the decision that the mouse does not exist at the site was not based on the most up-to-date information available to the Corps. Substantial questions were raised regarding the impacts on the Salt Marsh Harvest Mouse and the California Least Tern, both of which are endangered species. The Corps did not evaluate whether the air cargo buildings, the human traffic, and the airplane and vehicular traffic would add pollutants to the remaining wetlands. If the wetlands are affected by the pollutants, the wildlife in the wetlands will be endangered. These issues raise substantial questions about the effect on the environment which were not evaluated by the Corps. By ignoring these issues, the Corps violated NEPA's requirements to take a hard look at the impact on wildlife. The Corps could not reasonably conclude that there would not be a significant adverse environmental consequences with the incomplete information the Corps had before it." *Ibid.*

"The data the Corps relied upon in making their statement that the project would not measurably increase noise levels beyond the acceptable level in the vicinity of the airport is not in the Administrative Record. The Corps did not see the study it relied upon and instead accepted it at face value. The Corps neither independently verified the data it relied upon, nor did they take a hard look at the noise impacts of the proposed project. Thus the Corps violated NEPA's standards." *Ibid.*

The court also concluded that "[a] Federal agency must analyze and discuss the cumulative impacts of the proposed action considered together with past, present, and reasonably foreseeable future action [See 40 C.F.R. §§ 1508.7, 1508.27 (1987); *Kleppe v. Sierra Club*, 427 U.S. 390, 410, 96 S.Ct. 2718, 2730, 49 L.Ed.2d 576 (1975)]. The agency must consider other proposals and contemplated actions that are not yet formalized proposals. The agency must also consider actions that are not themselves subject to NEPA's requirements [See 40 C.F.R. § 1508.7 (1987); *Fritiofson v. Alexander*, 772 F.2d 1225, 1242-43 (5th Cir.1985)]." *Ibid.* at 500.

"The Corps did not independently evaluate the San Francisco Bay Conservation and Development Commission's report on the amount of tidal and nontidal wetlands, but instead used the information without concern for their lack of understanding of the figures in the report. The Corps was required to independently verify the information it relied upon [*Friends of the Earth v. Hintz*, 800 F.2d at 834-835]. The Corps must review the project in conjunction with all past, present and proposed projects to determine if the project may have a significant impact on the human environment. The Corps' lack of investigation into the cumulative impacts of the proposed project violated NEPA's requirements." *Ibid.*

The court held that "the Corps did not adequately address the wetlands, wildlfe, and endangered species impacts, water quality impacts, noise impacts, cumulative impacts, or the adequacy of the mitigation proposal." *Ibid.* at 501. Thus, the EAs were inadequate and these issues must be addressed in more detail to determine whether they would have a significant impact on the human environment.

Calvert Cliffs' Coordinated Committee v. Atomic Energy Commission, 449 F.2d 1109 (D.C. Cir. 1971), *cert. denied*, 404 U.S. 942 (1972)

ISSUE(S) ADDRESSED: judicial review, procedural requirements, compliance with environmental standards, reasonable alternatives

FACTS: The court was asked to review rules promulgated by the Atomic Energy Commission (AEC) on NEPA implementation. Although the rules required applicants for construction permits and operating licenses to prepare their own "environmental reports" and required the AEC's regulatory staff to prepare its own detailed statement of environmental costs, benefits, and alternatives, the rules did set limits on how environmental issues would be considered in the Commission's decision making process.

FINDINGS: The general substantive policy in Section 101 of NEPA is flexible. "It leaves room for a responsible exercise of discretion and may not require particular substantive results in particular problematic instances." The procedural provisions in NEPA Section 102 are not as flexible and indeed are designed to see that all Federal agencies do in fact exercise the substantive discretion given them. 449 F.2d at 1112.

NEPA makes environmental protection a part of the mandate of every Federal agency and department. Agencies are "not only permitted, but compelled, to take environmental values into account. Perhaps the greatest importance of NEPA is to require [all] agencies to consider environmental issues just as they *consider* other matters within their mandates." *Ibid.* (emphasis in original).

To insure that an agency balances environmental issues with its other mandates, NEPA Section 102 requires agencies to prepare a "detailed statement." The apparent purpose of the "detailed statement" is to aid in the agencies' own decision making process and to advise other interested agencies and the public of the environmental consequences of the planned action.

The procedural duties imposed by NEPA are to be carried out by the Federal agencies "to the fullest extent possible." "[T]his language does not provide an escape hatch for footdragging agencies; it does not make NEPA's procedural requirements somehow 'discretionary'. Congress did not intend the Act to be such a paper tiger." 449 F.2d at 1114. NEPA's procedural requirements "must be complied with to the fullest extent, unless there is a clear conflict of *statutory* authority." *Ibid.* at 1115 (emphasis in original).

Section 102 of NEPA mandates a careful and informed decision making process and creates judicially enforceable duties. The reviewing courts probably could not reverse a substantive decision on the merits, but if the decision were reached procedurally without consideration of environmental factors—conducted fully and in good faith—it is the responsibility of the courts to reverse.

The AEC's interpretation of its NEPA responsibilities was "crabbed" and made "a mockery of the Act." 449 F.2d at 1117. Section 102's requirement that the detailed statement accompany a proposal through agency review means more than physical proximity and the physical act of passing papers to reviewing officials. It is not enough that environmental data and evaluation merely "accompany" an application through the review process but receive no consideration from the hearing board as contemplated by the AEC regulations.

The AEC improperly abdicated its NEPA authority by relying on certifications by Federal, State, and regional agencies that the applicant complied with specific environmental quality standards. NEPA mandates a case-by-case balancing judgment on the part of Federal agencies; in each case, the particular economic and technical benefits of an action must be weighed against the environmental costs. Certification by another agency that its own environmental standards are satisfied involves an entirely different kind of judgment and attends to only one aspect of the problem—the magnitude of certain environmental costs. Their certification does not mean that they found no environmental damage, only that it was not high enough to violate applicable standards. The only agency in a position to balance environmental costs with economic and technical benefits is the agency with the overall responsibility for the project.

NEPA requires that an agency—to the fullest extent possible—consider alternatives to its actions which would reduce environmental damage. By refusing to consider requiring alterations of facilities (which received construction permits before NEPA was enacted) until construction is completed, the AEC may effectively foreclose the environmental protection envisioned by Congress.

Delay in the final operation of the facility may occur but is not a sufficient reason to reduce or eliminate consideration of environmental factors under NEPA. Some delay is inherent in NEPA compliance, but it is far more consistent with the purposes of the act to delay operation at a stage when real environmental protection may come about than at a stage where corrective action may be so costly as to be impossible.

Catron County Board of Commissioners v. United States Fish and Wildlife Service, 75 F.3d 1429 (10th Cir. 1996)

ISSUE(S) ADDRESSED: application of NEPA to Endangered Species Act actions

FACTS: In 1985, the Secretary of DOI proposed listing the spikedace and loach minnow as threatened species and establishing a critical habitat for them. The Secretary's proposed designation comprised approximately 74 miles of river habitat in the County. The notice also provided for a 60-day comment period, which was subsequently extended by several weeks, and scheduled three public meetings to gather additional information and comments on the proposed actions. Also in his proposal, the Secretary determined that he was not required to comply with the documentation requirements of NEPA, claiming that Secretarial actions under ESA § 1533, 16 U.S.C. §§ 1531-44, are exempt from NEPA. In April 1994, the County filed its motion for injunctive relief claiming that the Secretary had failed to comply with NEPA and seeking to prevent the Secretary from implementing and enforcing its designation of critical habitat.

FINDINGS: The court found that the FWS failed to comply with NEPA when designating critical habitat under the ESA. The court noted that agencies are exempted from complying with NEPA only if environmental review requirements were unavoidably in conflict with a statute, making compliance impossible, or if the procedural requirements of the statute were the functional equivalent of NEPA. The court also noted that the Ninth Circuit addressed exactly the same issue with a different result.

"The Ninth Circuit affirmed in part and reversed in part, holding that while *Douglas County* did have standing, NEPA did not apply. *Douglas County*, 48 F.3d at 1507-08. We disagree with the panel's reasoning. First, given the focus of the ESA together with the rather cursory directive that the Secretary is to take into account 'economic and other relevant impacts,' we do not believe that the ESA procedures have displaced NEPA requirements. Secondly, we likewise disagree with the panel that no actual impact flows from the critical habitat designation. Merely because the Secretary says it does not make it so. The record in this case suggests that the impact will be immediate and the consequences could be disastrous. The preparation of an EA will enable all involved to determine what the effect will be. Finally, we believe that compliance with NEPA will further the goals of the ESA, and not vice versa as suggested by the Ninth Circuit panel. For these reasons and in view of our own circuit precedent, we conclude that the Secretary must comply with NEPA when designating critical habitat under ESA." 75 F.2d at 1436.

"NEPA does not require particular results but rather a particular process. *Robertson v. Methow Valley Citizens Council*, 490 U.S. 332, 350 (1989); see also 40 C.F.R 1500.1(c). NEPA ensures that a Federal agency makes informed, carefully calculated decisions when acting in such a way as to affect the environment and also enables dissemination of relevant information to external audiences potentially affected by the agency's decision. *Robertson*, 490 U.S. at 349....By contrast, ESA's core purpose is to prevent the extinction of species by preserving and protecting the habitat upon which they depend from the intrusive activities of humans. See 16 U.S.C. 1531(b). While the protection of species through preservation of habitat may be an environmentally beneficial goal, Secretarial action under ESA is not inevitably beneficial or immune to improvement by compliance with NEPA procedure. The designation of critical habitat effectively prohibits all subsequent Federal or federally funded or directed actions likely to affect the habitat. *Ibid.* at 1536(a)(2)." *Ibid.* at 1437.

"'[E]ven if the Federal agency believes that on balance the effect [of the action] will be beneficial,' regulations promulgated by the Council on Environmental Quality (CEQ) nonetheless require an impact statement. 40 C.F.R. § 1508.27(b)(1); see also *Environmental Defense Fund v. Marsh*, 651 F.2d 983, 993 (5th Cir., 1981). NEPA's requirements are not solely designed to inform the Secretary of the environmental consequences of his action. NEPA documentation notifies the public and relevant government officials of the proposed action and its environmental consequences and informs the public that the acting agency has considered those consequences. A Federal agency could not know the potential alternatives to a proposed Federal action until it complies with NEPA and prepares at least an EA....To interpret NEPA as merely requiring an assessment of detrimental impacts upon the environment would significantly diminish the act's fundamental purpose—to 'help public officials make decisions that are based on understanding of environmental consequences, and take actions that protect, restore, and enhance the environment.' 40 C.F.R. 1500.1(c). Appellants' theory would cast the judiciary as final arbiter of what Federal actions protect or enhance the environment, a role for which the courts are not suited." *Ibid.*

Citizens Against Burlington v. Busey, 938 F.2d 190 (D.C. Cir. 1991), *cert. denied*, 502 U.S. 994 (1991)

ISSUES ADDRESSED: reasonable alternatives, purpose and need

FACTS: The Toledo Airport Authority in Toledo Ohio, sought permission from the FAA to expand its local airport to accommodate a cargo hub. According to the airport authority, the cargo hub would create new jobs and provide new revenue for the local economy. The FAA prepared an EIS for Federal approval action and gave detailed consideration to only two alternative actions: the operation of the Toledo Airport as a cargo hub (the preferred alternative) and the no-action alternative. In its EIS, the FAA defined the goal for its action as helping to launch a new hub in Toledo and thereby helping to fuel the Toledo economy. There were only two alternatives considered and alternative locations outside of the Toledo area were dismissed because they would not fulfill these objectives. After completion of the EIS, the FAA approved the cargo hub. Plaintiffs challenged the FAA action, arguing, among other things, that FAA violated NEPA and CEQ regulations by not assessing other alternatives such as creating a cargo hub at Fort Wayne, Indiana.

FINDINGS: In upholding the FAA decision, the court recognized that the identification of reasonable alternatives is limited by the purpose and need for the proposed action.

"We realize, as we stated before, that the word 'reasonable' is not self-defining. Deference, however, does not mean dormancy, and the rule of reason does not give agencies license to fulfill their own prophecies, whatever the parochial impulses that drive them. Environmental impact statements take time and cost money. Yet an agency may not define the objectives of its action in terms so unreasonably narrow that only one alternative from among the environmentally benign ones in the agency's power would accomplish the goals of the agency's action, and the EIS would become a foreordained formality." 938 F.2d at 196.

The court stated that an agency's definition of the objectives of a proposed Federal action should be upheld as long as the objectives the agency chooses are reasonable. Further, an agency need follow only a rule of reason in preparing an EIS, and this rule of reason extends to both choosing which alternatives the agency must discuss as well as the extent to which the agency must discuss them.

"[T]he FAA defined the goal for its action as helping to launch a new cargo hub in Toledo and thereby helping to fuel the Toledo economy. The agency then eliminated from detailed discussion the alternatives that would not accomplish this goal." *Ibid.* at 198.

In addition, EPA had criticized the methods used to analyze the noise issues, but the court found that "...a lead agency does not have to follow the EPA's comments slavishly—it just has to take them seriously." *Ibid.* at 201.

Citizens For Environmental Quality v. U.S., 731 F. Supp. 970 (D. Colo. 1989)

ISSUES ADDRESSED: programmatic EIS, cumulative impacts

FACTS: Plaintiffs challenged the comprehensive Land Resource Management Plan for the Rio Grande National Forest on the ground that, among other things, the EIS accompanying the plan was inadequate.

FINDINGS: The court upheld the EIS for the land management plans. "Defendants' EIS complied with NEPA since it provided for on-going, site-specific impact studies to take place prior to the implementation of soil disturbing activities; there is no requirement that the EIS set forth a discussion of cumulative impacts, since such a discussion is to take place prior to the issuance of the [site-specific] EIS." 731 F. Supp. at 982.

"The test which agencies must meet in dealing with environmental aspects of the proposed action is tied to the 'rule of reason' which may be stated as follows: If the environmental aspects of proposed actions are easily identifiable, they should be related in such detail that the consequences of the action are apparent. If, however, the effects cannot be readily ascertained and if the alternatives are deemed remote and only speculative possibilities, detailed discussion of environmental effects is not contemplated under NEPA." *Ibid.* at 995.

City of Tenakee Springs v. Clough, 915 F.2d 1308 (9th Cir. 1990)

ISSUES ADDRESSED: reasonable alternatives, cumulative impacts, programmatic EIS

FACTS: The litigation arose out of a 50-year timber sale contract which the Forest Service and Alaska Pulp Company entered into in 1956 for logging in the Tongass National Forest. Since 1971, the Service has prepared operating plans for successive five-year periods, each supported by an EIS as required by NEPA. The specific action is the consolidated challenge to the ten-volume Supplemental EIS which the USFS released in November 1989 concerning old growth timber harvesting in the Tongass National Forest in southeastern Alaska. The district court denied the injunction because it ruled that the appellants had not raised any serious legal questions or presented any likelihood of success on the merits of their claims that the USFS violated NEPA.

FINDINGS: On appeal, the Court of Appeals held that plaintiffs had demonstrated a likelihood of success on the merits and issued an injunction. Specifically, the court found that the EIS for the 5-year operating plan for a 50-year timber sales contract was not adequate because it failed to consider alternatives of "terminating, suspending or amending its contract". 915 F.2d at 1312

"Where there are large scale plans for regional development, NEPA requires both a programmatic and site-specific EIS....This court has held that where several foreseeable similar projects in a geographical region have a cumulative impact, they should be evaluated in a single EIS." *Ibid.*

NEPA requires consideration of the potential impact of an action before the action takes place. Emphasizing the likelihood of future timber sales, the court remanded to the agency for further consideration of cumulative impact because the agency had examined single projects in isolation without considering the net impact that all the projects in the area might have on the environment.

Coker v. Skidmore, 941 F.2d 1306 (5th Cir. 1991)

ISSUE(S) ADDRESSED: supplementation

FACTS: This case concerns the proposed construction by the Army Corps of approximately 5.4 miles of levee along the Yazoo River in Mississippi, as part of the Upper Yazoo portion of the Yazoo River Basin Flood Control Project. The Project covered 13,400 square miles in northwest Mississippi. In 1975, the Army Corps prepared a programmatic final EIS for the Project. Coker's complaint alleged that the Army Corps had violated NEPA in failing to issue a supplemental EIS. Prior to trial, the Army Corps issued an EA and a draft Finding of No Significant Impact. Prior to that time, the Army Corps had stated its plans to prepare a supplemental EIS for the channelization portion and also all other uncompleted portions of the Yazoo Headwater Project. The FONSI concluded, as to the levee, that a supplement to the final EIS was not required. The District Court had found that the 1975 EIS was outdated and thus had to be supplemented before the levee construction could proceed. The Army Corps appealed.

FINDINGS: In this decision, the Court of Appeals for the Fifth Circuit overturned the district court's determination that a supplemental EIS had to be prepared prior to construction of a 5.4-mile levee on the Yazoo River in Mississippi. The levee construction was part of the Yazoo River Basin Flood Control Project, for which the Army Corps prepared a programmatic EIS in 1975. The Court of Appeals, however, found that the lower court had not evaluated the case using the CEQ and Army Corps NEPA standards for supplementation. The CEQ regulations (40 CFR 1502.9 (c)) State that an agency must supplement an EIS if the agency makes substantial changes in the proposed action relevant to environmental concern, or if significant new circumstances or information relevant to environmental concerns and bearing on the proposed action or its impacts arise. The district court explicitly found no evidence that construction of the levee would have a significant environmental effect. The Court of Appeals noted that "[a]n EIS need not be supplemented whenever new information concerning a project comes to light...or when portions of it become out of date." 941 F.2d at 1310.

Commonwealth of Massachusetts v. Watt, 716 F.2d 946 (1st Cir. 1983)

ISSUES ADDRESSED: supplementation

FACTS: The government asked that a preliminary injunction stopping the auction of drilling rights near Georges Bank off the New England Coast be set aside. The district court had agreed that a significant reduction in the oil estimates had occurred since the final EIS.

FINDINGS: Plaintiffs contended that a 97% reduction in the estimates of oil likely to be found required the supplementation of an oil leasing EIS at Georges Bank. The court agreed, stating "[w]ithout a supplement, the FEIS did not describe the likely environmental harms well enough to allow the Secretary to make an informed decision." 716 F.2d at 948.

Conservation Law Foundation of New England v. General Services Administration, 707 F.2d. 626 (1st Cir. 1983)

ISSUES ADDRESSED: definition of major Federal action, secondary (indirect) impacts

FACTS: This case concerned the preparation of an EIS by the General Services Administration for the disposal of excess property under the Federal Property and Administrative Services Act.

FINDINGS: The court held 1) that disposal of excess Federal property is a major Federal action requiring the preparation of an EIS, 2) that the EIS must discuss the environmental effects of potential uses of the property by a new owner in order to permit a reasoned choice between retention or disposal of each parcel, and 3) that GSA is not required to obtain development plans from the party whose bid GSA intends to accept and to supplement the EIS because GSA has no power to see that the implementation plans are ever implemented. However, "[t]he fact that GSA cannot control the land once it is transferred is no reason not to take a hard look at whether the land should be sold. Such a hard look necessarily includes speculation about the consequences of sale, including speculation about likely reuses of the property." 707 F.2d at 633.

Conservation Law Foundation, Inc. v. Department of the Air Force, 864 F. Supp. 265 (D.N.H.1994); *aff'd in part, rev'd in part*, 79 F.3d 1250 (1st Cir. 1996)

ISSUES ADDRESSED: public involvement and disclosure, supplementation, mitigation

FACTS: This case was brought by an environmental group and local residents near Pease Air Force Base (AFB) to challenge the USAF's compliance with NEPA and other Federal statutes in the transfer of Pease AFB to a State agency for redevelopment into an international trade hub. The Commission on Base Realignment and Closure decided to close Pease AFB, New Hampshire. The USAF issued a final EIS on the disposal and reuse of the base in June 1991. The EIS concluded that the proposed redevelopment plans would impact on New Hampshire's ability to meet the air quality milestones mandated by the Clean Air Act Amendments of 1990. As a result of subsequent discussions with EPA, the USAF conducted further air quality analysis and the redevelopment authority entered into a Memorandum of Understanding (MOU) with EPA and the State. Under the terms and conditions specified in the MOU, the parties agreed that redevelopment of Pease could go forward in compliance with the Clean Air Act. In August 1991, the Air Force issued a ROD, addressing the air quality concerns by incorporating the MOU into the ROD. The ROD stated that, because of contamination on most of the reuse parcels, the Air Force could not transfer the affected parcels by deed because of the requirements of CERCLA §120(h)(3). However, the ROD provided for the long-term lease of the parcels to the redevelopment authority and stated that the leases would be converted to a transfer by deed after remediation was complete. In April 1992, the Air Force issued a Supplemental ROD which stated that, based on subsequent information, redevelopment of the AFB would not cause any new Clean Air Act standard violations and that the Air Force would allow the development authority to assume control of the property and proceed with redevelopment. The plaintiffs challenged the final EIS on the ground that it failed to fully address air quality impacts and that the USAF did not fully disclose the methods by which the agency would conform to Clean Air Act requirements.

FINDINGS: The court found that the USAF had violated the public disclosure requirements of NEPA by relying on post-EIS studies to satisfy its statutory obligations regarding air quality concerns, and by failing to include in the FEIS the decision to transfer parcels by long-term lease, as opposed to deed, until the USAF's CERCLA obligations were satisfied. "The procedural requirements of NEPA mandate that the USAF prepare an EIS detailing all relevant environmental information prior to a decision. This requirement acts to serve the underlying purpose of NEPA to disseminate the environmental information surrounding a particular agency decision and allow public comment prior to the final decision. The decisions made regarding the conformity of the project to the [Clean Air Act] amendments followed the EIS process and thus were never subject to the public comment. The EPA in their August 14, 1991 comments on the FEIS opined that this lack of public review constituted a violation of the NEPA public disclosure requirements." 864 F. Supp. at 284-85.

The USAF also violated NEPA in failing to prepare a supplemental EIS after conducting a Clean Air Act conformity analysis and developing conformity information after the final EIS. Additionally, the final EIS was inadequate because the USAF failed to analyze air quality mitigation measures related to the reuse and that transfer for reuse did not relieve the USAF of the responsibility to evaluate mitigation measures related to the reuse. *See Ibid.* at 288.

The court also found that "...in evaluating the adequacy of the FEIS the court must use the 'rule of reason' standard. However, even in giving the USAF the utmost deference, the response to wetland concerns is woefully inadequate. The USAF simply stated that while it may be possible to complete development without filling any wetlands, the ultimate responsibility lies with the developer." *Ibid.* at 292.

The court held that the final EIS was inadequate and directed that a supplemental EIS be prepared. *Ibid.*

Douglas County v. Babbitt, 48 F.3d 1495 (9th Cir. 1995), *cert. denied*, 116 S.Ct. 698 (1996)

ISSUES ADDRESSED: application of NEPA to Endangered Species Act actions

FACTS: The Department of the Interior policy on "critical habitat designation" first announced in the *Federal Register* in 1983 and routinely used since that time was that the Secretary did not need to prepare a NEPA document for this action. Douglas County sued the department on a critical habitat designation that affected lands in Douglas County, contending that a NEPA document was required. The district court (*Douglas County v. Lujan*, 810 F. Supp. 1470 (D. Ore. 1992)) granted a permanent injunction and set aside the critical habitat designation, but stayed the order pending appeal.

FINDINGS: The Court of Appeals affirmed the County's standing on procedural grounds, but reversed the lower court's finding that NEPA applied to the designation of critical habitat. "[T]he ESA has an important mandate that distinguishes it from NEPA. Congress gave a special guideline to the Secretary in the critical habitat process. Though the Secretary may exclude from the critical habitat any area, the exclusion of which, would be more beneficial than harmful, he or she must designate any area without which the species would become extinct...This mandate conflicts with the requirements of NEPA because in cases where extinction is at issue, the Secretary has no discretion to consider the environmental impact of his or her actions." 48 F.3d at 1503.

"More importantly, in 1983, the Secretary announced in the *Federal Register* his decision not to prepare EAs (and, therefore, EISs) before making critical habitat designations...In the 1988 amendments [to the ESA], Congress did not respond to this interpretation." *Ibid.* at 1504. The court found this inaction to be significant because Congress, in revisiting the ESA, could have changed the Secretary's interpretation but did not do so. Further, this inaction is significant because, before the 1988 amendments, in 1981, the Sixth Circuit, in *Pacific Legal Foundation*, 657 F.2d at 835, held that NEPA did not apply when the Secretary listed a species as threatened or endangered under the ESA and suggested in dicta that the process of designating a critical habitat might provide the 'functional equivalent' of an EIS." *Ibid.* at 1504.

"We find that the NEPA procedures do not apply to Federal actions that do nothing to alter the natural physical environment. When we consider the purpose of NEPA in light of Supreme Court guidance on the scope of the statute, we conclude that an EA or an EIS is not necessary for Federal actions that conserve the environment. The purpose of NEPA is to 'provide a mechanism to enhance or improve the environment and prevent further irreparable damage.'" *Ibid.* at 1505.

"If the purpose of NEPA is to protect the physical environment, and the purpose of preparing an EIS is to alert agencies and the public to potential adverse consequences to the land, sea or air, then an EIS is unnecessary when the action at issue does not alter the natural, untouched physical environment at all." *Ibid.* at 1505.

"We also find that NEPA does not apply to the designation of a critical habitat because the ESA furthers the goals of NEPA without demanding an EIS." *Ibid.* at 1506

"On the merits, we find that NEPA does not apply to the Secretary's decision to designate a habitat for an endangered or threatened species under the ESA because (1) Congress intended that the ESA critical habitat procedures displace the NEPA requirements, (2) NEPA does not apply to actions that do not change the physical environment, and (3) to apply NEPA to the ESA would further the purposes on neither statute." *Ibid.* at 1507-08

Environmental Defense Fund, Inc. v. Environmental Protection Agency, 489 F.2d 1247 (D.C. Cir. 1973)

ISSUE(S) ADDRESSED: functional equivalence

FACTS: EPA was challenged on the cancellation of almost all registrations of compounds using DDT under the Federal Insecticide, Fungicide, and Rodenticide Act (FIFRA). All parties agreed that the withdrawal of registration was a major Federal action that would significantly affect the human environment.

FINDINGS: "The court is asked to consider two other, somewhat interrelated questions concerning NEPA. First, is the EPA an agency subject to the requirements of the statute when it undertakes environmental actions such as the cancellation of DDT registrations here? Second, has EPA in effect complied with the requirements, despite the lack of a formal NEPA impact statement?" 489 F.2d at 1255.

"The rationale we first developed in *Portland Cement* is applicable here as well, and an exemption from the strict letter of the NEPA requirements is thus appropriate. The explicit language in FIFRA requires that pesticides be deregistered if they will be injurious to man and his environment." *Ibid.* at 1256.

"We conclude that where an agency is engaged primarily in an examination of environmental questions, where substantive and procedural standards ensure full and adequate consideration of environmental issues, then formal compliance with NEPA is not necessary, but functional compliance is sufficient." *Ibid.* at 1257.

"[W]e delineate a narrow exemption from the literal requirements for those actions which are undertaken pursuant to sufficient safeguards so that the purpose and policies behind NEPA will necessarily be fulfilled." *Ibid.*

Environmental Defense Fund v. Massey, 986 F.2d 528 (D.C. Cir. 1993)

ISSUE(S) ADDRESSED: extraterritorial application of NEPA

FACTS: Plaintiffs challenged the National Science Foundation's (NSF) plans to incinerate food waste at McMurdo Station in Antarctica, arguing that NEPA applies extraterritorially and, thus, that NSF should have prepared an EIS. Plaintiffs further alleged that NSF violated Executive Order 12114, requiring the preparation of environmental assessments for U.S. actions which have an impact overseas. After preparing an environmental assessment under Executive Order 12114, NSF issued its final decision regarding incineration. Environmental Defense Fund challenged the agency's decision under NEPA. NSF moved to dismiss, arguing that NEPA does not apply extraterritorially.

FINDINGS: The Court of Appeals for the District of Columbia Circuit held that despite NEPA's broad mandates, there is no clear congressional intent that NEPA should apply beyond the borders of the U.S. and that NEPA did not apply to NSF's decision to build waste incinerators in Antarctica. The court, however, criticized NSF's environmental impact assessment of the waste disposal determination. The Court of Appeals reversed the lower court's decision with specific language about the unique nature of Antarctica.

Specifically, the court held that the application of NEPA to Federal agency actions is not limited to actions occurring in, or having effects in, the United States. Rather, in its view, NEPA applies to Federal agency actions occurring anywhere in the world or outer space, since NEPA is designed "to control the decision making process...not the substance of agency decisions" and that decision making "take[s] place almost exclusively in this country...." 986 F.2d at 532.

However, the court relied on Antarctica's unique status as a place without a sovereign in reaching its holding that NEPA applies to this case and found that NSF's concern for adverse foreign policy impacts was unwarranted. In its conclusion, the court stated "We find it important to note, however, that we do not decide today how NEPA might apply to actions in a case involving an actual foreign sovereign or how other U.S. statutes might apply to Antarctica. We only hold that the alleged failure of NSF to comply with NEPA before resuming incineration in Antarctica does not implicate the presumption against extraterritoriality." *Ibid.* at 537.

Foundation on Economic Trends v. Heckler, 756 F.2d 143 (D.C. Cir. 1985)

ISSUE(S) ADDRESSED: significance

FACTS: The court addressed the question of the appropriate level of environmental review required of the National Institutes of Health (NIH) before it approved the deliberate release of genetically engineered, recombinant-DNA-containing organisms into the open environment. The court affirmed a lower court's issuance of an injunction temporarily enjoining NIH from approving deliberate release experiments without a greater level of environmental concern than the agency had shown.

FINDINGS: "Although the 'agency commencing Federal action has the initial and primary responsibility for ascertaining whether an EIS is required,' the courts must determine that this decision accords with traditional norms of reasoned decision making and that the agency has taken the 'hard look' required by NEPA." 756 F.2d at 151.

The court held that NIH must attempt to evaluate seriously the risk of ecological disruption from the deliberate release of genetically engineered organisms and that "ignoring possible environmental consequences will not suffice." *Ibid.* at 154.

"An environmental assessment that fails to address a significant environmental concern can hardly be deemed adequate for a reasoned determination that an EIS is not appropriate." *Ibid.*

Foundation on Economic Trends v. Department of Agriculture, 943 F.2d. 79 (D.C. Cir. 1991)

ISSUE(S) ADDRESSED: standing

FACTS: Plaintiffs challenged the lack of an EIS for a "germplasm" program within the Department of Agriculture. Their standing to sue was based upon harm to their ability to disseminate information or "informational standing."

FINDINGS: The court stated that it had never sustained an organization's standing in a NEPA case solely on the basis of informational injury, i.e., damage to the organization's interest in disseminating the environmental data that an EIS could be expected to contain. "If such injury alone were sufficient, a prospective plaintiff could bestow standing upon itself merely by requesting the agency to prepare the detailed statement NEPA contemplates, which in turn would prompt the agency to engage in 'agency action' by failing to honor the request." 943 F.2d at 85.

The court concluded that plaintiffs had failed to allege specific agency action that injured them and triggered a violation of NEPA. "As we have indicated, plaintiffs seeking judicial review under section 702 of the [Administrative Procedure Act] for an alleged violation of NEPA and claiming only an 'informational injury' must show the *particular* agency action—in addition to the agency's refusal to prepare an impact statement—that allegedly triggered the violation and thereby caused the injury. In this case, neither the complaint nor the materials plaintiffs submitted on summary judgment satisfied this requirement." *Ibid.* at 87.

Friends of Fiery Gizzard v. Farmers Home Administration, 61 F.3d 501 (6th Cir. 1995)

ISSUE(S) ADDRESSED: beneficial impacts

FACTS: Plaintiffs challenged an environmental assessment prepared by the Farmers Home Administration that indicated that there were no adverse environmental impacts and that the only significant environmental impacts associated with the proposed action (a water impoundment and treatment project) were beneficial ones. Plaintiffs claimed that in light of these significant beneficial impacts, NEPA required the agency to prepare an EIS.

FINDINGS: The court held that the conclusion that a dam project would have purely beneficial impacts did not require the preparation of an EIS, absent the forecast of any significant adverse impacts of the project. "The mere fact that [the project] will have a positive impact on the health and welfare of the people it serves does not compel the conclusion that the project may not go forward without an environmental impact statement that would not otherwise be required." 61 F. 3d at 505. However, if significant adverse effects can be predicted from a project and an agency is in the position of having to balance adverse effects against projected benefits, then NEPA requires that a full EIS be prepared. (See *Ibid.*) The agency's decision that the project would not have any significant adverse environmental impacts was not arbitrary or capricious. (See *Ibid.* at 506.)

Friends of the Bitterroot, Inc. v. U.S. Forest Service, 900 F. Supp. 1368 (D. Mont. 1994)

ISSUE(S) ADDRESSED: public involvement and disclosure, supplementation, reasonable alternatives, range of alternatives

FACTS: Plaintiffs filed a NEPA action challenging the Forest Service approval of a timber sale in a national forest.

FINDINGS: The district court held that (1) the Forest Service did not act arbitrarily and capriciously by considering issues of habitat fragmentation, biological diversity, and biological corridors in a separate environmental report prepared after the final EIS; (2) the fact that the national forest management plan designated land as suitable for timber harvesting did not obligate the Forest Service to proceed with timber sales; and (3) the EIS was inadequate because it failed to consider the action alternative of preserving roadless lands in the area.

The Forest Service did not act arbitrarily and capriciously by considering issues of potential impacts of the proposed national forest timber sale on habitat fragmentation, biological diversity, and biological corridors in a separate supplemental information report prepared after the final EIS in light of the failure of the plaintiff environmental groups to raise the issues until administrative appeals after the Forest Service had issued its record of decision.

"[T]he Forest Service took every reasonable step to develop and discuss the comments to the draft EIS and incorporate responses thereto in the final EIS. The administrative record reflects the plaintiffs failed to structure their participation in the NEPA process in a meaningful manner so as to alert the Forest Service to their concerns with the potential impacts on habitat fragmentation, biodiversity, and biological corridors. As a result, plaintiffs cannot take issue with the Forest Service's subsequent discussion of those particular issues in a separate document. Consequently, the court concludes the Forest Service's preparation of the SIR was not arbitrary and capricious under the facts and circumstances of this case." 900 F. Supp at 1372.

The agency must examine every reasonable alternative within the range dictated by the nature and scope of the proposed action in order to provide the decision maker with detailed and careful analysis of the relative environmental merits and demerits of the proposed action and alternatives. The court determined that "the Forest Service examined seven alternate courses of action with respect to the Trail Creek project: six 'action' alternatives (Alternatives B, C, D, E, F, and G) and one 'no action' alternative

(Alternative A). The 'action' alternatives proposed timber harvesting in varying locations, amounts, and methods in the Trail Creek area. Moreover, the action alternatives all called for varying degrees of timber harvesting in the Beaver Lakes roadless area." *Ibid.* at 1373.

The court also held that the range of alternatives in an EIS is reviewed under the rule of reason standard that requires an agency to set forth only those alternatives necessary to permit a reasoned choice. However, "NEPA does not require a separate analysis of alternatives which are not significantly distinguishable from alternatives actually considered or which have substantially similar consequences." *Ibid.* at 1373. Consideration of alternatives is sufficient if it examines a range of alternatives, even if it does not consider every available alternative.

"Given the contentious and long-standing debate in the State of Montana regarding the preservation of roadless lands and wilderness designation, the court concurs with plaintiffs' assertion that the NEPA process would have been properly serviced by development of an action alternative that preserved roadless lands in the Trail Creek area. Such an alternative would have afforded the opportunity for scientific and public participation and debate regarding the delicate balance between preserving natural resources and timber management." *Ibid.* at 1374. The EIS' failure to address an alternative preserving existing roadless lands rendered the EIS inadequate.

Friends of the Earth v. Hall, 693 F. Supp. 904 (W.D. Wash. 1988)

ISSUE(S) ADDRESSED: obligation to consider views of agencies with jurisdiction by law or special expertise, scientific uncertainty

FACTS: Plaintiff, Friends of the Earth (FOE), sought to halt the Navy's plans to dredge contaminated sediments in Everett Harbor and deposit them in Port Gardner Bay. Plaintiff contended that the EISs prepared by the Navy and the Army Corps did not fulfill NEPA's statutory mandate and that, in granting the Navy a dredge and fill permit, the Army Corps violated the Clean Water Act.

FINDINGS: "[T]he issue before the court is not whether CAD [confined aquatic disposal] will work or whether the court would choose CAD as a disposal method. Rather, the court must determine whether the EISs satisfy their primary purposes of (1) providing decision makers with 'an environmental disclosure sufficiently detailed to aid in the substantive decision whether to proceed with the project in light of the environmental consequences,' and (2) providing 'the public with information and an opportunity to participate in gathering information.' *Methow Valley*, 833 F.2d at 814. FOE argues that the Corps and Navy failed to meet their NEPA obligations with respect to three general areas: (1) technical/scientific issues; (2) treatment of a proposed upland alternative; and (3) reasonable mitigation measures." 693 F. Supp. at 922.

"The court concludes that, for two distinct reasons, the resource agencies' views should have been included in the body of the FEIS and the FSEIS. First, the [U.S. Fish and Wildlife Service and the National Marine Fisheries Service] clearly and repeatedly stated strong opposition to the project itself, rather than merely making substantive comments. Second, the body of the FEIS and the FSEIS never discusses the environmental problems raised by *any* responsible party, let alone the views of these key Federal agencies." *Ibid.* at 924 (emphasis in original).

"In summary, the court concludes that the Corps' and the Navy's EISs (1) failed to acknowledge the degree of uncertainty concerning the CAD technology and its use at REDCOAT depths; (2) failed to appropriately reveal the views of the Federal resource agencies on the subject, and (3) failed to identify the 'major' environmental consequences of a technology failure. NEPA requires an EIS to expose scientific uncertainty concerning safety and environmental risk of a proposed action...Moreover, an EIS 'must be particularly thorough when the environmental consequences of Federal action are great.'...Although an EIS 'need not discuss remote and highly speculative consequences,' ...the court concludes, along with the Ninth Circuit, FWS, NFS, and three members of the Shorelines Board, that the REDCOAT project is experimental and fraught with uncertainties. In such a case, the 'major' environmental consequences that would result from a failure cannot be said to be 'remote and highly speculative.' Because the EIS text failed to disclose and discuss crucial information concerning technological uncertainty and what major environmental impact would occur if the REDCOAT technology failed, the Corps and the Navy could not possibly have satisfied NEPA's requirement of informed decision making and informed public participation." *Ibid.* at 925.

Friends of Walker Creek Wetlands, Inc. v. Bureau of Land Management, [no official citation], 19 EPR 20852 (D. Ore. 1988)

ISSUE(S) ADDRESSED: public involvement and disclosure

FACTS: BLM wrote an EA in October 1987 and supplemented it in February 1988. The EA tiered to an area-wide EIS. Plaintiffs challenged the adequacy of the EA.

FINDINGS: "The plaintiffs have failed to raise substantial questions concerning any potential adverse effects of the proposed sale. I conclude that the BLM adequately considered the cumulative impact of the proposed sale and reasonably concluded that an EIS was unnecessary. However, the BLM did not include this information in the EA. The BLM must include or refer to this information in the EA. If the BLM makes references in the EA to information which is not included in the EA then the BLM must make this information readily available to the public." 19 EPR at 20853.

"I am disturbed by this case. The plaintiffs argue that an EIS is required in this situation. Actually a categorical exclusion would have been appropriate...This over story removal was planned for in the first timber sale EA. The sale is a follow-through on an earlier activity when the sale area was harvested by a shelterwood cut. There were no significant changes in the environment of this area between the first removal and now. For these reasons, the proposed project could have been categorically excluded from preparing a EA. However, it should be noted that a categorical exclusion is an environmental document and must comply with the requirements of public notice and participation. See 40 C.F.R. § 1506.6." *Ibid.*

"Plaintiffs contend that the BLM failed to adequately involve the public in the environmental assessment process. Furthermore, plaintiffs argue that the BLM did not give adequate notice. I agree." *Ibid.*

"There was no general public notice of the availability of the EA, although copies were provided to plaintiffs at their request. Furthermore, there was no public notice of the FONSI. On March 30, 1988, the BLM published a Notice of Sale of the PDQ MacMason Timber Sale. Notice of the sale does not qualify as notice for the purposes of NEPA. The purpose of the procedures promulgated under NEPA is to ensure that environmental information is available on an agency's proposed actions before the decision is made to take the action. Public participation is integral to the dual goals of NEPA, providing information to agency decision makers and facilitating public involvement in agency decision making. The BLM failed to give public notice of the EA and the FONSI. As a consequence, the BLM did not adequately provide for public participation to the extent that is practicable." *Ibid.* at 20854.

Fritiofson v. Alexander, 772 F.2d 1225 (5th Cir. 1985)

ISSUES ADDRESSED: cumulative actions, scope, cumulative impacts

FACTS: Plaintiff challenged an Army Corps' decision to prepare an EA on a Section 404 permit to fill wetlands for a development on Galveston Island (Texas). Further development plans affecting the wetlands were clearly planned, but those plans were not yet pending before the Army Corps. In addition, it was acknowledged that this particular proposal would not have significant effect and the Army Corps said that it had to go no further. The court disagreed.

FINDINGS: The court makes a distinction between the requirement to analyze cumulative actions and the requirement for an analysis of cumulative impacts. Specifically, with respect to cumulative actions, the court noted that CEQ scoping regulations require connected, cumulative, and similar actions to be considered together in the same EIS—where proposals up for decision are functionally or economically related, those proposals must be considered in one EIS. "If proceeding with one project will, because of functional or economic dependence, foreclose options or irretrievably commit resources to future projects, the environmental consequences of the projects should be evaluated together." 772 F.2d at 1241, n. 10.

Specifically, only actual proposals are considered sufficiently related to require preparation of a NEPA document. This means only actions or proposals that are ready for decision, e.g. several 404 permits pending before the Army Corps in one geographic region. Unlike the obligation to include cumulative actions in one EIS for analysis and decision, the obligation to address cumulative impacts is not limited to actual proposals. With respect to cumulative impacts, the court noted that the CEQ regulations require analysis of direct, indirect, and cumulative impacts and held that in this context, the impacts were not limited to those from actual proposals, but must also include impacts from actions which are merely being contemplated (i.e., are not yet ripe for decision). However, the court noted that contemplated actions must be "reasonably foreseeable," not speculative and not off in the distant future. See generally, *Ibid.* at 1242.

"In a case like this one ... where an EA constitutes the only environmental review ... the cumulative-impacts analysis plays a [particular] role...This distinction is clearly recognized in the CEQ regulations. Sections 1508.7 and 1508.27 require an analysis ...[of] whether it is 'reasonable to anticipate cumulatively significant impacts' from the specific impacts of the proposed project ... The regulation does not limit the inquiry to the cumulative impacts that can be expected from the proposed project; rather, the inquiry also extends to the effects that can be anticipated from 'reasonably foreseeable future actions.'...In other words, when deciding the significance of a single proposed action (i.e., whether to prepare an EIS at all), a [broad] analysis of cumulative impacts is required." *Ibid.* at 1242-43.

The court stated that a cumulative impact analysis must identify: (1) the area in which the effects of the proposed project will be felt; (2) the impacts that are expected in that area from the proposed project; (3) other past, present, and reasonably foreseeable actions that have or are expected to have impacts in the area; (4) the impacts or expected impacts from these other actions; and (5) the overall impact that can be expected if the individual impacts are allowed to accumulate. See generally, *Ibid.* at 1245.

Getty Oil Co. (Eastern Operation) v. Ruckelshaus, 467 F.2d 349 (3d Cir. 1972), *cert. denied,* 409 U.S. 1125 (1973)

ISSUE(S) ADDRESSED: functional equivalence

FACTS: At issue was whether EPA's approval of Delaware's State Implementation Plans required preparation of a NEPA document when there were Clean Air Act Section 307 questions on pre-enforcement review of the plans.

FINDINGS: The court held that EPA's actions pursuant to the Clean Air Act achieved the goals sought to be attained by NEPA and declined to rule that EPA was required to prepare an EIS. Congress later amended the Clean Air Act, stating that "No action taken under the Clean Air Act shall be deemed a major Federal action significantly affecting the quality of the human environment within the meaning of the National Environmental Policy Act".

Golden Beach v. Army Department, [no official citation] Southern District of Florida, No. 94-1816, September 22, 1994

ISSUE(S) ADDRESSED: public involvement and disclosure

FACTS: The Army Corps had begun a beach erosion control and hurricane surge protection project near the town of Golden Beach in Dade County, Florida. ACOE had contracted with Great Lakes

Dredge and Dock Company to dredge and relocate the sand to other beaches at Sunny Isles and Miami Beach. The town of Golden Beach was not notified of the expected dredge work or allowed to participate in the NEPA process.

FINDINGS: "The Court here is confronted with far more than abstract violations of NEPA. Interested persons that is, the Town of Golden Beach which have the greatest stake in bringing critical environmental information to the attention of the agency decision maker have been excluded from the process. As a result thereof, information bearing on the risk of the project to endangered species, for example, was not thoroughly addressed in the formulation of the original design specifications for this portion of the project as evidenced by the Florida Fish and Wildlife Services letter to the Corps."

"Specifically, with regard to the scoping notice, the CEQ regulations compel public notice and participation.... Here, the ACOE went to great lengths to solicit input from proponents of the action i.e., Miami Beach and others who will benefit from the renourishment yet ignored its explicit obligation to 'invite the participation' of the very local entity that was most likely to 'not be in accord with the action on environmental grounds.'"

"The ACOE's EA contains no discussion of feasible alternatives, including those which would not pose a threat to endangered sea turtles, or severe damage to the coral reefs and other aspects of the Golden Beach's atypical sea-life environment."

"With regard to the balancing of irreparable injuries, it is clear that where there is a fundamental breakdown in the NEPA process and where a project involves concerns of serious harm to the environment, preliminary injunctive relief is appropriate. In particular, where one party has been improperly and inexplicably excluded from a NEPA decision making process, and where there are serious environmental risks at stake which may be avoided entirely or at least ameliorated if the proper process is followed, preliminary injunctive relief is the only remedy that is appropriate under the circumstances."

Greenpeace USA v. Stone, 748 F. Supp. 749 (D. HI. 1990)

ISSUE(S) ADDRESSED: extraterritorial application of NEPA

FACTS: The district court of Hawaii examined the application of NEPA to the removal, transportation, and destruction of chemical munitions stored in the Federal Republic of Germany (FRG). Under a congressional mandate to proceed, the Army prepared separate EISs with respect to the construction and operation of the Johnston Atoll disposal facility. Additionally, an EA pursuant to Executive Order 12114 analyzed the impacts on the global commons of shipment of the munitions from FRG to Johnston Atoll, but no environmental impact assessment under NEPA or the Executive Order was conducted for the movement within the FRG. Plaintiffs filed suit against the Army to enjoin movement of the munitions from the FRG to Johnston Atoll on the grounds that the Army violated NEPA by failing to prepare a comprehensive EIS covering all aspects of the transportation and disposal of the FRG stockpile. The court denied the plaintiffs' request for a preliminary injunction.

FINDINGS: "First, absent evidence of Congressional intent to the contrary, a Federal statute should be construed as applying only within the territorial jurisdiction of the United States....Although the language of NEPA indicates that Congress was concerned with the global environment and the worldwide character of environmental problems, it does not explicitly provide that its requirements are to apply extraterritorially." 748 F. Supp. at 758-59

Further, the court stated that actions under NEPA "should be taken 'consistent with the foreign policy of the United States." *Ibid.* at 759.

The court also stated that "[a]n extraterritorial application of NEPA to the Army's action in the FRG with the approval and cooperation of the FRG would result in a lack of respect for the FRG's sovereignty, authority and control over actions taken within its borders. Although there is no question that the movement of the weapons is being effectuated in large measure by United States Army personnel to eliminate United States weapons, the removal operation takes place entirely within the FRG and the environmental impacts of the actual overland transportation of the stockpile are felt solely within that country. The West German government has reviewed and approved the operation. Imposition of NEPA requirements to that operation would encroach on the jurisdiction of the FRG to implement a political decision which necessarily involved a delicate balancing of risks to the environment and the public and the ultimate goal of expeditiously ridding West Germany of obsolete chemical munitions." *Ibid.* at 760.

In concluding that NEPA did not apply to the movement of munitions through and within West Germany, the court stated that its decision was limited to the specific facts of the case. "In other circumstances, NEPA *may* require a Federal agency to prepare an EIS for action taken abroad, especially where the United States agency's action abroad has direct environmental impacts within this country or where there has been a total lack of environmental assessment by the Federal agency or foreign country involved." *Ibid.* at 761 (emphasis in original).

"The foreign policy considerations which were critical to the preceding analysis of extraterritorial NEPA application are not implicated to the same extent by the transoceanic shipment of the European stockpile from West Germany to Johnston Atoll. The global commons portion of the Army's action does not take place within the sovereign borders of a foreign nation ore in concert with that foreign nation. Accordingly, the question of NEPA application to the transoceanic shipment of the chemical munitions presents a different question." *Ibid.*

"The court cannot conclude, as defendants would suggest, that Executive Order 12114 preempts application of NEPA to *all* Federal agency actions taken outside the United States. Such an application of an Executive Order would be inappropriate and not supported by law.... Nevertheless, the court is persuaded under the *specific facts* of this case that the Army's compliance with Executive Order 12114 is to be given weight in determining whether NEPA requires defendants to consider the global commons portion of the removal of the European stockpile in the same EIS which covers the JACADS project." *Ibid.* at 762 (emphasis in original).

Hanly v. Kleindienst, 471 F.2d 823 (2d Cir. 1972), *cert. denied*, 412 U.S. 908 (1973)

ISSUE(S) ADDRESSED: definition of major Federal action, significance

FACTS: This case challenged a GSA EA for construction of a jail and other facilities in New York City. GSA had issued an EA which described a number of environmental impacts and concluded that the project was not an action significantly affecting the quality of the human environment.

FINDINGS: The determination of whether an EIS was required turns on meaning of "significantly." Almost every major Federal action, no matter how limited in scope, has some adverse effect on the human environment. Congress could have decided that every major Federal action should be the subject of an EIS, but by adding "significantly" Congress required that the agency find a greater environmental impact would occur than from "any major Federal action." CEQ guidelines suggest that an EIS should be prepared where the impacts are controversial, referring not to the amount of public opposition, but to where there is a substantial technical or professional dispute as to the size, or effect of the major Federal action. "The term 'controversial' apparently refers to cases where a substantial dispute exists as to the size, nature or effect of the major Federal action rather than to the existence of opposition to a use, the effect of which is relatively undisputed." 471 F.2d at 830.

The court said that in deciding whether a major Federal action will "significantly" affect the environment, an agency should be required to review the proposed action in light of the extent to which the action will cause adverse environmental effects in excess of those created by existing uses in the area affected by it, and the absolute quantitative adverse environmental effects of the action itself, including the cumulative harm that results. Agencies in doubtful cases will prepare EISs rather than risk the delay and expense of protracted litigation on what is "significant."

"In the absence of any Congressional or administrative interpretation of the term, we are persuaded that in deciding whether a major Federal action will 'significantly' affect the quality of the human environment the agency in charge, although vested with broad discretion, should normally be required to review the proposed action in the light of at least two relevant factors: (1) the extent to which the action will cause adverse environmental effects in excess of those created by existing uses in the area affected by it, and (2) the absolute quantitative adverse environmental effects of the action itself, including the cumulative harm hat results from its contribution to existing adverse conditions or uses in the affected area. Where conduct conforms to existing uses, its adverse consequences will usually be less significant than when it represents a radical change. Absent some showing that an entire neighborhood is in the process of redevelopment, its existing environment, though frequently below an ideal standard, represents a norm that cannot be ignored. For instance, one more highway in an area honeycombed with roads usually has less of an adverse impact than if it were constructed through a roadless public park." *Ibid.* at 830-31.

Agencies must affirmatively develop a reviewable environmental record for the purposes of a threshold determination under Section 102(2)(C). Before a threshold determination of significance is made, the agency must give notice to the public of the proposed major Federal action and an opportunity to submit relevant facts which might bear upon the agency's threshold decision of significance. (See generally, *Ibid.* at 836.)

Hiram Clarke Civic Club v. Lynn, 476 F.2d 421 (5th Cir. 1973)

ISSUE(S) ADDRESSED: beneficial impacts

FACTS: Plaintiffs challenged a proposed low and moderate income apartment project in Houston, Texas, arguing that HUD was barred from funding the project because the agency had failed to prepare an EIS.

FINDINGS: The court concluded that HUD was not required to file an EIS covering the proposed apartment project. According to the court, the plaintiffs "have raised no environmental factors, either beneficial or adverse, that were not considered by HUD before it concluded that this apartment project would produce no significant environmental impact." 476 F.2d at 426.

Having made that ruling, the court went on to address the plaintiffs' claim that HUD's determination of "significance" improperly focused only on adverse environmental impacts, contrary to the CEQ Guidelines: "[Plaintiffs] argue that NEPA requires that an agency file an environmental impact statement if any significant environmental effects, whether adverse or beneficial, are forecast. Thus, they argue, by considering only *adverse* effects HUD in effect did but one-half the proper investigation. We think this contention raises serious questions about the adequacy of the investigatory basis underlying the HUD decision not to file an environmental impact statement." *Ibid.* at 426-27 (emphasis in original).

Without amplification or example, the court expressed its view that "[a] close reading of Section 102(2)(C) in its entirety discloses that Congress was not only concerned with just adverse effects but with all potential environmental effects that affect the quality of the human environment." *Ibid.* at 427. Despite this, the court agreed that the project in question was not a major Federal action significantly affecting the quality of the human environment. HUD was not required to prepare an EIS.

Jones v. Gordon. 621 F. Supp. 7 (D. AK 1985), aff'd, 792 F.2d 821 (9th Cir. 1986)

ISSUE(S) ADDRESSED: statutory conflict, functional equivalence

FACTS: Plaintiff filed suit claiming that the issuance of a National Marine Fisheries Service permit to Sea World to take orca whales required the agency to first prepare an EIS. The agency argued that, because its mission was to protect marine life, its activities were the functional equivalence of NEPA.

FINDINGS: The court first addressed plaintiffs' argument that NEPA did not apply because there was an irreconcilable conflict between NEPA and the Marine Mammal Protection Act under which the permit was being issued. The defendant agency did not believe that there was a conflict, and the court agreed. The court stated that only if there is an "irreconcilable" conflict between the statute and NEPA will the requirements of NEPA not apply. An irreconcilable conflict is created if a statute mandates a fixed time period that is too short to allow the agency to comply with NEPA. (See generally, 621 F. Supp. at 10.)

With respect to plaintiffs' functional equivalence argument, the court held that "[t]he mere fact that an agency has been given the role of implementing an environmental statute is insufficient to invoke the 'functional equivalent' exception. To extend the doctrine to all cases in which a Federal agency administers a statute which was designed to preserve the environment would considerably weaken NEPA, rendering it inapplicable in many situations." *Ibid.* at 13.

Macht v. Skinner, 916 F.2d 13 (D.C. Cir. 1990)

ISSUE(S) ADDRESSED: definition of major Federal action

FACTS: The District of Columbia Court of Appeals examined the extent to which Federal involvement in a non-Federal project may "federalize" the project for purposes of NEPA compliance. In this case, the Maryland Mass Transit Administration decided to build a 22.5-mile light rail line near Baltimore, to be financed solely by State and local governments. However, under the original plan, State and local governments were to finance $250 million of the estimated $290 million project, while the Urban Mass Transportation Administration (UMTA) was to contribute the remaining $40 million. As the planning progressed, however, Maryland officials realized that they were required to comply with NEPA in order to obtain UMTA funding. Because compliance with NEPA would delay construction of the project, Maryland officials decided in late 1988 to withdraw their request for UMTA funding and build a smaller light rail line entirely with State and local funds. Maryland began construction on the 22.5-mile State segment.

Federal involvement in the project included a $2.5-million UMTA grant to help the State complete alternative analyses and draft EISs for the proposed extensions. In addition, the State needed to obtain a Section 404 permit from the Army Corps for 3.58 acres of wetlands. Further, using Federal funds, Maryland began consideration of three extensions to the rail line.

The plaintiffs sued the Federal agencies, claiming that there was sufficient Federal involvement in the rail project to constitute a "major Federal action" requiring compliance with NEPA.

FINDINGS: Affirming the lower court, the court of appeals held that neither the Army Corps wetlands permit nor the UMTA grant was enough to transform the entirely state-funded project into a Federal action. With respect to the UMTA grant for the preliminary environmental analyses, the court stated that "NEPA does not require UMTA to prepare an EIS until it proposes or decides to participate in a project that will affect the environment." 916 F.2d. at 16.

Addressing the Army Corps permit issue, the court noted that the plaintiffs "correctly assert that Federal involvement in a nonfederal project may be sufficient to 'federalize' the project for purposes of NEPA." *Ibid.* at 18. The court characterized the issue as "whether the Federal participation in the project is so substantial that the State should not be allowed to go forward until all the Federal approvals have been granted in accordance with NEPA." *Ibid.* In this case, the court found that the Army Corps had discretion only over a negligible portion of the entire project, that the only Federal involvement in the 22.5-mile State portion of the project was the wetlands permits, and that the State had not entered into a financial partnership with the Federal government. "NEPA therefore provides no basis for enjoining Maryland's construction of the Light Rail Project." *Ibid.* at 20.

Marble Mountain Audubon Society v. Rice, 914 F.2d 179 (9th Cir. 1990)

ISSUE(S) ADDRESSED: judicial review

FACTS: After a forest fire in 1987, the Forest Service began to plan the salvage and rehabilitation of the damaged area, and prepared a draft and final EIS that considered the environmental impacts of nine alternative salvage and harvest proposals. The alternative selected called for logging of some green timber as well as the fire-killed timber and for the addition of six miles of logging roads. Alleging that the final EIS failed to adequately consider the unique value of the area as the only significant biological corridor between two wilderness areas, plaintiffs sought declaratory and injunctive relief. The district court granted summary judgment in favor of the Forest Service, stating that the NEPA claims were barred by Section 312 of Pub. L. No. 101-121 (which denies judicial review of Forest Service plans on the sole basis that the plans, in their entirety, are outdated) and, alternatively, that the final EIS adequately addressed the biological corridor issue.

FINDINGS: The Ninth Circuit reversed

Recognizing the "strong presumption in favor of judicial review of administrative action" and "narrowly constru[ing]" Section 312's prohibition against judicial review, the court found that the biological corridor issue was not a generic issue that would enable plaintiffs to challenge the entire Timber Management Plan for the Klamath National Forest in contravention of Section 312. 914 F.2d at 181.

The court also concluded that, based on the record before it, the Forest Service had not taken a "hard look" at the impact of the selected salvage and harvest alternative on the biological corridor. The court found that the Forest Service's conclusion that the preservation of a ½-mile corridor would be sufficient was "without any apparent study or supporting documentation" and found "no discussion" of the corridor issue in either of two underlying documents relied upon by the Forest Service (a 1967 Multiple Use Plan and a 1974 Klamath National Forest Timber Management Plan and accompanying EIS). *Ibid.* at 182.

"In response to public comments that the EIS does not discuss the importance of maintaining biological corridors, the FEIS characterizes the issue as 'a forest-planning matter and therefore beyond the scope of this document (V-16).' The underlying [timber management plan] and [multiple use plan], however, contain no discussion whatsoever of the corridor issue. We therefore reverse the district court's summary judgment on plaintiffs' NEPA claim and remand for further proceedings." *Ibid.*

Merrell v. Thomas, 807 F.2d 776 (9th Cir. 1986), *cert. denied*, 108 S.Ct. 145 (1987)

ISSUE(S) ADDRESSED: Functional equivalence

FACTS: The plaintiff challenged EPA's registration of pesticides under FIFRA without first complying with NEPA and requested the cancellation or suspension of the registration of several pesticides.

FINDINGS: Congress, under FIFRA, established a comprehensive scheme for the registration and regulation of pesticides, the purpose of which is to protect the environment. "In 1972, Congress comprehensively amended FIFRA, in part in response to 'increasing public concern over the uses and application of pesticides' [citing a congressional report]. Yet Congress gave no indication that it thought NEPA would apply. Instead, Congress created a registration procedure within FIFRA to ensure consideration of environmental impact - a procedure that apparently made NEPA superfluous." 807 F.2d at 778.

The court noted that FIFRA had been interpreted by EPA as not requiring compliance with NEPA, and that FIFRA had been amended in 1975, 1978, and 1984 without Congressional revision or repeal of

EPA's interpretation. (See *Ibid.* at 779.) "We infer that Congress believes that analyses in support of registration currently are an adequate substitute for an EIS in the FIFRA context. Congress did not intend to make NEPA apply." *Ibid.* at 780.

"We are confident that Congress did not intend NEPA to apply to FIFRA registrations." *Ibid.* at 781. EPA was not required to prepare a NEPA document for pesticide registration process.

Minnesota Public Interest Research Group v. Butz, 498 F.2d 1314 (8th Cir.1974)

ISSUE(S) ADDRESSED: definition of major Federal action, significance, secondary (indirect) impacts

FACTS: Plaintiffs sought to enjoin timber sales in the Boundary Waters Canoe Area until the Forest Service competed an EIS on the management of the area. The Forest Service argued that the phrase "major Federal actions significantly affecting the quality of the human environment" creates two tests: first it must be determined whether there is a major Federal action, and next, if there is a major Federal action, whether the impact of the action on the environment is major. The Forest Service asserted that timber sales were not "major Federal actions."

FINDINGS: The court noted that "...these actions (and their impacts) of the Forest Service cannot be quantified in terms of dollars to be spent or tons of earth to be moved." 498 F.2d at 1319. "NEPA is not only an environmental full-disclosure law, but was also intended to effectuate substantive changes in decision making." *Ibid.* at 1320.

"In view of the concern for environmental disclosure present in NEPA, the agency's discretion as to whether an impact statement is required is properly exercised only within narrow bounds. Action which could have a significant effect on the environment should be covered by an impact statement." *Ibid.*

The court concluded that the term "major Federal action significantly affecting the quality of the human environment" involved only one concept. "To separate the consideration of the magnitude of Federal action from its impact on the environment does little to foster the purposes of the Act, i.e., to 'attain the widest range of beneficial uses of the environment without degradation, risk to health and safety, or other undesirable and unintended consequences.' By bifurcating the statutory language, it would be possible to speak of a 'minor Federal action significantly affecting the quality of the human environment,' and to hold NEPA inapplicable to such an action....[T]he activities of Federal agencies cannot be isolated from their impact on the environment." *Ibid.* at 1321-22.

The court also rejected the Forest Service's conclusion that there was no effect on the "human" environment from the timber sales because there was no evidence that human users of the area had ever seen a timber sale. "This appears to be too restrictive a view of what significantly affects the human environment. We think NEPA is concerned with indirect effects as well as direct effects. There has been increasing recognition that man and all other life on this earth may be significantly affected by actions which on the surface appear insignificant." *Ibid.* at 1322.

Morgan v. Walter. 728 F. Supp. 1483 (D. Idaho 1989)

ISSUE(S) ADDRESSED: significance, mitigation, EAs, connected actions

FACTS: The defendant in this case proposed to build a fish propagation facility on his property. In order to support this facility, a diversion structure was to be built on lands owned by BLM. The BLM issued a right of way which authorized the construction and operation of the diversion facility and prepared an EA to support this decision. The right of way agreement contained 24 stipulations which imposed specific restrictions and requirements on both building the dam and maintaining the property. The Army Corps issued a 404 permit relying extensively on the EA prepared by BLM and its mitigation. Plaintiffs challenged the issuance of the right-of-way permit on the ground that an EIS should have been prepared.

FINDINGS: The court granted plaintiffs' request for a preliminary injunction, finding that there was substantial likelihood that they would succeed on the merits of the case. Specifically, the court noted that there were substantial questions raised regarding whether the project may have a significant effect on the environment. The court recognized that "mitigation measures may be considered by an agency in determining whether to prepare an EIS....An EIS must be prepared, however, where substantial questions are raised as to whether these mitigation efforts are adequate." 728 F. Supp. at 1491.

With respect to whether the proposed fish propagation facility was connected to the proposed diversion, the court noted that "the inquiry here, then, is whether the proposed diversion and the Blind Canyon Creek propagation facility are 'links in the same bit of chain.... [T]he fish propagation could not exist absent a diversion. Therefore, the propagation facility should probably have been considered by the Corps in preparing its EA." *Ibid.* at 1493. However, the court could not conclude that a potential hydroelectric plant that the plaintiffs asserted the landowner might construct at some time in the future was reasonably foreseeable. (See *Ibid.* at 1493.)

"The proposed mitigation proposal, wherein [the defendant, Hardy] designates a significant portion of his land as a preservation zone, is to be commended and demonstrates the sincere efforts which he has made toward reaching a sensible solution to the competing interests involved in this matter. Nevertheless, the law requires certain steps to be taken to ensure that agencies carefully consider the specific impacts that a major Federal action will have on the environment. One of these steps is the preparation of an environmental impact statement when the project may significantly affect the environment. Despite the efforts of the government to comply with the requirements of NEPA, the court is compelled, through the application of the 'reasonableness' standard, to find that the plaintiffs probably have raised substantial questions as to the significance the Hardy proposal, even with the proposed mitigation measures, may have on the human environment." *Ibid.* at 1494-95.

National Wildlife Federation v. Federal Energy Regulatory Commission, 912 F.2d 1471 (D.C. Cir. 1990)

ISSUE(S) ADDRESSED: Connected actions, cumulative actions, cumulative impacts

FACTS: The EIS prepared for this project looked only at the environmental impacts of Phase I, although construction of Phase II, while not inevitable, was believed to be reasonably foreseeable. The plaintiffs had challenged the issuance of the license for Phase, I, asserting that FERC violated NEPA by not assessing the potential impacts of Phase II in deciding whether to approve Phase I.

FINDINGS: The court reasoned that Phase II of the project was not yet proposed and that NEPA does not require that an EIS delve into the impacts of a hypothetical project, "but need only focus on the impact of the particular proposal at issue and other pending or recently approved proposals that might be connected to or act cumulatively with the proposal at issue." 912 F.2d at 1478.

Natural Resources Defense Council v. Callaway, 524 F.2d 79 (2d Cir. 1975)

ISSUE(S) ADDRESSED: reasonable alternatives, cumulative actions, purpose and need

FACTS: The court addressed further dumping by the Navy of polluted dredged spoils at the New London dumping site in Long Island Sound. Plaintiffs claimed, among other things, that the Navy had not looked at all reasonable alternatives.

FINDINGS: "We agree with the Navy that NEPA does not require it to make a 'crystal ball' inquiry, ...and that an EIS is required to furnish only such information as appears to be reasonably necessary under the circumstances for evaluation of the project rather than to be so all-encompassing in scope that the task of preparing it would become either fruitless or well nigh impossible....A government agency cannot be expected to wait until a perfect solution of environmental consequences of proposed action is devised before preparing and circulating an EIS." 524 F.2d at 88.

"On the other hand, an agency may not go to the opposite extreme of treating a project as an isolated 'single-shot' venture in the face of persuasive evidence that it is but one of several substantially similar operations, each of which will have the same polluting effect in the same area. To ignore the prospective cumulative harm under such circumstances could be to risk ecological disaster." *Ibid.*

Further, the court acknowledged that the content and scope of the discussion of alternatives to the proposed actions depends upon the nature of the proposal. "Although there is no need to consider alternatives of speculative feasibility or alternatives which could be changed only after significant changes in governmental policy or legislation,... the EIS must still consider such alternatives to the proposed action as may partially or completely meet the proposal's goal and it must evaluate their comparative merits." *Ibid.* at 93.

Natural Resources Defense Council, Inc. v. Hodel, 865 F.2d 288 (D.C. Cir. 1988)

ISSUE(S) ADDRESSED: reasonable alternatives, public involvement and disclosure, cumulative impacts

FACTS: Plaintiffs maintained that the Secretary of the Interior should have considered various conservation policies as a partial alternative to the five-year program eliminating the need for leasing in environmentally sensitive areas and did not adequately consider cumulative impacts.

FINDINGS: "[The] arguments rest on the premise that conservation strategies can, at least in part, achieve the goals of the five-year program as well as OCS (Outer Continental Shelf) leasing can....We reject the Secretary's contention that he need not consider partial conservation alternatives *at all* because the nation's energy demands are likely to increase even with gains in energy conservation and development of alternative energy sources. This argument provides too much because it would relieve the Secretary of his duty under NEPA to consider alternatives altogether....Moreover, the Secretary's argument overlooks the reasons for NEPA's requirement that agencies consider alternatives. The purpose is not merely to force the *agency* to reconsider its proposed action, but, more broadly, to inform Congress, other agencies, and the general public about the environmental consequences of a certain action in order to spur all interested parties to rethink the wisdom of the action." 865 F.2d at 295-296 (emphasis in original).

"Given this informational purpose of NEPA, then, the Secretary must consider alternatives even if they do not reduce the need for OCS leasing. The continuing need for development of the OCS, however, reduces the *scope* of the required consideration.... In these circumstances, NEPA's informational function is served by a less searching treatment of alternatives than otherwise required." *Ibid.* at 297 (emphasis in original).

With respect to plaintiffs' argument regarding cumulative impacts on migratory species, the court stated that "[w]hen the FEIS does address inter-regional cumulative impacts, it simply repeats the same boilerplate for each area, varying the language only slightly in each instance....These perfunctory references do not constitute analysis useful to a decision maker in deciding whether, or how, to alter the program to lessen cumulative environmental impacts....[O]ur examination of the FEIS satisfies us that the Secretary did *not* consider the effect of simultaneous *inter*-regional development on migratory species." *Ibid.* (emphasis in original).

Natural Resources Defense Council v. Morton, 458 F.2d 827 (D.C. Cir. 1972)

ISSUE(S) ADDRESSED: reasonable alternatives, range of alternatives, public involvement and disclosure

FACTS: The Secretary of DOI prepared an EIS for proposed oil and gas lease sales off the coast of Louisiana. The EIS dealt with the environmental impacts of the proposed sale, and did discuss modifications to the proposal to delete some of the tracks with higher environmental risks. Plaintiffs contended that the EIS did not adequately discuss reasonable alternatives. The lower court had found that "the defendants failed to comply with NEPA by failing to discuss some alternatives at all, such as meeting energy demands by Federal legislation or administrative action freeing current onshore and state-controlled offshore production from State market demand prorationing or a change in the Federal Power Commission's natural gas pricing policies."

FINDINGS: While an agency is obligated to consider only reasonable alternatives, "[w]e do not agree that this requires a limitation to measures the agency or official can adopt." 458 F.2d at 834.

An EIS provides a basis for evaluation of the benefits of a proposed project in light of its environmental risks and a comparison of the net balance for the proposed project with the environmental risks presented by alternative courses of action. An agency must look at "reasonable" alternatives, but this is not limited to measures which the agency itself can adopt.

"When the proposed action is an integral part of a coordinated plan to deal with a broad problem, the range of alternatives which must be evaluated is broadened." *Ibid.* at 835. While the Department of the Interior did not have authority to undertake certain alternatives (such as elimination of oil import quotas), such actions are within the purview of Congress and the President to whom the EIS goes. An EIS is not only for the agency, but also for the guidance of others and must provide them with the environmental effects of both the proposal and the alternatives for their consideration. "The impact statement is not only for the exposition of the thinking of the agency, but also for the guidance of these ultimate decision-makers, and must provide them with the environmental effects of both the proposal and the alternatives, for their consideration along with the various other elements of the public interest." *Ibid.*

"The discussion of alternatives need not be exhaustive. What is required is information sufficient to permit a reasoned choice of alternatives so far as environmental aspects are concerned, including alternatives not within the scope of authority of the responsible agency [when the action is part of a broad overall plan]. Nor is it appropriate to disregard alternatives merely because they do not offer a complete solution to the problem." *Ibid.* at 836.

"We reiterate that the discussion of environmental effects of alternatives need not be exhaustive. What is required is information sufficient to permit a reasoned choice of alternatives so far as environmental aspects are concerned." *Ibid.*

"Discussion of reasonable alternatives does not require a 'crystal ball' inquiry. The statute must be construed in the light of reason." *Ibid.* at 837.

"The mere fact that an alternative requires legislative implementation does not automatically establish it as beyond the domain of what is required for discussion, particularly since NEPA was intended to provide a basis for consideration and choice by the decision-makers in the legislative as well as the executive branch." *Ibid.*

Oregon Environmental Council v. Kunzman, 614 F. Supp. 657 (D. Ore. 1985)

ISSUE(S) ADDRESSED: readability, public involvement and disclosure

FACTS: This case involved the sufficiency of a USFS EIS for the suppression and eradication of gypsy moths. The court held that the "worst case" analysis required at the time (since rescinded) was a mandatory part of the EIS, but was not "readable."

FINDINGS: The court recognized that one of NEPA's purposes is to inform the public of possible environmental consequences of actions. For this reason, NEPA requires that EISs be "readable." The court cited CEQ's regulations: "40 CFR 1502.1 and 1502.2(b) State that the information in an EIS must be 'concise, clear and to the point' and that statements should be 'analytic rather than encyclopedic.' Section 1502.8 further states that the document should be written in 'plain language so that decision makers and the public can readily understand them.'" 614 F. Supp. at 664-65. The court held that the worst case analysis that was not "readable" and declared the EIS to be inadequate on that ground.

The court agreed that the "FEIS is highly technical, esoteric and incomprehensible not only to the general public and majority of decision makers, but also to readers with advanced scientific backgrounds." *Ibid.* at 665.

"A thorough search of the case law and relevant literature has failed to produce any precedent or discussion regarding the 'readability' of an EIS. Mention has been made in a few cases of the requirement of understandability in Section 1502.8. However, no court has ever invalidated an EIS on the grounds that the document was not 'readily understandable' by the public and decision makers." *Ibid.*

"Although the worst case analysis contains all the necessary information, it fails to communicate that to the persons entitled to be so informed....An EIS must translate technical data into terms that render it an effective disclosure of the environmental impacts of a proposed project to *all* of its intended readership." *Ibid.* (emphasis in original).

Pilchuck Audubon Society v. MacWilliams, [no official citation] (D. W. Wash. 1988)

ISSUE(S) ADDRESSED: supplementation

FACTS: Plaintiff asserted that a timber resale violated NEPA, because the USFS failed to update an eight-year-old EA and failed to provide plaintiff an opportunity to establish that changed circumstances required a new environmental review.

FINDINGS: "The USFS contends that plaintiff did not contest the 1979 [EA] and Finding of No Significant Impact, and therefore NEPA requirements, having already been satisfied, need not be revisited. The Court disagrees, and given the USFS's role as steward of our national forests, the Court is somewhat mystified by the USFS's position. As the Council on Environmental Quality ('CEQ') has stated, where a proposal has not yet been implemented, as was the case with the original Olo Too sale, a 'rule of thumb' exists requiring environmental assessments that are more than 5 years old to be 'carefully reexamined to determine if the criteria in [40 C.F.R. § 1502.9] compel preparation of a...supplement.' Forty Most Asked Questions, Question No. 32, 48 Fed. Reg. 18026-01."

Portland Cement Association v. Ruckelshaus, 486 F.2d 375 (D.C. Cir. 1973), *cert denied*, 417 U.S. 921 (1974)

ISSUE(S) ADDRESSED: functional equivalence

FACTS: Portland Cement Association sought review of an EPA action to promulgate stationary sources standards for new or modified cement plants on the grounds that a NEPA document was required.

FINDINGS: EPA, in issuing standards under the Clean Air Act, is not required by NEPA to file an EIS in view of the functional equivalency of the statement of reasons, setting forth environmental considerations, required under the Clean Air Act. Congress later amended the Clean Air Act, stating that "[n]o action taken under the Clean Air Act shall be deemed a major Federal action significantly affecting the quality of the human environment within the meaning of the National Environmental Policy Act".

"A primary purpose of NEPA, and specifically the impact statement requirement, was the design to co-ordinate disparate environmental policies of different Federal agencies. At the time NEPA was enacted, on January 1, 1970, EPA was not yet in existence." 486 F.2d at 380.

"What is decisive ultimately, is the reality that, section 111 of the Clean Air Act, properly construed, requires the functional equivalent of a NEPA impact statement..." *Ibid.* at 384.

"We add, finally, a word of clarification: we establish a narrow exemption from NEPA, for EPA determinations under section 111 of the Clean Air Act. NEPA must be accorded full vitality as to non-environmental agencies, as established by our outstanding precedents." *Ibid.* at 387.

Public Service Company of Colorado v. Idaho, 825 F. Supp. 1483 (D. Idaho 1993)

ISSUE(S) ADDRESSED: adequacy of an EA, cumulative impacts, continuing actions

FACTS: DOE conducted an EA for the transportation of spent nuclear fuel to Idaho National Engineering Laboratory (INEL). Based on the EA, DOE determined that the shipment of spent fuel did not require an EIS. The State of Idaho filed suit against DOE alleging that the EA was seriously flawed and that DOE abused its discretion in contravention of the NEPA requirements. Idaho complained that there had never been proper NEPA analysis of the shipment and storage of any spent nuclear fuel. The district court enjoined DOE from shipping spent nuclear fuel to the Idaho site pending completion of an EIS.

FINDINGS: When originally threatened with legal action, DOE conceded that the proposed actions at INEL constituted a "major Federal action" but gave its contractor, Ecology and Environment, Inc., only two weeks to complete the NEPA analysis and dictated what the EA would contain and who would be consulted. The court stated that "DOE conducted a superficial and result-oriented analysis of many key aspects of the proposal." 825 F. Supp. at 1496. In addition, the agency "relied on outdated reports and studies in drawing many of its conclusions,...paid only cursory attention to potential risks associated with transportation of the spent fuel,...failed to consider reasonable alternatives,...[and] should have more carefully considered the potential effects of an accident in transport." *Ibid.* The court also noted that "DOE failed to give adequate consideration to the cumulative impacts of the proposal in conjunction with the shipment and storage of all of the other nuclear waste at INEL." *Ibid.*

"DOE was aware at that time that Ecology and Environment, Inc., seriously questioned the validity of the EA and the finding of no significant impact and recommended further analysis." *Ibid.* at 1497.

The court rejected DOE's argument that NEPA does not apply to shipments from sources where the activities began prior to the enactment of NEPA, since NEPA requires agencies to analyze the environmental effects of a proposed action before such action is taken. The court pointed out that "significant changes in programs rising to the level of major Federal actions which have [changed] or will change the status quo must be studied under the procedures outlined in NEPA." *Ibid.* at 1500. The court found that the increases in the volume and frequency of nuclear waste shipments under the existing or ongoing programs constituted a "significant change in the status quo." *Ibid.*

On cross motions for summary judgment, the district court held that: (1) the State of Idaho had standing to seek judicial review under NEPA and the Administrative Procedure Act; (2) the original EA on shipments of spent nuclear fuel from Colorado to Idaho was inadequate, and DOE was required to prepare an EIS; (3) DOE was required to prepare a comprehensive site-wide EIS addressing all nuclear waste activities at INEL, including ongoing activities; and (4) the threat of irreparable environmental injury was sufficiently likely that an injunction would issue barring DOE from receiving any type of spent nuclear fuel at the laboratory until it prepared an EIS.

Save the Yaak Committee v. J.R. Block, 840 F.2d 714 (9th Cir. 1988)

ISSUE(S) ADDRESSED: adequacy of an EA, connected actions, cumulative impacts

FACTS: Plaintiffs brought action against USFS to halt paving operations on a portion of the Yaak River Road that winds through the Yaak and Eureka Range Districts of the Kootenai National Forest. The Mountain Pine Beetle had infested the extensive lodgepole pine stands located in the Upper Yaak Valley and portions of the Eureka district. The USFS proposed to accelerate the harvest of these trees to salvage as many as possible. In the late 1960s, the USFS began reconstructing the Yaak River Road in five separate sections. Although EAs were prepared for four of the five sections, construction of the fifth section began in 1982 without the preparation of an EA. No comprehensive EIS had ever been prepared for the reconstruction of the entire road. Plaintiffs argued that the USFS failed to comply with NEPA because each group of timber sales contracts was related to the reconstruction of a section of the Yaak River Road, the harvesting of timber, and the construction of secondary roadways necessary for the harvesting, and that these actions had a cumulative effect on the environment.

FINDINGS: The court found that the USFS violated NEPA and the Endangered Species Act by rebuilding the road in the national forest without proper analysis of environmental impacts. Specifically, the court found that: (1) the EA prepared by the USFS did not evaluate environmental impacts; (2) the ESA biological assessment did not qualify as a substitute for an EA; and (3) even if both had been adequate they were not prepared in a timely manner.

"In reviewing an agency decision not to prepare an EIS pursuant to NEPA, our inquiry is whether the 'responsible agency has reasonably concluded that the project will have no significant adverse environmental consequences.' If substantial questions are raised regarding whether the proposed action may have a significant effect upon the human environment, a decision not to prepare an EIS is unreasonable. Additionally, an agency's decision not to prepare an EIS will be considered unreasonable if the agency fails to 'supply a convincing statement of reasons why potential effects are insignificant.' Indeed, 'the statement of reasons is crucial' to determining whether the agency took a 'hard look' at the potential environmental impact of a project." 840 F.2d at 717.

"At issue then, is whether the road reconstruction and the timber sales are 'connected actions' within the meaning of section 1508.25(a)(1). Central to this inquiry is our analysis in *Thomas v. Peterson*. In Thomas, we concluded that logging operations and the construction of a road were 'connected actions.' In coming to this conclusion, we considered six factors. After reviewing these factors, we stated that '[i]t is clear that the timber sales cannot proceed without the road, and the road would not be built but for the contemplated timber sales.'" *Ibid.* at 719.

The EA "did not evaluate the environmental impacts of either the reconstruction or the ongoing and future accelerated timber harvest. The cumulative impact of these actions raises material issues of fact concerning the project's effect upon the human environment." *Ibid.* at 721.

Schalk v. Reilly, 900 F.2d 1091 (7th Cir.), *cert. denied*, 498 U.S. 981, 111 S.Ct. 509 (1990)

ISSUE(S) ADDRESSED: application of NEPA to CERCLA actions

FACTS: Plaintiffs contended that EPA was required to comply with NEPA in evaluating PCB contamination and in arriving at a consent decree for cleanup at a hazardous waste site under CERCLA.

FINDINGS: The court, citing the "obvious meaning" of the statute, concluded that when a CERCLA remedy has been selected, no challenge, including a NEPA challenge, to the cleanup may be made prior to completion of the remedy. "The statute precludes Federal court review at this stage—when a remedial plan has been chosen but not 'taken' or 'secured.'" 900 F.2d at 1095.

The court noted that under NEPA all review is through the APA and that "APA review is not available when a Federal statute specifically precludes judicial review." *Ibid.* at 1097.

Shoshone-Paiute Tribe v. United States, 889 F. Supp. 1297 (D. Idaho 1994)

ISSUE(S) ADDRESSED: definition of proposal, definition of major Federal action, connected actions, cumulative actions

FACTS: The Shoshone-Paiute Tribe challenged the legal sufficiency of a USAF EIS regarding proposed USAF projects. The EIS covered three proposals: the establishment of a composite aircraft wing at the

Mountain Home Air Force Base, the modification of existing airspace to accommodate Air Force and Idaho Air National Guard flying activities, and to analyze the environmental suitability of a proposal made by the Governor of the State of Idaho, Cecil Andrus, to create a new State managed air-to-ground training range to be used by the USAF and the Idaho Air National Guard; this new range was referred to as the Idaho Training Range (ITR). As stated in the USAF EIS, if the State's proposed range was found to be operationally suitable and the area's environmental resources appeared generally capable of accommodating a range, then the USAF would conduct a subsequent environmental analysis. The plaintiffs challenged the manner in which the third proposal was treated in the EIS and contended that the agency violated NEPA by not conducting a full environmental analysis on the ITR at the same time it studied the other two proposals.

FINDINGS: This case addressed whether the ITR was a "proposal" for a "major Federal action" and thus whether the USAF correctly separated the beddown of the composite wing and establishment of the ITR into two separate EISs.

"While the ITR was initially conceived by Governor Andrus, the Administrative Record shows that the Air Force--at the very least--'partially assisted' the development of the range....This evidence in the record establishes that the AF at least 'partially assisted' in the development of the ITR and hence the range was a 'major Federal action' under the CEQ regulations." 889 F. Supp. at 1305.

With respect to whether the ITR was a "proposal," the court found that "[t]he ITR proposal, by contrast, was detailed enough to be analyzed, and had moved far beyond the 'contemplation' stage when the AF EIS was being prepared. In fact, only a month after the AF EIS ROD was issued, the ITR was so detailed that work on the ITR EIS immediately began. But even before this point, the ITR had sufficient detail to be studied in an EIS." *Ibid.* at 1306.

"[B]y the time the AF EIS was being prepared, the general acreage and boundaries of the ITR had been established, and the target locations had been plotted with precise longitude and latitude coordinates. The Defendants would never have committed $90,000.00 for a multi-seasonal analysis if the ITR had merely been a vague, undefined 'area.'" *Ibid.* at 1306-07.

"The next issue is whether the ITR proposal should have been included within the AF EIS. While administrative agencies must be given considerable discretion in defining the scope of environmental impact statements, 'there are situations in which an agency is required to consider several related actions in a single EIS.' *Thomas v. Peterson*, 753 F.2d 754, 758 (9th Cir.1985). 'Not to require this would permit dividing a project into multiple actions, each of which individually has an insignificant environmental impact, but which collectively have a substantial impact.' *Ibid.*" *Ibid.* at 1308.

"The evidence shows conclusively that the ITR and the approximately seventy aircraft that make up the Composite Wing are 'inextricably intertwined' just as the road and timber sales were in the *Thomas* case. The evidence shows that the ITR was an interdependent part of the Composite Wing and that it depends on the Composite Wing for its justification, thereby triggering subsection (iii) of 40 C.F.R. § 1508.25(a)(1)." *Ibid.* at 1309.

Finally the court found that "there was a definite proposal in this case and reasonably foreseeable impacts. Thus, the ITR and Composite Wing were cumulative actions that must be considered together in a single EIS under 40 C.F.R. § 1508.25(a)(2)." *Ibid.* at 1310.

Scientists' Institute for Public Information, Inc. v. Atomic Energy Commission, 481 F.2d 1079 (D.C. Cir. 1973)

ISSUE(S) ADDRESSED: definition of proposal, programmatic EISs

FACTS: Plaintffs challenged the AEC's Liquid Metal Fast Breeder Reactor Program as a "major Federal action significantly affecting the quality of the human environment" under Section 102(2)(C) of NEPA and argued that the AEC was required to issue a "detailed statement" for the program. The district court had held that no statement was needed; the Court of Appeals reversed.

FINDINGS: "Taking into account the magnitude of the ongoing Federal investment in this program, the controversial environmental effects attendant upon future widespread deployment of breeder reactors should the program fulfill present expectations, the accelerated pace under which this program has moved beyond pure scientific research toward creation of a viable, competitive breeder reactor electrical energy industry and the manner in which investment in this new technology is likely to restrict future alternatives, we hold that the Commission's program comes within both the letter and the spirit of Section 102[(2)](C) and that a detailed statement about the program, its environmental impact, and alternatives thereto is presently required." 481 F.2d at 1082.

"NEPA requires a detailed statement not only for particular facilities, but also for analysis of overall effects of broad agency programs." *Ibid.* at 1086-87.

"The statutory phrase 'actions significantly affecting the quality of the environment' is intentionally broad...The legislative history of the Act indicates that the term 'actions' refers not only to construction of particular facilities, but includes 'project proposals, proposals for new legislation, regulations, policy statements, or expansion or revision of ongoing programs...Thus, there is 'Federal action'...not only when an agency proposes to build a facility itself, but also whenever an agency makes a decision which permits action by other parties that will affect the quality of the environment." *Ibid.* at 1088.

"To wait until a technology attains the stage of complete commercial feasibility before considering the possible adverse effects attendant upon the ultimate application of the technology will undoubtedly frustrate meaningful consideration and balancing of environmental costs against economic and other benefits." *Ibid.* at 1089.

The agency must describe the reasonably foreseeable environmental impacts of the program. "Reasonable forecasting and speculation is thus implicit in NEPA, and we must reject any attempt by agencies to shirk their responsibilities under NEPA by labeling any and all discussion of future environmental effects as 'crystal ball inquiry." *Ibid.* at 1092.

"NEPA requires predictions, but not prophesy..." *Ibid.* at 1093.

"Statements must be written late enough in the development process to contain meaningful information, but they must be written early enough so that whatever information is contained can practically serve as an input into the decision making process." *Ibid.* at 1094.

Sierra Club v. Marsh, 872 F.2d 497 (1st Cir. 1989)

ISSUE(S) ADDRESSED: standing, public involvement and disclosure

FACTS: This case involved the State of Maine's efforts to build a new six-berth marine dry cargo terminal at Searsport, one of the busiest ports in Maine. The Maine Department of Transportation wanted to build the terminal on Sears Island, a 940-acre, uninhabited, undeveloped piece of land directly opposite Mack Point, the site of a present two-berth terminal. The project would require the construction of a causeway from the mainland to the island, funded primarily by FHWA. FHWA was required to prepare an EIS for the project. Plaintiffs sought to enjoin the project, citing inadequacies in the EIS.

FINDINGS: The court noted that "NEPA is not designed to prevent all possible harm to the environment; it foresees that decision makers may choose to inflict such harm, for perfectly good reasons. Rather, NEPA is designed to influence the decision making process; its aim is to make government officials notice environmental considerations and take them into account. Thus, *when a decision to which NEPA obligations attach is made without the informed environmental consideration that NEPA requires, the* *harm that NEPA intends to prevent has been suffered.* NEPA in this sense differs from substantive environmental statutes..." 872 F.2d at 500 (emphasis in original).

"Moreover, to set aside the agency's action at a later date will not necessarily undo the harm. The agency as well as private parties may well have become committed to the previously chosen course of action, and new information—a new EIS—may bring about a new decision, but it is that much less likely to bring about a different one. It is far easier to influence an initial choice than to change a mind already made up." *Ibid.*

"It is appropriate for the courts to recognize this type of injury in a NEPA case, for it reflects the very theory upon which NEPA is based—a theory aimed at presenting governmental decision-makers with relevant environmental data before they commit themselves to a course of action. This is not to say that a likely NEPA violation automatically calls for an injunction; the balance of harms may point the other way." *Ibid.*

"[W]e would add one further word of explanation. We did not (and would not) characterize the harm described as a 'procedural' harm, as if it were a harm to procedure (as the district court apparently considered it, see *Sierra Club*, 701 F. Supp. at 907 ('harm to the NEPA process itself')). Rather, the harm at stake is a harm to the *environment*, but the harm consists of the added *risk* to the environment that takes place when governmental decision makers make up their minds without having before them an analysis (with prior public comment) of the likely effects of their decision upon the environment. NEPA's object is to minimize that risk, the risk of uninformed choice, a risk that arises in part from the practical fact that bureaucratic decision makers (when the law permits) are less likely to tear down a nearly completed project than a barely started project. In *Watt* [Commonwealth of Massachusetts v. Watt, 716 F.2d 946 (1st Cir. 1983)] we simply held that the district court should take account of the potentially irreparable nature of this decision making risk to the environment when considering a request for preliminary injunction." *Ibid.* at 500-501 (emphasis in original).

"To repeat, the harm at stake in a NEPA violation *is* a harm to the environment, not merely to a legalistic 'procedure,' nor, for that matter, merely to psychological well-being." *Ibid.* at 504 (emphasis in original).

Sierra Club v. Marsh. 714 F. Supp. 539 (D. ME 1989), aff'd 976 F.2d. 763 (1st Cir. 1992)

ISSUE(S) ADDRESSED: supplementation, use of consultants, secondary (indirect) impacts, reasonable alternatives

FACTS: In this case challenging the adequacy of an EIS prepared by FHWA for a proposed marine dry cargo terminal, plaintiffs requested declaratory and injunctive relief halting construction of the terminal on the grounds that the agency had failed to comply with NEPA.

FINDINGS: The court made an extensive analysis of the case law, including the U.S. Supreme Court's decision in *Marsh* in deciding to what extent an agency must examine and document the need to supplement an EIS. Plaintiffs had asserted that the environmental effect of a newly proposed, larger port complex was new information that should have been assessed in a supplemental EIS. The court recognized that an agency is not required to prepare a supplemental EIS in response to every change in circumstance that occurs after approval of a final EIS. However, the court noted that the administrative record of the agency "does not provide the kind of detailed explanation contemplated by NEPA; it neither evinces careful consideration of the decision not to prepare a supplemental EIS, nor the rationale for the decision, much less that the agency evaluated specific potential impacts." 714 F. Supp. at 570.

The court, citing CEQ's regulations and "Forty Questions" guidance, found that where a consultant had actually prepared sections of an EIS, the agency must list those preparers in the EIS and must obtain conflict of interest disclosure statements from the consultant, even where a State agency oversaw the preparation of that EIS. The court also found that, while an agency should disclose a consultant's prior involvement in a project, this did not automatically disqualify them from working on an EIS. The agency's failure to obtain conflict of interest disclosure statements and its failure to list the consulting firms which prepared significant background papers in the list of preparers did not create a likelihood of harm to the environment. (See *Ibid.* at 582-83.)

The court found that FHWA failed to show that it was reasonable to assume that only four targeted industries would locate at the proposed industrial park in evaluating secondary impacts of the proposed cargo terminal. Inadequate consideration of secondary impacts created the risk of uninformed decision making necessary to support the issuance of a preliminary injunction. (See *Ibid.* at 583-584.)

"Therefore, it appears that agency decision makers had before them the information necessary to enable an informed decision of the likely environmental consequences of [the proposed project], but not [of project alternatives]. In addition to not presenting decision makers with the environmental effects of [project alternatives], the FEIS does not provide sufficient information to enable decision makers or the public to make an informed judgment as to whether [the proposed project] is economically necessary or viable, or whether the economic benefits of [the proposed project] would be worth the additional costs." *Ibid.* at 585. Failure to evaluate the partially expandable cargo terminal as a reasonable alternative to the proposed fully expandable terminal, in violation of NEPA, created a sufficient risk of uninformed decision making to support the issuance of a preliminary injunction. (See *Ibid.* at 586-87.)

"Because NEPA's goal is to minimize the '*risk* to the environment when governmental decision makers make up their minds without having before them an analysis (with prior public comment) of the likely effects of their decision upon the environment' it is 'perfectly proper' for the courts to consider the 'difficulty of stopping the bureaucratic steam roller,' and the 'practical fact that bureaucratic decision makers (where the law permits) are less likely to tear down a nearly completed project than a barely started project'....Courts 'should take account of the harm from inadequately informed decision making and its potentially irreparable nature.'" *Ibid.* at 590, quoting *Sierra Club v. Marsh*, 872 F.2d 497, 500, 504 (1st Cir. 1989).

Sierra Club v. United States Forest Service. 843 F.2d 1190 (9th Cir. 1988)

ISSUE(S) ADDRESSED: adequacy of an EA, cumulative impacts

FACTS: Plaintiffs challenged the USFS' award of nine timber sale contracts in the Sequoia National Forest. The EAs supporting these sales were found inadequate because they failed to consider cumulative impacts.

FINDINGS: With respect to plaintiffs' argument that the USFS neglected to consider cumulative impacts, the court noted that even the USFS witness acknowledged that the EAs failed to "identify the cumulative effects of past and future harvests on watersheds....This testimony raises substantial questions as to whether the sales may significantly affect the human environment." 843 F.2d at 1195.

"Moreover, such testimony leads to speculation on potential cumulative effects. The purpose of an EIS is to obviate the need for such speculation by insuring that available data are gathered and analyzed prior to the implementation of the proposed action. Although the Forest Service maintains it discusses the past and future cumulative impacts in its draft EIS for the Forest, none of the EAs incorporated these discussions in any way." *Ibid.*

Because substantial questions had been raised concerning the potential adverse effects of harvesting these timber sales, an EIS should have been prepared. *Ibid.*

State of Louisiana v. Lee, 758 F.2d 1081 (5th Cir. 1985), *cert. denied*, 475 U.S. 1044 (1986)

ISSUE(S) ADDRESSED: mitigated finding of no significant impact

FACTS: Plaintiff argued that a Army Corps' decision to issue a finding of no significant impact and not to prepare an EIS for the renewal of six five-year permits for holders to dredge shells off the Louisiana Gulf Coast was arbitrary and capricious. The District Court upheld the FONSI and dismissed plaintiffs' action.

FINDINGS: The Court of Appeals agreed with the lower court on the use of mitigation measures to eliminate significant impacts. Plaintiffs cited CEQ's Forty Most Asked Questions which states "..mitigation measures may be relied upon to make a finding of no significant impact only if they are imposed by statute or regulation or submitted by an applicant or agency as part of the original proposal." Both courts disagreed with CEQ on this point noting that "although NEPA regulations issued by the Council are binding on all Federal agencies, this publication [CEQ's Forty Most Asked Questions] is not a regulation, but merely an informal statement. Therefore, it is not a controlling authority." 758 F.2d at 1083.

"... NEPA was intended to address reality, not a hypothetical situation. The conditions at issue are embodied in the permits themselves. This is not an instance where the proposed mitigating conditions consist of vague statements of good intentions by third parties not within the control of the agency...Rather, here the conditions are legally enforceable by the Corps. The dredging must be conducted in accordance with these restrictions. Therefore, the only realistic course of action is to consider the conditions in reviewing the Corp's decision not to file the impact statement." *Ibid.*

"An environmental impact statement is intended to detail the environmental and economic effects of any proposed Federal action so that those not directly involved can understand and give meaningful consideration to and make appropriate comment on the factors involved. It also ensures that the decision-maker gives serious weight to environmental factors in making discretionary choices." *Ibid.* at 1084.

"Any decision based on an environmental assessment alone is necessarily more speculative than one made after the preparation and full consideration required by an impact statement." *Ibid.* The court noted that plaintiffs need show only that a significant degradation may result and that "plaintiffs must establish only that the Corps was unreasonable in concluding there was no reasonable possibility that the proposed action would significantly degrade any environmental factor" in order to find a FONSI inadequate. *Ibid.* at 1084-85.

"The Corps correctly asserts that the mere existence of differing opinions [among agencies] does not make its decision erroneous." *Ibid.* at 1084-85

State of Maryland v. Train. 415 F. Supp. 116 (D. MD. 1976)

ISSUE(S) ADDRESSED: functional equivalence

FACTS: States brought an action against EPA challenging the issuance of a permit allowing Camden, New Jersey to use an ocean dumping site for sewage sludge on the ground that EPA was required to comply with NEPA prior to issuing a permit under the Ocean Dumping Act.

FINDINGS: The court found EPA was not required to file an EIS in order to issue a dumping permit. Citing "[a] host of cases [that] support EPA's position based on functional equivalence," the court stated: "Where Federal regulatory action is circumscribed by extensive procedures, including public participation, for evaluating environmental issues and is taken by an agency with recognized environmental expertise, formal adherence to the NEPA requirements is not required unless Congress has specifically so directed." *Ibid.* at 121, 122.

Stein v. Barton, 740 F. Supp. 743 (D.Alaska 1990)

ISSUE(S) ADDRESSED: reasonable alternatives, purpose and need, mitigation

FACTS: In 1951, the USFS signed a long-term timber sale contract with Ketchikan Pulp Company providing for logging of more than 8.25 billion board feet of timber over a 50-year period in an area of the Tongass National Forest in southeastern Alaska, including Prince of Wales, Revilla, and Heceta Islands (primary sale area). Since 1964, planning had been divided into five-year operating periods. The USFS prepared a final EIS for the 1989-94 Operating Period for the Ketchikan Pulp Company Long-Term Sale Area and, in a ROD dated June 2, 1989, the Regional Forester adopted the latest five-year operating plan for the sale area. Plaintiffs contended that the final EIS prepared by the USFS and the agency's choice of mitigation options were invalid for several reasons under NEPA.

FINDINGS: "NEPA does not require a Federal agency to consider alternatives which do not achieve the purpose contemplated for the proposed action, and NEPA does not circumscribe the agency's discretion in designating the project's purpose." 740 F. Supp. at 748.

In reference to mitigation, the court noted that "[e]ven if the court assumes, for the sake of argument, that the Federal defendants' rejoinder [that past experience is a poor indicator of future occurrence] is true, the FEIS does not articulate and explain this proposition sufficiently to withstand review under the 'arbitrary and capricious' standard. The 'elaborate monitoring plan' alluded to by the Federal defendants in their opposition is given only cursory treatment in the FEIS. The FEIS states, 'All action alternatives are subject to monitoring and reporting requirements contained in Forest Service manuals and handbooks. The monitoring requirements will be part of the implementation for all of the alternatives.' This vague declaration is supplemented by one short table entry explaining that the program for monitoring fisheries mitigation will be implemented by district rangers, who will measure the percent effectiveness of mitigation measures in five to fifteen percent of harvested units annually and who will record their findings on a form which is exemplified at the back of the table. This explanation of mitigation monitoring is wholly insufficient to rebut the inferences raised by plaintiffs' evidence. It is true that NEPA does not require an agency to mitigate adverse environmental impacts. However, where an agency's decision to proceed with a project is based on unconsidered, irrational, or inadequately explained assumptions about the efficacy of mitigation measures, the decision must be set aside as 'arbitrary and capricious.' The court concludes that plaintiffs have shown a likelihood of success on the merits of their claim that the Forest Service's decision to adopt option B should be set aside for this reason." *Ibid.* at 754.

Texas Committee on Natural Resources v. Bergland, 573 F.2d 201 (5th Cir.), *cert. denied*, 439 U.S. 966 (1978)

ISSUE(S) ADDRESSED: Statutory conflict, functional equivalence

FACTS: Plaintiffs alleged that the USFS's failure to file an EIS before deciding to use even-aged timber management was a violation of NEPA.

FINDINGS: The court found the USFS was not exempted from complying with NEPA in preparing land management guidelines under National Forest Management Act (NFMA) because the USFS's statutory responsibilities under the act are not in fundamental and irreconcilable conflict with NEPA and do not amount to the "functional equivalent" of an EIS under NEPA.

"We are certain, however that Congress did not intend entirely to exempt the Forest Service from NEPA compliance in establishing those new management guidelines....We also hold that the Forest Service must prepare environment impact statements as dictated by the NFMA and that it is responsible for the development of management guidelines that conform to the NFMA." 573 F.2d at 212.

Town of Huntington v. Marsh, 859 F.2d 1134 (2d Cir. 1988)

ISSUE(S) ADDRESSED: connected actions, cumulative impacts

FACTS: The Long Island Sound is host to many recreational and industrial uses, including swimming, boating and fishing. Marinas and harbors which line the Sound must be dredged periodically to provide berthing for pleasure craft, commercial fishing boats, and military ships. The spoil from these dredging operations have for decades been dumped into the Sound. This litigation arises out of the ongoing effort of citizens and the Federal government to balance the use of the Sound as a waste dumpsite with the need to protect its increasingly fragile waters. The Army Corps prepared an EIS to consider the impacts of disposing of the dredge spoil in a new dumpsite in the western area of the Sound. The Army Corps used generic analyses of dumping in the Sound, saying that specific impacts would be addressed on a dredging project-specific basis at a later stage when individual permit applications were considered. In addition, the Army Corps planned to use the new area for additional disposal from its own dredging operations, but did not analyze those impacts.

FINDINGS: "The fundamental flaw in the Corps' EIS is its too-circumscribed view of the 'project' which is the subject of its impact analysis. The Corps conceives of its 'project' as the designation of a disposal site. It has rigidly adhered to the position that site designation and permit issuance are two distinct and unrelated actions. It has steadfastly maintained that particularized discussion of types, quantities and cumulative effects of dredged wastes to be deposited at WLIS III is outside the scope of the EIS and must await analysis on a case-by-case basis. We disagree. This is merely a variant of 'segmentation' which has been uniformly rejected by courts. 'Segmentation' or 'piecemealing' occurs when an action is divided into component parts, each involving action with less significant environmental effects.... Segmentation is to be avoided in order to 'insure that interrelated projects[,] the overall effect of which is environmentally significant, not be fractionalized into smaller, less significant actions.'" 859 F.2d at 1142.

"Even if the Corps were satisfied with its action, public scrutiny of the basis for the Corps' decision is 'essential to implementing NEPA.' 40 C.F.R. § 1500.1(b)....We note in particular the comments by agency experts from the Department of Interior Office of Environmental Project Review, the Department of Commerce Office of Marine Pollution Assessment, and the Fish and Wildlife Service which indicated that evaluation of the merits of WLIS III as a dumpsite was made difficult or impossible by the lack of sufficient data in the EIS submitted. For these reasons, we hold that the Corps violated NEPA by not including analysis of the types, quantities and cumulative effects of waste disposal in its EIS." *Ibid.* at 1143.

U.S. v. 95 Acres of Land, 994 F.2d 696 (9th Cir. 1993)

ISSUE(S) ADDRESSED: definition of major Federal action

FACTS: The USFS filed declarations of taking, and landowners challenged the action, claiming that a change in land title was a major Federal action requiring compliance with NEPA. The district court agreed and vacated the declarations of taking.

FINDINGS: The Court of Appeals reversed the lower court, stating that "in condemnation actions, Federal courts have jurisdiction only to review whether property is being taken for authorized public use....NEPA cannot be used as a defense to the condemnation action. The filing of the condemnation action and the subsequent transfer of legal title are not 'major Federal actions significantly affecting the environment.' Actions that fall under NEPA's umbrella may immediately follow a condemnation action; NEPA applies to newly acquired land in the same way it applies to land the government has long owned. In an appropriate action, the district court may enjoin the proposed road system [for which the land was condemned]. The district court cannot, however, address the ownership of the land." 994 F.2d at 699.

Valley Citizens' for a Safe Environment v. Vest, [no official citation] No. 91-30007-F (D. MA, May 6, 1991)

ISSUE(S) ADDRESSED: emergency actions

FACTS: In 1987, Westover Air Force Base issued an EIS to evaluate the likely effects that the presence and operation of C-5A transport planes would have on the environment. Pursuant to the EIS, night flights were prohibited. In September 1990, the Air Force began to fly the planes in and out on a 24-hour schedule, due to the events relating to the war in the Persian Gulf and Operation Desert Storm. CEQ determined that the developing situation in the Middle East constituted an emergency within the meaning of its regulations, and allowed the Air Force to continue to operate the flights while preparing an EA to address the environmental impacts of the flights and possible mitigation. Plaintiffs challenged both CEQ's authority to allow such arrangements in an emergency, as well as the application of the regulation to the situation at Westover.

FINDINGS: The court upheld CEQ's authority to issue the emergency regulation and its application to Westover. The court first noted that NEPA requires compliance "to the fullest extent possible," indicating that an EIS is not mandatory in all circumstances. Thus, the court noted that "before a Federal agency takes environmentally significant action, emergency circumstances may make completion of an EIS...unnecessary." Section 4331 of NEPA also acknowledges that other goals and interest of the United States may make strict compliance with NEPA impossible. The court also held that the decision by CEQ and the USAF to deem the Westover situation an emergency was reasonable, given the military's operational and scheduling difficulties during "the hostile and unpredictable" Persian Gulf crisis.

"The C-5A operations furnish fuel, tools, spare parts, and other critical supplies to American and international troops in the troubled Middle East region. The C-5As also bring back to the United States, via Westover AFB, equipment and personnel essential to the maintenance of military readiness at home and broad. The Court finds that defendants could reasonably interpret the present crisis to be an emergency within NEPA, given the military's operational and scheduling difficulties and the hostile and unpredictable nature of the Persian Gulf region. The Air Force has not attempted to justify the nighttime C-5A operations by speaking vaguely of national security or world peace. Rather, defendants have pointed to specific military concerns with regard to troop redeployment, flight scheduling, cargo transport, and other operations that necessitate the use of Westover AFB for C-5A operations on a twenty-four hour basis. In short, the Court must hold that the Air Force and CEQ are not acting in an arbitrary and capricious manner by categorizing the instant situation as an emergency."

Village of Palatine v. United States Postal Service, 742 F. Supp. 1377 (N.D. Ill. 1990)

ISSUE(S) ADDRESSED: reasonable alternatives, range of alternatives

FACTS: In this condemnation action, the village sought to enjoin the U. S. Postal Service (USPS) from constructing a mail distribution center on land the USPS had purchased from a private owner. In 1987, before conducting any environmental analysis, the USPS purchased an option on the parcel of land in question for a non-refundable $400,000; if the option were exercised, the purchase price was to be $9.5 million. The option was good until March 31, 1988. The USPS issued a draft EA on March 23; the option was exercised on March 31; and a final EA and FONSI were issued in May 1988. At the urging of the village, the USPS agreed in late 1988 to consider an alternative site. As the court stated, although the USPS agreed to study another site and even conceded that the alternative was viable, the agency indicated that it wanted to proceed at the original site because of the time and money it had already invested in that location. The village filed suit, seeking to enjoin the USPS from constructing the facility on the site it had acquired until after it had complied with NEPA and other pertinent statutes and regulations.

FINDINGS: In ruling on the USPS motion to dismiss, the court recognized that the USPS had substantially modified the proposed facility after issuance of the EA in May 1988, and concluded that the record did not demonstrate that the USPS had fully considered all the relevant environmental factors in its EA. Further, the court stated that the USPS was obligated to evaluate a range of alternatives, including alternative sites. While the EA indicated that the USPS has considered 28 sites, it failed to adequately explain why the USPS had rejected those alternative sites.

"The Postal Service argues that section 102(2)(E) does not require that it evaluate the environmental impact of building on alternative sites. The Postal Service argues that the law requires only that it consider the environmental impact of 'reasonable alternatives.' To fulfill this duty, the Postal Service argues, it evaluated the environmental impact of three alternatives: (1) no action; (2) leasing an existing building already owned or leased by the government; and (3) buying or leasing an existing building. After rejecting these three alternatives, the Postal Service decided to build a new facility. According to the Postal Service, this inquiry and decision exhausted its obligation to explore the environmental consequences of alternative plans. We disagree." 742 F. Supp. at 1392.

The USPS motion to dismiss was denied.

Warm Springs Dam Task Force v. Gribble, 621 F.2d 1017 (9th Cir. 1980)

ISSUE(S) ADDRESSED: supplementation

FACTS: This case involved the adequacy of an EIS prepared by the Army Corps for the construction of the Warm Springs Dam in Northern California. The central issue was whether the Army Corps was required to supplement its EIS further when it became aware of a USGS study indicating that a fault located six miles from the proposed dam might be capable of generating an earthquake of greater magnitude that the dam was designed to withstand.

FINDINGS: "We start with the premise that a Federal agency has a continuing duty to gather and evaluate new information relevant to the environmental impact of its actions...This does not mean, however, that supplementation s required whenever new information becomes available." 621 F.2d at 1023-24.

"When new information comes to light the agency must consider it, evaluate it, and make a reasoned determination whether it is of such significance as to require implementation of formal NEPA filing procedures. Reasonableness depends on such factors as the environmental significance of the new information, the probable accuracy of the information, the degree of care with which the agency considered the information and evaluated its impact, and the degree to which the agency supported its decision not to supplement with a statement of explanation or additional data." *Ibid.* at 1024.

EPA'S POLICY AND PROCEDURES FOR THE REVIEW OF FEDERAL ACTIONS IMPACTING THE ENVIRONMENT

1640
10/3/84

Chapter 1 - Purpose, Policy, and Mandates

1. Purpose

A. This manual establishes policies and procedures for carrying out the Environmental Protection Agency's (EPA's) responsibilities to review and comment on Federal actions affecting the quality of the environment. EPA has general statutory authority under the National Environmental Policy Act of 1969 and the Council on Environmental Quality's implementing regulations, and has specific authority and responsibility under Section 309 of the Clean Air Act to conduct such reviews, comment in writing, and make those comments available to the public. These responsibilities have been combined into one process and are referred to throughout this manual as the Environmental Review Process.

B. This manual contains EPA's policies and procedures for carrying out the Environmental Review Process, assigns specific responsibilities, and outlines mechanisms for resolving problems that arise in the Environmental Review Process. This manual is supplemented by, and should be read in conjunction with, the following manuals, which are also prepared, distributed, and maintained by the Office of Federal Activities:

1. *Office of Federal Activities Policies and Procedures Manual.* Contains current guidance and detailed information related to the Environmental Review Process; and

2. *Environmental Review Process Data Management Manual.* Contains detailed guidance and reporting requirements for the national level computerized tracking system.

2. Statutory Authorities

A. The National Environmental Policy Act of 1969 (NEPA), as amended, (42 U.S.C. 4321 *et seq.*, Public Law 91-190, 83 Stat. 852) requires that all Federal agencies proposing legislation and other major actions significantly affecting the quality of the human environment consult with other agencies having jurisdiction by law or special expertise over such environmental considerations, and thereafter prepare a detailed statement of these environmental effects. The Council on Environmental Quality (CEQ) has published regulations and associated guidance to implement NEPA (40 CFR Parts 1500-1508).

B. Section 309 of the Clean Air Act, as amended, (42 U.S.C. 7609, Public Law 91-604 12(a), 84 Stat. 1709) requires the EPA to review and comment in writing on the environmental impact of any matter relating to the duties and responsibilities granted pursuant to the Act or other provisions of the authority of the Administrator, contained in any: (1) legislation proposed by a Federal department or agency; (2) newly authorized Federal projects for construction and as major Federal action, or actions, other than a project for construction, to which Section 102(2)(C) of Public Law 91-190 applies; and (3) proposed regulations published by any department or agency of the Federal Government. Such written comments must be made public at the conclusion of any review. In the event such legislation, action, or regulation is determined to be unsatisfactory from the standpoint of public health, welfare, or environmental quality, the determination will be published and the matter referred to the CEQ.

C. Federal environmental laws require, in most circumstances, facilities of the Executive Branch of the Federal Government to comply with Federal, State, and local pollution control requirements promulgated pursuant to, or effective under, those statutes. The review of proposed Federal projects for compliance with these national environmental standards is the responsibility of the EPA through the Environmental Review Process and the Federal Facilities Compliance Program. In addition to these general statutory authorities, the reviews required under Section 1424(e) of the Safe Drinking Water Act (42 U.S.C. 300 h-3, Public Law 93-523, 88 Stat. 1678) and Section 404(r) of the Federal Water Pollution Control Act (Clean Water Act) (33 U.S.C. 1344(r), Public Law 92-500, Public Law 95-217, 86 Stat. 884, 91 Stat 1600) are integrated into the Environmental Review Process.

3. Policy

A. The objective of the Environmental Review Process is to foster the goals of the NEPA process by ensuring that the EPA's environmental expertise, as expressed in its comments on Federal actions and other interagency liaison activity, is considered by agency decision makers. It is EPA's policy to carry out the Environmental Review Process in conjunction with EPA's other authorities to:

1. Participate in interagency coordination early in the planning process to identify significant environmental issues that should be addressed in completed documents;

2. Conduct follow-up coordination on actions where EPA has identified significant environmental impacts to ensure a full understanding of the issues and to ensure implementation of appropriate corrective actions; and

3. Identify environmentally unsatisfactory proposals and consult with other agencies, including the CEQ, to achieve timely resolution of the major issues and problems.

B. In implementing this policy, EPA will assist Federal agencies in:

1. Achieving the goals set forth in the NEPA;

2. Meeting the objectives and complying with the requirements of the laws and regulations administered by the EPA; and

3. Developing concise, well-reasoned decision documents which identify project impacts, a range of project alternatives, and mitigation measures that will avoid or minimize adverse effects on the environment.

Chapter 2 - Management of the Environmental Review Process

1. General Responsibilities

The EPA Administrator has delegated responsibility for carrying out the Environmental Review Process to the Assistant Administrator for External Affairs and the Regional Administrators but has retained the responsibility to refer matters to the CEQ. The Assistant Administrator, Office of External Affairs, has in turn delegated program management to the Director, Office of Federal Activities, but has retained the responsibility for concurring on proposed comment letters that have the potential for referral to the CEQ.

2. Office of Federal Activities

The Office of Federal Activities (OFA) within the Office of External Affairs (OEA) is the program manager for the Environmental Review Process and for the overall coordination and policy development for activities associated with this process. To carry out these responsibilities, the OFA will maintain management support functions consisting of Federal Agency Liaison staff assigned to coordinate with the Headquarters offices of all Federal agencies and a Management Information Unit. The Director, Federal Agency Liaison Division, working through the Director, OFA, has overall policy development and management oversight responsibility for the Environmental Review Process.

A.   Federal Agency Liaisons. Each Federal Agency Liaison (FAL), working through their Division Director and other appropriate elements within the OFA, has the following responsibilities:

    1.   Conduct Headquarters-level liaison with other Federal agencies to identify those actions that should be reviewed and to provide information on how the EPA can most effectively review other agencies' proposed actions pursuant to the Environmental Review Process;

    2.   Provide management oversight of regional review actions carried out under the requirements of this Manual, and provide policy guidance on the Environmental Review Process to Headquarters program offices and regional EIS reviewers;

    3.   Ensure appropriate Headquarters involvement and support for actions that are elevated under these Procedures; and

    4.   Coordinate the EPA review of proposed regulations, national level Environmental Impact Statements (EISs), and other national level activities and other national level actions.

B.   Management Information Unit.

    1.   The Management Information Unit (MIU) is responsible for the operation of a centralized data management and reporting system for the Environmental Review Process, and for the public availability of comments pursuant to Section 309 of the Clean Air Act. The procedures and requirements for this centralized data system are described in the Environmental Review Process Data Management Manual. The MIU is also responsible for the official filing of all EISs in accordance with 40 CFR Section 1506.9.

    2.   The MIU is responsible for preparing the following reports to inform EPA officials and the public of EISs and other Federal actions received by the EPA for review and comment.

COMDATE. This weekly computerized report contains a list of all EISs filed, pursuant to 40 CFR Section 1506.9, during the previous week. COMDATE lists, in part, the EIS title, official filing date, EPA control numbers, location, *Federal Register* notice date (40 CFR 1506.10(a)), date comments are due to the lead agency, and regional assignment. Other relevant information is also noted such as overall extensions of time granted by lead agencies and EPA ratings of previously filed draft EISs.

CEQ Notice of EIS Availability. A Notice of Availability is published in the *Federal Register* each Friday for EISs filed during the previous week, pursuant to 40 CFR Section 1506.10(a). The minimum periods for review of the EISs are calculated from the *Federal Register* date of this notice.

Notice of Availability of EPA Comments. A notice will be published weekly announcing the availability of EPA comments on EISs, regulations, and any other action for which an unsatisfactory determination has been made. The notice will include, in part, the title, a summary of comments, and the rating (if applicable) of each review completed.

3. Regional Office

Each EPA regional office is responsible for carrying out the Environmental Review Process in accordance with the policies and procedures of this manual for proposed Federal actions affecting its region. Each EPA regional office will designate a regional environmental review coordinator who has overall management responsibility for the Environmental Review Process in that region. It is the responsibility of the regional environmental review coordinator to:

A.   Ensure that the region is maintaining effective liaison with other Federal agencies at the regional level;

B.   Carry out lead responsibilities for the review of proposed EISs and other Federal actions assigned to the coordinator's region or other actions for which it has lead responsibility (see paragraph 6 of this chapter); and

C.   Ensure that the region is maintaining the official agency files and is properly tracking correspondence generated under the regional Environmental Review Process.

4. Program Offices

EPA program offices are responsible for providing technical assistance and policy guidance on review actions directly related to their areas of responsibility. When acting as principal or associate reviewer in accordance with paragraph 5 of this chapter, program offices will follow the policies and procedures set forth in this Manual.

5. Specific Review Management Responsibilities

A.   Headquarters and Regional Environmental Review Coordinators. The term Environmental Review Coordinator (ERC) is used in this manual to mean either a regional environmental review coordinator or the OFA Division Director managing FAL responsibilities for a particular action agency. It is the ERC's responsibility to manage the environmental review of actions to ensure EPA compliance with the procedures in this Manual and to:

   1.   Ensure the timely receipt of all assigned EISs listed in COMDATE, and ensure completion of MIU reporting requirements;

   2.   Designate a principal reviewer for each assigned action;

   3.   Coordinate determination of the level of participation in EIS scoping efforts and manage participation efforts;

   4.   Coordinate determination of EPA's involvement as a cooperating agency under Section 1501.6 of the CEQ regulations;

   5.   Determine the case-by-case need for reviewing the adequacy of the contents of draft EISs;

   6.   Determine the case-by-case need for preparation of comments on final EISs;

   7.   Determine the appropriate rating to be assigned to each draft EIS in the comment letter;

   8.   Determine the need for preparation of comments on non-EIS actions;

   9.   Ensure timely distribution and public availability of comments; and

10. Initiate and manage agency follow-up efforts on comment letters identifying significant problem areas.

B. Principal Reviewer. The principal reviewer (PR) within a person designated by the ERC to coordinate the review of the action and to prepare the EPA comment letter on the proposed Federal action. The PR will be responsible for ensuring that the views of other EPA offices are adequately represented in the comment letter, and that the comment letter is consistent with agency policy and reflects all applicable EPA environmental responsibilities. In general, the PR for Headquarters lead reviews will be the FAL assigned to the lead agency. The PR will have the responsibility to:

1. Select associate reviewers (ARs) ensuring that all appropriate regional and Headquarters EPA offices are asked to participate;

2. Set due dates for AR comments that will ensure adequate time for review by the signing official;

3. Coordinate with ARs to ensure timely receipt of comments and timely receipt of disagreements or inconsistencies between reviewers;

4. Review and assure the validity of all comments included in the final EPA response;

5. Resolve and record the disposition of any disagreements with or between AR comments in accordance with subparagraph D, below;

6. Ensure consistency of EPA comments with any previous comments on the action;

7. Recommend the most appropriate rating of the environmental impacts of the proposal and/or the adequacy of the EIS, and include the rating in all draft EIS comment letters; and

8. Ensure the distribution of copies of the signed comment letter to all ARs and other appropriate parties.

C. Associate Reviewer. The associate reviewer (AR) is a person designated by the PR to provide technical and policy advice in specific review areas and to provide the views of the office in which the AR is located. ARs will have the responsibility to:

1. Review assigned actions within their areas of responsibility taking into account the policies and procedures of this manual;

2. Submit comments to the PR on actions in a timely manner;

3. Obtain the appropriate level of concurrence on comments submitted;

4. If significant issues are identified, assist the PR in determining the most appropriate rating for the proposed action; and

5. Upon the request of the PR and within the limits of available resources, provide liaison with, and technical assistance to, the agency that initiated the EIS or other Federal action.

D. Consolidation of Comments. The PR will consider all AR comments during preparation of the EPA comment letter. If the PR disagrees with substantive AR comments, the PR will attempt to resolve the differences directly with the AR. If this is not possible, the ERC will be informed and will coordinate resolution of the issue. On comment letters where substantive changes are made to comments generated by an AR, the PR will obtain AR concurrence on the final letter. If major policy issues are involved, the ERC should be informed and policy level concurrence by the AR office should be obtained. All AR comments, with applicable PR notations on disposition of the specific issue, will be retained in the official project file.

6. Routing and Lead Responsibility of EISs and Other Federal Actions

A. Distribution of EISs should be accomplished by lead agencies on or before the EIS filing date. To ensure that all EISs are properly distributed, the ERC will check the weekly COMDATE report to make sure that all assigned EISs have been received. If the ERC has not received an EIS identified in COMDATE, the ERC will inform the MIU immediately and work with the MIU to obtain the EIS. If appropriate, a request for a time extension due to lack of availability of the EIS will be coordinated by the MIU at that time. The following represents the normal routing and lead responsibility assignment of review actions:

Action directed to Legislation (not accompanied by EIS) Office of Legislative Analysis Policy statements, regulations, procedures, and legislation accompanied by an EIS Office of Federal Activities

Actions that embody a high degree of national controversy or significance, or pioneer Agency policy Office of Federal Activities

All other actions appropriate regional office.

B. In general, a regional office will have the lead responsibility for reviewing all EISs and other Federal actions it receives. Specific exceptions occur where:

1. The EIS or other Federal action pertains to an action that is to take place in another region. In such cases, that regional office will have the lead, the MIU will be informed immediately, and the EIS will be forwarded to the lead region.

2. The EIS pertains to more than one region. In this case, the affected regions should refer to COMDATE to determine which is the lead region and which is an AR. If there is a disagreement with the COMDATE assignments, the designated lead region will inform the MIU.

3. The EIS or other Federal action pertains primarily to national EPA policy, regulations, or procedures, or to an action which does not have a geographical focus (e.g., overlapping several regions), or to an action concerning areas in which the regional office does not have adequate expertise. If the ERC suspects this to be the case, the ERC will contact the appropriate FAL to determine lead responsibility. Unless otherwise agreed upon, such cases will be forwarded immediately to the MIU for reassignment of the action.

C. A regional or Headquarters office may at any time request that a particular EIS or other Federal action be evaluated by the OFA to determine lead responsibility.

Chapter 3 - Pre-EIS Review Activities

1. Policy

It is EPA's policy to participate early in the NEPA compliance efforts of other Federal agencies to the fullest extent practicable in order to identify EPA matters of concern with proposed agency actions and to assist in resolving these concerns at the earliest possible stage of project development. The ERC will make a concerted effort to resolve project concerns through early coordination, where possible, rather than rely on submission of critical comments on completed documents.

2. General Liaison

A. The regional environmental review coordinator and the FALs will establish and maintain contact at the appropriate levels of other agencies in order to foster an effective working relationship between agencies, to understand the agencies' programs and policies, and to be kept informed of projects of interest to the EPA.

B. To the fullest extent practicable, the ERC will assist the action agencies in:

    1. Early identification of potential project impacts and the need to prepare assessments or EISs;

    2. Identification of appropriate environmental assessment techniques and methodologies; and

    3. Incorporation of all reasonable alternatives and impact mitigation measures in the planning and development of projects.

3. EPA's Participation in Scoping

A. General. Scoping is the formal early coordination process required by CEQ's 1979 Regulations (40 CFR 1501.7) and is intended to ensure that problems are identified early and are properly studied, that issues of little significance do not consume time and effort, that the draft EIS is thorough and balanced, and that delays occasioned by an inadequate draft EIS are avoided. To help achieve these objectives, EPA will participate in scoping processes to the fullest extent practicable, emphasizing attendance at scoping meetings.

B. Responding to Scoping Requests.

    1. The ERC will review and respond by letter to all scoping requests specifically made to the EPA. Although *Federal Register* Notices of Intent to prepare an EIS are not considered specific, the ERC is responsible for being aware of all relevant scoping requests and for participating in those of special interest to the EPA. Responses to these non-EPA specific scoping requests may be made by telephone, but a record of the communication must be kept in the official project file.

    2. Scoping letters can be either a form letter of acknowledgment with a list of generic concerns (related to project type or project area), or a letter with detailed action-specific comments. A generic scoping letter or telephone response must define EPA's anticipated level of participation in the scoping process and include at least the following information:

        1. For the general type of project being proposed:

            1. A list of all EPA permits that might be required;

            2. Significant environmental issues that should be emphasized in preparation of the EIS; and

            3. References to publications, including guidelines and current research, that would be useful in analyzing the environmental impacts of various alternatives.

        2. A statement regarding EPA's intention to carry out its independent environmental review responsibilities under Section 309 of the Clean Air Act; and

---

3. The name, title, and telephone number of the appropriate working-level contact in the EPA. The level of EPA participation in scoping processes will be determined by the ERC on a case-by-case basis, taking into account the following factors:

EPA's statutory responsibility;

Severity of potential environmental impacts;

Priority concerns identified in the Administrator's Agency Operating Guidance; and

Available staff and travel resources.

C. Input to the Scoping Process. For those scoping requests where the ERC determines that more substantive EPA participation is warranted, the generic information listed in subparagraph 3b(2) should be supplemented with further detailed guidance to the lead agency. Such guidance will, to the extent possible, include:

1. Specific environmental issues that should be analyzed;

2. Specific information or data related to the area of interest;

3. Specific assessment techniques and methodologies that EPA program offices use or have approved for use;

4. Reasonable alternatives to the proposed action that may avoid potential adverse impacts, including suggestions for an environmentally preferred alternative; and

5. Mitigation measures that should be considered to reduce or substantially eliminate adverse environmental impacts.

4. EPA as a Cooperating Agency

A. General. Under 40 CFR 1501.6, the lead agency may request any other Federal agency to serve as a cooperating agency if it has jurisdiction or special expertise (statutory responsibility, agency mission, or related program experience) regarding any environmental issue that should be addressed in the statement. EPA may also request that the lead agency designate it as a cooperating agency. The ERC is responsible for determining whether the EPA will become a cooperating agency. The ERC is encouraged to accept cooperating agency status as often as possible, taking into account the criteria in subparagraph 3b(3).

B. Responding to Requests to be a Cooperating Agency.

1. If EPA determines in response to a formal request or makes an independent request to be a cooperating agency, the ERC must inform the lead agency of this decision in writing. The response must clearly State that every effort will be made to raise and resolve issues during scoping and EIS preparation, but that EPA has independent obligations under Section 309 of the Clean Air Act to review and comment on every draft EIS. EPA's response to a request to become a cooperating agency should clearly outline EPA's role in the preparation of the EIS. EPA's participation may range from participation in the scoping process and reviewing the scope of work, any preliminary drafts, or technical documents to assuming responsibility for developing information, preparing environmental analyses, and actually drafting portions of the EIS.

2. If the ERC determines that resource limitations preclude any involvement in the preparation of another agency's EIS, or preclude the degree of involvement requested by the lead agency, it

must inform the lead agency in writing (40 CFR 1501.6(c)). The letter should clearly State that EPA's status as a cooperating agency does not affect its independent responsibilities under Section 309 of the Clean Air Act to review and comment on other agencies' EISs. A copy of this reply will be submitted to the CEQ.

C. Providing Guidance as a Cooperating Agency. Information and/or guidance should be given to the lead agency in those areas where the EPA has special expertise as related to EPA's duties and responsibilities and in those subject areas described in subparagraph 3C. Specific guidance will be given in those areas where the EPA intends to exercise regulatory responsibility.

5. EPA as Lead Agency

Determining Lead Agency. When, in accordance with 40 CFR Part 6, EPA has an action which is subject to 102(2)(C) of NEPA and the action involves another Federal agency, the ERC and the other Federal agency will determine the lead agency status in accordance with the guidance contained in 40 CFR 1501.5(c), taking into account any relevant Memorandum of Understanding which EPA has executed with the Federal agency in question. Selection of the lead agency should be made at the earliest possible time. If the EPA is the lead agency, EPA will not review the EIS under the Environmental Review Process.

6. Reporting and Control

All responses related to scoping, cooperating, or lead agency issues, together with follow-up correspondence must be made a part of the official project file. Copies of letters in which EPA declines an agency's request to become a cooperating agency must be sent to the CEQ.

Chapter 4 - Review of Draft Environmental Impact Statements

1. Policy

It is EPA's policy to review and comment in writing on all draft EISs officially filed with the EPA, to provide a rating of the draft EIS which summarizes EPA's level of concern, and to meet with the lead agency to resolve significant issues. The EPA review will be primarily concerned with identifying and recommending corrective action for the significant environmental impacts associated with the proposal. Review of the adequacy of the information and analysis contained in the draft EISs will be done as needed to support this objective.

2. Draft EIS Review Management

Except as noted below, the review management procedures and responsibilities given in chapter 2 apply to the review of draft EISs.

A. Establishing Deadlines and Time Extensions.

   1. Deadlines. Unless a different deadline is officially established for receiving comments, EPA will provide comments on a draft EIS to the lead agency within 45 days from the start of the official review period. The official EIS due dates are listed in COMDATE. The PR will set internal deadlines to ensure EPA's comments are received within the official comment period.

   2. Time Extensions. Requests for extensions of review periods on draft EISs should be kept to a minimum. In general, review period extensions O.E.M. on draft EISs should not be requested unless important environmental issues are involved, and detailed substantive comments are being prepared. Time extensions should normally not exceed 15 days.

B. Categorization and Agency Notification System for Draft EISs.

1. After completing the review of a draft EIS, the PR will categorize or rate the EIS according to the alpha numeric system described below and in paragraph 4 of this chapter, and include the designated rate in the comment letter. In general, the rating will be based on the lead agency's preferred alternative. If, however, a preferred alternative is not identified, or if the preferred alternative has significant environmental problems that could be avoided by selection of another alternative, or if there is reason to believe that the preferred alternative may be changed at a later stage, the reviewer should rate individual alternatives. The purpose of the rating system is to synthesize the level of EPA's overall concern with the proposal and to define the associated follow-up that will be conducted with the lead agency.

2. The alphabetical categories LO, EC, EO, and EU signify EPA's evaluation of the environmental impacts of the proposal. Numerical categories 1, 2, and 3 signify an evaluation of the adequacy of the draft EIS. A summary of the rating definitions and the associated follow-up action is given in figure 4-1 [This figure is not included here. Editors' note.] at the end of this chapter. This figure should be attached to draft EIS comment letters when the lead agency may be unfamiliar with the EPA rating system. To the maximum extent possible, assignments of the alphabetical rating will be based on the overall environmental impact of the proposed project or action, including those project impacts that are not adequately addressed in the draft EIS. When there is insufficient information in the draft EIS, the determination of potential project impact may be based on other documents, information, or on-site surveys. The comment letter should clearly identify the source of information used by the EPA in evaluating the proposal.

3. The rating of a draft EIS will consist of one of the category combinations shown in the table below. As noted in the table and described in chapter 5, the ERC must follow up with the lead agency in those cases where significant problem areas are identified.

Category	Lead Agency Pre-Notification	Follow-up on Draft EIS Comment Letter
LO	None	None
EC-1, EC-2	None	Phone Call
EO-1, EO-2	Phone Call	Meeting
EO-3, EU-1, EU-2, EU-3, 3	Meeting	Meeting

4. For categories EO, EU, or 3, the ERC will ensure that the lead agency is notified of the general EPA concerns prior to receipt of EPA's comment letter. For categories EU and 3, the ERC must attempt to meet with the lead agency to discuss EPA's concerns prior to submission of the comment letter to the lead agency. The purposes of such a meeting are to describe the specific EPA concerns and discuss ways to resolve those concerns, to ensure that the EPA review has correctly interpreted the proposal and supporting information, and to become aware of any ongoing lead agency actions that might resolve the EPA concerns. To assure the objectivity and independence of the EPA review responsibility, the EPA comment letter itself and the assigned rating are not subject to negotiation and should not be changed on the basis of the meeting unless errors are discovered in EPA's understanding of the issues. However, the reviewer may add in the letter an acknowledgment of any relevant new lead agency activities that the reviewer believes could resolve the EPA concerns.

3. Scope of Comments on the Draft EIS

A. General. In general, EPA's comments will focus on the proposal but will, if necessary, review the complete range of alternatives, identifying those that are environmentally unacceptable to EPA and identifying EPA's preferred alternative. EPA's comment letter on the draft EIS will reflect all of EPA's environmental responsibilities that may bear on the action. The review will include EPA's assessment of the expected environmental impacts of the action and, if substantive impacts are identified, an evaluation of the adequacy of the supporting information presented in the EIS with suggestions for additional information that is needed. The EPA comment letter on draft EISs will:

   1. Explicitly reference EPA's review responsibilities under NEPA/Section 309;

   2. Acknowledge positive lead agency responses to EPA scoping suggestions or early coordination efforts;

   3. Provide a clear and concise description of EPA's substantive concerns and recommendations with supporting details given in attachments;

   4. Include a rating of the proposal and, if appropriate, the adequacy of the EIS in accordance with the criteria established in paragraphs 2 and 4 of this chapter; and

   5. Give the name and phone number of an appropriate EPA contact person.

B. Mitigation (40 CFR 1508.20). EPA's comments should include measures to avoid or minimize damage to the environment, or to protect, restore, and enhance the environment. Suggestions for mitigation should be oriented toward selection of mitigation measures that are technically feasible, of long-term effectiveness, and have a high likelihood of being implemented.

C. Statutory Authorities Special efforts should be made to identify project impacts that may lead to possible violation of national environmental standards or that might preclude or bias future issuance of EPA related environmental permits. EPA comments regarding potential violations of standards must be clearly stated in the letter, and an offer should be made to work with the proposing agency to develop appropriate measures to reduce impacts.

D. Alternatives. If significant impacts are associated with the proposal and they cannot be adequately mitigated, EPA's comments should suggest an environmentally preferable alternative, including if necessary, a new alternative. The suggested alternatives should be both reasonable and feasible. In this context, such an alternative is one that is practical in the technical, economic, and social sense, even if the alternative is outside the jurisdiction of the lead agency.

E. Purpose and Need. If a detailed review of alternatives is required, the reviewer may have to address the purpose of and need for the proposed action in order to determine to what degree an alternative would meet project objectives. In these cases, the reviewer may comment on the technical adequacy and accuracy of the EISs methods for estimating the need for the proposed action in cases where this affects the definition of reasonable and feasible alternatives. Within the context of reviewing purpose and need, the EPA may also comment on the economic justification of the project, and the relationship between the lead agency's economic analysis and any unquantified environmental impacts, values, and amenities. The comments may also address the technical validity and adequacy of the supporting data for the EISs economic analyses.

F. Projects Subject to Section 404(r) of the Clean Water Act. The Section 404 Coordinator will serve as an associate reviewer for those projects for which an agency is seeking an exemption under Section 404(r), and shall concur with the EPA comment letter. Section 404(r) provides that discharges of dredged or fill material which are part of Federal construction projects specifically authorized by Congress are not subject to regulation under Sections 301, 402, or 404 of the Clean

Water Act if the information on the effects of such discharge including consideration of the Section 404(b)(1) Guidelines, is included in the EIS for the project, and the EIS has been submitted to Congress before the discharge occurs and before the authorization for the project occurs. In accordance with the CEQ's guidance of November 17, 1980, EPA's comments on the EIS will serve as the vehicle for informing the agency of EPA's determination whether the proposed Section 404(r) exemption will be in compliance with the requirements of the Section 404(b)(1) Guidelines. The comments should reference the CEQ Memorandum for Heads of Agencies, which provides guidance on applying Section 404(r) and should include EPA's determination regarding:

1. Whether the EIS contains requisite information on the proposed discharges and other effects; and

2. Whether the proposal is consistent with Section 404(b)(1) Guidelines.

G. Projects Potentially Affecting a Designated "Sole Source" Aquifer Subject to Section 1424(e) of the Safe Drinking Water Act.

1. The regional office responsible for implementing the Safe Drinking Water Act (SDWA) will act as an AR on any EIS for a project potentially affecting a sole source aquifer designated under Section 1424(e) of the SDWA. EPA's comments on the draft EIS will serve as EPA's preliminary comments for the groundwater impact evaluation required under Section 1424(e), which stipulates that no commitment to a project of Federal financial assistance may be made, if the Administrator determines that a project has the potential to contaminate a designated aquifer, so as to create a significant hazard to public health. (Rules proposed to implement 1424(e) are found at 42 FR 51620, September 29, 1977.)

2. If it is determined that a project may contaminate the aquifer through the recharge zone so as to create a significant hazard to public health, the ERC will, in consultation with the drinking water staff, prepare a briefing memorandum and comment letter for the Regional Administrator. Copies of the briefing memorandum and the proposed comment letter shall first be sent to the appropriate FAL, who will coordinate concurrence by the appropriate Headquarters offices. The comment letter should cite EPA's authorities under Section 309/NEPA and Section 1424(e) of SDWA, and State that the project is a candidate for both referral to the CEQ and a Section 1424(e) determination.

4. Rating System Criteria

A. Rating the Environmental Impact of the Action.

1. LO (Lack of Objections). The review has not identified any potential environmental impacts requiring substantive changes to the preferred alternative. The review may have disclosed opportunities for application of mitigation measures that could be accomplished with no more than minor changes to the proposed action.

2. EC (Environmental Concerns). The review has identified environmental impacts that should be avoided in order to fully protect the environment. Corrective measures may require changes to the preferred alternative or application of mitigation measures that can reduce the environmental impact.

3. EO (Environmental Objections). The review has identified significant environmental impacts that should be avoided in order to adequately protect the environment. Corrective measures

may require substantial changes to the preferred alternative or consideration of some other project alternative (including the no action alternative or a new alternative). The basis for environmental objections can include situations:

1. Where an action might violate or be inconsistent with achievement or maintenance of a national environmental standard;

2. Where the Federal agency violates its own substantive environmental requirements that relate to EPA's areas of jurisdiction or expertise;

3. Where there is a violation of an EPA policy declaration;

4. Where there are no applicable standards or where applicable standards will not be violated but there is potential for significant environmental degradation that could be corrected by project modification or other feasible alternatives; or

5. Where proceeding with the proposed action would set a precedent for future actions that collectively could result in significant environmental impacts.

4. EU (Environmentally Unsatisfactory). The review has identified adverse environmental impacts that are of sufficient magnitude that EPA believes the proposed action must not proceed as proposed. The basis for an environmentally unsatisfactory determination consists of identification of environmentally objectionable impacts as defined above and one or more of the following conditions:

1. The potential violation of or inconsistency with a national environmental standard is substantive and/or will occur on a long-term basis;

2. There are no applicable standards but the severity, duration, or geographical scope of the impacts associated with the proposed action warrant special attention; or

3. The potential environmental impacts resulting from the proposed action are of national importance because of the threat to national environmental resources or to environmental policies.

B. Adequacy of the Impact Statement.

1.1 (Adequate). The draft EIS adequately sets forth the environmental impact(s) of the preferred alternative and those of the alternatives reasonably available to the project or action. No further analysis or data collection is necessary, but the reviewer may suggest the addition of clarifying language or information.

2.2 (Insufficient Information). The draft EIS does not contain sufficient information to fully assess environmental impacts that should be avoided in order to fully protect the environment, or the reviewer has identified new reasonably available alternatives that are within the spectrum of alternatives analyzed in the draft EIS, which could reduce the environmental impacts of the proposal. The identified additional information, data, analyses, or discussion should be included in the final EIS.

3.3 (Inadequate). The draft EIS does not adequately assess the potentially significant environmental impacts of the proposal, or the reviewer has identified new, reasonably available, alternatives, that are outside of the spectrum of alternatives analyzed in the draft EIS, which should be analyzed in order to reduce the potentially significant environmental impacts. The identified additional information, data, analyses, or discussions are of such a magnitude that they should have full public review at a draft stage. This rating indicates EPA's belief that the draft EIS does not meet the purposes of NEPA and/or the Section 309 review, and thus should be formally revised and made available for public comment in a supplemental or revised draft EIS.

5. Approving and Distributing Comments on Draft EISs

A. Categories LO, EC, EO, 1, or 2. For draft EISs rated LO, EC, EO, 1, or 2 the comments will be signed by the appropriate regional or Headquarters official and the ERC will distribute EPA's comments in accordance with subparagraph 5C of this chapter.

B. Categories EU or 3. For draft EISs where the ERC is proposing a rating of EU or 3, the EPA comment letter must be cleared by the Assistant Administrator for External Affairs prior to release. If the review is within a regional action, the draft letter will be submitted through the OFA for clearance. The draft comment letter must be submitted at least 5 working days prior to the due date and the proposed rating must have been approved by the regional signing official. In every case where a draft statement has been rated EU or 3, the Assistant Administrator, OEA, will send a copy of the EPA comment letter to the CEQ. In addition, where the EPA has commented to a regional office of the originating agency, appropriate officials within the headquarters office of the originating agency will also be informed. If a communications strategy has been developed for the action, the release of information should follow that strategy.

C. Checklist for Distribution of Agency Comments on the Draft EIS.

Addressee	Number of Copies
Agency submitting statement	Original
CEQ (if EU or 3) with transmittal letter	1 copy
Office of Public Affairs (if comments are rated EU or 3)	1 copy
EPA offices which served as associate reviewers	1 copy
Office of Federal Activities	2 copies
Attn: MIU	

6. Reporting and Control

All draft EISs under review, all time extensions, and all comment letters on draft EISs will be entered in the MIU data management system. All EPA comment letters and associated correspondence on draft EISs will he retained in the official project file. To the maximum extent practicable, the comment letter should not be distributed to parties outside of the EPA until after the original has been received by the lead agency.

Chapter 5 - Post-Draft EIS Follow-Up

1. Policy

It is EPA's policy to conduct follow-up discussions with the lead agency to ensure that EPA's concerns raised at the draft EIS stage are fully understood and considered by the lead agency. To the extent resources allow, follow-up efforts should exceed the minimum required by this chapter and paragraph 2b(3) of chapter 4.

2. Post-draft Consultations

In cases where a draft EIS is rated EO, EU, or 3, the ERC must initiate consultation with the lead agency. Agency consultation will continue at increasing levels of management, through the EPA Assistant Administrator level, as appropriate, until EPA's concerns are resolved or further negotiations are pointless. For those actions where the region is the PR, the ERC will work through the appropriate FAL to coordinate the consultation efforts at the regional and Headquarters levels. The ERC and/or FAL should be prepared to review the project in the field, to develop additional information, and/or to work with the agency to improve the proposed action and the supporting final EIS. When substantive consultation meetings are held, the ERC must document the outcome and, as appropriate, respond in writing to the lead agency to acknowledge any points of agreement, and to restate any unresolved issues.

3. Status Reports

A. After consulting or meeting with the lead agency concerning draft EISs rated EU or 3, the ERC will prepare a status memorandum for the Assistant Administrator, OEA, through the Director, OFA, and, if it is a regional action, for the Regional Administrator. This memorandum should summarize: (1) the progress of the consultations; (2) the remaining unresolved issues; (3) the positions of other affected Federal agencies; and (4) a prognosis for the resolution of remaining issues.

B. The ERC will periodically assess the lead agency's progress in respond to EPA's concerns on draft EISs rated EU or 3. It's the ERC's responsibility to anticipate, and make early preparation for, those final EISs which will be so unresponsive to EPA's concerns that a recommendation for referral of the final EIS to the CEQ will be required.

4. Reporting and Control

All correspondence regarding post-draft consultations and agreements must be retained in the official project file. For all draft EISs which have been rated EU or 3, the official file must also contain all material that may be needed for a formal referral package.

Chapter 6 - Review of Final EISs

1. Policy

It is EPA's policy to conduct detailed reviews of those final EISs which had significant issues raised by the EPA at the draft EIS stage. Each final EIS will be checked to determine whether the statement adequately resolves the problems identified in the EPA review of the draft EIS, or whether there has been a substantive change in the proposal. A detailed review and submission of comments on the final EIS will be done for those actions rated EO, EU, or 3 at the draft stage. A detailed review on other final EISs may be done if the ERC determines that conditions warrant it.

2. Final EIS Review Management

Except as noted below, the review management procedures and responsibilities given in chapter 2 apply to the review of final EISs.

A. Designating Lead Responsibility and Principal and Associate Reviewers. Lead responsibility for the final EIS will be the same as for the draft EIS unless other arrangements have been made with the MIU. If possible, the same principal and associate reviewers who dealt with the draft EIS will be assigned to review the final EIS.

B. Establishing Deadlines and Time Extensions.

1. Deadlines. Unless a different deadline is officially established for receiving comments, EPA will respond to a final EIS within 30 days from the start of the official review period. The official EIS due dates are listed in COMDATE. The PR will set internal deadlines to ensure EPA's comments are received within the official comment period. All final EISs which are candidates

for referral to the CEQ, will be given priority review in accordance with the internal deadlines specified in chapter 9.

2.   Time Extensions. Requests for extensions of review periods on final EISs should be kept to a minimum. In general, review period extensions on final EISs should not be requested unless important environmental issues are involved and detailed substantive comments are being prepared. Time extensions should normally not exceed 15 days. Time extensions for a referral 8 line will be requested in accordance with the procedures in chapter 9.

C.   Categorizing Final EISs. The alpha numeric rating system used for draft EISs will be applied to final EISs for internal management purposes only (see chapter 4, paragraph 4). The EPA rating is not to be included in comment letters on final EISs. Instead, the comments will rely wholly on narrative explanations to describe the environmental impact of the proposed action or the responsiveness or unresponsiveness of the EIS. The PR will include the assigned rating when entering the action into the MIU data management system.

3. Scope of Comments on Final EISs

A.   General.

1.   Except in unusual circumstances, the review of final EISs will be directed to the major unresolved issues, focusing on the impacts of the project rather than on the adequacy of the statement. Except in unusual circumstances, the scope of review will be limited to issues raised in EPA's comments on the draft EIS that have not been resolved in the final EIS, and any new, potentially significant impacts that have been identified as a result of information made available after publication of the draft EIS.

2.   Within 5 days after the start of the review period for the final EIS, the PR will make a preliminary determination as to whether the action meets the criteria for "environmentally unsatisfactory" as set forth in chapter 4, paragraph 4 of this Manual. If the action is determined to be environmentally unsatisfactory, the procedures set forth in chapter 9 of this Manual will be followed.

3.   For final EISs which had drafts categorized as LO, the PR may decide that no formal comments on the final EIS will be submitted to the lead agency. Written comments will be prepared in other cases and when the agency has made substantive modifications in the proposed action in comparison to the draft EIS. In addition, written comments will be prepared for final EISs that involve Section 404(r) or Section 1424(e) issues.

4.   In those cases involving significant mitigation requirements or where the proposed agency action is not clear, EPA's comments on the final EIS will also include a request for a copy of the Record of Decision.

B.   Mitigation Measures. If a final EIS identifies for the first time, or modifies the agency's preferred alternative, EPA's review should include consideration of any additional specific mitigation measures necessary to reduce any adverse impacts of that alternative. When mitigation measures are recommended, the comment letter should suggest that the lead agency include these measures in their Record of Decision as specific conditions on their permits or grants. Where mitigation measures are directly related to the acceptability of the action, the comment letter should include a request that the lead agency keep EPA informed of progress in carrying out the mitigation measures proposed by the EPA.

C. Projects Under Section 404(r) of the Clean Water Act.

1. The Section 404 Coordinator will serve as an associate reviewer on all final EISs involving a potential 404 permit. In order to satisfy the provisions of Section 404(r), the EIS process must be completed before Congress approves requests for authorizations and appropriations. Pursuant to the CEQ Memorandum for Heads of Agencies, November 17, 1980, completion of the EIS process includes resolution of any pre-decision referrals.

2. The comment letter on a final EIS seeking a 404(r) exemption will include EPA's determination regarding: (a) whether the EIS contains requisite information on the proposed discharges and other effects, and (b) whether the proposal is consistent with the 404(b)(1) Guidelines.

3. If a negative determination on either (2)(a) or (b) is made, the appropriate FAL will be informed and will coordinate with the lead agency to ensure that the required statement of EPA's determination is included in the lead agency's congressional submission. The FAL will also ensure that EPA's views regarding an exemption are effectively represented in the Office of Management and Budget's (OMB's) legislative and budget processes.

D. Projects Subject to Groundwater Evaluation Under Section 1424(e) of the SDWA.

1. The regional drinking water program staff will serve as an AR on the review of any EIS for a project potentially affecting a designated "sole source" aquifer and will be responsible for the preliminary determination of project compliance with the requirements of Section 1424(e) of the SDWA.

2. If the regional drinking water program staff determines that a project may contaminate the aquifer through the recharge zone so as to create a significant hazard to public health, the ERC will, in consultation with the regional drinking water staff and appropriate Headquarters FAL, prepare a briefing memorandum and comment letter for the Regional Administrator. Upon approval, the Regional Administrator shall submit the package to the Director, OFA, who shall coordinate the appropriate Headquarters approval and submission to the Administrator for action.

4. Unresponsive Final EIS

1. If the lead agency prepares a final EIS rather than a supplement or revised draft EIS in response to an EPA "3" rating, or if there are significant new circumstances or information relevant to areas of significant environmental impact, the review should follow the procedures of chapter 4 to determine if the proposal is either "environmentally unsatisfactory" or "inadequate." If it is determined that either of these situations apply, the procedures of chapter 9 should be initiated to determine if a referral of the proposal to the CEQ is warranted.

2. If a referral is not warranted, but the EIS contains insufficient information to assess potentially significant environmental impacts of the proposed action, a request should be made for the agency to prepare a supplemental EIS. In such cases, the EPA comment letter must demonstrate that the final EIS is unresponsive to EPA's comments on the draft EIS and State EPA's belief that the final EIS is inadequate to meet the purposes of the NEPA and/or the EPA review, and therefore should be formally supplemented (40 CFR 1502.9(c)).

5. Distribution of the Final EIS Comment Letter

The ERC will coordinate distribution of the final EIS comment letter in accordance with chapter 4, paragraph 5 of this manual (or in the case of a referral, chapter 9, paragraph 5) and any applicable communications strategy. To the maximum extent practicable, the comment letter will not be distributed externally until after the lead agency has received the original.

6. Reporting and Control

All final EISs, comment letters, no comment memoranda, and correspondence related to time extensions will be entered in the MIU data management system and retained in the official project file. The final EIS rating must also be entered into the MIU system (even if no comment letter was sent).

Chapter 7 - Monitoring and Follow-Up

1. Policy

It is EPA's policy to conduct, on a selected basis, follow-up activities on comments on final EISs to ensure that: (1) the EPA participates as fully as possible in any post-EIS efforts designed to assist agency decision making; (2) agreed upon mitigation measures are identified in the Record of Decision; and (3) the agreed upon mitigation measures are fully implemented (e.g., permit conditions, operating plan stipulations, etc.).

2. Monitoring and Follow-Up

A.   After transmittal of EPA's comments on the final EIS, the PR will, as appropriate, ensure that:

   1.   EPA receives a copy of the Record of Decision;

   2.   The lead agency has incorporated into the Record of Decision all agreed upon mitigation and other impact reduction measures; and

   3.   The lead agency has included all agreed upon measures as conditions in grants, permits, or other approvals, where appropriate.

B.   Officials who could be subsequently involved in the proposed action should be informed of the final EPA position on the EIS (e.g., regional or State enforcement officials for NPDES permitting, regional enforcement officials for Section 404 enforcement, regional air program or enforcement officials for transportation control strategy compliance and State implementation plan requirements).

C.   Where resources allow, the ERC is encouraged to assess the level of compliance and effectiveness of Federal agency mitigation measures. The ERC is responsible for determining when and how EPA's final EIS follow-up and monitoring should be carried out.

3. Review of the Record of Decision

A.   The PR should review the Record of Decision on all final EISs on which the EPA has expressed environmental Objections, and/or those where the EPA has negotiated mitigation measures or changes in project design.

B.   The ERC will bring problems or discrepancies between the Record of Decision and agreed upon mitigation measures to the attention of the lead agency. Any unresolved issues should be coordinated with the appropriate FAL, and, through the FAL, with the lead agency's headquarters office, and if appropriate, with the CEQ.

4. Reporting and Control

All correspondence regarding the Record of Decision will be recorded in the official project file.

Chapter 8 - Review of Documents Other than EISs

1. Policy

The Environmental Review Process will include review of those proposed Federal agency actions, legislation, regulations, and notices which may not be contained in an EIS, but which could lead to or have significant environmental impacts.

2. General Review Procedures

A.   Lead Responsibility for Review of Other Actions. Lead responsibilities for non-EIS actions are, in general, as defined below but may be adjusted, in accordance with the procedures in chapter 2 of this manual.

   1.   The OFA will have lead responsibility on all regulation reviews and the appropriate FAL will determine which proposed regulations should be reviewed;

   2.   The Office of Legislative Analysis (OLA), within the Office of External Affairs, will have lead responsibility on all non-EIS legislation reviews and will determine when the EPA will prepare formal comments on legislation; and

   3.   Overall management of the review of non-EIS agency actions, including environmental assessments and Findings of No Significant Impact (FONSIs), license applications, etc., is the responsibility of the ERC managing the liaison activity that involves the action.

B.   Conducting Reviews of Other Actions. The ERC will follow the review coordination procedures of chapter 2 to ensure that EPA's comments are coordinated and comprehensive and are received by the originating agency within its decision making period. If the ERC believes that an EIS is needed on the proposed action, the procedures found in paragraph 6 of this chapter should be followed.

C.   Rating Other Federal Actions. Except for the referral criteria, the rating system for draft impact statements pursuant to chapter 4 of this Manual will not be used for non-EIS actions. If the PR determines that a Federal agency action covered by this chapter is environmentally unsatisfactory in accordance with the the criteria listed in chapter 4, thus warranting a referral to the CEQ, then the procedures found in paragraph 7 of this chapter will apply.

3. Legislation Reviews

The OLA has lead responsibility on all proposed legislation not accompanied by an EIS. The OLA is responsible for coordinating with other EPA program and regional offices, and for preparing EPA's comments on all legislation. Any ERC receiving proposed legislation from another Federal agency should forward it directly to the OLA for action.

4. Regulation Reviews

The FALs will monitor the *Federal Register* regularly to determine which environmental regulations proposed by their assigned Federal agencies are significant and should be reviewed. FALs will normally act as PRs for regulations proposed by the agencies assigned to them. The Director, OFA, will be the signatory official for comments on these regulations. The FAL will be responsible for ensuring that the regions and EPA program offices impacted by the regulations will be designated as ARs.

5. Other Agency Action Reviews

The ERC may determine that other non-EIS Federal actions such as environmental assessments (40 CFR 1508.9), FONSIs (40 CFR 1508.13), issue papers, or technical support documents should be

---

reviewed. The ERC's decision to review these actions will take into account the relationship of the proposed action to other Federal actions and how the document fits into the overall decision making process.

6. Determining The Need For an EIS

Whenever the ERC determines on the basis of investigating a public inquiry, reviewing a regulation or environmental assessment/FONSI, or by other means, that a Federal agency has not or does not intend to prepare an EIS on an action that the EPA believes could significantly affect the quality of the human environment, the following procedures pertain.

A.   If it is a regional action, the ERC will immediately contact the appropriate FAL and develop a coordinated regional/headquarters approach for working with the lead agency.

B.   The ERC will initiate consultation with the Federal agency responsible for the major action to explore the necessity for EIS preparation. Discussions with the agency will be couched in terms of suggested action for the Federal agency's consideration rather than as an EPA requirement. It is the lead agency's responsibility to decide if an EIS will be prepared.

C.   If, after such consultation, the ERC believes that the requirements of Section 102(2)(C) of NEPA are applicable, the PR will prepare a comment letter to the Federal agency responsible for the proposed action. The comment letter should include EPA's assessment of the action and reasons why the EPA believes the agency should prepare an EIS.

7. Environmentally Unsatisfactory Actions

If the ERC determines that a non-EIS action is environmentally unsatisfactory at the draft stage (in accordance with the EU criteria specified in chapter 4), the proposed comment letter must be cleared by the Assistant Administrator, OEA, prior to release. The procedures of chapter 4 must be followed in obtaining this clearance. At the time of the clearance request, or if the non-EIS action is a final action, the ERC and/or appropriate FAL will set up internal consultation and referral procedures similar to those outlined in chapter 9 of this manual. The procedures will also consider the option of request an EIS. The procedures will ensure that the referral will take place no later than 5 days before the "final" lead agency action. For example, in the case of proposed regulations, the referral must occur prior to publication of the final rule.

8. Reporting and Control

Regulations under review and the resulting comment letters, as well as comment letters on any other non-EIS action determined to be environmentally unsatisfactory, will be entered into the MIU data management system. All agency comment letters and official agency actions related to the Environmental Review Process will be retained in the official project file.

Chapter 9 - Referrals to the Council on Environmental Quality

1. Policy

The EPA authority for referring proposed regulations or major Federal actions to the Council on Environmental Quality (40 CFR 1504 and Section 309 of the Clean Air Act) will be used only when significant environmental issues are involved and only after every effort to resolve these issues at the agency level has been exhausted.

2. Criteria for Referral

In order to meet a determination of "unsatisfactory from the standpoint of public health or welfare or environmental quality," the proposed action must satisfy the "environmentally unsatisfactory" criteria given in chapter 4.

3. Referral Procedures

A. The CEQ has established a 25-day time period, starting from the date of the Notice of Availability of the final EIS the *Federal Register*, for referring final EISs (40 CFR 1504.3(b)). Extensions of EIS referral periods can be granted only by the lead agency (40 CFR 1504.3(b)) and must be specific to the 25-day referral period rather than the overall comment period.

B. Since EPA has author quality under Section 309 of the Clean Air Act to refer proposed regulations and major Federal actions for which no EIS has been prepared, the intent of the 25-day deadline is incorporated in the procedures of this section by requiring all EPA referrals to be made no later than 5 days before the end of the comment period or, in any case, 5 days before the final action takes place.

4. Referral Package Development Sequence

A. The objective of the referral package development sequence requirements in this section is to ensure that the referral package is ready within the rigid 25-day time limit and, simultaneously, allow for a final attempt to resolve EPA's concerns with the lead agency. The key elements in this sequence are:

1. Early identification of the potential referral action by the PR/ERC;

2. Approval of the referral action by the Regional Administrator (if a regional action) and the Assistant Administrator, OEA;

3. An attempt to meet with the lead agency and work out EPA's concerns; and

4. Preparation of the referral package to preserve the referral option if discussions with the lead agency do not resolve EPA's concerns.

B. Specific procedures for the referral development sequence are described below. To facilitate this description, it is assumed that the referral action is taken by a region. The same procedures apply where Headquarters has the referral action except there would be no regional requirements.

1. Within 5 days after the beginning of the review period the PR, in consultation with the ERC, will make a preliminary determination as to whether the action is unsatisfactory from the standpoint of public health, welfare, or environmental quality in accordance with the EU criteria in chapter 4. If a referral is indicated, the ERC will notify the appropriate FAL and proceed with development of the materials described below.

2. Within 10 days from the start of the 25-day referral period, the ERC, in consultation with the FAL, will prepare and submit to the Regional Administrator and the Assistant Administrator, OEA, through the Director, OFA, a briefing memorandum and interim response to the lead agency. The interim response will State that the EPA is considering a referral to the CEQ and will request a meeting and time extension to allow for a resolution of EPA's concerns. The briefing memorandum will contain the following information:

   1. Brief description of the proposed action;

2. Reason the action is environmentally unsatisfactory;

3. Description of the attempts to resolve differences with the lead agency;

4. Positions of other affected Federal agencies, groups, and public officials; and

5. Recommended strategy for resolution of remaining issues.

3. If the lead agency grants a time extension, EPA negotiations will take place and, if necessary, the referral package will be developed according to the extended referral time period. If the lead agency grants a time extension of the referral period by phone, the ERC will immediately prepare a letter to the lead agency documenting the agreement. If a time extension is not granted, the referral preparation will proceed on the basis of the original referral deadline.

4. No later than 10 days before the referral deadline, the FAL will prepare a short information memorandum for the Administrator describing the potential referral and the status of unresolved issues; a one page "talking points" paper; and an outline of a communication strategy for notifying all interested groups of EPA's action. Development of the communication strategy is to be coordinated with the immediate Office of the Assistant Administrator for External Affairs.

5. No later than 7 days before the referral deadline, the final referral package, prepared in accordance with paragraph 6 of this chapter and approved by the Regional Administrator, will be forwarded to the Director, OFA.

6. No later than 5 days before the referral deadline, the Director, OFA, will ensure that the referral package is in final form with all letters and appropriate concurrences ready for the Administrator's signature, and working through the Assistant Administrator for OEA, to ensure that a briefing has been arranged for the Administrator.

5. Content and Organization of the Referral Packages

A. Administrator's Referral Package. The referral package for the Administrator will include the package to be submitted to the CEQ and the lead agency, and the following:

1. An action memorandum to the Administrator (not to exceed two pages) briefly outlining the proposed action, EPA's concerns with the proposed action, and positions of other affected Federal agencies, public interest groups, and congressional delegations.

2. A communications strategy for notifying all interested groups of the referral. This strategy will be coordinated with the immediate Office of the Assistant Administrator for External Affairs and will follow the established strategy development format.

B. CEQ Referral Package. The CEQ referral package will consist of a letter for the Administrator's signature to the Chairman of the CEQ setting forth the basis of EPA's determination and the lead agency referral package described below.

C. Lead Agency Referral Package. This package will consist of the following:

1. A letter for the Administrator's signature to the head of the lead agency informing the lead agency of EPA's unsatisfactory determination, and of the referral of the matter to the CEQ. The letter should request that no action be taken on the proposed action until the CEQ acts on the matter.

2. Detailed comments supporting EPA's conclusion that the matter is unsatisfactory from the standpoint of public health, welfare, or environmental quality. The detailed comments will include the following information:

1. The unacceptable impacts related to EPA's areas of jurisdiction or expertise;

2. The reasons EPA believes the matter is unsatisfactory;

3. Description of those national resources or environmental policies that would be adversely affected;

4. Identification of environmentally preferable alternatives;

5. Identification of agreed upon facts;

6. Identification of material facts in controversy; and

7. Brief review of attempts by the EPA to resolve the concerns with the lead agency.

6. Approving and Distributing the Referral Package

After the Administrator signs the referral comment letters to the lead agency and to the CEQ, the letters will be hand carried to the addressees. The appropriate FAL will then ensure follow-up distribution of the CEQ referral package as follows and/or in accordance with the communications strategy:

Addressee	Number of Copies
Lead agency	3 copies
CEQ	4 copies
EPA Administrator	2 copies
Assistant Administrator, OEA	2 copies
Headquarters Office of Public Affairs	2 copies
Appropriate regional office	3 copies
Appropriate regional Office of Public Affairs	2 copies
Director, OFA	1 copy
Management Information Unit, OFA	1 copy
EPA offices which served as associate reviewers	1 copy
Appropriate elected officials	Determined by the Office of Congressional Liaison

7. Reporting and Control

The referral package, all related correspondence, and documentation of time extensions will be retained in the official project file. Time extensions will be entered into the MIU data management system.

Appendix

Summary of Rating Definitions and Follow-Up Action

Environmental Impact of the Action

LO–Lack of Objections. The EPA review has not identified any potential environmental impacts requiring substantive changes to the proposal. The review may have disclosed opportunities for application of mitigation measures that could be accomplished with no more than minor changes to the proposal.

EC–Environmental Concerns. The EPA review has identified environmental impacts that should be avoided in order to fully protect the environment. Corrective measures may require changes to the preferred alternative or application of mitigation measures that can reduce the environmental impact. EPA would like to work with the lead agency to reduce these impacts.

EO–Environmental Objections. The EPA review has identified significant environmental impacts that must be avoided in order to provide adequate protection for the environment. Corrective measures may require substantial changes to the preferred alternative or consideration of some other project alternative (including the no action alternative or a new alternative). EPA intends to work with the lead agency to reduce these impacts.

EU–Environmentally Unsatisfactory. The EPA review has identified adverse environmental impacts that are of sufficient magnitude that they are unsatisfactory from the standpoint of public health or welfare or environmental quality. EPA intends to work with the lead agency to reduce these impacts. If the potential unsatisfactory impacts are not corrected at the final EIS stage, this proposal will be recommended for referral to the CEQ.

Adequacy of the Impact Statement

Category 1–Adequate. EPA believes the draft EIS adequately sets forth the environmental impact(s) of the preferred alternative and those of the alternatives reasonably available to the project or action. No further analysis or data collection is necessary but the reviewer may suggest the addition of clarifying language or information.

Category 2–Insufficient Information. The draft EIS does not contain sufficient information for EPA to fully assess environmental impacts that should be avoided in order to fully protect the environment or the EPA reviewer has identified new reasonably available alternatives that are within the spectrum of alternatives analyzed in the draft EIS which could reduce with the environmental impacts of the action. The identified additional information data analyses or discussion should be included in the final EIS.

Category 3–Inadequate. EPA does not believe that the draft EIS adequately assesses potentially significant environmental impacts of the action, or that the EPA reviewer his identified new reasonably available alternatives that are outside of the spectrum of alternatives analyzed in the draft EIS, which should be analyzed in order to reduce the potentially significant environmental impacts. EPA believes that the identified additional information data analyses or discussions are of such magnitude that they should have full public review at a draft stage. EPA does not believe that the draft EIS is adequate for the purposes of the NEPA and/or Section 309 review, and thus should be formally revised and made available for public comment in a supplemental or revised draft EIS. On the basis of the potential significant impacts involved, this proposal could be a candidate for referral to the CEQ.

SELECTED EXECUTIVE ORDERS

Executive Order 11514. Protection and Enhancement of Environmental Quality

HISTORY: March 5, 1970; 35 FR 4247, 3 CFR, 1966-1970 Comp., p. 902; As amended by Executive Order 11991, May 24, 1977, 42 FR 26967, 3 CFR, 1977 Comp., p. 123

By virtue of the authority vested in me as President of the United States and in furtherance of the purpose and policy of the National Environmental Policy Act of 1969 (Public Law No. 91-190, approved January 1, 1970), it is ordered as follows:

Sec. 1. Policy. The Federal Government shall provide leadership in protecting and enhancing the quality of the Nation's environment to sustain and enrich human life. Federal agencies shall initiate measures needed to direct their policies, plans and programs so as to meet national environmental goals. The Council on Environmental Quality, through the Chairman, shall advise and assist the President in leading this national effort.

Sec. 2. Responsibilities of Federal agencies. Consonant with Title I of the National Environmental Policy Act of 1969, hereafter referred to as the "Act", the heads of Federal agencies shall:

(a) Monitor, evaluate, and control on a continuing basis their agencies' activities so as to protect and enhance the quality of the environment. Such activities shall include those directed to controlling pollution and enhancing the environment and those designed to accomplish other program objectives which may affect the quality of the environment. Agencies shall develop programs and measures to protect and enhance environmental quality and shall assess progress in meeting the specific objectives of such activities. Heads of agencies shall consult with appropriate Federal, State and local agencies in carrying out their activities as they affect the quality of the environment.

(b) Develop procedures to ensure the fullest practicable provision of timely public information and understanding of Federal plans and programs with environmental impact in order to obtain the views of interested parties. These procedures shall include, whenever appropriate, provision for public hearings, and shall provide the public with relevant information, including information on alternative courses of action. Federal agencies shall also encourage State and local agencies to adopt similar procedures for informing the public concerning their activities affecting the quality of the environment.

(c) Insure that information regarding existing or potential environmental problems and control methods developed as part of research, development, demonstration, test, or evaluation activities is made available to Federal agencies, States, counties, municipalities, institutions, and other entities, as appropriate.

(d) Review their agencies' statutory authority, administrative regulations, policies, and procedures, including those relating to loans, grants, contracts, leases, licenses, or permits, in order to identify any deficiencies or inconsistencies therein which prohibit or limit full compliance with the purposes and provisions of the Act. A report on this review and the corrective actions taken or planned, including such measures to be proposed to the President as may be necessary to bring their authority and policies into conformance with the intent, purposes, and procedures of the Act, shall be provided to the Council on Environmental Quality not later than September 1, 1970.

(e) Engage in exchange of data and research results, and cooperate with agencies of other governments to foster the purposes of the Act.

(f) Proceed, in coordination with other agencies, with actions required by section 102 of the Act.

(g) In carrying out their responsibilities under the Act and this Order, comply with the regulations issued by the Council except where such compliance would be inconsistent with statutory requirements.

Sec. 3. Responsibilities of Council on Environmental Quality. The Council on Environmental Quality shall:

(a) Evaluate existing and proposed policies and activities of the Federal Government directed to the control of pollution and the enhancement of the environment and to the accomplishment of other objectives which affect the quality of the environment. This shall include continuing review of procedures employed in the development and enforcement of Federal standards affecting environmental quality. Based upon such evaluations the Council shall, where appropriate, recommend to the President polices and programs to achieve more effective protection and enhancement of environmental quality and shall, where appropriate, seek resolution of significant environmental issues.

(b) Recommend to the President and to the agencies priorities among programs designed for the control of pollution and for enhancement of the environment.

(c) Determine the need for new policies and programs for dealing with environmental problems not being adequately addressed.

(d) Conduct, as it determines to be appropriate, public hearings or conferences on issues of environmental significance.

(e) Promote the development and use of indices and monitoring systems (1) to assess environmental conditions and trends, (2) to predict the environmental impact of proposed public and private actions, and (3) to determine the effectiveness of programs for protecting and enhancing environmental quality.

(f) Coordinate Federal programs related to environmental quality.

(g) Advise and assist the President and the agencies in achieving international cooperation for dealing with environmental problems, under the foreign policy guidance of the Secretary of State.

(h) Issue regulations to Federal agencies for the implementation of the procedural provisions of the Act (42 USC 4332(2)). Such regulations shall be developed after consultation with affected agencies and after such public hearings as may be appropriate. They will be designed to make the environmental impact statement process more useful to decisionmakers and the public; and to reduce paperwork and the accumulation of extraneous background data, in order to emphasize the need to focus on real environmental issues and alternatives. They will require impact statements to be concise, clear, and to the point, and supported by evidence that agencies have made the necessary environmental analyses. The Council shall include in its regulations procedures (1) for the early preparation of environmental impact statements, and (2) for the referral to the Council of conflicts between agencies concerning the implementation of the National Environmental Policy Act of 1969, as amended, and Section 309 of the Clean Air Act, as amended, for the Council's recommendation as to their prompt resolution.

(i) Issue such other instructions to agencies, and request such reports and other information from them, as may be required to carry out the Council's responsibilities under the Act.

(j) Assist the President in preparing the annual Environmental Quality Report provided for in section 201 of the Act.

(k) Foster investigations, studies, surveys, research, and analyses relating to (i) ecological systems and environmental quality, (ii) the impact of new and changing technologies thereon, and (iii) means of preventing or reducing adverse effects from such technologies.

Sec. 4. Amendments of E.O. 11472.

[E.O. 11472 expired January 5, 1977. Editor's note.]
/s/ RICHARD NIXON
THE WHITE HOUSE
March 5, 1970

Executive Order 11593. Protection and Enhancement of the Cultural Environment

May 13, 1971, 36 F.R. 8921

By virtue of the authority vested in me as President of the United States and in furtherance of the purposes and policies of the National Environmental Policy Act of 1969 (83 Stat. 852, 42 U.S.C. 4321 et seq.), the National Historic Preservation Act of 1966 (80 Stat. 915, 16 U.S.C. 470 et seq.), the Historic Sites Act of 1935 (49 Stat. 666, 16 U.S.C. 461 et seq.), and the Antiquities Act of 1906 (34 Stat. 225, 16 U.S.C. 431 et seq.), it is ordered as follows:

Sec 1. Policy. The Federal Government shall provide leadership in preserving, restoring and maintaining the historic and cultural environment of the Nation. Agencies of the executive branch of the Government (hereinafter referred to as 'Federal agencies') shall (1) administer the cultural properties under their control in a spirit of stewardship and trusteeship for future generations, (2)initiate measures necessary to direct their policies, plans and programs in such a way that federally owned sites, structures, and objects of historical, architectural or archaeological significance are preserved, restored and maintained for the inspiration and benefit of the people, and (3), in consultation with the Advisory Council on Historic Preservation 16 U.S.C. 470i), institute procedures to assure that Federal plans and programs contribute to the preservation and enhancement of non-federally owned sites, structures and objects of historical, architectural or archaeological significance.

Sec. 2. Responsibilities of Federal agencies. Consonant with the provisions of the acts cited in the first paragraph of this order, the heads of Federal agencies shall:

(a) No later than July 1, 1973, with the advice of the Secretary of the Interior, and in cooperation with the liaison officer for historic preservation for the State or territory involved, locate, inventory, and nominate to the Secretary of the Interior all sites, buildings, districts, and objects under their jurisdiction or control that appear to qualify for listing on the National Register of Historic Places.

(b) Exercise caution during the interim period until inventories and evaluations required by subsection (a) are completed to assure that any federally owned property that might qualify for nomination is not inadvertently transferred, sold, demolished or substantially altered. The agency head shall refer any questionable actions to the Secretary of the Interior for an opinion respecting the property's eligibility for inclusion on the National Register of Historic Places. The Secretary shall consult with the liaison officer for historic preservation for the State or territory involved in arriving at his opinion. Where, after a reasonable period in which to review and evaluate the property, the Secretary determines that the property is likely to meet the criteria prescribed for listing on the National Register of Historic Places, the Federal agency head shall reconsider the proposal in light of national environmental and preservation policy. Where, after such reconsideration, the Federal agency head proposes to transfer, sell, demolish or substantially alter the property he shall not act with respect to the property until the Advisory Council on Historic Preservation shall have been provided an opportunity to comment on the proposal.

(c) Initiate measures to assure that where as a result of Federal action or assistance a property listed on the National Register of Historic Places is to be substantially altered or demolished, timely steps be taken to make or have made records, including measured drawings, photographs and maps, of the property, and that copy of such records then be deposited in the Library of Congress as part of the Historic American Buildings Survey or Historic American Engineering Record for future use and reference. Agencies may call on the Department of the Interior for advice and technical assistance in the completion of the above records.

(d) Initiate measures and procedures to provide for the maintenance, through preservation, rehabilitation, or restoration, of federally owned and registered sites at professional standards prescribed by the Secretary of the Interior.

(e) Submit procedures required pursuant to subsection (d) to the Secretary of the Interior and to the Advisory Council on Historic Preservation no later than January 1, 1972, and annually thereafter, for review and comment.

(f) Cooperate with purchasers and transferees of a property listed on the National Register of Historic Places in the development of viable plans to use such property in a manner compatible with preservation objectives and which does not result in an unreasonable economic burden to public or private interests.

Sec. 3. Responsibilities of the Secretary of the Interior.

The Secretary of the Interior shall:

(a) Encourage State and local historic preservation officials to evaluate and survey federally owned historic properties and, where appropriate, to nominate such properties for listing on the National Register of Historic Places.

(b) Develop criteria and procedures to be applied by Federal agencies in the reviews and nominations required by section 2(a). Such criteria and procedures shall be developed in consultation with the affected agencies.

(c) Expedite action upon nominations to the National Register of Historic Places concerning federally owned properties proposed for sale, transfer, demolition or substantial alteration.

(d) Encourage State and Territorial liaison officers for historic preservation to furnish information upon request to Federal agencies regarding their properties which have been evaluated with respect to historic, architectural or archaeological significance and which as a result of such evaluations have not been found suitable for listing on the National Register of Historic Places.

(e) Develop and make available to Federal agencies and State and local governments information concerning professional methods and techniques for preserving, improving, restoring and maintaining historic properties.

(f) Advise Federal agencies in the evaluation, identification, preservation, improvement, restoration and maintenance of historic properties.

(g) Review and evaluate the plans of transferees of surplus Federal properties transferred for historic monument purposes to assure that the historic character of such properties is preserved in rehabilitation, restoration, improvement, maintenance and repair of such properties.

(h) Review and comment upon Federal agency procedures submitted pursuant to section 2(e) of this order.

Signed, RICHARD NIXON
THE WHITE HOUSE
Last updated on August 19, 1995

Executive Order 11644. Use of Off-Road Vehicles on the Public Lands

HISTORY: Feb. 8, 1972, 37 FR 2877, Feb. 9, 1972; Amended by Executive Order 11989, May 25, 1977, 42 FR 26959; E.O. 12608, Sept. 14, 1987, 52 FR 34617

An estimated 5 million off-road recreational vehicles—motorcycles, minibikes, trial bikes, snowmobiles, dune-buggies, all-terrain vehicles, and others—are in use in the United States today, and their popularity continues to increase rapidly. The widespread use of such vehicles on the public lands—often for legitimate purposes but also in frequent conflict with wise land and resource management practices, environmental values, and other types of recreational activity—has demonstrated the need for a unified Federal policy toward the use of such vehicles on the public lands.

NOW, THEREFORE, by virtue of the authority vested in me as President of the United States by the Constitution of the United States and in furtherance of the purpose and policy of the National Environmental Policy Act of 1969 (42 U.S.C. 4321), it is hereby ordered as follows:

Sec 1. Purpose.

It is the purpose of this order to establish policies and provide for procedures that will ensure that the use of off-road vehicles on public lands will be controlled and directed so as to protect the resources of those lands, to promote the safety of all users of those lands, and to minimize conflicts among the various uses of those lands.

Sec. 2. Definitions.

As used in this order, the term:

(1) "Public lands" means (A) all lands under the custody and control of the Secretary of the Interior and the Secretary of Agriculture, except Indian lands, (B) lands under the custody and control of the Tennessee Valley Authority that are situated in western Kentucky and Tennessee and are designated as "Land Between the Lakes," and (C) lands under the custody and control of the Secretary of Defense;

(2) "Respective agency head" means the Secretary of the Interior, the Secretary of Defense, the Secretary of Agriculture, and the Board of Directors of the Tennessee Valley Authority, with respect to public lands under the custody and control of each;

(3) "Off-road vehicle" means any motorized vehicle designed for or capable of cross-country travel on or immediately over land, water, sand, snow, ice, marsh, swampland, or other natural terrain; except that such term excludes (A) any registered motorboat, (B) any fire, military, emergency or law enforcement vehicle when used for emergency purposes, and any combat or combat support vehicle when used for national defense purposes, and (C) any vehicle whose use is expressly authorized by the respective agency head under a permit, lease, license, or contract; and

(4) "Official use" means use by an employee, agent, or designated representative of the Federal Government or one of its contractors in the course of his employment, agency, or representation. [§2 amended by E.O. 11989, 42 FR 26959, May 25, 1977]

Sec. 3. Zones of Use

(a) Each respective agency head shall develop and issue regulations and administrative instructions, within six months of the date of this order, to provide for administrative designation of the specific areas and trails on public lands on which the use of off-road vehicles may be permitted, and areas in which the use of off-road vehicles may not be permitted, and set a date by which such designation of all public lands shall be completed. Those regulations shall direct that the designation of such areas and trails will be based upon the protection of the resources of the public lands, promotion of the safety of all users of those lands, and minimization of conflicts among the various uses of those lands. The regulations shall further require that the designation of such areas and trails shall be in accordance with the following—

(1) Areas and trails shall be located to minimize damage to soil, watershed, vegetation, or other resources of the public lands.

(2) Areas and trails shall be located to minimize harassment of wildlife or significant disruption of wildlife habitats.

(3) Areas and trails shall be located to minimize conflicts between off-road vehicle use and other existing or proposed recreational uses of the same or neighboring public lands, and to ensure the compatibility of such uses with existing conditions in populated areas, taking into account noise and other factors.

(4) Areas and trails shall not be located in officially designated Wilderness Areas or Primitive Areas. Areas and trails shall be located in areas of the National Park system, Natural Areas, or National Wildlife Refuges and Game Ranges only if the respective agency head determines that off-road vehicle use in such locations will not adversely affect their natural, aesthetic, or scenic values.

(b) The respective agency head shall ensure adequate opportunity for public participation in the promulgation of such regulations and in the designation of areas and trails under this section.

(c) The limitations on off-road vehicle use imposed under this section shall not apply to official use.

Sec. 4. Operating Conditions.

Each respective agency head shall develop and publish, within one year of the date of this order, regulations prescribing operating conditions for off-road vehicles on the public lands. These regulations shall be directed at protecting resource values, preserving public health, safety, and welfare, and minimizing use conflicts.

Sec. 5. Public Information.

The respective agency head shall ensure that areas and trails where off-road vehicle use is permitted are well marked and shall provide for the publication and distribution of information, including maps, describing such areas and trails and explaining the conditions on vehicle use. He shall seek cooperation of relevant State agencies in the dissemination of this information.

Sec. 6. Enforcement.

The respective agency head shall, where authorized by law, prescribe appropriate penalties for violation of regulations adopted pursuant to this order, and shall establish procedures for the enforcement of those regulations. To the extent permitted by law, he may enter into agreements with State or local governmental agencies for cooperative enforcement of laws and regulations relating to off-road vehicle use.

Sec. 7. Consultation.

Before issuing the regulations or administrative instructions required by this order or designating areas or trails as required by this order and those regulations and administrative instructions, the Secretary of the Interior shall, as appropriate, consult with the Secretary of Energy and the Nuclear Regulatory Commission. [§7 amended by E.O. 12608, 52 FR 34617, Sept. 14, 1987]

Sec 8. Monitoring of Effects and Review.

(a) The respective agency head shall monitor the effects of the use of off-road vehicles on lands under their jurisdictions. On the basis of the information gathered, they shall from time to time amend or rescind designations of areas or other actions taken pursuant to this order as necessary to further the policy of this order.

(b) The Council on Environmental Quality shall maintain a continuing review of the implementation of this order.

Sec. 9. Special Protection of The Public Lands.

(a) Notwithstanding the provisions of Section 3 of this Order, the respective agency head shall, whenever he determines that the use of off-road vehicles will cause or is causing considerable adverse effects on the soil, vegetation, wildlife, wildlife habitat or cultural or historic resources of particular areas or trails of the public lands, immediately close such areas or trails to the type of off-road vehicle causing such effects, until such time as he determines that such adverse effects have been eliminated and that measures have been implemented to prevent future recurrence.

(b) Each respective agency head is authorized to adopt the policy that portions of the public lands within his jurisdiction shall be closed to use by off-road vehicles except those areas or trails which are suitable and specifically designated as open to such use pursuant to Section 3 of this Order. [§9 added by E.O. 11989, 42 FR 26959, May 25, 1977]

Executive Order 11988. Floodplain Management

HISTORY: May 24, 1977; 42 FR 26951, 3 CFR, 1977 Comp., p. 117; Amended by Executive Order 12148, July 20, 1979; 44 FR 43239, 3 CFR, 1979 Comp., p. 412

[Executive Order 12148–Federal Emergency Management, July 20, 1979, substituted "Director of the Federal Emergency Management Agency" for "Federal Insurance Administration" in Section 2(d).]

By virtue of the authority vested in me by the Constitution and statutes of the United States of America, and as President of the United States of America, in furtherance of the National Environmental Policy Act of 1969, as amended (42 USC 4321 et seq.) the National Flood Insurance Act of 1968, as amended, (42 USC 4001 et seq.) and the Flood Disaster Protection Act of 1973 (Public Law 93-234, 87 Stat. 975), in order to avoid to the extent possible the long and short term adverse impacts associated with the occupancy and modification of floodplains and to avoid direct or indirect support of floodplain development wherever there is a practicable alternative, it is hereby ordered as follows:

Sec. 1.

Each agency shall provide leadership and shall take action to reduce the risk of flood loss, to minimize the impact of floods on human safety, health and welfare, and to restore and preserve the natural and beneficial values served by floodplains in carrying out its responsibilities for (1) acquiring, managing, and disposing of Federal lands and facilities; (2) providing Federally undertaken, financed, or assisted construction and improvements; and (3) conducting Federal activities and programs affecting land use, including but not limited to water and related land resources planning, regulating, and licensing activities.

Sec. 2.

In carrying out the activities described in Section 1 of this Order, each agency has a responsibility to evaluate the potential effects of any actions it may take in a floodplain; to ensure that its planning programs and budget requests reflect consideration of flood hazards and floodplain management; and to prescribe procedures to implement the policies and requirements of this Order, as follows:

(a)(1) Before taking an action, each agency shall determine whether the proposed action will occur in a floodplain —for major Federal actions significantly affecting the quality of the human environment, the evaluation required below will be included in any statement prepared under Section 102(2)(C) of the National Environmental Policy Act. This determination shall be made according to a Department of Housing and Urban Development (HUD) floodplain map or a more detailed map of an area, if available. If such maps are not available, the agency shall make a determination of the location of the floodplain based on the best available information. The Water Resources Council shall issue guidance on this information not later than October l, 1977.

(2) If an agency has determined to, or proposes to, conduct, support, or allow an action to be located in a floodplain, the agency shall consider alternatives to avoid adverse effects and incompatible development in the floodplains. If the head of the agency finds that the only practicable alternative consistent with the law and with the policy set forth in this Order requires siting in a floodplain, the agency shall, prior to taking action, (i) design or modify its action in order to minimize potential harm to or within the floodplain, consistent with regulations issued in accord with Section 2(d) of this Order, and (ii) prepare and circulate a notice containing an explanation of why the action is proposed to be located in the floodplain.

(3) For programs subject to the Office of Management and Budget Circular A-95, the agency shall send the notice, not to exceed three pages in length including a location map, to the State and areawide A-95 clearinghouses for the geographic areas affected. The notice shall include: (i) the reasons why the action is proposed to be located in a floodplain; (ii) a statement indicating whether the action conforms to applicable State or local floodplain protection standards and (iii) a list of the alternatives considered. Agencies shall endeavor to allow a brief comment period prior to taking any action.

---

(4) Each agency shall also provide opportunity for early public review of any plans or proposals for actions in floodplains, in accordance with Section 2(b) of Executive Order No. 11 514, as amended, including the development of procedures to accomplish this objective for Federal actions whose impact is not significant enough to require the preparation of an environmental impact statement under Section 102(2)(C) of the National Environmental Policy Act of 1969, as amended.

(b) Any requests for new authorizations or appropriations transmitted to the Office of Management and Budget shall indicate, if an action to be proposed will be located in a floodplain, whether the proposed action is in accord with this Order.

(c) Each agency shall take floodplain management into account when formulating or evaluating any water and land use plans and shall require land and water resources use appropriate to the degree of hazard involved. Agencies shall include adequate provision for the evaluation and consideration of flood hazards in the regulations and operating procedures for the licenses, permits, loan or grants-in-aid programs that they administer. Agencies shall also encourage and provide appropriate guidance to applicants to evaluate the effects of their proposals in floodplains prior to submitting applications for Federal licenses, permits, loans or grants.

(d) As allowed by law, each agency shall issue or amend existing regulations and procedures within one year to comply with this Order. These procedures shall incorporate the Unified National Program for Floodplain Management of the Water Resources Council, and shall explain the means that the agency will employ to pursue the nonhazardous use of riverine, coastal and other floodplains in connection with the activities under its authority. To the extent possible, existing processes, such as those of the Council on Environmental Quality and the Water Resources Council, shall be utilized to fulfill the requirements of this Order. Agencies shall prepare their procedures in consultation with the Water Resources Council, the Director of the Federal Emergency Management Agency, and the Council on Environmental Quality, and shall update such procedures as necessary.

Sec. 3.

In addition to the requirements of Section 2, agencies with responsibilities for Federal real property and facilities shall take the following measures:

(a) The regulations and procedures established under Section 2(d) of this Order shall, at a minimum, require the construction of Federal structures and facilities to be in accordance with the standards and criteria and to be consistent with the intent of those promulgated under the National Flood Insurance Program. They shall deviate only to the extent that the standards of the Flood Insurance Program are demonstrably inappropriate for a given type of structure or facility.

(b) If, after compliance with the requirements of this Order, new construction of structures or facilities are to be located in a floodplain, accepted floodproofing and other flood protection measures shall be applied to new construction or rehabilitation. To achieve flood protection, agencies shall, wherever practicable, elevate structures above the base flood level rather than filling in land.

(c) If property used by the general public has suffered flood damage or is located in an identified flood hazard area, the responsible agency shall provide on structures, and other places where appropriate, conspicuous delineation of past and probable flood height in order to enhance public awareness of and knowledge about flood hazards.

(d) When property in floodplains is proposed for lease, easement, right-of-way, or disposal to non-Federal public or private parties, the Federal agency shall (1) reference in the conveyance those uses that are restricted under identified Federal, State or local floodplain regulations; and (2) attach other appropriate restrictions to the uses of properties by the grantee or purchaser and any successors, except where prohibited by law; or (3) withhold such properties from conveyance.

Sec. 4.

In addition to any responsibilities under this Order and Sections 202 and 205 of the Flood Disaster Protection Act of 1973, as amended, (42 U.S.C. 4106 and 4128) agencies which guarantee, approve, regulate, or insure any financial transaction which is related to an area located in a floodplain shall, prior to completing action on such transaction, inform any private parties participating in the transaction of the hazards of locating structures in the floodplain.

Sec. 5.

The head of each agency shall submit a report to the Council on Environmental Quality and to the Water Resources Council on June 30, 1978, regarding the status of their procedures and the impact of this Order on the agency's operations. Thereafter, the Water Resources Council shall periodically evaluate agency procedures and their effectiveness.

Sec. 6.

As used in this Order: (a) The term "agency" shall have the same meaning as the term "Executive agency" in Section 105 of Title 5 of the United States Code and shall include the military departments; the directives contained in this Order, however, are meant to apply only to those agencies which perform the activities described in Section I which are located in or affecting floodplains.

(b) The term "base flood" shall mean that flood which has a one percent or greater chance of occurrence in any given year.

(c) The term "floodplain" shall mean the lowland and relatively flat areas adjoining inland and coastal waters including floodprone areas of offshore islands, including at a minimum, that area subject to a one percent or greater chance of flooding in any given year.

Sec. 7.

Executive Order No. 11296 of August 10, 1966, is hereby revoked. All actions, procedures, and issuances taken under that Order and still in effect shall remain in effect until modified by appropriate authority under the terms of this Order.

Sec. 8.

Nothing in this Order shall apply to assistance provided for emergency work essential to save lives and protect property and public health and safety, performed pursuant to Sections 305 and 306 of the Disaster Relief Act of 1974 (88 Stat. 148, 42 U.S.C. 5145 and 5146).

Sec. 9.

To the extent the provisions of Section 2(a) of this Order are applicable to projects covered by Section 104(h) of the Housing and Community Development Act of 1974, as amended, (88 Stat. 640, 42 U.S.C. 5304(h)) the responsibilities under those provisions may be assumed by the appropriate applicant, if the applicant has also assumed, with respect to such projects, all of the responsibilities for environmental review, decision making, and action pursuant to the National Environmental Policy Act of 1969, as amended.

/s/ JIMMY CARTER
THE WHITE HOUSE
May 24, 1977

Executive Order 11990. Protection of Wetlands

HISTORY: May 24, 1977; 42 FR 26961, 3 CFR, 1977 Comp., p. 121

By virtue of the authority vested in me by the Constitution and statutes of the United States of America, and as President of the United States of America, in furtherance of the National Environmental Policy Act of 1969, as amended (42 USC 4321 et seq.), in order to avoid to the extent possible the long and short term adverse impacts associated with the destruction or modification of wetlands and to avoid direct or indirect support of new construction in wetlands wherever there is a practicable alternative, it is hereby ordered as follows:

Sec. 1.

(a) Each agency shall provide leadership and shall take action to minimize the destruction, loss or degradation of wetlands, and to preserve and enhance the natural and beneficial values of wetlands in carrying out the agency's responsibilities for (1) acquiring, managing, and disposing of Federal lands and facilities; and (2) providing Federally undertaken, financed, or assisted construction and improvements; and (3) conducting Federal activities and programs affecting land use, including but not limited to water and related land resources planning, regulating, and licensing activities.

(b) This Order does not apply to the issuance by Federal agencies of permits, licenses, or allocations to private parties for activities involving wetlands on non-Federal property.

Sec. 2.

(1) In furtherance of Section 101(b)(3) of the National Environmental Policy Act of 1969 (42 USC 4331(b)(3)) to improve and coordinate Federal plans, functions, programs and resources to the end that the Nation may attain the widest range of beneficial uses of the environment without degradation and risk to health or safety, each agency, to the extent permitted by law, shall avoid undertaking or providing assistance for new construction located in wetlands unless the head of the agency finds (1) that there is no practicable alternative to such construction, and (2) that the proposed action includes all practicable measures to minimize harm to wetlands which may result from such use. In making this finding the head of the agency may take into account economic, environmental and other pertinent factors.

(b) Each agency shall also provide opportunity for early public review of any plans or proposals for new construction in wetlands, in accordance with Section 2(b) of Executive Order No. 11514, as amended, including the development of procedures to accomplish this objective for Federal actions whose impact is not significant enough to require the preparation of an environmental impact statement under Section 102(2)(C) of the National Environmental Policy Act of 1969, as amended.

Sec. 3.

Any requests for new authorizations or appropriations transmitted to the Office of Management and Budget shall indicate, if an action to be proposed will be located in wetlands, whether the proposed action is in accord with this Order.

Sec. 4.

When Federally-owned wetlands or portion wetlands are proposed for lease, easement, right-of or disposal to non-Federal public or private parties Federal agency shall (a) reference in the conveyance those uses that are restricted under identified Federal, State or local wetlands regulations; and (b) attach other appropriate restrictions to the uses of properties by the grantee or purchaser and any successor, except where prohibited by law; or (c) withhold such properties from disposal.

Sec. 5.

In carrying out the activities described in Section 1 of this Order, each agency shall consider factors relevant to a proposal's effect on the survival and quality of the wetlands. Among these factors are:

      (a) Public health, safety, and welfare, including water supply, quality, recharge and discharge; pollution; flood and storm hazards; and sediment and erosion;

      (b) Maintenance of natural systems, including conservation and long term productivity of existing flora and fauna, species and habitat diversity and stability, hydrologic utility, fish, wildlife, timber, and food and fiber resources; and

      (c) Other uses of wetlands in the public interest, including recreational, scientific, and cultural uses.

Sec. 6.

As allowed by law, agencies shall issue or amend their existing procedures in order to comply with this Order. To the extent possible, existing processes, such as those of the Council on Environmental Quality and the Water Resources Council, shall be utilized to fulfill the requirements of this Order.

Sec. 7.

As used in this Order:

      (a) The term "agency" shall have the same meaning as the term "Executive agency" in Section 105 of Title 5 of the United States Code and shall include the military departments; the directives contained in this Order, however, are meant to apply only to those agencies which perform the activities described in Section 1 which are located in or affecting wetlands.

      (b) The term "new construction" shall include draining, dredging, channelizing, filling, diking, impounding, and related activities and any structures or facilities begun or authorized after the effective date of this Order.

      (c) The term "wetlands" means those areas that are inundated by surface or ground water with a frequency sufficient to support and under normal circumstances does or would support a prevalence of vegetative or aquatic life that requires saturated or seasonally saturated soil conditions for growth and reproduction. Wetlands generally include swamps, marshes, bogs, and similar areas such as sloughs, potholes, wet meadows, river overflows, mud flats, and natural ponds.

Sec. 8.

This Order does not apply to projects presently under construction, or to projects for which all of the funds have been appropriated through Fiscal Year 1977, or to projects and programs for which a draft or final environmental impact statement will be filed prior to October 1, 1977. The provisions of Section 2 of this Order shall be implemented by each agency not later than October 1, 1977.

Sec. 9.

Nothing in this Order shall apply to assistance provided for emergency work, essential to save lives and protect property and public health and safety, performed pursuant to Sections 305 and 306 of the Disaster Relief Act of 1974 (88 Stat. 148, 42 U.S.C. 5145 and 5146).

Sec. 10.

To the extent the provisions of Sections 2 and 5 of this Order are applicable to projects covered by Section 104(h) of the Housing and Community Development Act of 1974, as amended, (88 Stat. 640, 42 U.S.C. 5304(h)) the responsibilities under those provisions may be assumed by the appropriate applicant, if the applicant has also assumed, with respect to such projects, all of the responsibilities for environmental review, decision making, and action pursuant to the National Environmental Policy Act of 1969, as amended.

/s/ JIMMY CARTER
THE WHITE HOUSE
May 24, 1977

Executive Order 12114. Environmental Effects Abroad of Major Federal Actions

HISTORY: Jan. 4, 1979; 44 FR 1957, 3 CFR, 1979 Comp., p. 356

By virtue of the authority vested in me by the Constitution and the laws of the United States, and as President of the United States, in order to further environmental objectives consistent with the foreign policy and national security policy of the United States, it is ordered as follows:

Sec. 1

Sec. 1-1. Purpose and Scope.

The purpose of this Executive Order is to enable responsible officials of Federal agencies having ultimate responsibility for authorizing and approving actions encompassed by this Order to be informed of pertinent environmental considerations and to take such considerations into account, with other pertinent considerations of national policy in making decisions regarding such actions. While based on independent authority, this Order furthers the purpose of the National Environmental Policy Act and the Marine Protection Research and Sanctuaries Act and the Deepwater Port Act consistent with the foreign policy and national security policy of the United States and represents the United States government's exclusive and complete determination of the procedural and other actions to be taken by Federal agencies to further the purpose of the National Environmental Policy Act, with respect to the environment outside the United States, its territories and possessions.

Sec. 2

2-1. Agency Procedures.

Every Federal agency taking major Federal actions encompassed hereby and not exempted herefrom having significant effects on the environment outside the geographical borders of the United States and its territories and possessions shall within eight months after the effective date of this Order have in effect procedures to implement this Order. Agencies shall consult with the Department of State and the Council on Environmental Quality concerning such procedures prior to placing them in effect.

2-2. Information Exchange.

To assist in effectuating the foregoing purpose, the Department of State and the Council on Environmental Quality in collaboration with other interested Federal agencies and other nations shall conduct a program for exchange on a continuing basis of information concerning the environment. The objectives of this program shall be to provide information for use by decisionmakers, to heighten awareness of and interest in environmental concerns and, as appropriate, to facilitate environmental cooperation with foreign nations.

2-3 Actions Included.

Agencies in their procedures under Section 2-1 shall establish procedures by which their officers having ultimate responsibility for authorizing and approving actions in one of the following categories encompassed by this Order, take into consideration in making decisions concerning such actions, a document described in Section 2-4(a):

(a) Major Federal actions significantly affecting the environment of the global commons outside the jurisdiction of any nation (e.g., the oceans or Antarctica;)

(b) Major Federal actions significantly affecting the environment of a foreign nation not participating with the United States and not otherwise involved in the action;

(c) Major Federal actions significantly affecting the environment of a foreign nation which provide to that nation:

(1) A product or physical project producing a principal product or an emission or effluent which is prohibited or strictly regulated by Federal law in the United States because its toxic effects on the environment create a serious public health risk; or

(2) A physical project which in the United States is prohibited or strictly regulated by Federal law to protect the environment against radioactive substances.

(d) Major Federal actions outside the United States, its territories and possessions which significantly affect natural or ecological resources of global importance designated for protection under this subsection by the President, or, in the case of such a resource protected by international agreements binding on the United States by the Secretary of State. Recommendations to the President under this subsection shall be accompanied by the views of the Council of Environmental Quality and the Secretary of State.

2-4 Applicable Procedures.

(a) There are the following types of documents to be used in connection with actions described in Section 2-3;

(i) Environmental impact statements (including generic program and specific statements);

(ii) Bilateral or multilateral environmental studies, relevant or related to the proposed action, by the United States and one more foreign nations, or by an international body or organization in which the United States is a member or participant; or

(iii) Concise reviews of the environmental, issues involved, including environmental assessments, summary environmental analyses or other appropriate documents.

(b) Agencies shall in their procedures provide for preparation of documents described in Section 2-4(a), with respect to actions described in Section 2-3 as follows:

(i) For effects described in Section 2-3(a), an environmental impact statement described in Section 2-4(a)(1).

(ii) For effects described in Section 2-3(b), a document described in Section 2-4(a)(ii) or (iii), as determined by the agency;

(iii) For effects described in Section 2-3(c), a document described in Section 2-4(a)(ii) or (iii), as determined by the agency;

(iv) For effects described in Section 2-3(d), a document described in Section 2-4(a)(i), (ii) or (iii), as determined by the agency. Such procedures may provide that an agency need not prepare a new document when a document described in Section 2-4(a) already exists.

(c) Nothing in this Order shall serve to invalidate any existing regulations of any agency which have been adopted pursuant to court order or pursuant to judicial settlement of any case or to prevent any agency from providing in its procedures for measures in addition to those provided for herein to further the purpose of the National Environmental Policy Act and other environmental laws, including the Marine Protection Research and Sanctuaries Act and the Deepwater Port Act, consistent with the foreign and national security policies of the United States.

(d) Except as provided in Section 2-5(b), agencies taking action encompassed by this Order shall, as soon as feasible, inform other Federal agencies with relevant expertise of the availability of environmental documents prepared under this Order.

Agencies in their procedures under Section 2-1 shall make appropriate provision for determining when an affected nation shall be informed in accordance with Section 3-2 of this Order of the availability of environmental documents prepared pursuant to those procedures.

In order to avoid duplication of resources, agencies in their procedures shall provide for appropriate utilization of the resources of other Federal agencies with relevant environmental jurisdiction or expertise.

2-5 Exemptions and Considerations:

(a) Notwithstanding Section 2-3, the following actions are exempt from this Order;

(i) Actions not having a significant effect on the environment outside the United States as determined by the agency;

(ii) Actions taken by the President;

(iii) Actions taken by or pursuant to the direction of the President or Cabinet officer when the national security or interest is involved or when the action occurs in the course of an armed conflict;

(iv) Intelligence activities and arms transfers;

(v) Export licenses or permits or export approvals, and actions relating to nuclear activities except actions providing to a foreign nation a nuclear production or utilization facility as defined in the Atomic Energy Act of 1954, as amended, or a nuclear waste management facility;

(vi) Votes and other actions in international conferences and organizations;

(vii) Disaster and emergency relief action.

(b) Agency procedures under Section 2-1 implementing Section 2-4 may provide for appropriate modifications in the contents, timing and availability of documents to other affected Federal agencies and affected nations, where necessary to:

(i) Enable the agency to decide and act promptly as and when required:

(ii) Avoid adverse impacts on foreign relations or infringement in fact or appearance of other nations, sovereign responsibilities, or

(iii) Ensure appropriate reflection of:

(1) Diplomatic factors;

(2) International commercial, competitive and export promotion factors;

(3) Needs for governmental or commercial confidentiality;

(4) National security considerations;

(5) Difficulties of obtaining information and agency ability to analyze meaningfully environmental effects of a proposed action; and

(6) The degree to which the agency is involved in or able to affect a decision to be made.

(c) Agency procedure under Section 2-1 may provide for categorical exclusions and for such exemptions in addition to those specified in subsection (a) of this Section as may be necessary to meet emergency circumstances, situations involving exceptional foreign policy and national security sensitivity and other such special circumstances. In utilizing such additional exemptions agencies shall, as soon as feasible, consult with the Department of State and the Council on Environmental Quality.

(d) The provisions of Section 2-5 do not apply to actions described in Section 2-3(a) unless permitted by law.

Sec. 3.

3-1. Rights of Action.

This Order is solely for the purpose of establishing internal procedures for Federal agencies to consider the significant effects of their actions on the environment outside the United States, its territories and possessions, and nothing in this Order shall be construed to create a cause of action.

3-2. Foreign Relations.

The Department of State shall coordinate all communications by agencies with foreign governments concerning environmental agreements and other arrangements in implementation of this Order.

3-3. Multi-Agency Actions.

Where more than one Federal agency is involved in an action or program, a lead agency, as determined by the agencies involved, shall have responsibility for implementation of this Order.

3-4. Certain Terms.

For purposes of this Order, "environment" means the natural and physical environment and excludes social, economic and other environments; and an action significantly affects the environment if it does significant harm to the environment even though on balance the agency believes the action to be beneficial to the environment. The term "export approvals" in Section 2-5(a)(v) does not mean or include direct loans to finance exports.

3-5. Multiple Imports.

If a major Federal action having effects on the environment of the United States or the global commons requires preparation of an environmental impact statement, and if the action also has effects on the environment of a foreign nation, an environmental impact statement need not be prepared with respect to the effects on the environment of the foreign nation.

/s/ JIMMY CARTER
THE WHITE HOUSE
January 4, 1979

Executive Order 12898. Federal Actions to Address Environmental Justice in Minority Populations and Low-Income Populations

HISTORY: Feb. 11, 1994; 59 FR 7629, Feb. 16, 1994

By the authority vested in me as President by the Constitution and the laws of the United States of America, it is hereby ordered as follows:

Sec. 1-1. Implementation.

1-101. Agency Responsibilities. To the greatest extent practicable and permitted by law, and consistent with the principles set forth in the report on the National Performance Review, each Federal agency shall make achieving environmental justice part of its mission by identifying and addressing, as appropriate, disproportionately high and adverse human health or environmental effects of its programs, policies, and activities on minority populations and low-income populations in the United States and its territories and possessions, the District of Columbia, the Commonwealth of Puerto Rico, and the Commonwealth of the Mariana Islands.

1-102. Creation of an Interagency Working Group on Environmental Justice. (a) Within 3 months of the date of this order, the Administrator of the Environmental Protection Agency ("Administrator") or the Administrator's designee shall convene an interagency Federal Working Group on Environmental Justice ("Working Group"). The Working Group shall comprise the heads of the following executive agencies and offices, or their designees: (a) Department of Defense; (b) Department of Health and Human Services; (c) Department of Housing and Urban Development; (d) Department of Labor; (e) Department of Agriculture; (f) Department of Transportation; (g) Department of Justice; (h) Department of the Interior; (i) Department of Commerce; (j) Department of Energy; (k) Environmental Protection Agency; (l) Office of Management and Budget; (m) Office of Science and Technology Policy; (n) Office of the Deputy Assistant to the President for Environmental Policy; (o) Office of the Assistant to the President for Domestic Policy; (p) National Economic Council; (q) Council of Economic Advisers; and (r) such other Government officials as the President may designate. The Working Group shall report to the President through the Deputy Assistant to the President for Environmental Policy and the Assistant to the President for Domestic Policy.

(b) The Working Group shall: (1) provide guidance to Federal agencies on criteria for identifying disproportionately high and adverse human health or environmental effects on minority populations and low-income populations;

(2) Coordinate with, provide guidance to, and serve as a clearinghouse for, each Federal agency as it develops an environmental justice strategy as required by section 1-103 of this order, in order to ensure that the administration, interpretation and enforcement of programs, activities and policies are undertaken in a consistent manner;

(3) Assist in coordinating research by, and stimulating cooperation among, the Environmental Protection Agency, the Department of Health and Human Services, the Department of Housing and Urban Development, and other agencies conducting research or other activities in accordance with section 3-3 of this order;

(4) Assist in coordinating data collection, required by this order;

(5) Examine existing data and studies on environmental justice;

(6) Hold public meetings as required in section 5-502(d) of this order; and

(7) Develop interagency model projects on environmental justice that evidence cooperation among Federal agencies.

1-103. Development of Agency Strategies. (a) Except as provided in section 6-605 of this order, each Federal agency shall develop an agency-wide environmental justice strategy, as set forth in subsections (b)-(e) of this section that identifies and addresses disproportionately high and adverse human health or environmental effects of its programs, policies, and activities on minority populations and low-income populations. The environmental justice strategy shall list programs, policies, planning and public participation processes, enforcement, and/or rulemakings related to human health or the environment that should be revised to, at a minimum: (1) promote enforcement of all health and environmental statutes in areas with minority populations and low-income populations; (2) ensure greater public participation; (3) improve research and data collection relating to the health of and environment of minority populations and low-income populations; and (4) identify differential patterns of consumption of natural resources among minority populations and low-income populations. In addition, the environmental justice strategy shall include, where appropriate, a timetable for undertaking identified revisions and consideration of economic and social implications of the revisions.

(b) Within 4 months of the date of this order, each Federal agency shall identify an internal administrative process for developing its environmental justice strategy, and shall inform the Working Group of the process.

(c) Within 6 months of the date of this order, each Federal agency shall provide the Working Group with an outline of its proposed environmental justice strategy.

(d) Within 10 months of the date of this order, each Federal agency shall provide the Working Group with its proposed environmental justice strategy.

(e) Within 12 months of the date of this order, each Federal agency shall finalize its environmental justice strategy and provide a copy and written description of its strategy to the Working Group. During the 12 month period from the date of this order, each Federal agency, as part of its environmental justice strategy, shall identify several specific projects that can be promptly undertaken to address particular concerns identified during the development of the proposed environmental justice strategy, and a schedule for implementing those projects.

(f) Within 24 months of the date of this order, each Federal agency shall report to the Working Group on its progress in implementing its agency-wide environmental justice strategy.

(g) Federal agencies shall provide additional periodic reports to the Working Group as requested by the Working Group.

1-104. Reports to the President. Within 14 months of the date of this order, the Working Group shall submit to the President, through the Office of the Deputy Assistant to the President for Environmental Policy and the Office of the Assistant to the President for Domestic Policy, a report that describes the implementation of this order, and includes the final environmental justice strategies described in section 1-103(e) of this order.

Sec. 2-2. Federal Agency Responsibilities for Federal Programs.

Each Federal agency shall conduct its programs, policies, and activities that substantially affect human health or the environment, in a manner that ensures that such programs, policies, and activities do not have the effect of excluding persons (including populations) from participation in, denying persons (including populations) the benefits of, or subjecting persons (including populations) to discrimination under, such programs, policies, and activities, because of their race, color, or national origin.

Sec. 3-3. Research, Data Collection, and Analysis.

3-301. Human Health and Environmental Research and Analysis. (a) Environmental human health research, whenever practicable and appropriate, shall include diverse segments of the population in epidemiological and clinical studies, including segments at high risk from environmental hazards, such as minority populations, low-income populations and workers who may be exposed to substantial environmental hazards.

(b) Environmental human health analyses, whenever practicable and appropriate, shall identify multiple and cumulative exposures.

(c) Federal agencies shall provide minority populations and low-income populations the opportunity to comment on the development and design of research strategies undertaken pursuant to this order.

3-302. Human Health and Environmental Data Collection and Analysis. To the extent permitted by existing law, including the Privacy Act, as amended (5 USC. section 552a):

(a) each Federal agency, whenever practicable and appropriate, shall collect, maintain, and analyze information assessing and comparing environmental and human health risks borne by populations identified by race, national origin, or income. To the extent practical and appropriate, Federal agencies shall use this information to determine whether their programs, policies, and activities have disproportionately high and adverse human health or environmental effects on minority populations and low-income populations;

(b) In connection with the development and implementation of agency strategies in section 1-103 of this order, each Federal agency, whenever practicable and appropriate, shall collect, maintain and analyze information on the race, national origin, income level, and other readily accessible and appropriate information for areas surrounding facilities or sites expected to have a substantial environmental, human health, or economic effect on the surrounding populations, when such facilities or sites become the subject of a substantial Federal environmental administrative or judicial action. Such information shall be made available to the public, unless prohibited by law; and

(c) Each Federal agency, whenever practicable and appropriate, shall collect, maintain, and analyze information on the race, national origin, income level, and other readily accessible and appropriate information for areas surrounding Federal facilities that are: (1) subject to the reporting requirements under the Emergency Planning and Community Right-to-Know Act, 42 U.S.C. section 11001-11050 as mandated in Executive Order No. 12856; and (2) expected to have a substantial environmental, human health, or economic effect on surrounding populations. Such information shall be made available to the public, unless prohibited by law.

(d) In carrying out the responsibilities in this section, each Federal agency, whenever practicable and appropriate, shall share information and eliminate unnecessary duplication of efforts through the use of existing data systems and cooperative agreements among Federal agencies and with State, local, and tribal governments.

Sec. 4-4. Subsistence Consumption of Fish and Wildlife.

4-401. Consumption Patterns. In order to assist in identifying the need for ensuring protection of populations with differential patterns of subsistence consumption of fish and wildlife, Federal agencies, whenever practicable and appropriate, shall collect, maintain, and analyze information on the consumption patterns of populations who principally rely on fish and/or wildlife for subsistence. Federal agencies shall communicate to the public the risks of those consumption patterns.

4-402. Guidance. Federal agencies, whenever practicable and appropriate, shall work in a coordinated manner to publish guidance reflecting the latest scientific information available concerning methods for evaluating the human health risks associated with the consumption of pollutant-bearing fish or wildlife. Agencies shall consider such guidance in developing their policies and rules.

Sec. 5-5. Public Participation and Access to Information.

(a) The public may submit recommendations to Federal agencies relating to the incorporation of environmental justice principles into Federal agency programs or policies. Each Federal agency shall convey such recommendations to the Working Group.

(b) Each Federal agency may, whenever practicable and appropriate, translate crucial public documents, notices, and hearings relating to human health or the environment for limited English speaking populations.

(c) Each Federal agency shall work to ensure that public documents, notices, and hearings relating to human health or the environment are concise, understandable, and readily accessible to the public.

(d) The Working Group shall hold public meetings, as appropriate, for the purpose of fact-finding, receiving public comments, and conducting inquiries concerning environmental justice. The Working Group shall prepare for public review a summary of the comments and recommendations discussed at the public meetings.

Executive Order 12962. Recreational Fisheries

of June 7, 1995

By the authority vested in me as President by the Constitution and the laws of the United States of America, and in furtherance of the purposes of the Fish and Wildlife Act of 1956 (16 U.S.C. 742a-d, and e-j), the Fish and Wildlife Coordination Act (16 U.S.C. 661-666c), the National Environmental Policy Act of 1969 (42 U.S.C. 4321 et seq.), and the Magnuson Fishery Conservation and Management Act (16 U.S.C. 1801-1882), and other pertinent statutes, and in order to conserve, restore, and enhance aquatic systems to provide for increased recreational fishing opportunities nationwide, it is ordered as follows:

Sec. 1. Federal Agency Duties.

Federal agencies shall, to the extent permitted by law and where practicable, and in cooperation with the States and Tribes, improve the quantity, function, sustainable productivity, and distribution of U.S. aquatic resources for increased recreational fishing opportunities by:

(a) Developing and encouraging partnerships between governments and the private sector to advance aquatic resource conservation and enhance recreational fishing opportunities;

(b) Identifying recreational fishing opportunities that are limited by water quality and habitat degradation and promoting restoration to support viable, healthy, and where feasible, self-sustaining recreational fisheries;

(c) Fostering sound aquatic conservation and restoration endeavors to benefit recreational fisheries;

(d) Providing access to and promoting awareness of opportunities for public participation and enjoyment of U.S. recreational fishery resources;

(e) Supporting outreach programs designed to stimulate angler participation in the conservation and restoration of aquatic systems;

(f) Implementing laws under their purview in a manner that will conserve, restore, and enhance aquatic systems that support recreational fisheries;

(g) Establishing cost-share programs, under existing authorities, that match or exceed Federal funds with non-Federal contributions;

(h) Evaluating the effects of Federally funded, permitted, or authorized actions on aquatic systems and recreational fisheries and document those effects relative to the purpose of this order; and

(i) Assisting private landowners to conserve and enhance aquatic resources on their lands.

Sec. 2. National Recreational Fisheries Coordination Council.

A National Recreational Fisheries Coordination Council ("Coordination Council") is hereby established. The Coordination Council shall consist of seven members, one member designated by each of the following Secretaries–Interior, Commerce, Agriculture, Energy, Transportation, and Defense–and one by the Administrator of the Environmental Protection Agency. The Coordination Council shall:

(a) Ensure that the social and economic values of healthy aquatic systems that support recreational fisheries are considered by Federal agencies in the course of their actions;

(b) Reduce duplicative and cost-inefficient programs among Federal agencies involved in conserving or managing recreational fisheries;

(c) Share the latest resource information and management technologies to assist in the conservation and management of recreational fisheries;

(d) Assess the implementation of the Conservation Plan required under section 3 of this order; and

(e) Develop a biennial report of accomplishments of the Conservation Plan.

The representatives designated by the Secretaries of Commerce and Interior shall co-chair the Coordination Council.

Sec. 3. Recreational Fishery Resources Conservation Plan.

(a) Within 12 months of the date of this order, the Coordination Council, in cooperation with Federal agencies, States, and Tribes, and after consulting with the Federally chartered Sport Fishing and Boating Partnership Council, shall develop a comprehensive Recreational Fishery Resources Conservation Plan ("Conservation Plan").

(b) The Conservation Plan will set forth a 5-year agenda for Federal agencies identified by the Coordination Council. In so doing, the Conservation Plan will establish, to the extent permitted by law and where practicable;

(1) Measurable objectives to conserve and restore aquatic systems that support viable and healthy recreational fishery resources,

(2) Actions to be taken by the identified Federal agencies,

(3) A method of ensuring the accountability of such Federal agencies, and

(4) A comprehensive mechanism to evaluate achievements.

The Conservation Plan will, to the extent practicable, be integrated with existing plans and programs, reduce duplication, and will include recommended actions for cooperation with States, Tribes, conservation groups, and the recreational fisheries community.

Sec. 4. Joint Policy for Administering the Endangered Species Act of 1973.

All Federal agencies will aggressively work to identify and minimize conflicts between recreational fisheries and their respective responsibilities under the Endangered Species Act of 1973 ("ESA") (16 U.S.C. 1531 et seq.). Within 6 months of the date of this order, the Fish and Wildlife Service and the National Marine Fisheries Service will promote compatibility and reduce conflicts within the administration of the ESA and recreational fisheries by developing a joint agency policy that will;

(1) Ensure consistency in the administration of the ESA between and within the two agencies,

(2) Promote collaboration with other Federal, State, and Tribal fisheries managers, and

(3) Improve and increase efforts to inform nonfederal entities of the requirements of the ESA.

Sec. 5. Sport Fishing and Boating Partnership Council.

To assist in the implementation of this order, the Secretary of the Interior shall expand the role of the Sport Fishing and Boating Partnership Council to:

(a) Monitor specific Federal activities affecting aquatic systems and the recreational fisheries they support;

(b) Review and evaluate the relation of Federal policies and activities to the status and conditions of recreational fishery resources; and

(c) Prepare an annual report of its activities, findings, and recommendations for submission to the Coordination Council.

Sec. 6. Judicial Review.

This order is intended only to improve the internal management of the executive branch and it is not intended to create any right, benefit or trust responsibility, substantive or procedural, enforceable at law or equity by a party against the United States, its agencies, its officers, or any other person.

WILLIAM J. CLINTON
THE WHITE HOUSE
June 7, 1995

Executive Order 13006. Locating Federal Facilities on Historic Properties in Our Nation's Central Cities

By the authority vested in me as President by the Constitution and the laws of the United States of America, including the National Historic Preservation Act (16 U.S.C. 470 et seq.) and the Public Buildings Cooperative Use Act of 1976 (90 Stat. 2505), and in furtherance of and consistent with Executive Order No. 12072 of August 16, 1978, and Executive Order No. 11593 of May 13, 1971, it is hereby ordered as follows:

Sec. 1. Statement of Policy.

Through the Administration's community empowerment initiatives, the Federal Government has undertaken various efforts to revitalize our central cities, which have historically served as the centers for growth and commerce in our metropolitan areas. Accordingly, the Administration hereby reaffirms the commitment set forth in Executive Order No. 12072 to strengthen our Nation's cities by encouraging the location of Federal facilities in our central cities. The Administration also reaffirms the commitments set forth in the National Historic Preservation Act to provide leadership in the preservation of historic resources, and in the Public Buildings Cooperative Use Act of 1976 to acquire and utilize space in suitable buildings of historic, architectural, or cultural significance.

To this end, the Federal Government shall utilize and maintain, wherever operationally appropriate and economically prudent, historic properties and districts, especially those located in our central business areas. When implementing these policies, the Federal Government shall institute practices and procedures that are sensible, understandable, and compatible with current authority and that impose the least burden on, and provide the maximum benefit to, society.

Sec. 2. Encouraging the Location of Federal Facilities on Historic Properties in Our Central Cities.

When operationally appropriate and economically prudent, and subject to the requirements of Section 601 of title Vi of the Rural Development Act of 1972, as amended, (42 U.S.C. 3122) and Executive Order No. 12072, when locating Federal facilities, Federal agencies shall give first consideration to historic properties within historic districts.

If no such property is suitable, then Federal agencies shall consider other developed or undeveloped sites within historic districts. Federal agencies shall then consider historic properties outside of historic districts, if no suitable site within a district exists. Any rehabilitation or construction that is undertaken pursuant to this order must be architecturally compatible with the character of the surrounding historic district or properties.

Sec. 3. Identifying and Removing Regulatory Barriers.

Federal agencies with responsibilities for leasing, acquiring, locating, maintaining, or managing Federal facilities or with responsibilities for the planning for, or managing of, historic resources shall take steps to reform, streamline, and otherwise minimize regulations, policies, and procedures that impede the Federal Government's ability to establish or maintain a presence in historic districts or to acquire historic properties to satisfy Federal space needs, unless such regulations, policies, and procedures are designed to protect human health and safety or the environment. Federal agencies are encouraged to seek the assistance of the Advisory Council on Historic Preservation when taking these steps.

Sec. 4. Improving Preservation Partnerships.

In carrying out the authorities of the National Historic Preservation Act, the Secretary of the Interior, the Advisory Council on Historic Preservation, and each Federal agency shall seek appropriate partnerships with States, local governments, Indian tribes, and appropriate private organizations with the goal of enhancing participation of these parties in the National Historic Preservation Program. Such partnerships should embody the principles of administrative flexibility, reduced paperwork, and increased service to the public.

Sec. 5. Judicial Review.

This order is not intended to create, nor does it create, any right or benefit, substantive or procedural, enforceable at law by a party against the United States, its agencies or instrumentalities, its officers or employees, or any other person.

WILLIAM J. CLINTON
THE WHITE HOUSE,
May 21, 1996.

Executive Order 13007. Indian Sacred Sites

By the authority vested in me as President by the Constitution and the laws of the United States, in furtherance of Federal treaties, and in order to protect and preserve Indian religious practices, it is hereby ordered:

Sec. 1. Accommodation of Sacred Sites.

(a) In managing Federal lands, each executive branch agency with statutory or administrative responsibility for the management of Federal lands shall, to the extent practicable, permitted by law, and not clearly inconsistent with essential agency functions,(1) accommodate access to and ceremonial use of Indian sacred sites by Indian religious practitioners and (2) avoid adversely affecting the physical integrity of such sacred sites. Where appropriate, agencies shall maintain the confidentiality of sacred sites.

(b) For purposes of this order:

(i) "Federal lands" means any land or interests in land owned by the United States, including leasehold interests held by the United States, except Indian trust lands;

(ii) "Indian tribe" means an Indian or Alaska Native tribe, band, nation, pueblo, village, or community that the Secretary of the Interior acknowledges to exist as an Indian tribe pursuant to Public Law No. 103-454, 108 Stat. 4791, and "Indian" refers to a member of such an Indian tribe; and

(iii) "Sacred site" means any specific, discrete, narrowly delineated location on Federal land that is identified by an Indian tribe, or Indian individual determined to be an appropriately authoritative representative of an Indian religion, as sacred by virtue of its established religious significance to, or ceremonial use by, an Indian religion; provided that the tribe or appropriately authoritative representative of an Indian religion has informed the agency of the existence of such a site.

Sec. 2. Procedures.

(a) Each executive branch agency with statutory or administrative responsibility for the management of Federal lands shall, as appropriate, promptly implement procedures for the purposes of carrying out the provisions of section 1 of this order, including, where practicable and appropriate, procedures to ensure reasonable notice is provided of proposed actions or land management policies that may restrict future access to or ceremonial use of, or adversely affect the physical integrity of, sacred sites. In all actions pursuant to this section, agencies shall comply with the Executive memorandum of April 29, 1994, "Government-to- Government Relations with Native American Tribal Governments."

(b) Within 1 year of the effective date of this order, the head of each executive branch agency with statutory or administrative responsibility for the management of Federal lands shall report to the President, through the Assistant to the President for Domestic Policy, on the implementation of this order. Such reports shall address, among other things, (i) any changes necessary to accommodate access to and ceremonial use of Indian sacred sites; (ii) any changes necessary to avoid adversely affecting the physical integrity of Indian sacred sites; and (iii) procedures implemented or proposed to facilitate consultation with appropriate Indian tribes and religious leaders and the expeditious resolution of disputes relating to agency action on Federal lands that may adversely affect access to, ceremonial use of, or the physical integrity of sacred sites.

Sec. 3.

Nothing in this order shall be construed to require a taking of vested property interests. Nor shall this order be construed to impair enforceable rights to use of Federal lands that have been granted to third parties through final agency action. For purposes of this order, "agency action" has the same meaning as in the Administrative Procedures Act (5 U.S.C.551(13).

Sec. 4.

This order is intended only to improve the internal management of the executive branch and is not intended to, nor does it, create any right, benefit, or trust responsibility, substantive or procedural, enforceable at law or equity by any party against the United States, its agencies officers, or any person.

WILLIAM J. CLINTON
THE WHITE HOUSE,
May 24, 1996.

Executive Order 13045. Protection of Children from Environmental Health Risks and Safety Risks

[*Federal Register*: April 23, 1997 (Volume 62, Number 78)]
[Presidential Documents]

Executive Order 13045 of April 21, 1997

Protection of Children From Environmental Health Risks and Safety Risks

By the authority vested in me as President by the Constitution and the laws of the United States of America, it is hereby ordered as follows:

Sec. 1. Policy.

1-101. A growing body of scientific knowledge demonstrates that children may suffer disproportionately from environmental health risks and safety risks. These risks arise because: children's neurological, immunological, digestive, and other bodily systems are still developing; children eat more food, drink more fluids, and breathe more air in proportion to their body weight than adults; children's size and weight may diminish their protection from standard safety features; and children's behavior patterns may make them more susceptible to accidents because they are less able to protect themselves. Therefore, to the extent permitted by law and appropriate, and consistent with the agency's mission, each Federal agency:

(a) Shall make it a high priority to identify and assess environmental health risks and safety risks that may disproportionately affect children; and

(b) Shall ensure that its policies, programs, activities, and standards address disproportionate risks to children that result from environmental health risks or safety risks.

1-102. Each independent regulatory agency is encouraged to participate in the implementation of this order and comply with its provisions.

Sec. 2. Definitions.

The following definitions shall apply to this order.

2-201. "Federal agency" means any authority of the United States that is an agency under 44 U.S.C. 3502(1) other than those considered to be independent regulatory agencies under 44 U.S.C. 3502(5). For purposes of this order, "military departments," as defined in 5 U.S.C. 102, are covered under the auspices of the Department of Defense.

2-202. "Covered regulatory action" means any substantive action in a rulemaking, initiated after the date of this order or for which a Notice of Proposed Rulemaking is published 1 year after the date of this order, that is likely to result in a rule that may:

(a) Be "economically significant" under Executive Order 12866 (a rulemaking that has an annual effect on the economy of $100 million or more or would adversely affect in a material way the economy, a sector of the economy, productivity, competition, jobs, the environment, public health or safety, or State, local, or tribal governments or communities); and

(b) Concern an environmental health risk or safety risk that an agency has reason to believe may disproportionately affect children.

2-203. "Environmental health risks and safety risks" mean risks to health or to safety that are attributable to products or substances that the child is likely to come in contact with or ingest (such as the air we breath, the food we eat, the water we drink or use for recreation, the soil we live on, and the products we use or are exposed to).

Sec. 3. Task Force on Environmental Health Risks and Safety Risks to Children.

3-301. There is hereby established the Task Force on Environmental Health Risks and Safety Risks to Children ("Task Force").

3-302. The Task Force will report to the President in consultation with the Domestic Policy Council, the National Science and Technology Council, the Council on Environmental Quality, and the Office of Management and Budget (OMB).

3-303. Membership. The Task Force shall be composed of the:

(a) Secretary of Health and Human Services, who shall serve as a Co-Chair of the Council;

(b) Administrator of the Environmental Protection Agency, who shall serve as a Co-Chair of the Council;

(c) Secretary of Education;

(d) Secretary of Labor;

(e) Attorney General;

(f) Secretary of Energy;

(g) Secretary of Housing and Urban Development;

(h) Secretary of Agriculture;

(i) Secretary of Transportation;

(j) Director of the Office of Management and Budget;

(k) Chair of the Council on Environmental Quality;

(l) Chair of the Consumer Product Safety Commission;

(m) Assistant to the President for Economic Policy;

(n) Assistant to the President for Domestic Policy;

(o) Assistant to the President and Director of the Office of Science and Technology Policy;

(p) Chair of the Council of Economic Advisers; and

(q) Such other officials of executive departments and agencies as the President may, from time to time, designate.

Members of the Task Force may delegate their responsibilities under this order to subordinates.

3-304. Functions. The Task Force shall recommend to the President Federal strategies for children's environmental health and safety, within the limits of the Administration's budget, to include the following elements:

(a) Statements of principles, general policy, and targeted annual priorities to guide the Federal approach to achieving the goals of this order;

(b) A coordinated research agenda for the Federal Government, including steps to implement the review of research databases described in section 4 of this order;

(c) Recommendations for appropriate partnerships among Federal, State, local, and tribal governments and the private, academic, and nonprofit sectors;

(d) Proposals to enhance public outreach and communication to assist families in evaluating risks to children and in making informed consumer choices;

(e) An identification of high-priority initiatives that the Federal Government has undertaken or will undertake in advancing protection of children's environmental health and safety; and

(f) A statement regarding the desirability of new legislation to fulfill or promote the purposes of this order.

3-305. The Task Force shall prepare a biennial report on research, data, or other information that would enhance our ability to understand, analyze, and respond to environmental health risks and safety risks to children. For purposes of this report, cabinet agencies and other agencies identified by the Task Force shall identify and specifically describe for the Task Force key data needs related to environmental health risks and safety risks to children that have arisen in the course of the agency's programs and activities. The Task Force shall incorporate agency submissions into its report and ensure that this report is publicly available and widely disseminated. The Office of Science and Technology Policy and the National Science and Technology Council shall ensure that this report is fully considered in establishing research priorities.

3-306. The Task Force shall exist for a period of 4 years from the first meeting. At least 6 months prior to the expiration of that period, the member agencies shall assess the need for continuation of the Task Force or its functions, and make appropriate recommendations to the President.

Sec. 4. Research Coordination and Integration.

4-401. Within 6 months of the date of this order, the Task Force shall develop or direct to be developed a review of existing and planned data resources and a proposed plan for ensuring that researchers and Federal research agencies have access to information on all research conducted or funded by the Federal Government that is related to adverse health risks in children resulting from exposure to environmental health risks or safety risks. The National Science and Technology Council shall review the plan.

4-402. The plan shall promote the sharing of information on academic and private research. It shall include recommendations to encourage that such data, to the extent permitted by law, is available to the public, the scientific and academic communities, and all Federal agencies.

Sec. 5. Agency Environmental Health Risk or Safety Risk Regulations.

5-501. For each covered regulatory action submitted to OMB's Office of Information and Regulatory Affairs (OIRA) for review pursuant to Executive Order 12866, the issuing agency shall provide to OIRA the following information developed as part of the agency's decision making process, unless prohibited by law:

(a) A evaluation of the environmental health or safety effects of the planned regulation on children; and

(b) An explanation of why the planned regulation is preferable to other potentially effective and reasonably feasible alternatives considered by the agency.

5-502. In emergency situations, or when an agency is obligated by law to act more quickly than normal review procedures allow, the agency shall comply with the provisions of this section to the extent practicable. For those covered regulatory actions that are governed by a court-imposed or statutory deadline, the agency shall, to the extent practicable, schedule any rulemaking proceedings so as to permit sufficient time for completing the analysis required by this section.

5-503. The analysis required by this section may be included as part of any other required analysis, and shall be made part of the administrative record for the covered regulatory action or otherwise made available to the public, to the extent permitted by law.

Sec. 6. Interagency Forum on Child and Family Statistics.

6-601. The Director of the OMB ("Director") shall convene an Interagency Forum on Child and Family Statistics ("Forum"), which will include representatives from the appropriate Federal statistics and research agencies. The Forum shall produce an annual compendium ("Report") of the most important indicators of the well-being of the Nation's children.

6-602. The Forum shall determine the indicators to be included in each Report and identify the sources of data to be used for each indicator. The Forum shall provide an ongoing review of Federal collection and dissemination of data on children and families, and shall make recommendations to improve the coverage and coordination of data collection and to reduce duplication and overlap.

6-603. The Report shall be published by the Forum in collaboration with the National Institute of Child Health and Human Development. The Forum shall present the first annual Report to the President, through the Director, by July 31, 1997. The Report shall be submitted annually thereafter, using the most recently available data.

Sec. 7. General Provisions.

7-701. This order is intended only for internal management of the executive branch. This order is not intended, and should not be construed to create, any right, benefit, or trust responsibility, substantive or procedural, enforceable at law or equity by a party against the United States, its agencies, its officers, or its employees. This order shall not be construed to create any right to judicial review involving the compliance or noncompliance with this order by the United States, its agencies, its officers, or any other person.

7-702. Executive Order 12606 of September 2, 1987 is revoked.

WILLIAM J. CLINTON
THE WHITE HOUSE,
April 21, 1997.

Executive Order 13089. Coral Reef Protection

THE WHITE HOUSE
June 11, 1998

By the authority vested in me as President by the Constitution and the laws of the United States of America and in furtherance of the purposes of the Clean Water Act of 1977, as amended, (33 U.S.C. 1251, *et seq.*) Coastal Zone Management Act (16 U.S.C. 1451, *et seq.*), Magnuson-Stevens Fishery Conservation and Management Act (16 U.S.C. 1801, *et seq.*), National Environmental Policy Act of 1969, as amended, (42 U.S.C. 4321, *et seq.*) National Marine Sanctuaries Act, (16 U.S.C. 1431, *et seq.*), National Park Service Organic Act (16 U.S.C. 1, *et seq.*), National Wildlife Refuge System Administration Act (16 U.S.C. 668dd-ee), and other pertinent statutes, to preserve and protect the biodiversity, health, heritage, and social and economic value of U.S. coral reef ecosystems and the marine environment, it is hereby ordered as follows:

Sec. 1. Definitions.

(a) "U.S. coral reef ecosystems" means those species, habitats, and other natural resources associated with coral reefs in all maritime areas and zones subject to the jurisdiction or control of the United States (e.g., Federal, State, territorial, or commonwealth waters), including reef systems in the south Atlantic, Caribbean, Gulf of Mexico, and Pacific Ocean.

(b) "U.S. Coral Reef Initiative" is an existing partnership between Federal agencies and State, territorial, commonwealth, and local governments, non-governmental organizations, and commercial interests to design and implement additional management, education, monitoring, research, and restoration efforts to conserve coral reef ecosystems for the use and enjoyment of future generations. The existing U.S. Islands Coral Reef Initiative strategy covers approximately 95 percent of U.S. coral reef ecosystems and is a key element of the overall U.S. Coral Reef Initiative.

(c) "International Coral Reef Initiative" is an existing partnership, founded by the United States in 1994, of governments, intergovernmental organizations, multilateral development banks, non-governmental organizations, scientists, and the private sector whose purpose is to mobilize governments and other interested parties whose coordinated, vigorous, and effective actions are required to address the threats to the world's coral reefs.

Sec. 2. Policy.

(a) All Federal agencies whose actions may affect U.S. coral reef ecosystems shall: (a) identify their actions that may affect U.S. coral reef ecosystems; (b) utilize their programs and authorities to protect and enhance the conditions of such ecosystems; and (c) to the extent permitted by law, ensure that any actions they authorize, fund, or carry out will not degrade the conditions of such ecosystems.

(b) Exceptions to this section may be allowed under terms prescribed by the heads of Federal agencies:

(1) During time of war or national emergency;

(2) When necessary for reasons of national security, as determined by the President;

(3) During emergencies posing an unacceptable threat to human health or safety or to the marine environment and admitting of no other feasible solution; or

(4) In any case that constitutes a danger to human life or a real threat to vessels, aircraft, platforms, or other man-made structures at sea, such as cases of force majeure caused by stress of weather or other act of God.

Sec. 3. Federal Agency Responsibilities.

In furtherance of section 2 of this order, Federal agencies whose actions affect U.S. coral reef ecosystems, shall, subject to the availability of appropriations, provide for implementation of measures needed to research, monitor, manage, and restore affected ecosystems, including, but not limited to, measures reducing impacts from pollution, sedimentation, and fishing. To the extent not inconsistent with statutory responsibilities and procedures, these measures shall be developed in cooperation with the U.S. Coral Reef Task Force and fishery management councils and in consultation with affected States, territorial, commonwealth, tribal, and local government agencies, non-governmental organizations, the scientific community, and commercial interests.

Sec. 4. U.S. Coral Reef Task Force.

The Secretary of the Interior and the Secretary of Commerce, through the Administrator of the National Oceanic and Atmospheric Administration, shall co-chair a U.S. Coral Reef Task Force ("Task Force"), whose members shall include, but not be limited to, the Administrator of the Environmental Protection Agency, the Attorney General, the Secretary of the Interior, the Secretary of Agriculture, the Secretary of Commerce, the Secretary of Defense, the Secretary of State, the Secretary of Transportation, the Director of the National Science Foundation, the Administrator of the Agency for International Development, and the Administrator of the National Aeronautics and Space Administration. The Task Force shall oversee implementation of the policy and Federal agency responsibilities set forth in this order, and shall guide and support activities under the U.S. Coral Reef Initiative ("CRI"). All Federal agencies whose actions may affect U.S. coral reef ecosystems shall review their participation in the CRI and the strategies developed under it, including strategies and plans of State, territorial, commonwealth, and local governments, and, to the extent feasible, shall enhance Federal participation and support of such strategies and plans. The Task Force shall work in cooperation with State, territorial, commonwealth, and local government agencies, non-governmental organizations, the scientific community, and commercial interests.

Sec. 5. Duties of the U.S. Coral Reef Task Force.

(a) Coral Reef Mapping and Monitoring. The Task Force, in cooperation with State, territory, commonwealth, and local government partners, shall coordinate a comprehensive program to map and monitor U.S. coral reefs. Such programs shall include, but not be limited to, territories and commonwealths, special marine protected areas such as National Marine Sanctuaries, National Estuarine Research Reserves, National Parks, National Wildlife Refuges, and other entities having significant coral reef resources. To the extent feasible, remote sensing capabilities shall be developed and applied to this program and local communities should be engaged in the design and conduct of programs.

(b) Research. The Task Force shall develop and implement, with the scientific community, research aimed at identifying the major causes and consequences of degradation of coral reef ecosystems. This research shall include fundamental scientific research to provide a sound framework for the restoration and conservation of coral reef ecosystems worldwide. To the extent feasible, existing and planned environmental monitoring and mapping programs should be linked with scientific research activities. This Executive order shall not interfere with the normal conduct of scientific studies on coral reef ecosystems.

(c) Conservation, Mitigation, and Restoration. The Task Force, in cooperation with State, territorial, commonwealth, and local government agencies, non-governmental organizations, the scientific community and commercial interests, shall develop, recommend, and seek or secure implementation of measures necessary to reduce and mitigate coral reef ecosystem degradation and to restore damaged coral reefs. These measures shall include solutions to problems such as land-based sources of water pollution, sedimentation, detrimental alteration of salinity or temperature, over-fishing, over-use, collection of coral reef species, and direct destruction caused by activities such as recreational and commercial vessel traffic and treasure salvage. In developing these measures, the Task Force shall review existing legislation to determine whether additional legislation is necessary to complement the policy objectives of this order and shall recommend such legislation if appropriate. The Task Force shall further evaluate existing navigational aids, including charts, maps, day markers, and beacons to determine if the designation of the location of specific coral reefs should be enhanced through the use, revision, or improvement of such aids.

(d) International Cooperation. The Secretary of State and the Administrator of the Agency for International Development, in cooperation with other members of the Coral Reef Task Force and drawing upon their expertise, shall assess the U.S. role in international trade and protection of coral reef species and implement appropriate strategies and actions to promote conservation and sustainable use of coral reef resources worldwide. Such actions shall include expanded collaboration with other International Coral Reef Initiative ("ICRI") partners, especially governments, to implement the ICRI through its Framework for Action and the Global Coral Reef Monitoring Network at regional, national, and local levels.

Sec. 6.

This order does not create any right or benefit, substantive or procedural, enforceable in law or equity by a party against the United States, its agencies, its officers, or any person.

WILLIAM J. CLINTON
THE WHITE HOUSE,
June 11, 1998.

Executive Order 13112. Invasive Species
February 3, 1999

By the authority vested in me as President by the Constitution and the laws of the United States of America, including the National Environmental Policy Act of 1969, as amended, (42 U.S.C. 4321 *et seq.*) Nonindigenous Aquatic Nuisance Prevention and Control Act of 1990, as amended, (16 U.S.C. 4701 *et seq.*) Lacey Act, as amended (18 U.S.C. 42), Federal Plant Pest Act (7 U.S.C. 150aa *et seq.*), Federal Noxious Weed Act of 1974, as amended, (7 U.S.C. 2801 *et seq.*) Endangered Species Act of 1973, as amended, (16 U.S.C. 1531 *et seq.*) and other pertinent statutes, to prevent the introduction of invasive species and provide for their control and to minimize the economic, ecological, and human health impacts that invasive species cause, it is ordered as follows:

Sec. 1. Definitions.

(a) "Alien species" means, with respect to a particular ecosystem, any species, including its seeds, eggs, spores, or other biological material capable of propagating that species, that is not native to that ecosystem.

(b) "Control" means, as appropriate, eradicating, suppressing, reducing, or managing invasive species populations, preventing spread of invasive species from areas where they are present, and taking steps such as restoration of native species and habitats to reduce the effects of invasive species and to prevent further invasions.

(c) "Ecosystem" means the complex of a community of organisms and its environment.

(d) "Federal agency" means an executive department or agency, but does not include independent establishments as defined by 5 U.S.C. 104.

(e) "Introduction" means the intentional or unintentional escape, release, dissemination, or placement of a species into an ecosystem as a result of human activity.

(f) "Invasive species" means an alien species whose introduction does or is likely to cause economic or environmental harm or harm to human health.

(g) "Native species" means, with respect to a particular ecosystem, a species that, other than as a result of an introduction, historically occurred or currently occurs in that ecosystem.

(h) "Species" means a group of organisms all of which have a high degree of physical and genetic similarity, generally interbreed only among themselves, and show persistent differences from members of allied groups of organisms.

(i) "Stakeholders" means, but is not limited to, State, tribal, and local government agencies, academic institutions, the scientific community, nongovernmental entities including environmental, agricultural, and conservation organizations, trade groups, commercial interests, and private landowners.

(j) "United States" means the 50 States, the District of Columbia, Puerto Rico, Guam, and all possessions, territories, and the territorial sea of the United States.

Sec. 2. Federal Agency Duties.

(a) Each Federal agency whose actions may affect the status of invasive species shall, to the extent practicable and permitted by law,

(1) Identify such actions;

---

(2) Subject to the availability of appropriations, and within Administration budgetary limits, use relevant programs and authorities to: (i) prevent the introduction of invasive species; (ii) detect and respond rapidly to and control populations of such species in a cost-effective and environmentally sound manner; (iii) monitor invasive species populations accurately and reliably; (iv) provide for restoration of native species and habitat conditions in ecosystems that have been invaded; (v) conduct research on invasive species and develop technologies to prevent introduction and provide for environmentally sound control of invasive species; and (vi) promote public education on invasive species and the means to address them; and

(3) Not authorize, fund, or carry out actions that it believes are likely to cause or promote the introduction or spread of invasive species in the United States or elsewhere unless, pursuant to guidelines that it has prescribed, the agency has determined and made public its determination that the benefits of such actions clearly outweigh the potential harm caused by invasive species; and that all feasible and prudent measures to minimize risk of harm will be taken in conjunction with the actions.

(b) Federal agencies shall pursue the duties set forth in this section in consultation with the Invasive Species Council, consistent with the Invasive Species Management Plan and in cooperation with stakeholders, as appropriate, and, as approved by the Department of State, when Federal agencies are working with international organizations and foreign nations.

Sec. 3. Invasive Species Council.

(a) An Invasive Species Council (Council) is hereby established whose members shall include the Secretary of State, the Secretary of the Treasury, the Secretary of Defense, the Secretary of the Interior, the Secretary of Agriculture, the Secretary of Commerce, the Secretary of Transportation, and the Administrator of the Environmental Protection Agency. The Council shall be Co-Chaired by the Secretary of the Interior, the Secretary of Agriculture, and the Secretary of Commerce. The Council may invite additional Federal agency representatives to be members, including representatives from subcabinet bureaus or offices with significant responsibilities concerning invasive species, and may prescribe special procedures for their participation. The Secretary of the Interior shall, with concurrence of the Co-Chairs, appoint an Executive Director of the Council and shall provide the staff and administrative support for the Council.

(b) The Secretary of the Interior shall establish an advisory committee under the Federal Advisory Committee Act, 5 U.S.C. App., to provide information and advice for consideration by the Council, and shall, after consultation with other members of the Council, appoint members of the advisory committee representing stakeholders. Among other things, the advisory committee shall recommend plans and actions at local, tribal, State, regional, and ecosystem-based levels to achieve the goals and objectives of the Management Plan in section 5 of this order. The advisory committee shall act in cooperation with stakeholders and existing organizations addressing invasive species. The Department of the Interior shall provide the administrative and financial support for the advisory committee.

Sec. 4. Duties of the Invasive Species Council.

The Invasive Species Council shall provide national leadership regarding invasive species, and shall:

(a) Oversee the implementation of this order and see that the Federal agency activities concerning invasive species are coordinated, complementary, cost-efficient, and effective, relying to the extent feasible and appropriate on existing organizations addressing invasive species, such as the Aquatic Nuisance Species Task Force, the Federal Interagency Committee for the Management of Noxious and Exotic Weeds, and the Committee on Environment and Natural Resources;

(b) Encourage planning and action at local, tribal, State, regional, and ecosystem-based levels to achieve the goals and objectives of the Management Plan in section 5 of this order, in cooperation with stakeholders and existing organizations addressing invasive species;

(c) Develop recommendations for international cooperation in addressing invasive species;

(d) Develop, in consultation with the Council on Environmental Quality, guidance to Federal agencies pursuant to the National Environmental Policy Act on prevention and control of invasive species, including the procurement, use, and maintenance of native species as they affect invasive species;

(e) Facilitate development of a coordinated network among Federal agencies to document, evaluate, and monitor impacts from invasive species on the economy, the environment, and human health;

(f) Facilitate establishment of a coordinated, up-to-date information-sharing system that utilizes, to the greatest extent practicable, the Internet; this system shall facilitate access to and exchange of information concerning invasive species, including, but not limited to, information on distribution and abundance of invasive species; life histories of such species and invasive characteristics; economic, environmental, and human health impacts; management techniques, and laws and programs for management, research, and public education; and

(g) Prepare and issue a national Invasive Species Management Plan as set forth in section 5 of this order.

Sec. 5. Invasive Species Management Plan.

(a) Within 18 months after issuance of this order, the Council shall prepare and issue the first edition of a National Invasive Species Management Plan (Management Plan), which shall detail and recommend performance-oriented goals and objectives and specific measures of success for Federal agency efforts concerning invasive species. The Management Plan shall recommend specific objectives and measures for carrying out each of the Federal agency duties established in section 2(a) of this order and shall set forth steps to be taken by the Council to carry out the duties assigned to it under section 4 of this order. The Management Plan shall be developed through a public process and in consultation with Federal agencies and stakeholders.

(b) The first edition of the Management Plan shall include a review of existing and prospective approaches and authorities for preventing the introduction and spread of invasive species, including those for identifying pathways by which invasive species are introduced and for minimizing the risk of introductions via those pathways, and shall identify research needs and recommend measures to minimize the risk that introductions will occur. Such recommended measures shall provide for a science-based process to evaluate risks associated with introduction and spread of invasive species and a coordinated and systematic risk-based process to identify, monitor, and interdict pathways that may be involved in the introduction of invasive species. If recommended measures are not authorized by current law, the Council shall develop and recommend to the President through its Co-Chairs legislative proposals for necessary changes in authority.

(c) The Council shall update the Management Plan biennially and shall concurrently evaluate and report on success in achieving the goals and objectives set forth in the Management Plan. The Management Plan shall identify the personnel, other resources, and additional levels of coordination needed to achieve the Management Plan's identified goals and objectives, and the Council shall provide each edition of the Management Plan and each report on it to the Office of Management and Budget. Within 18 months after measures have been recommended by the Council in any edition of the Management Plan, each Federal agency whose action is required to implement such measures shall either take the action recommended or shall provide the Council with an explanation of why the action is not feasible. The Council shall assess the effectiveness of this order no less than once each 5 years after the order is issued and shall report to the Office of Management and Budget on whether the order should be revised.

Sec. 6. Judicial Review and Administration.

(a) This order is intended only to improve the internal management of the executive branch and is not intended to create any right, benefit, or trust responsibility, substantive or procedural, enforceable at law or equity by a party against the United States, its agencies, its officers, or any other person.

(b) Executive Order 11987 of May 24, 1977, is hereby revoked.

(c) The requirements of this order do not affect the obligations of Federal agencies under 16 U.S.C. 4713 with respect to ballast water programs.

(d) The requirements of section 2(a)(3) of this order shall not apply to any action of the Department of State or Department of Defense if the Secretary of State or the Secretary of Defense finds that exemption from such requirements is necessary for foreign policy or national security reasons.

WILLIAM J. CLINTON
THE WHITE HOUSE,
February 3, 1999.

ABIOTIC - Not biotic or not living; often referring to the nonliving components of the ecosystem such as soils, water, and climate.

ACID RAIN - A complex chemical and atmospheric phenomenon that occurs when emissions of sulfur and nitrogen compounds and other substances are transformed by chemical processes in the atmosphere, often far from the original sources, and then deposited on earth in either a wet or dry form.

ACTION - A desired outcome. For example, a major construction project.

ACTION - (ESA§) All activities or programs of any kind authorized, funded, or carried out, in whole or in part, by Federal agencies in the United States or upon the high seas [50 CFR §402.02].

ACTION AREA - (ESA§) All areas to be affected directly or indirectly by the Federal action and not merely the immediate area involved in the action [50 CFR §402.02].

ADAPTION - The result of a process usually involving long-term evolutionary adjustment of a population to environmental changes.

ADAPTIVE MANAGEMENT - (1) The process of implementing policy decisions as scientifically driven management experiments that test predictions and assumptions in management plans; and using the resulting information to improve the plans; (2) A mechanism for integrating scientific knowledge and experience for the purpose of understanding and managing natural systems.

ADVISORY COUNCIL - (NHPA§) Advisory Council on Historic Preservation (ACHP) or Council. The ACHP, an independent Federal agency composed of 19 members, is charged with advising the President and the Congress on historic preservation matters and administering the provisions of Section 106 of the National Historic Preservation Act. The various duties of the Council that are defined by regulations at 36 CFR Part 800 are carried out by Council members, the Council Chairman, and the Council Executive Director, according to an internal delegation of authority.

AESTHETIC ATTRIBUTES - Perceptual stimuli that provide diverse and pleasant surroundings for human enjoyment and appreciation. Included in this category are sights, sounds, scents, tastes, and tactile impressions, and the interactions of these sensations, of natural and cultural resources. Examples are the sight of a pristine landscape, the view of a historic fortress, the sound of a waterfall or brook, the scent of a hedgerow of honeysuckle or a pine forest, and the taste of mineral water.

AESTHETIC QUALITY - The distinctive property of a landscape determined by professional, public, or personal values and the intrinsic physical properties of the landscape.

AESTHETIC RESOURCE - Those natural man-made features of the environment which can be perceived by the senses. That is, what is seen and what is perceived by the other senses. Aesthetic resources elicit one or more sensory reactions and evaluations by the observer, particularly in regards to their pleasurable effects. Aesthetic

resources include the combination of what can be perceived at a particular site. This involves the unified combination of water resources, landform, vegetation, and user characteristics at a site. An aesthetic resource may be a particular landscape, viewshed, or view.

AFFECTED INTERESTS - Those persons and organizations impacted by the proposed action, either directly or indirectly. These impacts include economic, recreational, or lifestyle changes and changes to the physical or biological environment (e.g., hydrology, vegetation, or wildlife).

AFFECTING - (NEPA§) Will or may have an effect on [40 CFR §1508.3].

AICUZ - Air Installation Compatible Use Zone. A process for predicting the impact of an air program on the surrounding area, involving the measurement of various noise levels.

ALLEE EFFECT - The phenomenon of a population dropping below a threshold density or number of individuals from which it cannot recover; named after the animal ecologist W.C. Allee.

ALLELE - One of a pair of genes at a particular genetic locus.

ALLUVIUM - A general term for clay, silt, sand, gravel, or similar unconsolidated detrital material deposited during comparatively recent geologic time by a stream or other body of running water as a sorted or semisorted sediment in the bed of the stream.

ALPHA DIVERSITY - Species diversity within a habitat.

ALTERNATIVE COURSES OF ACTION - (ESA§) All alternatives and thus is not limited to original project objectives and agency jurisdiction.

ALTERNATIVES - (NEPA§) Methods of accomplishing the proposed action, with each alternative at least partially satisfying the desired outcome [40 CFR §1502.14 and 1508.25 (b)].

AMBIENT MONITORING - Monitoring within natural systems (e.g., lakes, rivers, estuaries, wetlands) to determine existing conditions.

ANCIENT FOREST - Forest in late successional stages, or a shifting mosaic of forest patches in various ages after natural disturbances.

ANADROMOUS FISH - (ESA§) Fish that spend most of their lives in salt water but migrate into fresh water to spawn, e.g., salmon, shad, and striped bass.

ANTICIPATORY DEMOLITION - (NHPA§) An action of an applicant who, with intent to avoid the requirements of NHPA§ 106, has intentionally significantly adversely affected a historic property to which an agency grant of a loan, loan guarantee, permit, license, or other assistance relates, or an inaction of an applicant who, having the legal power to prevent it, allowed such a significant adverse effect to occur.

APPLICANT - (ESA§) Any person (an individual, corporation, partnership, trust, association, or any other private entity; or any officer, employee, agent, department, or instrumentality of the Federal Government, of any State, municipality, or political subdivision of a State, or of any foreign government; any State, municipality, or political subdivision of a State; or any other entity subject to the jurisdiction of the United States) who requires formal approval or authorization from the Service as a prerequisite to conducting the action [50 CFR §402.02].

APPROVAL OF THE EXPENDITURE OF FUNDS - (NHPA§) Any final agency decision approving the eligibility of an undertaking for Federal funds or financial assistance, including any agency decision that may be subject to an administrative appeal or rehearing procedure and conditional decisions subject to reevaluation by the agency.

AQUIFER - An underground bed or layer of earth, gravel, or porous stone that contains water that typically is capable of yielding a significant amount of water.

AREA/PERIMETER RATIO - The ratio of internal area to edge habitat of a region. The area/perimeter ratio is an indication of the amount of interior habitat with respect to edge habitat, and may indicate potential success of a reserve in protecting interior species.

ARCHAEOLOGICAL RESOURCE - Any material remains of past life or activities which are of archeological interest [16 USC §470bb].

ARCHAEOLOGICAL SITE - Any location containing evidence such as artifacts or features.

ARCHITECTURAL RESOURCES - Structures, landscaping, or other human constructions that possess artistic merit, and particularly representative of their class or period, or represent achievements in architecture, engineering, technology, design or scientific research and development; such resources may be important for their archaeological or historical value as well.

AREA OF POTENTIAL EFFECTS - (NHPA§) The geographic area or areas within which an undertaking may directly or indirectly cause changes, whether beneficial or adverse, to the character or use of historic properties, if any such properties exist. The area of potential effects is not limited to land under Federal jurisdiction or control or land within a Federal construction, right-of-way, or permit area.

ARTIFACT - In the broadest sense, any product or by-product of human activity.

ARTIFICIAL RECHARGE - Replenishment of the groundwater supply by means of spreading basins, recharge wells, irrigation, or induced infiltration of surface water.

ASSEMBLAGE - A given taxonomic subset of a larger community (e.g., a bird assemblage in a deciduous forest).

ASSIMILATIVE CAPACITY - The capacity of a natural body of water to receive: (1) water, without deleterious effects, (2) humans who consume the water, and (3) BOD, within prescribed dissolved oxygen limits.

ASSOCIATED FUNERARY OBJECTS - Objects that, as a part of the death rite or ceremony of a culture, are reasonably believed to have been placed with individual human remains either at the time of death or later, and both the human remains and associated funerary objects are presently in the possession or control of a Federal agency or museum, except for other items exclusively made for burial purposes or to contain human remains shall be considered as associated funerary objects [PL 101-601 §2].

ASSOCIATED RECORDS - Original records (or copies thereof) that are prepared assembled and document efforts to locate, evaluate, record, study, preserve, or recover a prehistoric or historic resource [36 CFR §79.4].

ASSOCIATION - A definite or characteristic assemblage of plants and animals living together in an area essentially uniform in environmental conditions; any ecological unit of more than one species.

AUTECOLOGY - The study of the ecology of a single species.

BACKGROUND EXTINCTION RATE - Historical rates of extinction due to environmental causes not influenced by human activities, such as the rate of species going extinct because of long-term climate change.

BANK STORAGE - Water entering the banks of stream channels during high stages of stream flow, most of which returns to stream flow during falling stages.

BASELINE DATA - Environmentally related information collected from a site, either undisturbed or disturbed. Baseline data are collected to provide a reference point to which future changes in the environment resulting from an action can be compared.

BASE RUNOFF - Sustained or fair weather runoff. In most streams, base runoff is composed largely of groundwater effluent.

BEAUTIFICATION - Improvement of project lands for the primary purpose of aesthetic quality, usually involving landscaping, restoring construction scars, etc.

BED LOAD - Course material moving on or near the bed of a flowing stream.

BENCHMARK AREAS - Areas of natural or minimally disturbed habitat that can serve as control or comparison areas to measure the effects of an activity or management practice on similar habitat in the same region.

BENTHOS - Those organisms which live on the bottom of a body of water.

BETA DIVERSITY - Species diversity between habitats or along an environmental gradient.

BIODIVERSITY - See BIOLOGICAL DIVERSITY.

BIOLOGICAL ASSESSMENT - (ESA§) Information prepared by or under the direction of a Federal agency using the procedures in 50 CFR §402.12 concerning listed and proposed species and designated and proposed critical habitat that may be present in the action area and the evaluation of potential effects of the action on such species and habitat.

BIOLOGICAL DIVERSITY - The variety of genetic combinations, species functions and associations, both biotic and abiotic, occurring in an area, and typically with the degree representative of the indigenous flora and fauna as a benchmark. Biological diversity does not simply equal species richness as defined here.

BIOLOGICAL OPINION - (ESA§) Document stating the opinion of the Fish and Wildlife Service or the National Marine Fisheries Service on whether or not a Fish and Wildlife Service action is likely to jeopardize the continued existence of listed species, or result in the destruction or adverse modification of critical habitat [50 CFR §402.02].

BIOMASS - The total weight of matter incorporated into (living and dead) organisms.

BIOME - Any of the major terrestrial ecosystems of the world such as tundra, deciduous forest, desert, taiga.

BIOPHILIA - A term coined by E.O. Wilson to describe humans' seemingly innate, positive attitudes about, and love for, nature and natural diversity.

BIOTA - All of the organisms, including animals, plants, fungi, and microorganisms, found in a given area.

BIOTIC - Pertaining to any aspect of life.

BUILDING - A structure created to shelter any form of human activity, such as a house, barn, church, hotel, or similar structure. Building may refer to a historically related complex such as a courthouse and jail, or a house and barn [36 CFR §60.3].

BURIAL SITE - Any natural or prepared physical location, whether originally below, on, or above the surface of the earth, into which as a part of the death rite or ceremony of a culture, individual human remains are deposited [PL 101-601 §2].

CANDIDATE SPECIES - (ESA§) Under the 1996 revised listing policy, candidate species are species for which the Fish and Wildlife Service has enough scientific information to warrant proposing them for listing as endangered or threatened under the Endangered Species Act. Only those species for which there is enough information to support a listing proposal will be called "candidates." These species were formerly known as "Category 1 Candidate Species."

PRE 1996 CANDIDATE SPECIES definitions - Any species being considered by the Secretary of the Interior for listing as an endangered or threatened species [50 CFR §424.02].

Category 1 - Taxa for which substantial information exists to support proposal to list the taxon as endangered or threatened.

Category 2 - Taxa for which information exists to support proposal to list the taxon as endangered or threatened, but for which conclusive data on biological vulnerability and threat are not currently available to support proposed rules.

Category 3 - Taxa that were once being considered for listing as endangered or threatened, but are not currently receiving such consideration.

Subcategory 3A - Taxa for which persuasive evidence of extinction is available. If rediscovered, such taxa might warrant high priority for addition to the List of Endangered and Threatened Wildlife.

Subcategory 3B - Taxonomic names that, on the basis of current taxonomic understanding, usually as represented in published revisions and monographs, do not represent taxa meeting the legal definition of species in the Endangered Species Act. Future investigation could lead to re-evaluation of the listing qualifications of such entities.

Subcategory 3C - Taxa that are now considered to be more abundant and/or widespread than previously thought. Should new information suggest that any such taxon is experiencing a numerical or distributional decline, or is under a substantial threat, it may be considered for transfer to Category 1 or 2.

CARRYING CAPACITY - (Biological) The maximum population size of a given species in an area beyond which no significant increase can occur without damage occurring to the area and to the species.

CARRYING CAPACITY - (Training or outdoor recreation) The maximum amount of training or recreation activity and number of participants that a land or water area can support in a manner compatible with the objectives of the natural resources management plan without degrading existing natural resources.

CATEGORICAL EXCLUSION - (NEPA§) "Categorical Exclusion" means a category of actions which do not individually or cumulatively have a significant effect on the human environment and which have been found to have no such effect in procedures adopted by a Federal agency in implementation of these regulations [40 CFR §1507.3) and for which, therefore, neither an environmental assessment nor an environmental impact statement is required. An agency may decide in its procedures or otherwise, to prepare environmental assessments for the reasons stated in 40 CFR §1508.9 even though it is not required to do so. Any procedures under this section shall provide for extraordinary circumstances in which a normally excluded action may have significant environmental effect [40 CFR §1508.4].

CHANNEL IMPROVEMENT - The improvement of the flow characteristics of a channel by clearing, excavation, realignment, lining, or other means in order to increase its capacity; sometimes used to connote channel stabilization.

CHANNEL STABILIZATION - Erosion prevention and stabilization of velocity distribution in a channel using jetties, drops, revetments, vegetation, and other measures.

CHANNELIZATION - To straighten and deepen streams so water will move faster, a flood reduction or marsh drainage tactic that can interfere with waste assimilation capacity and disturb fish habitat.

CIRQUE - A deep steep-walled half-bowl-like recess or hollow situated high on the side of a mountain and commonly at the head of a glacial valley, and produced by the erosive activity of a mountain glacier [Bates and Jackson, 1980].

CLIMAX - The theoretical culminating stage in the succession of a natural community at a given site, at which the community is self-reproducing and thus has reached a stable State.

CLIMAX COMMUNITY - The final, stable community in an ecological succession which is able to reproduce itself indefinitely under existing conditions.

CLONE - A population of individuals all derived asexually from the same single parent.

CO-ADAPTED GENE COMPLEXES - A concept in which particular gene combinations, presumably acting in concert through a long association, function particularly well together.

COARSE FILTER - Biological inventory and land protection approach that focuses on communities, ecosystems, habitats, or landscapes.

COASTAL ZONE - The coastal waters (including lands therein and thereunder) and the adjacent shorelands (including the waters therein and thereunder) strongly influenced by each other and in proximity to the shoreline of the several coastal states. Includes islands, transitional and intertidal areas, salt marshes, wetlands, and beaches [PL 92-583].

COLD-DECIDUOUS BROADLEAF - Woody angiosperms with wide, flat leaves (e.g., paper birch) that are shed by plants during the dormant season (that portion of the year when frosts occur).

COLLUVIUM - A general term applied to any loose, heterogeneous, and incoherent mass of soil material and/or rock fragments deposited by rainwash, sheetwash, or slow continuous downslope creep, usually collecting at the base of gentle slopes or hillsides [Bates and Jackson, 1980].

COLONIZATION - The immigration of a species into a new habitat and the founding of a new population.

COMMENT - (NHPA§) The findings and recommendations of the Council membership formally provided in writing to the head of a Federal agency under §106.

COMMERCIAL ACTIVITY - (ESA§) All activities of industry and trade, including, but not limited to, the buying or selling of commodities and activities conducted for the purpose of facilitating such buying and selling; however, it does not include exhibitions of commodities by museums or similar cultural or historical organizations.

COMMUNITY - All of the plants, animals, and microbes in an area or volume; a complex association usually containing both animals and plants.

CONDITIONAL NO ADVERSE EFFECT AGREEMENT - (NHPA§) An agreement between an Agency Official and a State Historic Preservation Officer that an undertaking will have no adverse effect because the undertaking is being conducted in accordance with specified conditions.

CONFERENCE - (ESA§) A form of intra-agency cooperation involving discussions within the Service pursuant to section 7(a)(4) of the ESA. Conferences are required for Service actions likely to jeopardize species proposed for listing or category I candidates, or likely to adversely modify proposed critical habitat. Such conferences are designed to help the Service identify and resolve potential conflicts between an action and species conservation early in a project's planning. They should identity recommendations to minimize or avoid adverse effects [50 CFR §402.02, §402.10].

CONSERVE/CONSERVATION - (ESA§) To use/the use of all methods and procedures to bring any endangered species or threatened species to the point at which the measures provided pursuant to the ESA are no longer necessary.

CONSERVATION - The protection, improvement, and use of natural resources according to principles that will provide optimum public benefit.

CONSERVATION - (ESA§) The terms "conserve," "conserving," and "conservation" mean to use, or the use of, all methods and procedures necessary to restore a listed species to the point at which ESA protection no longer is necessary. These methods and procedures include, but are not limited to, all activities associated with scientific resources management. Examples of such activities are research, census, law enforcement, habitat acquisition and maintenance, propagation, live trapping, and transportation, and—in the extraordinary case where population pressures within a given ecosystem cannot otherwise be relieved—regulated taking [ESA §3(3)].

CONSERVATION BIOLOGY - An integrative approach to the protection and management of biological diversity that uses appropriate principles and experiences from basic biological fields such as genetics and ecology, from natural resource management fields such as fisheries and wildlife, and from social sciences such as anthropology, sociology, philosophy, and economics.

CONSERVATION RECOMMENDATIONS - (ESA§) Suggestions resulting from formal or informal consultation that (1) identify discretionary measures the Service can take to minimize or avoid the adverse effects of a proposed action on listed species or critical habitat; (2) identify studies, monitoring, or research to develop new information on listed species or critical habitat; and (3) include suggestions on how the Service can assist species conservation, in association with the project, under the authority of section 7(a)(1) of ESA [50 CFR §402.02].

CONSULTATION - (NHPA§) The good faith process of seeking, discussing, and considering the views of other participants in the §106 process as set forth in §800.1(b). Consultation is required per the NHPA, 36 CFR 800, and/or a MOA or CRMP.

CONSTITUENT ELEMENTS - (ESA§) Physical and biological features of critical habitat including, but not limited to: (1) space for individual and population growth, and for normal behavior; (2) food, water, air, light, minerals, or other nutritional or physiological requirements; (3) cover or shelter; (4) sites for breeding, reproduction, rearing of offspring, germination, or seed dispersal; and generally, (5) habitats that are protected from disturbance or are representative of the historic geographic and ecological distributions of a species [50 CFR 424.12(b)].

CONSUMER - An organism that consumes another.

CONSUMER (PRIMARY) - An organism which consumes green plants.

CONSUMER (SECONDARY) - An organism which consumes a primary consumer.

CONTRIBUTING PROPERTY - (NHPA§) A property in a historic district which adds to the historic architectural qualities, historic associations, or archeological values for which a property is significant because it was present during the period of significance, and time or is capable of yielding important information about a period, or it independently meets the National Register criteria.

COOPERATING AGENCY - (NEPA§) Any Federal agency other than a lead agency with jurisdiction by law or special expertise with respect to any environmental impact involved in a proposal, legislation, or other Federal action that significantly affects the quality of the human environment [40 CFR §1508.5].

CORRIDOR - A route that allows movement of individuals or taxa from one region or place to another.

COUNCIL MEMBERSHIP - (NHPA§) The full membership of the Council or a subgroup of members, numbering not less than three, appointed by the Chairman to carry out specific responsibilities under this part.

COUNCIL ON ENVIRONMENTAL QUALITY (CEQ) - The body charged with monitoring progress toward achieving the national environmental goals as set forth in NEPA. The CEQ promulgates regulations governing the NEPA process for all Federal agencies.

CREATED WETLAND - A wetland at a site where it did not formerly occur. Created wetlands are designed to meet a variety of human benefits including, but not limited to, the treatment of water pollution discharges (e.g., municipal wastewater, stormwater) and the mitigation of wetland losses permitted under Section 404 of the Clean Water Act. This term encompasses the term "constructed wetland" as used in some EPA guidance and documents.

CRITICAL ECOLOGICAL PROCESSES - The diversity and complexity of ecosystems seem to depend on a small set of biotic and abiotic, or physical processes, each operating over different scale ranges. For example, ecological conditions at the scale of the patch in a forest may depend on natural fire cycles.

CRITICAL HABITAT - (ESA§) Specific areas within the geographic area commonly occupied by a species which contain features essential to the conservation of the species and which may require special management consideration or protection. Specific areas outside of the currently occupied range of a threatened or endangered species may be determined by the Secretary of the Interior as areas essential for the conservation of the species [50 CFR §424.02].

CUESTA - A hill or ridge with a gentle slope on one side and a steep slope on the other; formed by uplifted rock outcrop consisting of strata having different resistance to erosion. [Bates and Jackson, 1980].

CULTURAL ATTRIBUTES - Evidence of past and present habitation that can be used to reconstruct or preserve human lifeways. Included in this category are structures, sites, artifacts, environments, and other relevant information, and the contexts in which these occur. Cultural attributes are found in archaeological remains of prehistoric and historic aboriginal occupations; historic European and American areas of occupation and activities; and objects and places related to the beliefs, practices, and products of existing folk or traditional communities and native American groups. Examples are campsites of prehistoric mammoth hunters, a 19th century farmstead, and a stream crossing in long-standing use by an Appalachian community for baptizing church members.

CULTURAL HISTORY RESOURCE - Potential knowledge about human cultural systems, in the form of historic and prehistoric products and by-products of man.

CULTURAL RESOURCES - Refers to those tangible and intangible aspects of cultural systems, both living and dead, that are valued by or representative of a given culture or that contain information about a culture. These resources are finite and nonrenewable and include, but are not limited to, sites, structures, districts, objects, and historic documents associated with or representative of peoples, cultures, and human activities and events either in the present or in the past. Cultural resources can also include the primary written and verbal data for interpreting and understanding those tangible resources.

CULTURAL RESOURCES MANAGEMENT - An umbrella term for activities affecting cultural resources, including the preservation, conservation, use, protection, selective investigation of, or decision not to preserve, prehistoric and historic remains. Cultural resources management specifically includes the development of ways and means, including legislation and actions to safeguard extant evidences or preserve records of the past.

CUMULATIVE EFFECTS - (ESA§) An analysis of those effects of future State, local, or private activities, not involving Federal activities, that are reasonably certain to occur within the action area of the Service action subject to consultation [50 CFR §402.02].

CUMULATIVE IMPACT - (NEPA§) "Cumulative impact" is the impact on the environment which results from the incremental impact of the action when added to other past, present, and reasonably foreseeable future actions regardless of what agency (Federal or non-Federal) or person undertakes such other actions [40 CFR §1508.7]. Cumulative impacts can result from individually minor but collectively significant actions taking place over a period of time.

DATA RECOVERY (ARCHAEOLOGICAL) - (a) Recovery and preservation (including long-term curation of a representative sample of archaeological and scientific data sufficient to address questions posed in the approved research design for the work, and the published analysis and interpretation of the meaning of such data in terms of the cultural sequence, settlement patterns, subsistence strategies and environmental conditions prevailing at the time(s) the project area was previously occupied or otherwise utilized by humans; (b) Recording, through architectural quality photographs and/or measured drawings of buildings, structures, districts, sites and objects, and deposition of such documentation in the Library of Congress as a part of the National Architectural and Engineering Record.

DECISION MAKER - Person who is responsible by regulation or position for making a given decision.

DEMOGRAPHIC BOTTLENECK - A significant, usually temporary, reduction in genetically effective population size, either from a population "crash" or a colonization event by a few founders.

DEMOGRAPHIC STOCHASTICITY - The effects of random events on the survival and reproduction of individuals.

DENSITY STRATIFICATION - The arrangement of water masses into separate, distinct horizontal layers as a result of differences in density; may be caused by differences in temperature or dissolved and suspended solids.

DESTRUCTION or **ADVERSE MODIFICATION** - (ESA§) A direct or indirect alteration that appreciably diminishes the value of critical habitat for both the survival and recovery of a listed species [50 CFR §402.02]. Such alterations include, but are not limited to, alterations adversely modifying any of those physical or biological features that were the basis for determining the habitat to be critical.

DETERMINATION OF ELIGIBILITY - A decision by the Department of the Interior that a district, site, building, structure or object meets the National Register criteria for evaluation although the property is not formally listed in the National Register [36 CFR §60.3].

DESTRUCTION or **ADVERSE MODIFICATION** - A direct or indirect alteration that appreciably diminishes the value of critical habitat for both the survival and recovery of a listed species [50 CFR §402.02].

DISCOVERY - (NHPA§) To find a cultural resource in an unexpected location or of a class not covered by previous review under the NHPA, Section 106.

DISTRICT - (NHPA§) A geographically definable area, urban or rural, that possesses a significant concentration, linkage or continuity or sites, structures, buildings, or objects united by past events or aesthetically by plan or physical development. A district may also compromise individual elements separated geographically but linked by association or history [36 CFR §60.3].

DIVERSITY - Ecological measure of number of species and their relative abundance (evenness) in a community; a low diversity refers to relatively fewer species or more uneven abundance, whereas a high diversity refers to a higher number of species or more even abundance.

DIVISION - An ecological unit in the ecoregion planning and analysis scale of the National Hierarchical Framework corresponding to subdivisions of a Domain that have the same regional climate.

DOCUMENTATION - (NHPA§) A documentary, photographic, and graphic record of a historic property. Buildings and structures are documented according to the guidelines of NPS (HABS/HAER) for deposit in the Library of Congress. Also includes documents associated with archeological effect. See 36 CFR 800.

DOMAIN - An ecological unit in the ecoregion planning and analysis scale of the National Hierarchical Framework corresponding to subcontinental divisions of broad climatic similarity that are affected by latitude and global atmospheric conditions.

DOMINANCE - The degree of influence (usually inferred from the amount of area covered) that a species exerts over a community.

DRAFT EIS - First draft of an EIS circulated for comment from other agencies and the public. It is prepared to satisfy, to the fullest extent possible, the requirements of a final statement [40CFR, §1502.9 (a)].

DREDGING - To remove earth from the bottom of water bodies.

DRUMLIN - An elongated hill or ridge of glacial drift.

DYNAMIC EQUILIBRIUM - A State of relative balance between forces or processes having opposite effects.

ECOLOGICAL ATTRIBUTES - Components of the environment and the interactions among all its living (including people) and non-living components that directly or indirectly sustain dynamic, diverse, viable ecosystems. In this category are functional and structural aspects of the environment, including aspects that require special consideration because of their unusual characteristics.

ECOLOGY - The study of the interrelationships of organisms with and within their environment.

ECOLOGICAL SUCCESSION - The natural, sequential change of species composition of a community in a given area.

ECOREGION - (1) Regions of relative homogeneity with respect to ecological composition, structure, and function. (2) A scale of planning and analysis in the National Hierarchical Framework that has broad applicability for modeling and sampling, strategic planning and assessment, and international planning. Ecoregions include Domain, Division, and Province ecological units.

ECOSYSTEM - A dynamic complex of plant, animal, fungal, and microorganism communities and their associated abiotic environment interacting as an ecological unit.

ECOSYSTEM ANALYSIS - Examination of structure, function and control mechanisms present and operating in an ecosystem.

ECOSYSTEM INTEGRITY - The ability to support and maintain a balanced, integrated, adaptive community of organisms having a species composition, diversity, and functional organization comparable to that of natural habitat of the region [Angermeier and Karr, 1994].

ECOSYSTEM SERVICES - Services provided by nature free of charge, which we collectively use in our daily lives. Examples include the production of oxygen and removal of aerials pollutants by plants, the filtration and storage of water by wetlands and streams, and the protection of soils from erosion by forests and grasslands.

EDGE EFFECTS - The ecological changes that occur at the boundaries of ecosystems. Many edge effects have negative ecological consequences (i.e., forest interior species have population reduction by edge effects).

EFFECTS (NEPA§) - "Effects" include: (a) Direct effects, which are caused by the action and occur at the same time and place. (b) Indirect effects, which are caused by the action are later in time or farther removed in distance, but are still reasonably foreseeable [40 CFR §1508.8]. Indirect effects may include growth inducing effects and other effects related to induced changes in the pattern of land use, population density or growth rate, and related effects on air and water and other natural systems, including ecosystems. Effects include ecological (such as the effects on natural resources and on the components, structures, and functioning of affected ecosystems), aesthetic, historic, cultural, economic, social, or health, whether direct, indirect, or cumulative. Effects may also include those resulting from actions which may have both beneficial and detrimental effects, even if on balance the agency believes that the effect will be beneficial.

"EFFECT", "NO EFFECT", AND "ADVERSE EFFECT" (NHPA§) - These are evaluations of the impacts of projects upon identified cultural resources. Criteria for determining effect are specifically defined in 36 CFR §800. These procedures, which must be followed by all Federal agencies for projects involving cultural resources, are outlined in 36 CFR §800.

EFFECTIVENESS MONITORING - Monitoring to determine if some activity is having the predicted or desired effect.

EFFLUENT STREAM - A stream or reach of stream fed by ground water. It is also called a gaining stream.

EMERGENCY UNDERTAKINGS - Agency actions taken in response to an officially declared disaster or State of emergency. Council regulations make special provisions for such situations at 36 CFR 800.12.

ENDANGERED PROPERTY - (NHPA§) A historic property which is or is about to be subjected to a major impact that will destroy or seriously damage the qualities of significance that make it eligible for National Historic Landmark or National Register of Historic Places designation [36 CFR §65.3].

ENDANGERED SPECIES - (ESA§) The term "endangered species" means any species which is in danger of extinction throughout all or a significant portion of the range other than a species of the Class Insecta determined by the Secretary to constitute a pest whose protection under the provisions of this chapter would present an overwhelming and overriding risk to man. Federally listed endangered species are officially designated by the DOI [50 CFR §81.1].

   a. *Endangered species.* Any species, plant or animal, which is in danger of extinction throughout all or a significant portion of its range as listed by the U.S. Department of the Interior.

   b. *Threatened species.* Any species, plant or animal, which is likely to become an endangered species within the foreseeable future throughout all or a significant portion of it's range, as listed by the U.S. Department of the Interior.

   c. *Candidate species.* Any species, plant or animal, which has sufficient data to be considered for listing as threatened or endangered by the U.S. Department of the Interior (See "Candidate Species").

   d. *State listed species.* Any species, plant or animal, which is listed by the appropriate State as threatened or endangered within the State, but may not be listed by the U.S. Department of the Interior.

ENDANGERED SPECIES PERMIT - (ESA§) A document issues by the FWS under authority of Section 10 allowing an action otherwise prohibited under Section 9 of the ESA.

ENDEMIC - A species or race native to a particular place and found only there (i.e., restricted to a specified locality).

ENDEMISM - The relative number of endemic species found within a geographic area or region. High endemism indicates that there are many native species found only in that area or region. Low endemism indicates that most species found in that area or region are also found in other places.

ENERGY BUDGET - A quantitative account sheet of inputs, transformations, and outputs of energy in an ecosystem. May apply to the long-wave radiation (heat) of an organism or a lake, or to the food taken in and subsequently reduced to heat by an individual or population.

ENERGY FLOW - The one-way passage of energy (largely chemical) through the system, entering via photosynthesis, being exchanged through feeding interactions, and at each stage, being reduced to heat.

ENHANCEMENT - An activity increasing one or more natural or artificial wetland functions. For example, the removal of a point source discharge impacting a wetland.

ENVIRONMENTAL ASSESSMENT (EA) - (NEPA§) (a) Refers to a concise public document for which a Federal agency is responsible that serves to: (1) Briefly provide sufficient evidence and analysis for determining whether to prepare an environmental impact statement or a finding of no significant impact. (2) Aid an agency's compliance with the Act when no environmental impact statement is necessary. (3) Facilitate preparation of a statement when one is necessary. (b) Shall include brief discussions of the need for the proposal, of alternatives of the environmental impacts of the proposed action and alternatives, and a listing of agencies and persons consulted [40 CFR §1508.9].

ENVIRONMENTAL GRADIENTS - The change in ecological or environmental features across space, such as changes in elevation, moisture, temperature, or soils.

ENVIRONMENTAL IMPACT STATEMENT (EIS) - (NEPA§) A detailed written statement required by NEPA for all major Federal action significantly affecting the quality of the human environment [40 CFR §1508.11].

ENVIRONMENTAL QUALITY (EQ) RESOURCE - An EQ resource is a natural or cultural form, process, system, or other phenomenon that—(1) is related to land, water, atmosphere, plants, animals, or historic or cultural objects, sites, buildings, structures, or districts; and (2) has one or more EQ attributes (ecological, cultural, aesthetic).

ENVIRONMENTAL STRESS - Perturbations likely to cause observable changes in ecosystems; usually departures from normal or optimum conditions.

ENVIRONMENTAL STOCHASTICITY - Refers to rare abiotic (e.g., unusual weather, storms) or biotic (e.g., food supply, diseases, new predators) events that affect a population and are unpredictable over relevant time and space scales.

EPILMNION - The turbulent upper layer of a lake between the surface and the horizontal plane marked by the maximum gradient of temperature and density change.

ERRATA SHEET - (NEPA§) A listing of minor factual errors and changes in a draft EIS [40 CFR $1503.4 (c)].

EUTROPHICATION - The slow aging process of a lake. During eutrophication the lake is choked by abundant plant life. Human activities that add nutrients to a water body can speed up this action.

EUTROPHIC LAKES - Lake or other contained water body rich in nutrients. Characterized by a large quantity of planktonic algae, low water transparency with high dissolved oxygen in upper layer, zero dissolved oxygen in deep layers during summer months, and large organic deposits colored brown to black. Hydrogen sulfide often present in water and deposits.

EVENNESS - The component of diversity indices that refers to the variance in relative abundance of species.

EVOLUTIONARY-ECOLOGICAL LAND ETHIC - A philosophical approach to conservation derived from the evolutionary and ecological perspective, first advanced by Aldo Leopold. In this perspective, nature is seen not as a collection of independent parts, to be used as needed, but as an integrated system of interdependent processes and components, in which the disruption of some components may greatly affect others. This ethic is the philosophical foundation for modem conservation biology.

EXOTIC SPECIES - Species that have been introduced deliberately or accidentally into an area which they are not native.

EXTANT - Living, not extinct.

EXTINCT - No longer living or existing.

EXTIRPATION - Local extinction of a taxa disappearing from a locality without becoming extinct throughout its range.

FAUNA - The animals of a given region taken collectively; as in the taxonomic sense, the species, or kinds, of animals in a region.

FEDERAL AGENCY - (NEPA§) "Federal agency" means all agencies of the Federal Government [§1508.12]. It does not mean the Congress, the Judiciary, or the President, including the performance of staff functions for the President in his Executive Office. It also includes for purposes of these regulations States and units of general local govern-ment and Indian tribes assuming NEPA responsibilities under §104(h) of the Housing and Community Development Act of 1974.

FEDERAL REGISTER - U.S. Government publication that officially publishes all Federal rules and regulations and other public notices and statements covering Federal agency actions.

FENCEROW SCALE - With respect to corridors, the connection of habitat patches by narrow rows of habitat, usually effective only for small, edge tolerant species.

FINAL EIS (FEIS)- (NEPA§) EIS published in compliance with NEPA including consideration of public comments on the draft EIS [40 CFR §1502.9(b) and 1503.4].

FINE FILTER - Biological inventory and land protection activities focused on individual rare species (Noss and Cooperrider, 1994].

FINDING OF NO SIGNIFICANT IMPACT (FONSI or FNSI) - (NEPA§) "Finding of No Significant Impact" means a document by a Federal agency briefly presenting the reasons why an action, not otherwise excluded [40 CFR §1508.4], will not have a significant effect on the human environment and for which an environmental impact

statement therefore will not be prepared. It shall include the environmental assessment or a summary of it and shall note any other environmental documents related to it [40 CFR §1501.7(a)(5)]. If the assessment is included, the finding need not repeat any of the discussion in the assessment but may incorporate it by reference.

FINE FILTER - Biological inventory and land protection activities focused on individual species.

FISH OR WILDLIFE - (ESA§) Any member of the animal kingdom, including without limitation any mammal, fish, bird, amphibian, reptile, mollusk, crustacean, arthropod or other invertebrate, and includes any part, product, egg, or offspring thereof, or the dead body or parts thereof.

FITNESS - The relative contribution of an individual's genotype to the next generation in context of the population gene pool. Relative reproductive success.

FLAGSHIP SPECIES - Species that are popular and charismatic with the public and which therefore attract popular support for their conservation.

FLOOD - A general and temporary condition of partial or complete inundation of normally dry land areas from the overflow of inland and/or tidal waters, and/or the unusual and rapid accumulation or runoff of surface waters from any source.

FLOOD CONTROL POOL - Reservoir volume above the conservation or joint-use pool that is kept empty to catch flood runoff and then evacuated as soon as possible to keep it in readiness for the next flood.

FLOOD FREQUENCY - The average interval of time between floods equal to or greater than a specified discharge or stage. It is generally expressed in years.

FLOOD PLAIN - (1) The extent of a flood plain obviously fluctuates with the size of overbank stream flows. Thus, no simple, absolute flood plain commonly exists. As a conse-quence, flood plains are delineated in terms of some specified flood size (e.g., the 50-year flood plain, the area that would be flooded by the largest stream that will, on the average occur once within a 50-year period). Such expected flood-return frequencies are estimated from historic records of stream flows. The largest, absolute flood plain that is ever likely to occur is sometimes referred to as the flood basin. The lowlands and relatively flat areas adjoining inland and coastal waters including flood-prone areas of offshore islands, including at a minimum, that area subject to a one percent or greater chance of flooding in any given year. The base floodplain is used to designate the 100-year floodplain (one percent chance floodplain). The critical action floodplain is defined as the 500-year floodplain (0.2 percent chance floodplain).

FLORA - Plants, organisms of the plant kingdom; specifically, the plants growing in a geographic area, as the Flora of Texas.

FORECLOSURE - (NHPA§) The action or inaction of a Federal agency which precludes the Agency Official from obtaining, considering and acting on the Council's comments on the full range of measures to avoid or minimize the adverse effects in accordance with §800.12(b).

FORMAL CONSULTATION - (ESA§) a process that determines whether a proposed Service action is likely to jeopardize the continued existence of listed species or destroy or adversely modify designated critical habitat. If a proposed Service action is likely to adversely affect listed species or designated critical habitat, formal consultation is required. The process (1) begins with the Service's written request and submittal of a complete initiation package; and (2) concludes with the issuance of a biological opinion and incidental take statement. Activities subject to consultation include proposed Service actions that are intended to benefit listed species but adversely affect other listed species or critical habitat in the process, or actions leaving residual adverse effects [50 CFR §402.02, 50 CFR §402.14].

FOREST MANAGEMENT - The science and practice of managing and using for human benefit the natural resources that occur on or in association with forest lands.

FOUNDER EFFECT - The principle that the founders of a new population carry only a random fraction of the genetic diversity found in the larger, parent population.

FUNCTIONS - The roles that wetlands serve, which are of value to society or the environment.

GAGING STATION - A selected section of a stream channel equipped with a gage, recorder, or other facilities for determining stream discharge.

GAME SPECIES - Fish and wildlife that may be harvested in accordance with Federal and State laws.

GAMMA DIVERSITY - Diversity at the regional scale.

GAP ANALYSIS - An assessment of the protection status of biodiversity in a specified region which looks for gaps in the representation of species or ecosystems in protected areas.

GAP DYNAMICS- The formation and replacement of patches or gaps in a landscape, as in the fall of trees and growth of new trees in that opening.

GAP FORMATION - The generation of patches in a landscape, such as the generation of openings in a forest as a result of trees falling down or dying and losing their canopy leaves.

GAP-PHASE REPLACEMENT- The regeneration of landscape, such as a forest, by succession in small patches or gaps.

GENE FLOW - The uni- or bidirectional exchange of genes between populations due to migration of individuals and subsequent successful reproduction in the new population.

GENE POOL - The sum total of genes in a sexually reproducing population.

GENETIC DRIFT - Random change in gene frequencies in small populations, where, by chance alone, some alleles will not be "sampled" or represented in the next generation.

GENETIC STOCHASTICITY - The result of random changes in the genetic makeup of individuals of a small population.

GEOGRAPHIC INFORMATION SYSTEM (GIS) - A computer system capable of storing and manipulating spatial data.

GLOBAL WARMING - The projected increase in global temperature due to the release of the by-products of fossil-fuel combustion, caused by a buildup of carbon dioxide, and other gases, that allows light from the sun's rays to heat the Earth but prevent loss of heat.

GOD SQUAD - A nickname for the Endangered Species Committee, a Cabinet-level committee that can be summoned to decide whether, in particular cases, there should be exemptions to the Act for economic reasons.

GOOD MANAGEMENT PRACTICE (GMP) - Practices that, although not mandated by law, are encouraged to promote safe operating procedures. In some states these are called Best Management Practices (BMPs).

FRAGMENTATION - The disruption of extensive habitats into isolated and small patches. Fragmentation has two negative components of biota: loss of total habitat area, and smaller, more isolated remaining habitat patches.

GREENBELT - A plot of vegetated land separating or surrounding areas of intensive residential or industrial use and devoted to recreation or park uses.

GUIDELINES - A guideline is a standard, criterion, threshold, optimum, or other desirable level for an indicator that provides a basis for judging whether an effect is beneficial or adverse. Guidelines are to be based on institutional, public, or technical recognition.

HABITAT - The environment occupied by individuals of a particular species, population, or community.

HABITAT FRAGMENTATION - Process by which habitats are increasingly subdivided into smaller units, resulting in their increased insularity as well as losses of total habitat area.

HEAD OF THE AGENCY - (NHPA§) The chief official of the agency responsible for all aspects of the agency's actions. If a State, local or tribal government has been delegated responsibility for compliance with §106, the head of that unit of government shall be considered the head of the agency.

HETEROZYGOUS - The situation in which an individual has two different alleles at a given gene locus.

HISTORIC AMERICAN BUILDINGS SURVEY (HABS) - A program established in 1933 to survey and have measured drawings made of those structures identified as nationally significant. The drawings are stored at the Library of Congress in Washington, D.C.

HISTORIC DISTRICT - (NHPA§) A geographically definable area, urban or rural, that possesses a significant concentration, linkage, or continuity of historic sites, structures, or objects unified by past events or aesthetically by plan or physical developments or by similarity of human use. A district also may be composed of individual elements that are separated geographically but are linked by association or history.

HISTORIC PRESERVATION - Identification, evaluation, documentation, curation, acquisition, protection, rehabilitation, restoration, management, stabilization, maintenance, recording, and reconstruction of cultural resources, and any combination of the foregoing [16 USC §470w(8)].

HISTORIC PROPERTY - (NHPA§) Any prehistoric or historic district, site, building, structure, or object included in, or eligible for, inclusion on the Nation Register. The term includes artifacts, records, and material remains related to such property [16 USC §470w(5)]. The term further includes properties of traditional religious and cultural importance to an Indian tribe or Native Hawaiian organization which meet the criteria for inclusion in the National Register of Historic Places. The term "eligible for inclusion in the National Register" includes both properties formally determined as such in accordance with regulations of the Secretary of the Interior and all other properties that meet National Register listing criteria.

HISTORIC RESOURCES - Evidence of human activities that represent facets of the history or prehistory of the nation, State or locality; places where historic or prehistoric events occurred even though no evidence of the event remains; places associated with a personality important in history or structures or evidence representative of traditional lifeways or practices. Cultural resources can also include districts, sites, structures, and objects important to an indigenous culture, a subculture, or a community for traditional spiritual, religious, or magical reasons, as well as places important for the artistic, recreational, or other community activities that take place there.

HISTORICAL ARCHAEOLOGY - The subdiscipline of archaeology concerned with the remains left by literate societies (in contrast to prehistoric archaeology, although the distinction is not always clear-cut). In the United States, historical archaeology generally deals with the evidences of Euro-American societies and with the evidences of aboriginal societies after the time of major cultural disruption or material change due to Euro-American contact.

HUMAN ENVIRONMENT - (NEPA§) "Human Environment" is interpreted comprehensively to include the natural and physical environment and the relationship of people with that environment. (See the definition of "effects" [40 CFR §1508.8)]. This means that economic or social effects are not intended by themselves to require preparation of an environmental impact statement. When an environmental impact statement is prepared and economic or social and natural or physical environmental effects are interrelated, then the environmental impact statement will discuss all of these effects on the human environment.

HYDROLOGIC CYCLE - The continual exchange of moisture between the earth and the atmosphere, consisting of evaporation, condensation, precipitation (rain or snow), stream runoff, absorption into the soil, and evaporation in repeating cycles.

HYDROLOGY - The science dealing with the properties, distribution, and circulation of water both on the surface and under the earth.

HYPOLIMNION - Colder bottom zone of a stratified lake, extending from the thermocline to the bottom.

IMPACTS - See **EFFECTS**.

IMPLEMENTATION MONITORING - Monitoring to determine if a planned action is being taken, sometimes referred to as compliance monitoring.

INBREEDING - The mating of individuals who are more closely related than by chance alone.

INBREEDING DEPRESSION - A reduction in fitness and vigor of individuals as a result of increased homozygosity through inbreeding in a normally outbreeding population.

INCIDENTAL TAKE - (ESA§) Takings otherwise prohibited, that result from, but are not the purpose of, carrying out an otherwise lawful activity conducted by the Federal agency [50 CFR §402.02].

INCREMENTAL - Amount of change occurring in an environmental system during some measurable time period.

INDIAN LANDS - All lands under the jurisdiction or control of an Indian Tribe [36 CFR §800.2].

INDIAN TRIBE or TRIBE - (NHPA§) An Indian Tribe, band, nation, or other organized group or community including a Native village, Regional corporation or Village Corporation as those terms are defined in Section 3 of the Alaska Native Claims Settlement Act [42 USC §1602], which is recognized as eligible for the special programs and services provided by the United States to Indians because of their status as Indians [NHPA §301(4)].

INDICATOR - An indicator is a characteristic of a EQ resource that serves as a direct or indirect means of measuring or otherwise describing changes in the quantity and/or quality of an EQ attribute. (1) Quantity indicators describe how much of a resource attribute is present in terms of physical size, magnitude or dimension. They are usually measurable in numeric units (example: The indicator "depth" is measurable in meters, feet, etc.); but they may be described in non-numeric terms (example: The indicator "amount" could be described on a scale of "abundant/adequate/scarce/unique"). The diversity or stability of an ecosystem or natural community may be a numeric or non-numeric indicator. (2) Quality indicators are characteristics that describe the degree or grade of an attribute's desirability (how good or how bad). Some quality indicators are measurable in numeric units (example: The indicator "landscape beauty" measured by an ordinal ranking of landscapes); some represent composites of numeric measurements (example: The indicator "Class 'A' water quality" is a composite of measurements of concentrations of dissolved oxygen, suspended solids, etc.); some are described in non-numeric units (example: The indicator "desirability of scent" described on a scale of "offensive/neutral/pleasant").

INFILTRATION - The penetration of water through the ground surface into subsurface soil.

INFORMAL CONSULTATION - (ESA§) An optional process that includes all intra-Service discussions and correspondence to determine whether a proposed Service action is likely to adversely affect listed species or critical habitat. If a proposed Service action is likely to result in adverse effects to listed species or designated critical habitat, formal consultation is required. This formal consultation requirement includes activities that will have an overall beneficial effect on a listed species, but would result in some adverse effects [50 CFR §402.02, 50 CFR §402.13].

INTEGRITY - The authenticity of a property's historic identity, evidenced by the survival of physical characteristics that existed during the property's historic or prehistoric period.

INTENSITY - (NEPA§) Severity of an impact [40 CFR §1508.27(b)].

INTERESTED PARTY - (NHPA§) Any individual or organization that has indicated to the Agency Official, State Historic Preservation Officer or Council its concern with the effects of an undertaking on historic properties.

INTERRELATED ACTIONS - (ESA§) Actions that are part of a larger action and depend on the larger action for their justification [50 CFR §402.02].

INTERSPECIFIC VARIATION - Variation between species.

INTRASPECIFIC VARIATION - Variation among individuals or populations of the same species.

INVENTORY - The data base or data bases compiled through the processes of identifying and evaluating cultural or natural resources.

IRREVERSIBLE and **IRRETRIEVABLE** - Cannot be corrected, or reversed; cannot be retrieved; impossible to recoup, repair, or overcome.

IS LIKELY TO ADVERSELY AFFECT - (ESA§) The appropriate conclusion if any adverse effect to listed species or critical habitat may occur as a direct or indirect result of the proposed action or its interrelated or interdependent actions. In the event the overall effect of the proposed action is beneficial to listed species or critical habitat, but is also likely to cause some adverse effects, the proposed action must be determined "is likely to adversely affect." Such a determination requires formal intra-Service Section 7 consultation.

IS LIKELY TO JEOPARDIZE PROPOSED SPECIES, CATEGORY 1 CANDIDATES, OR ADVERSELY MODIFY PROPOSED CRITICAL HABITAT - (ESA§) The appropriate conclusion when the Service identifies situations in which the proposed action is likely to jeopardize the continued existence of a species proposed for listing, Category 1 candidates, or adversely modify an area proposed for designation as critical habitat. If this conclusion is reached, intra-Service conference is required.

IS NOT LIKELY TO ADVERSELY AFFECT - (ESA§) The appropriate conclusion when effects on the species or critical habitat are expected to be beneficial, discountable, or insignificant. Beneficial effects have contemporaneous positive effects without any adverse effects to the species or habitat. Insignificant effects relate to the size of the impact and should never reach the scale where take occurs. Discountable effects are those extremely unlikely to occur. Based on best judgment, a person would not (1) be able to meaningfully measure, detect, or evaluate insignificant effects or (2) expect discountable effects to occur.

JEOPARDIZE THE CONTINUED EXISTENCE OF - (ESA§) To engage in an action that reasonably would be expected, directly or indirectly, to reduce appreciably the likelihood of both the survival and recovery of a listed species in the wild by reducing the genetic diversity, reproduction, numbers, or distribution of that species [50 CFR §402.02].

JURISDICTION BY LAW - (NEPA§) "Jurisdiction by law" means agency authority to approve, veto, or finance all or part of the proposal [§1508.15].

KEYSTONE SPECIES - A species that plays a pivotal role in an ecosystem and upon which a large part of the community depends.

LAKE TURNOVER - The complete top-to-bottom circulation of water in a lake which occurs when the density of the surface water is the same or slightly greater than that at the lake bottom; most temperate zone lakes circulate in spring and again in fall.

LANDMARK - A National Historic Landmark is a district, site, building, structure, or object, in public or private ownership, judged by the Secretary of Interior to possess national significance in American history, archaeology, architecture, engineering, and culture, and so designated by the Secretary [36 CFR §65.3].

LANDSCAPE - Landform, water, and landcover forming a distant visual pattern; an expanse of natural and man-made scenery seen by the eye in one view.

LANDSCAPE COMPATIBILITY - The degree to which landscape elements/characteristics are unified within their setting.

LANDSCAPE COMPOSITION - The arrangement of objects and voids in the landscape that can be categorized by their spatial arrangement. Some spatial compositions, especially those which are distinctly focal, enclosed, detail or feature oriented landscape, are more vulnerable to modifications than panoramic, canopied or ephemeral landscapes.

LANDSCAPE MOSAIC SCALE - With respect to corridors, the connection of major landscape features using broad habitats, including representation of interior habitat, as corridors.

LEACHATE - Materials that pollute water as it seeps through solid waste.

LEACHING - The process by which nutrient chemicals or contaminants are dissolved and carried away by water, or are moved into a lower layer of soil.

LEAD AGENCY - (NEPA§) Agency or agencies preparing or having taken primary responsibility for preparing the environmental impact statement [40 CFR §1508.16].

LEGISLATION - (NEPA§) "Legislation" includes a bill or legislative proposal to Congress developed by or with the significant cooperation and support of a Federal agency, but does not include requests for appropriations. The test for significant cooperation is whether the proposal is in fact predominantly that of the agency rather than another source. Drafting does not by itself constitute significant cooperation. Proposals for legislation include requests for ratification of treaties. Only the agency which has primary responsibility for the subject matter involved will prepare a legislative environmental impact statement [§1508.17].

LEGISLATIVE EIS - (NEPA§) An EIS included in a recommendation or report on a legislative proposal to Congress [40 CFR, §1506.8 and 1508.18].

LIFE ZONES - A classification of macroclimatic conditions based on temperature and precipitation that has been widely applied in tropical environments to delineate zones dominated by vegetative communities of characteristic physiognomy and composition.

LIMITING FACTOR - (1) An environmental factor (or factors) which limits the distribution and/or abundance of an organism or its population, i.e., the factor which is closest to the physiological limits of tolerance of that organism. (2) A particular element of the natural or man-made resources which limits the development or use of a recreation or natural resource.

LISTED SPECIES - (ESA§) Any species of fish, wildlife, or plant which has been determined to be endangered or threatened under §4 of the ESA. Listed species are found in 50 CFR §17.11-17.12.

LOCAL GOVERNMENT - (NHPA§) A city, county, parish, township, municipality, borough, or other general purpose political subdivision of a State.

LONG-TERM IMPACT - One that continues a relatively long time after an action is completed. (See Short-term use.)

MACROINVERTEBRATES - The larger or more prominent invertebrates; abundance and species composition of macroinvertebrates in freshwater streams is often measured as an indication of impacts to a stream or watershed.

MAGNITUDE - Size of an impact.

MAJOR FEDERAL ACTION - (NEPA§) "Major Federal action" includes actions with effects that may be major and which are potentially subject to Federal control and responsibility. Major reinforces but does not have a meaning independent of significantly [40 CFR §1508.27]. Actions include the circumstance where the responsible officials fail to act and that failure to act is reviewable by courts or administrative tribunals under the Administrative Procedure Act or other applicable law as agency action.

MATERIAL REMAINS - Artifacts, objects, specimens, and other physical evidence that are excavated or removed in connection with efforts to locate, evaluate, document, study, preserve or recover a prehistoric or historic resource [36 CFR §79.4].

MATRIX - The most extensive and most connected habitat type in a landscape, which often plays the dominant role in landscape processes.

MATTER - (NEPA§) "Matter" includes for purposes of Part 1504: (a) With respect to the Environmental Protection Agency, any proposed legislation, project, action or regulation as those terms are used in §309 (a) of the Clean Air Act [42 U.S.C. 7609]. (b) With respect to all other agencies, any proposed major Federal action to which §102(2)(C) of NEPA applies [§1508.19].

MAXIMUM PROBABLE FLOOD - The largest flood for which there is any reasonable expectancy in the geographical region involved.

MEAN HIGH WATER - A tidal datum: the arithmetic average of the high water heights observed over a specific 18.6 Metonic Cycle (the National Datum Epoch).

MESOPREDATORS - Medium sized predators (i.e., raccoons and coyotes).

METAPOPULATION - A network of semi-isolated populations with some level of regular or intermittent migration and gene flow among them, in which individual populations may go extinct but then be recolonized from other populations.

MIGRATORY BIRDS - Birds, whatever their origin, which belong to a species listed in 50 CFR §10.13, or which has a mutation or a hybrid of any such species, including any part, nest, or egg of such birds, or any product, whether or not manufactured, which consists, or is composed in whole or part of any such bird species or any part, nest, or egg thereof [50 CFR §10.12].

MINIMUM DYNAMIC AREA - The smallest area necessary for a reserve to have a complete, natural disturbance regime in which discrete habitat patches may be colonized from other patches within the reserve.

MITIGATION - (NEPA§) "Mitigation" includes: (a) Avoiding the impact altogether by not taking a certain action or parts of an action. (b) Minimizing impacts by limiting the degree or magnitude of the action and its implementation. (c) Rectifying the impact by repairing, rehabilitating, or restoring the affected environment. (d) Reducing or eliminating the impact over time by preservation and maintenance operations during the life of the action. (e) Compensating for the impact by replacing or providing substitute resources or environments [40 CFR §1508.20].

MITIGATION - (NHPA§)Treatment of an adverse effect on cultural resources by taking actions such as; archeological data recovery, architectural documentation, or design of new construction to be compatible with existing architectural fabric.

MORAINE - A mound, ridge, or other distinct accumulation of unsorted, unstratified glacial drift, predominantly till, deposited chiefly by direct action of glacier ice, in a variety of topographic land forms that are independent of control by the surface on which the drift lies [Bates and Jackson, 1980].

MULTIPLE-USE - The integrated management of all natural resources, each with the other, to achieve the optimum use and enjoyment while maintaining the environmental qualities, ecological relationships and aesthetic values in proper balance.

MUTAGENIC - Causing mutations.

MUTATION - Broadly defined as any genetic change in an organism, either from an alteration of DNA composing individual genes or from a shift in the structure or number of chromosomes. Mutations create the new raw material on which evolution is based.

MUTUALISM - Symbiosis in which both of the partner species benefit.

NATURAL CATASTROPHE - A major environmental cause of mortality, such as a volcanic eruption, that can affect the probability of survival for both large and small populations.

NATIONAL ENVIRONMENTAL POLICY ACT (NEPA) of 1969, as amended, Public Law 91-190, 42 U.S.C. Section 4321, et seq.

NATIONAL HISTORIC LANDMARK (NHL) - (NHPA§) A district, site, building, structure or object that the Secretary of the Interior has determined possesses exceptional value in commemorating or illustrating the history of the United

States and which has been so designated under the authority of the Historic Sites Act of 1935, 16 U.S.C. 461 et seq. NHLs are listed in the National Register. Effects to NHLs are reviewed in accordance with the NHPA, section 110(f), and 36 CFR 800.10.

NATIONAL HISTORIC LANDMARKS PROGRAM - The program that identifies, designates, recognizes, lists, and monitors National Historic Landmarks conducted by the Secretary of Interior through the National Park Service [36 CFR §65.3].

NATIONAL HISTORIC PRESERVATION ACT OF 1966 - NHPA

NATIONAL REGISTER - (NHPA§) The National Register of Historic Places maintained by the Secretary of the Interior.

NATIONAL REGISTER CRITERIA - (NHPA§) The criteria established by the Secretary of the Interior for use in evaluating the eligibility of properties for the National Register [36 CFR Part 60].

NATIONAL REGISTER OF HISTORIC PLACES - The National Register is the official record of all districts, sites, structures, and objects of local, State, and national significance. It was established by the NHPA of 1966, which expanded the 1935 national landmarks concept [36 CFR §65.3]. To be eligible for inclusion in the National Register, properties can be publicly or privately owned but must meet the criteria found in 36 CFR §800 or 36 CFR §1202.6. The program is administered by NPS.

NATIONAL TRAILS SYSTEM - A network of nationally significant scenic and recreation trails: (1) Scenic; extended trails which provide outdoor recreation opportunities and conserve nationally significant scenic, historic, natural or cultural qualities of areas through which they pass, (2) Recreation; trails which provide a variety of outdoor recreation uses in or reasonably accessible to urban areas.

NATIONAL WILD AND SCENIC RIVERS SYSTEM - Rivers and their immediate environments which possess outstanding scenic, recreational, geologic, fish and wildlife, historic, cultural and other similar values, and are preserved in a free flowing condition: (1) Recreation; rivers or sections of rivers readily accessible by road or railroad, that may have some development along their shoreline and that may have undergone some impoundment or diversion in the past, (2) Scenic; rivers or sections of rivers free of impoundments, with shorelines or watersheds still largely undeveloped, but accessible in places by roads, and (3) Wild: rivers or sections of rivers free of impoundments and generally inaccessible except by trails, with watersheds or shorelines essentially primitive and waters unpolluted.

NATIVE - A naturally occurring species that has not been introduced from somewhere else by humans.

NATIVE AMERICAN - Of, or relating to, a tribe, people, or culture that is indigenous to the United States.

NATIVE HAWAIIAN - (NHPA§) Any individual which is a descendent of the aboriginal people who, prior to 1778, occupied and exercised sovereignty in the area that now constitutes the State of Hawaii.

NATURAL RESOURCES - The viable and/or renewable products of nature.

NATURAL SELECTION - The differential contribution of offspring to the next generation by various genetic types belonging to the same population; the mechanism of evolution proposed by Darwin.

NEEDLE-LEAVED EVERGREEN - Woody gymnosperms with green, needle-shaped, or scale-like leaves (e.g., black spruce) that are retained by plants throughout the year.

NEOTROPICAL - Relating to or being from the region from southern Mexico and the West Indies to South America (i.e., neotropical birds).

NEPA PROCESS - (NEPA§) "NEPA process" means all measures necessary for compliance with the requirements of Section 2 and Title I of NEPA [§1508.21].

NICHE - A vague but useful term, meaning the range of sets of environmental conditions which an organism's behavioral morphological and physiological adaptations enable it to occupy; the role an organism plays in the functioning of a natural system, in contrast to habitat.

NON-CONTRIBUTING PROPERTY - A property in a historic district which does not add to the historic architectural qualities, historic associations, or archeological values for which a property is significant; or due to alterations, disturbances, additions, or other changes, it no longer possesses historic integrity reflecting its character at that time or is incapable of yielding important information about the period; or it does not independently meet the National Register criteria.

NONGAME SPECIES - Species not harvested for recreation or subsistence purposes.

NONPOINT SOURCE - A contributing factor to water pollution that can't be traced to a specific spot; like agricultural fertilizer runoff, sediment from construction.

NOMINATE - To complete and submit National Park Service forms proposing that a resource be included in the National Register. Nominations can be made for individual resources, multiple resources, or thematic groups [36 CFR §60.4].

NOTICE OF AVAILABILITY (NOA) - Notification placed in the *Federal Register* by an agency announcing that an EIS or other environmental document is available for public review.

NOTICE OF INTENT (NOI) - (NEPA§) Notice that a draft EIS will be prepared and considered. It should contain: (1) a description of the proposed action and possible alternatives, (2) the proposed scoping process and schedule, (3) the name and address of the person who can give more information [40 CFR §1508.22].

NOTICE OF VIOLATION - (NHPA§) A notification from the Council of its finding in accordance with Sec. 800.12(d) that an Agency Official has failed to comply with Section 106.

NOXIOUS WEEDS - Plant species identified by Federal or several State laws as requiring control or eradication.

NUTRIENTS - Inorganic compounds (e.g., phosphates, nitrates) essential for plant growth. Waters with heavy growth of aquatic weeds and algae generally have high levels of nutrients.

OLIGOTROPHIC LAKES - Usually, deep clear lakes with low nutrient supplies. They contain little organic matter and have a relatively high dissolved oxygen level.

OVERTURN - The complete circulation or mixing of the upper and lower waters of a lake when the temperatures (and densities) are similar.

OVERVIEW - (NHPA§) A report based on the collection and analysis of existing information that summarizes what is known about the cultural resources on the installation, suggests the likelihood of additional cultural resources, and provides recommendations for meeting the requirements of this regulation.

PALEONTOLOGICAL AREA - Areas which have been designated by the Forest Service as containing significant remains (usually fossilized) by flora and fauna (nonhuman) of geologic time periods before the appearance of man.

PANMICTIC - Random breeding among individuals of a population.

PARADIGM - An established pattern of thinking. Often applied to a dominant ecological or evolutionary viewpoint, e.g., during earlier decades the dominant paradigm held that communities were shaped by equilibrial processes.

PATCH DYNAMICS - A conceptual approach to ecosystem and habitat analysis that emphasizes dynamics of heterogeneity within a system. Diverse patches of habitat created by natural disturbance regimes are seen as critical to maintenance of diversity.

PHENOTYPE - The observed traits of an organism, created by an interaction of the organism's genotype and the environment in which it developed.

PLANNING AREA - The planning area is a geographic space with an identified boundary that includes: (a) The area identified in the study's authorizing document; (b) The locations of alternative plans, often called "project areas"; and (c) The locations of resources that would be directly, indirectly, or cumulatively affected by alternative plans, often called the "affected area."

PLANT - (ESA§) Any member of the plant kingdom, including seeds, roots and other parts thereof [ESA §3(14)].

PLANT ASSOCIATION - A potential natural plant community of definite floristic composition and uniform appearance.

PLANT COMMUNITY - A group of one or more populations of plants in a common spatial arrangement.

PLASTICITY - Genetically based, environmentally induced variation in characteristics of an organism.

PLAYA - A term used in the southwestern U.S. for a dry, vegetation-free, flat area at the lowest part of an undrained desert basin, underlain by stratified clay, silt, or sand, and commonly by soluble salts [Bates and Jackson, 1980].

POLAR - A classification of climate based on the Koppen System for regions where the warmest month is colder than 50°F (10°C). [Bailey, 1980].

POPULATION - A grouping of organisms from the same species occurring more or less contiguously.

POPULATION VIABILITY ANALYSIS (PVA) - A comprehensive analysis of the many environmental and demographic factors that affect survival of a population, usually applied to small populations at risk of extinction.

POTENTIAL NATURAL COMMUNITY - The biotic community that would be established if all successional sequences of its ecosystem were completed without additional human-caused disturbance under present environmental conditions. Grazing by native fauna, natural disturbances, such as drought, floods, fire, insects, and disease, are inherent in the development of potential natural communities which may include naturalized exotic species.

POTENTIAL NATURAL VEGETATION - The vegetation that would exist today if man were removed from the scene and if the plant succession after his removal were telescoped into a single moment. The time compression eliminates the effects of future climatic fluctuations, while the effects of man's earlier activities are permitted to stand. The maps and descriptions of potential natural vegetation developed by Kuchler (1964) for the 48 conterminous States are among the most widely used.

POTHOLE - A shallow depression, generally less than 10 acres in area, occurring between dunes on a prairie, often containing an intermittent pond or marsh and serving as a nesting place for waterfowl.

PREPARATION PLAN - Guidance and management document prepared to assist in the scoping, formulation, and preparation of an EIS.

PRESCRIBED BURNING - Skillful application of fire to natural fuels under conditions of weather, fuel moisture, soil moisture, etc., to allow confinement of the fire to a predetermined area while producing the intensity of heat and rate of spread required to accomplish certain planned benefits. These benefits may include all or one or more objectives of silviculture, wildlife management, grazing, hazard reduction, etc. Its objective is to employ fire scientifically to realize maximum net benefits at minimum damage and acceptable cost.

PRESERVATION - (NHPA§) Preservation or historic preservation includes identification, evaluation, recordation, documentation, curation, acquisition, protection, management, rehabilitation, restoration, stabilization, maintenance and reconstruction, or any combination of Programmatic Agreement (PA). A form of a Memorandum of Agreement developed by a Federal agency for a large or complex project or a class of undertakings that would otherwise require numerous individual requests for Advisory Council comments under Section 106. Procedures for developing a Programmatic Agreement are contained in the Council regulations at 36 CFR 800.13.

PRESERVATIONIST - A person concerned with natural things for their intrinsic value rather than for some utilitarian purpose; alternately, a person interested in stopping human-induced changes.

PRIMARY IMPACT - (NEPA§) Direct effect of the proposed action or alternatives [40 CFR $1508.8].

PRIMARY SUCCESSION - Succession beginning with bare rock or soil.

PRISTINE State - A State of nature without human effect or with negligible human effect.

PRODUCER - PRODUCER ORGANISM - An organism which can synthesize organic material using inorganic materials and an external energy source (light or chemical). See autotroph; also, biotic pyramIbid.

PRODUCTION - The amount of organic material produced by biological activity in an area or volume.

PRODUCTIVITY - The rate of production or organic matter produced by biological activity in an area or volume (e.g., grams per square meter per day, or other units of weight or energy per area or volume and time).

PRODUCTIVITY, GROSS PRIMARY - The rate of synthesis of organic material produced by photosynthesis (or chemosynthesis), including that which is used up in respiration by the producer organism.

PRODUCTIVITY, NET PRIMARY - The rate of accumulation of organic material in plant tissues. Gross primary productivity less respiratory utilization by the producer organism.

PRODUCTIVITY, SECONDARY - The rate of production of organic materials by consumer organisms (animals) which eat plants (which are the primary producers).

PROGRAMMATIC EIS - (NEPA§) An EIS that evaluates environmental impacts of broad agency action such as the setting of national policies or the development of programs [40 CFR §1502.4 and 1508.28].

PROTECTION - The act or process of applying measures designed to affect the physical condition of a property by defending or guarding it from deterioration, loss or attack, or to cover or shield the property from danger or injury. In the case of buildings, structures, and landscapes, such treatment is generally of a temporary nature and anticipates future historic preservation treatment. In the case of archeological sites, the protective measure may be temporary or permanent.

PROPERTY - A site, building, object, structure, or a collection of such items that forms a district [36 CFR §65.3].

PROPONENT- (NEPA§) The proponent is the organization/person that has the need for the proposed action to meet his mission requirements and typically will be the primary user of the project. If no one identifies themselves as the proponent, none being interested in having the project implemented, there is no need to continue the NEPA process or the project. Proponent identification is dependent on the nature and scope of a proposed action.

PROPOSAL- (NEPA§) "Proposal" exists at that stage in the development of an action when an agency subject to the Act has a goal and is actively preparing to make a decision on one or more alternative means of accomplishing that goal and the effects can be meaningfully evaluated. Preparation of an environmental impact statement on a proposal should be timed [§1502.5] so that the final statement may be completed in time for the statement to be included in any recommendation or report on the proposal. A proposal may exist in fact as well as by agency declaration that one exists [§1508.23].

PROPOSED CRITICAL HABITAT - (ESA§) Habitat proposed in the *Federal Register* to be designated or revised as critical habitat for any listed or proposed species.

PROPOSED SPECIES - A fish, wildlife, or plant species that is proposed in the *Federal Register* to be listed as endangered or threatened under the ESA.

PROVINCE - An ecological unit in the ecoregion planning and analysis scale of the National Hierarchical Framework corresponding to subdivisions of a Division that conform to climatic subzones controlled mainly by continental weather patterns.

PUBLIC LANDS - Lands owned and administered by the Federal agencies including the national park system, national wildlife refuge system, and national forest system.

REASONABLE and PRUDENT ALTERNATIVES - (ESA§) Alternative actions identified during formal consultation that can be implemented in a manner consistent with the intended purpose of the action, that can be implemented consistent with the scope of the Federal agency's legal authority and jurisdiction, that are economically and technologically feasible, and that the FWS or NMFS believes would avoid the likelihood of jeopardizing the continued existence of listed species or result in the destruction or adverse modification of critical habitat.

REASONABLE and PRUDENT MEASURES - (ESA§) Those nondiscretionary actions the FWS or NMFS believes necessary or appropriate to minimize the impacts, that is, the amount or extent, of incidental take.

RECHARGE AREA - (1) An area in which water is absorbed that eventually reaches the zone of saturation in one or more aquifers. (2) Area where underground aquifers meet the land surfaces and replenish the groundwater supply. Composed of highly permeable material, recharge areas are usually located in topographical positions that permit runoff to be channeled or concentrated onto their surfaces from upslope drainage areas; they are described in terms of permeability and area (either in acres or square miles).

RECLAMATION - Actions taken to restore a disturbed area to an environmentally stable and productive condition.

RECORD OF DECISION (ROD) - (NEPA§) The written record of the decision made on a proposal after completion of an EIS. Must State what the decision was, identify all alternatives considered and specify which alternative was environmentally preferable, and State whether all practicable means to avoid or minimize environmental harm from the selected alternative have been adopted and if not, why not. Additionally, it states the monitoring and mitigation program adopted, and may discuss preferences among alternatives based on non-environmental factors.

RECORD OF ENVIRONMENTAL CONSIDERATION (REC) - (NEPA§) A document used to explain how an action is covered by a categorical exclusion or by an existing EA/EIS.

RECOVERY - The improvement in the status of listed species to the point at which listing is no longer appropriate under the criteria set out in §4(a)(1) of the ESA.

RECOVERY PLAN - A plan developed by the FWS or NMFS, as required by the ESA, for the conservation, survival, and recovery of a listed species. This document delineates, justifies, and schedules the research and management actions necessary to support recovery of a species, including those actions that, if successfully undertaken, are likely to permit reclassification or delisting of the species.

RECREATION AREA - A tract of land and water area of substantial size which may contain one or several recreational activities on a project. Usually reached by a single access road for control purposes.

RECREATION BENEFITS - The tangible and intangible gains to the public directly attributable to recreation activities at a water resources project.

RECREATION DAY - A measure of recreation use consisting of a visit by one individual to a recreation site, area or project for recreation purposes during all or any portion of a 24-hour day. May consist of several activity days.

RECREATIONAL DEVELOPMENT - Any type of facility or improvement which are planned, designed, developed and managed for recreational purposes.

RECREATIONAL EXPERIENCE - The physical and psychological benefits or liabilities which are derived from the pursuit of recreational activities.

RECRUITMENT - (ESA§) The designation and management of habitat for the purpose of attracting T&E populations to that habitat area.

REFERRING AGENCY - (NEPA§) "Referring agency" means the Federal agency which has referred any matter to the Council after a determination that the matter is unsatisfactory from the standpoint of public health or welfare or environmental quality [§1508.24].

REGIONAL SCALE - With respect to corridors, the largest scale of activity, in which major swaths of habitat connect regional networks of reserves.

REHABILITATION - The act or process of returning a property to a State of utility through repair or alteration which makes possible an efficient contemporary use while preserving those portions or features of the property which are significant to its historical, architectural and cultural values.

RELIGIOUS REMAINS - Material remains that have been determined are of traditional, religious, or sacred importance to an Indian tribe or other group because of customary use in religious rituals or spiritual activities. This determination is made in consultation with appropriate Indian tribes or other groups [36 CFR §79.4].

RELOCATION - The act or process of moving a structure from its original location to protect it from an adverse effect.

RESCUE EFFECT - The recolonization of a habitat with a sub-population from a metapopulation that has gone locally extinct.

RESIDENCE - The ability of any system, e.g., and ecosystem, to resist or to recover from stress.

RESILIENT - A measure of the rate at which a community will rebound following a single disturbance (Pimm 1984].

RESOURCE CONSERVATION ETHIC - A philosophical approach to conservation derived from the views of forester Gifford Pinchot, based on the utilitarian philosophy of John Stuart Mill. Nature is seen as a collection of natural resources to be used for "the greatest good of the greatest number for the longest time."

RESTORATION - An activity returning a wetland from a disturbed or altered condition with lesser acreage or functions to a previous condition with greater wetland acreage or functions. For example, restoration might involve the plugging of a drainage ditch to restore the hydrology to an area that was a wetland before the installation of the drainage ditch.

RESTORATION - The act or process of accurately recovering the form and details of property and its setting as it appeared at a particular period of time by means of the removal of later work or by the replacement of missing earlier work [36 CFR §68.2].

RIFFLE-POOL CONCENTRATION - Arrangement within a stream of alternation riffles (i.e., deep, rapidly-flowing, shallow areas) and pools (i.e., deep slow-moving areas). Riffles are areas of high productivity by phytoplankton; pools provide resting places for fish and other organisms. The specific configuration of riffles and pools is important to the potential of a stream as aquatic habitat.

RIPARIAN - Areas next to or substantially influenced by water. These may include areas adjacent to rivers, lakes, or estuaries. These areas often include wetlands.

RIPRAP - Material placed on a stream bank and bed for protection from stream or wave action; can consist of broken rock or other materials such as car bodies or trees.

RISK - Situations of risk are conventionally defined as those in which the potential outcomes can be described in reasonably well known probability distributions. For example, if it is known that a river will flood to a specific level on the average of once in 20 years, a situation of risk, rather than uncertainty, exists.

ROMANTIC - TRANSCENDENTAL CONSERVATION ETHIC - A philosophical approach to conservation derived from the writings of Emerson, Thoreau, and Muir, in which nature is seen in a quasi-religious sense, and as having uses other than human economic gain. This ethic strives to preserve nature in a wild and pristine State.

SACRED OBJECT - Specific ceremonial objects which are needed by traditional Native American religious leaders for the practice of their traditional Native American religions by their present adherents.

SALMONIDS - Fish of the family Salmonidae, which includes the trout and salmon.

SALT WATER INTRUSION - The movement of salt water inland into subterranean aquifers.

SCALE - The degree of resolution at which ecological processes, structures, and changes across space and time are observed and measured.

SCENIC RIVER - Wild and Scenic River Act usage. Those rivers or selections of rivers that are free of impoundments, with shorelines of watersheds still largely primitive and shorelines largely undeveloped, but accessible in places by roads.

SCOPE - (NEPA§) Scope consists of the range of actions, alternatives, and impacts to be considered in an environmental impact statement. The scope of an individual statement may depend on its relationships to other statements [40 CFR §1502.28]. To determine the scope of environmental impact statements, agencies shall consider 3 types of actions, 3 types of alternatives, and 3 types of impacts. They include: (a) Actions (other than unconnected single actions) which may be: (1) Connected actions, which means that they are closely related and therefore should be discussed in the same impact statement. Actions are connected if they: (i) Automatically trigger other actions which may require environmental impact statements. (ii) Cannot or will not proceed unless other actions are taken previously or simultaneously. (iii) Are interdependent parts of a larger section and depend on the larger action for their justification. (2) Cumulative actions, which when viewed with other proposed actions have cumulatively significant impacts and should therefore be discussed in the same impact statement. (3) Similar actions, which when viewed with other reasonably foreseeable or proposed agency actions, have similarities that provide a basis for evaluating their environmental consequences together, such as common timing or geography. An agency may wish to analyze these actions in the same impact statement. It should do so when the best way to assess adequately the combined impacts of similar actions or reasonable alternatives to such actions is to treat them in a single impact statement. (b) Alternatives which include: (1) No action alternative, (2) Other reasonable courses of actions. (3) Mitigation measures (not in the proposed action). (c) Impacts, which may be: (1) Direct, (2) Indirect, and (3) Cumulative.

SCOPING PROCESS - (NEPA§) Early and open process for determining the scope of issues to be addressed and for identifying the significant issues related to a proposed action [40 CFR §1501.7].

SECTION - An ecological unit in the subregion planning and analysis scale of the National Hierarchical Framework corresponding to subdivisions of a Province having broad areas of similar geomorphic process, stratigraphy, geologic origin, drainage networks, topography, and regional climate. Such areas are often inferred by relating geologic maps to potential natural vegetation groupings as mapped by Kuchler (1964).

SECTION 7 CONSULTATION - (ESA§) The ESA formal requirement for consultation with the FWS or NMFS whenever a Federal agency anticipates taking any action or is engaging in an ongoing action that may affect, beneficially or adversely, a listed species or critical habitat.

SECTION 106, OR "106" - (NHPA§) This applies to the process stated in §106 of the 1966 Historic Preservation Act, which requires the responsible Federal agency official to take into account the effect of any proposed undertaking upon cultural resources included in or eligible for inclusion in the National Register of Historic Places. It also requires the

agency official to permit the Advisory Council on Historic Preservation (established by the act) a reasonable opportunity to comment with regard to the undertaking. Compliance with §106 is required for any Federal or federally controlled or licensed undertaking [36 CFR §800.3 through 800.9].

SELECTION - A process by which differential reproductive success of individuals in a population results from differences in one or more hereditary characteristics. Natural selection is a function of genetically based variation in a trait, fitness differences (differential reproductive success) among individuals possessing different forms of that trait, and inheritance of that trait by offspring.

SHORELINE - The line along which the land surface meets the water surface of a lake, sea, or ocean. Strictly speaking, it is not a line, but a narrow strip or area embracing that part of the land surface which comes in contact with wave action both above and below the surface of the water. The term does not apply to tidal flats or marshes which are inundated by the tides, but essentially to strips where land surface has an appreciable slope toward the water.

SHORT-TERM USE - One that continues over a relatively short period of time and does not continue after the action is completed.

SIGNIFICANT - (NHPA§) Having a characteristic that makes a property eligible for listing on the National Register [DOD Directive 4710.0].

SIGNIFICANTLY - (NEPA§) "Significantly" as used in NEPA requires considerations of both context and intensity: (a) Context. This means that the significance of an action must be analyzed in several contexts such as society as a whole (human, national), the affected region, the affected interests, and the locality. Significant varies with the setting of the proposed action. For instance, in the case of a site-specific action, significance would usually depend upon the effects in the locale rater than in the world as a whole. Both short- and long-term effects are relevant. (b) Intensity. This refers to the severity of the impact. Responsible officials must bear in mind that more than one agency may make decisions about partial aspects of a major action. The following should be considered in evaluating intensity: (1) Impacts that may be both beneficial and adverse. A significant effect may exist even if the Federal agency believes that on balance the effect will be beneficial. (2) The degree to which the proposed action affects public health or safety. (3) Unique characteristics of the geographic area such as proximity to historic or cultural resources, park lands, prime farmlands, wetlands, wild and scenic rivers, or ecologically critical areas. (4) The degree to which the effects on the quality of the human environment are likely to be highly controversial. (5) The degree to which the possible effects on the human environment are highly uncertain or involve unique or unknown risks. (6) The degree to which the action may establish a precedent for future actions with significant effects or represents a decision in principle about a future consideration. (7) Whether the action is related to other actions with individually insignificant but cumulatively significant impact on the environment. Significance exists if it is reasonable to anticipate a cumulatively significant impact on the environment. Significance cannot be avoided by terming an action temporary or by breaking it down into small component parts. (8) The degree to which the action may adversely affect districts, sites, highways, structures, or objects listed in or eligible for listing in the National Register of Historic Places or may cause loss or destruction of significant scientific, cultural, or historical resources. (9) The degree to which the action may adversely affect an endangered or threatened species or its habitat that has been determined to be critical under the Endangered Species Action of 1973. (10) Whether the action threatens violation of Federal, State, or local law or requirements imposed for the protection of the environment.

SINK POPULATION - A population in a low-quality habitat in which birth rate is generally less than the death rate and population density is maintained by immigrants from source populations.

SOURCE AND SINK DYNAMICS - Spatial linkage of population dynamics such that high-quality habitats (sources) provide excess individuals that maintain population density, through migration, in low-quality habitats (sinks).

SOURCE POPULATION - A population in a high-quality habitat in which birth rate greatly exceeds death rate and the excess individuals leave as migrants.

SPECIAL EXPERTISE - (NEPA§) "Special expertise" means statutory responsibility, agency mission, or related program experience [§1508.26].

SPECIATION - The process of species formation; the full sequence of events leading to the splitting of one population of organisms into two or more populations reproductively isolated from one another.

SPECIES - (ESA§) The term "species" includes any subspecies of fish or wildlife or plants, and any distinct population segment of any species or vertebrate fish or wildlife which interbreeds when mature.

SPECIES DIVERSITY - Refers to the number of species or other kinds in an area, and, for purposes of quantification, to their relative abundance as well (both species richness and evenness).

SPECIES DIVERSITY INDEX - Any of several mathematical indices which express in one term the number of kinds of species and the relative numbers of each in an area (both species richness and evenness).

SPECIES RICHNESS - The total number of species within a defined area.

STABILITY (ecological) - The tendency of systems, especially ecosystems, to persist, relatively unchanged, through time; also, persistence of a component of a system.

STAKEHOLDER - Those organizations and/or individuals having a vested interest in the outcome of a decision making process.

STANDING CROP - The biological mass (biomass) of certain or all living organisms of an area or volume at some specific time, i.e., what could be harvested.

State HISTORIC PRESERVATION OFFICER (SHPO) - (NHPA§) This is an official within each State appointed by the governor to administer the State historic preservation program. In addition, the SHPO has specific responsibilities relating to Federal undertakings that affect cultural resources within the State [36 CFR §60.3].

STOCHASTIC - Any random process, such as mortality, due to weather extremes.

STRUCTURAL DIVERSITY - Diversity in a community that results from having many horizontal or vertical physical elements (i.e., layers or tiers of canopy).

SUBCLIMAX - A stage in a community's development, i.e., succession before its final (climax) stage; a community simulating climax because of its further development being inhibited by some disturbing factor (e.g., fire, poor soil).

SUBENVELOP - The general altitude of the drainage network that portrays differences in stream gradient from one geomorphic unit to another.

SUBREGION - A scale of planning and analysis in the National Hierarchical Framework that has applicability for strategic, multi-forest, statewide, and multi-agency analysis and assessment. Subregions include Section and Subsection ecological units.

SUBSECTION - An ecological unit in the subregion planning and analysis scale of the National Hierarchical Framework corresponding to subdivisions of a Section into areas with similar surficial geology, lithology, geomorphic process, soil groups, subregional climate, and potential natural communities.

SUBTROPICAL - A classification of climate based on the Koppen System for regions where there are eight months or more warmer than 50°F (10°C) and the coolest month is warmer than 32°F (0°C) but colder than 65°F (18°C) [Bailey, 1980].

SUCCESSION - The more or less predictable replacement of one community by another; the definition includes the (controversial or hypothetical) possibility of "retrograde" succession.

SUCCESSION, PLANT - The replacement of one kind of plant assemblage by another through time.

SUCCESSION, PRIMARY - Refers to succession which begins on bare, unmodified substrata.

SUCCESSION, SECONDARY - Refers to succession which occurs on formerly vegetated areas (i.e., having an already developed soil) after disturbance or clearing.

SUPPLEMENTAL EIS - An EIS required to supplement an existing draft or final EIS [40 CFR §1502.9(c)].

SUSTAINED YIELD - Production of renewable natural resources that a land or water area can maintain at a given intensity of management for an extended period of time.

SYMBIOSIS - The living together of dissimilar organisms, by definition when the relationship is both mutually beneficial and essential.

SYNERGISM - The nonadditive effect of two or more substances or organisms acting together.

SYSTEMS ECOLOGY - That branch of ecology which incorporates the viewpoints and techniques of systems analysis and engineering, especially those having to do with the simulation of systems using computers and mathematical models.

TAILWATER - In hydraulics, water, in a river or channel, immediately downstream from a structure.

TAKE OR TAKING - (ESA§) To harass, harm, pursue, hunt, shoot, wound, kill, trap, capture, or collect, or to attempt to engage in any such conduct. Harm is further defined to include significant habitat modification or degradation that results in death or injury to listed species by significantly impairing behavioral patterns such as breeding, feeding, or sheltering. Harass is defined as actions that create the likelihood of injury to listed species to such an extent as to significantly disrupt normal behavioral patterns which include, but are not limited to, breeding, feeding, or sheltering.

TAXON- A taxonomic category or unit, as a species, genus, or higher grouping.

TEMPERATE - A classification of climate based on the Koppen System for regions where there are four to eight months warmer than 50°F (10°C) and the coldest month is cooler than 32°F (0°C).

THERMAL POLLUTION - The excessive raising or lowering of water temperatures above or below normal seasonal ranges in streams, lakes, or estuaries or oceans as the result of discharge of hot or cold effluents into such waters.

THERMAL STRATIFICATION - The seasonal formation of horizontal layers of water in lakes and oceans (warm surface, cool bottom) of markedly varying temperature, separated by a zone with a steep temperature gradient.

THERMOCLINE - A narrow (horizontal) zone of water in lakes and oceans with a steep temperature gradient, separating a warmer surface layer (epilmnion, epithalassa) from a cooler bottom layer (hypolimnion, hypothalassa); as a thermocline is a plane, but a zone is observed, the preference or usual term is metalimnion.

THREAT ASSESSMENT - The identification, evaluation, and ranking of stresses and sources of stress to populations, species, ecological communities, or ecosystems at a site or within a landscape.

THREATENED SPECIES - Any species which is likely to become an endangered species within the foreseeable future throughout all or a significant portion of its range. Federally listed threatened species are officially designated by the DOI [50 CFR §81.21].

THRESHOLD VALUE - Level of environmental contamination or change above which environmental impact or change is detectable.

TIERING - (NEPA§) "Tiering" refers to the coverage of general matters in broader environmental impact statements (such as national program or policy statements) with subsequent narrower statements or environmental analyses (such as regional or basinwide program statements or ultimately site-specific statements) incorporating by reference the general discussions and concentrating solely on the issues specific to the statement subsequently prepared. Tiering is appropriate when the sequence of statements of analyses is: (a) From a program, plan, or policy environmental impact statement to a program, plan, or policy statement or analysis of lesser scope or to a site-specific statement or analysis. (b) From an environmental impact statement on a specific action at an early stage (such as needed and site selection) to a supplement (which is preferred) or a subsequent statement or analysis at a later stage (such as environmental mitigation). Tiering in such cases is appropriate when it helps the lead agency to focus on the issues which are ripe for decision and exclude from consideration issues already decided or not yet ripe.

TOLERANCE - An organism's capacity to endure or adapt to (usually temporary) unfavorable environmental factors.

TRADITIONAL COMMUNITY - (NHPA§) The members of a recognizable ethnic group who continue to live according to beliefs and traditions passed down from previous generations.

TRADITIONAL CULTURAL AUTHORITY - (NHPA§) An individual or a group of individuals in an Indian tribe, Native Hawaiian organization, or other social or ethnic group who is recognized by members of the group as knowledgeable in the group's traditional history and cultural practices.

TRANSLOCATION - (ESA§) The relocation of one or more individuals from a given population to another area of equally suitable habitat.

TRIBAL LANDS - (NHPA§) All lands within the exterior boundaries of any Indian reservation and all dependent Indian communities.

TROPICAL - A classification of climate based on the Koppen System for regions where the coolest month is warmer than 65°F (18°C).

TUNDRA - A classification of climate based on the Koppen System for regions where the warmest month is colder than 50°F (10°C) but warmer than 32°F (0°C).

TURNOVER - A process whereby the water on the bottom of a deep lake exchanges with the water on the top. The process is generally caused by warming of weather with concomitant seasonal wind patterns. The same process occurs as the weather cools into winter season.

UMBRELLA SPECIES - Species that require large areas to maintain viable populations and by which protection of their habitat may protect the habitat and populations of many other more restricted or less wide-ranging species.

UNCERTAINTY - In situations of uncertainty, potential outcomes cannot be described in objectively known probability distributions. Uncertainty is characteristic of many aspects of water resources planning. Because there are no known probability distributions to describe uncertain outcomes, uncertainty is substantially more difficult to analyze than risk.

UNDERTAKING - (NHPA§) A project, activity, or program funded in whole or in part under the direct or indirect jurisdiction of a Federal agency that can result in changes in the character or use of historic properties, if any such historic properties are located in the area of potential effects. It includes any project, activity, or program that is carried out by or on behalf of the agency; is financed in whole or in part with Federal financial assistance; requires a Federal permit, license or approval, including agency authority to disapprove or veto the project, activity, or program; or is subject to State or local regulation administered pursuant to a delegation or approval by a Federal agency. Undertakings include new and continuing projects, technical assistance pertaining to a specific site and related to the provision of Federal financial assistance, activities, or programs, renewals or reapprovals of such assistance, activities, or programs, and any of their elements not previously considered under §106 [NHPA, §301(7)].

UNIT DAY VALUE - A monetary value per visitor day of use which is assigned to a recreation activity or activities to determine the recreation benefits generated by an overall plan of those activities. May be applied to recreation opportunities foregone or proposed for comparison.

UPLAND - Any area that does not qualify as wetland because the associated hydrologic regime is not sufficiently wet to elicit development of vegetation, soils and/or hydrologic characteristics associated with wetlands, or is defined as open waters.

UTILITARIAN - A philosophical term applied to any activity that produces a product useful to humans, typically in some economic sense. Also used to describe a system of values which is measured by its contribution to human well-being, usually in terms of health and economic standard of living.

VIABLE POPULATION - A population that contains an adequate number of individuals appropriately distributed to ensure a high probability of long-term survival without significant human intervention.

VISITOR DAY - A measure of recreation use by one person for one day or part of a day.

VISUAL CHARACTER - The character of a landscape is composed of patterns which consist of elements of form, line, color and texture.

VISUAL COMPATIBILITY - The degree to which development with specific visual characteristics is visually unified with its setting.

VISUAL CONTRAST - The difference in appearance between two (or more) elements and/or an element and its background.

VISUAL DOMINANCE - That visual objects(s) which exerts the greatest influence on the visual character of the landscape.

VISUAL IMPACT - The significance and/or severity of change in visual resource quality as a result of activities or land use changes.

VISUAL QUALITY - The visual significance given to a landscape determined by professional, public, or personal values and intrinsic physical properties of the landscape.

VISUAL RESOURCE - Those natural and cultural features of the environment which can potentially be viewed.

WATERS OF THE UNITED STATES [40 CFR $ 232.2(q)] - (1) All waters which are currently used, were used in the past, or may be susceptible to use in interstate or foreign commerce, including all waters which are subject to the ebb and flow of the tide; (2) All interstate waters including interstate wetlands; (3) All other waters such as intrastate lakes, rivers, streams (including intermittent streams), mudflats, sandflats, wetlands, sloughs, prairie potholes, wet meadows, playa lakes, or natural ponds, the use, degradation or destruction of which would or could affect interstate or foreign commerce including any such waters: (i) Which are or could be used by interstate or foreign travelers for recreational or other purposes; or (ii) From which fish or shellfish could be taken and sold in interstate or foreign commerce; and (iii) Which are used or could be used for industrial purposes by industries in interstate commerce;* (4) All impoundments of waters otherwise defined as waters of the United States under this definition; (5) Tributaries of waters identified in paragraphs 1-4; (6) The territorial sea; and (7) Wetlands adjacent to waters (other than waters that are themselves wetlands) identified in 1-6; waste treatment systems, including treatment ponds or lagoons designed to meet the requirements of CWA (other than cooling ponds as defined in 40 CFR 423.11(m) which also meet criteria in this definition) are not waters of the United States. (*Note: EPA has clarified that waters of the U.S. under the commerce connection in (3) above also include, for example, waters: which are or would be used as habitat by birds protected by Migratory Bird Treaties or migratory birds which cross State lines; which are or would be used as habitat for endangered species; used to irrigate crops sold in interstate commerce.)

WETLANDS - Those areas that are inundated or saturated by surface or ground water at a frequency and duration sufficient to support, and that under normal circumstances do support, a prevalence of vegetation typically adapted for life in saturated soil conditions. Wetlands generally include swamps, marshes, bogs, and similar areas [33 CFR §328.3

(b), 40 CFR Parts 122.2, 230.3, and 232.2. and 40 CFR §230.3 (t)].

WILD RIVER AREA - Wild and Scenic River Act Usage. Those rivers or sections of rivers that are free of impoundments and generally inaccessible except by trail, with watersheds or shorelines essentially primitive and waters unpolluted. These represent vestiges of primitive America.

WILDLIFE MANAGEMENT - The practical application of scientific and technical principles to wildlife populations and habitats so as to maintain such populations essentially for ecological, recreational, and/or scientific purposes.

WITHOUT-PLANS CONDITION - The without-plans condition is an estimation of the most probable future condition expected to occur in the absence of any of the study's alternative plans. The without-plans condition includes any changes expected to directly, indirectly, or cumulatively result from all reasonably foreseeable actions without any of the study's alternative plans. For example, if it is most probable that within the next 20 years 60 percent of a woodland will be cleared for agricultural purposes without any of the plans being considered by the agency, the effects of such clearing would be included in the without-plans conditions. Similarly, if existing legislation, such as the Clean Water Act, expected to improve water quality in a river, such improvement would be included in the without-plans conditions. The without-plans condition is synonymous with "No Action" as used in NEPA [40 CFR 1502.14(d)].

XERIC - Characterized by, relating to, or requiring only a small amount of moisture.

ZONE OF INTEREST- The range of concerns under a statute (i.e., NEPA, ESA, etc) that are protected by that statute.

Index

A

88

abuse of discretion . . . C-126

action(s)

agency . . . A-10, R-19, R-22, R-34, R-39, R-41, Q-55, T-95,T-97, J-100, J-102-105, J-107, J-108, C-114, C-120, C-121,C-135, C-136, C-142, M-169, M-173, M-179, M-182 ,M-183, O-205, O-215, O-216, gl-235, gl-236, gl-240, gl-243,gl-245

alternative . . . C-130, gl-243

connected . . . R-41, C-124, C-125, C-146, C-147, C-151, C-152, C-159, gl-245

federal . . . L-3, R-15, R-19, R-20, R-27, R-30, R-37, R-39, R-40, Q-47, Q-50, Q-51, Q-54, G-68-70, G-73, P-91, P-94, T-95-97, J-99-101, J-108,C-111, C-112, C-114, C-116, C-117, C-125,C-126, C-130, C-132, C-134, C-135, C-136, C-138, C-140, C-142-144,C-146, C-147, C-150-153, C-157, C-159, 164-167, M-168, M-169, M-182-184, O-191, gl-240,O-196, O-197, O-199, O-202, O-203, O-205, O-206, gl-229, gl-233, gl-235

foreseeable . . . Q-55, C-140, gl-249

future . . . R-37, R-41, C-140, M-176, gl-233, gl-245

proposed . . . 1, L-3, R-16-18, R-21-23, R-25-27, R-31-34, R-38, R-40, R-41, Q-45-48, Q-50, Q-52-54, Q-59-63, G-67, G-68, G-70, G-72, G-74, S-76, S-77, S-82, S-87, P-94, T-96, T-98, J-102-108, C-113, C-116, C-119, C-120, C-125-127, C-130-132, C-137, C-138, C-140, C-142, C-143, C-147-149, C-151, C-152, C-156-158, M-168, M-171, M-174-176, M-178-185, O-196, O-197, O-199, O-203, O-204, gl-229, gl-232, gl-235, gl-239, gl-241-243, gl-245

related . . . Q-47, Q-55, C-153

similar . . . R-41, Q-55, C-140, gl-245

action area . . . gl-229, gl-230, gl-233

action-forcing . . . C-114

adequacy . . . 1, L-4, I-8, R-23, R-25, R-26, R-31, Q-45, Q-59, G-74, T-96, C-111, C-112, C-116, C-126, C-127, C-133, C-139, C-143, C-151, C-155, C-156, C-161, M-167, M-168, M-172-174, M-176, M-179, M-187

Adequacy of the EA . . . C-139

Administrative Procedure Act (APA) . . . R-29, R-34, R-39, Q-55, C-151, gl-240, Q-55, C-121, C-122, C-152

administrative record . . . R-21, G-68, G-69, C-124, C-127, C-137, C-153, C-155, O-220

adoption . . . L-3, R-20, R-31, R-39, Q-55, Q-59, Q-62, G-69, G-70, G-73

Advance or Xerox Copies . . . Q-57

adverse

effect(s) . . . I-8, R-12, R-24, Q-64, J-107, C-118, C-119, C-137, C-139, C-142,C-143, C-154, C-156, M-165, O-189, O-195, O-196, gl-229, gl-232, gl-235--239

impacts . . . R-19, R-25, P-94, C-137, M-171, M-179, O-196, O-199, O-204

adverse modification . . . gl-231, gl-234, gl-243

Advisory Council on Historic Preservation (ACHP) . . . O-191, O-192, O-213, gl-229, gl-245

AEC . . . C-128, C-129, C-154

aesthetic . . . L-4, R-38, J-102, C-121, O-194, gl-229, gl-230, gl-234, gl-235, gl-240

affected environment . . . R-21-23, R-40, Q-55, J-103, J-105, gl-240

agency

ability . . . O-204

activities . . . M-173, O-225

authority . . . R-14, R-39, gl-239, gl-248

capability . . . R-35

comments . . . R-12, Q-45, G-66, S-78, M-177

compliance . . . 11, R-13

control . . . R-39

cooperation . . . R-17, Q-47, gl-232

decision . . . R-19, R-29, R-34, J-105, C-120, C-125, C-133, C-139, C-141, C-152, C-156, M-165, M-181, gl-230

determines . . . R-16, R-21, Q-50, Q-51, Q-59, G-71, G-73, G-74

discretion . . . P-90, C-119

disputes . . . R-14, R-15

flexibility . . . R-35

head . . . O-191, O-193-195

may . . . R-13, R-14, R-16-18, R-24-26, R-28, R-30, R-31, R-34, R-37, R-41, Q-45, Q-50, Q-58-62, Q-64, G-70, C-124, C-130, C-148, M-171, M-173, O-199, O-209, gl-231, gl-245

mission . . . R-41, M-171, gl-246

official . . . Q-46, gl-232, gl-236, gl-239, gl-241, gl-245

L=NEPA; I = Environmental Quality Improvement Act; A= Clean Air Act; R= CEQ Regulations for implementing the procedural Provisions of the National Environmental Policy Act; Q= Forty Most Asked Question Concerning CEQ's NEPA Regulations; G= CEQ 1983 Memorandum; S= CEQ 1981 Memorandum, Scoping Guidance; P= CEQ 1993 Memorandum, Guidance on Pollution Prevention; T= CEQ 1997 Guidance on NEPA Analyses for Transboundary Impacts; J= CEQ guidance on Environmental Justice; C= NEPA Case Law; M= EP's Policy and Procedure for the Review of Federal Actions Impacting the Environment; O= Selected Executive Orders; and gl= the Glossary.

Index   d-251

L=NEPA; I = Environmental Quality Improvement Act; A= Clean Air Act; R= CEQ Regulations for implementing the procedural
Provisions of the National Environmental Policy Act; Q= Forty Most Asked Question Concerning CEQ's NEPA Regulations;
G= CEQ 1983 Memorandum; S= CEQ 1981 Memorandum, Scoping Guidance; P= CEQ 1993 Memorandum, Guidance on
Pollution Prevention; T= CEQ 1997 Guidance on NEPA Analyses for Transboundary Impacts; J= CEQ guidance on Environmental
Justice; C= NEPA Case Law; M= EP's Policy and Procedure for the Review of Federal Actions Impacting the Environment;
O= Selected Executive Orders; and gl= the Glossary.

E

L=NEPA; I = Environmental Quality Improvement Act; A= Clean Air Act; R= CEQ Regulations for implementing the procedural Provisions of the National Environmental Policy Act; Q= Forty Most Asked Question Concerning CEQ's NEPA Regulations; G= CEQ 1983 Memorandum; S= CEQ 1981 Memorandum, Scoping Guidance; P= CEQ 1993 Memorandum, Guidance on Pollution Prevention; T= CEQ 1997 Guidance on NEPA Analyses for Transboundary Impacts; J= CEQ guidance on Environmental Justice; C= NEPA Case Law; M= EP's Policy and Procedure for the Review of Federal Actions Impacting the Environment; O= Selected Executive Orders; and gl= the Glossary.

L=NEPA; I = Environmental Quality Improvement Act; A= Clean Air Act; R= CEQ Regulations for implementing the procedural Provisions of the National Environmental Policy Act; Q= Forty Most Asked Question Concerning CEQ's NEPA Regulations; G= CEQ 1983 Memorandum; S= CEQ 1981 Memorandum, Scoping Guidance; P= CEQ 1993 Memorandum, Guidance on Pollution Prevention; T= CEQ 1997 Guidance on NEPA Analyses for Transboundary Impacts; J= CEQ guidance on Environmental Justice; C= NEPA Case Law; M= EP's Policy and Procedure for the Review of Federal Actions Impacting the Environment; O= Selected Executive Orders; and gl= the Glossary.

G

H

I

L=NEPA; I = Environmental Quality Improvement Act; A= Clean Air Act; R= CEQ Regulations for implementing the procedural
Provisions of the National Environmental Policy Act; Q= Forty Most Asked Question Concerning CEQ's NEPA Regulations;
G= CEQ 1983 Memorandum; S= CEQ 1981 Memorandum, Scoping Guidance; P= CEQ 1993 Memorandum, Guidance on
Pollution Prevention; T= CEQ 1997 Guidance on NEPA Analyses for Transboundary Impacts; J= CEQ guidance on Environmental
Justice; C= NEPA Case Law; M= EP's Policy and Procedure for the Review of Federal Actions Impacting the Environment;
O= Selected Executive Orders; and gl= the Glossary.

L=NEPA; I = Environmental Quality Improvement Act; A= Clean Air Act; R= CEQ Regulations for implementing the procedural Provisions of the National Environmental Policy Act; Q= Forty Most Asked Question Concerning CEQ's NEPA Regulations; G= CEQ 1983 Memorandum; S= CEQ 1981 Memorandum, Scoping Guidance; P= CEQ 1993 Memorandum, Guidance on Pollution Prevention; T= CEQ 1997 Guidance on NEPA Analyses for Transboundary Impacts; J= CEQ guidance on Environmental Justice; C= NEPA Case Law; M= EP's Policy and Procedure for the Review of Federal Actions Impacting the Environment; O= Selected Executive Orders; and gl= the Glossary.

L=NEPA; I = Environmental Quality Improvement Act; A= Clean Air Act; R= CEQ Regulations for implementing the procedural
Provisions of the National Environmental Policy Act; Q= Forty Most Asked Question Concerning CEQ's NEPA Regulations;
G= CEQ 1983 Memorandum; S= CEQ 1981 Memorandum, Scoping Guidance; P= CEQ 1993 Memorandum, Guidance on
Pollution Prevention; T= CEQ 1997 Guidance on NEPA Analyses for Transboundary Impacts; J= CEQ guidance on Environmental
Justice; C= NEPA Case Law; M= EP's Policy and Procedure for the Review of Federal Actions Impacting the Environment;
O= Selected Executive Orders; and gl= the Glossary.

L=NEPA; I = Environmental Quality Improvement Act; A= Clean Air Act; R= CEQ Regulations for implementing the procedural
Provisions of the National Environmental Policy Act; Q= Forty Most Asked Question Concerning CEQ's NEPA Regulations;
G= CEQ 1983 Memorandum; S= CEQ 1981 Memorandum, Scoping Guidance; P= CEQ 1993 Memorandum, Guidance on
Pollution Prevention; T= CEQ 1997 Guidance on NEPA Analyses for Transboundary Impacts; J= CEQ guidance on Environmental
Justice; C= NEPA Case Law; M= EP's Policy and Procedure for the Review of Federal Actions Impacting the Environment;
O= Selected Executive Orders; and gl= the Glossary.

W

L=NEPA; I = Environmental Quality Improvement Act; A= Clean Air Act; R= CEQ Regulations for implementing the procedural
Provisions of the National Environmental Policy Act; Q= Forty Most Asked Question Concerning CEQ's NEPA Regulations;
G= CEQ 1983 Memorandum; S= CEQ 1981 Memorandum, Scoping Guidance; P= CEQ 1993 Memorandum, Guidance on
Pollution Prevention; T= CEQ 1997 Guidance on NEPA Analyses for Transboundary Impacts; J= CEQ guidance on Environmental
Justice; C= NEPA Case Law; M= EP's Policy and Procedure for the Review of Federal Actions Impacting the Environment;
O= Selected Executive Orders; and gl= the Glossary.